RELIGION, GENDER, AND CULTURE IN THE
PRE-MODERN WORLD

Religion/Culture/Critique
Series editor: Elizabeth A. Castelli

How Hysterical: Identification and Resistance in the Bible and Film
By Erin Runions
(2003)

Connected Places: Region, Pilgrimage, and Geographical Imagination in India
By Anne Feldhaus
(2003)

Representing Religion in World Cinema: Filmmaking, Mythmaking, Culture Making
Edited by S. Brent Plate
(2003)

Derrida's Bible (Reading a Page of Scripture with a Little Help from Derrida)
Edited by Yvonne Sherwood
(2004)

Feminist New Testament Studies: Global and Future Perspectives
Edited by Kathleen O'Brien Wicker, Althea Spencer Miller, and Musa W. Dube
(2005)

Women's Renunciation in South Asia: Nuns, Yoginis, Saints, and Singers
Edited by Meena Khandelwal, Sondra L. Hausner, and Ann Grodzins Gold
(2006)

Retheorizing Religion in Nepal
By Gregory Price Grieve
(2006)

The Religious Dimensions of Advertising
By Tricia Sheffield
(2006)

Religion, Gender, and Culture in the Pre-Modern World
Edited by Alexandra Cuffel and Brian Britt
(2007)

RELIGION, GENDER, AND CULTURE IN THE PRE-MODERN WORLD

EDITED BY

ALEXANDRA CUFFEL AND BRIAN BRITT

First published in 2007 by
PALGRAVE MACMILLAN™
175 Fifth Avenue, New York, N.Y. 10010 and
Houndmills, Basingstoke, Hampshire, England RG21 6XS
Companies and representatives throughout the world.

PALGRAVE MACMILLAN is the global academic imprint of the Palgrave Macmillan division of St. Martin's Press, LLC and of Palgrave Macmillan Ltd. Macmillan® is a registered trademark in the United States, United Kingdom and other countries. Palgrave is a registered trademark in the European Union and other countries.

ISBN-13: 978–1–4039–7218–7
ISBN-10: 1–4039–7218–4

Library of Congress Cataloging-in-Publication Data

Religion, gender, and culture in the pre-modern world / edited by Alexandra Cuffel and Brian Britt.
    p. cm.—(Religion / culture / critique)
  Includes bibliographical references and index.
  ISBN 1–4039–7218–4 (alk. paper)
    1. Gender identity—History. 2. Sex differences—History.
  3. Anthropology of religion. 4. Ethnic relations—History. I. Cuffel, Alexandra. II. Britt, Brian M., 1964–

HQ21.R427 2007
306.7089—dc22   2006049108

A catalogue record for this book is available from the British Library.

Design by Newgen Imaging Systems (P) Ltd., Chennai, India.

First edition: March 2007

10 9 8 7 6 5 4 3 2 1

Printed in the United States of America.

Contents

Acknowledgments

This book began as a series of lectures in 2001 and 2002 sponsored by the Dean of Arts and Sciences at Virginia Tech. We would like to thank Dean Robert Bates and the Departments of History and Interdisciplinary Studies for supporting the series, and Paulette Jayabalan for designing and organizing the publicity. We would also like to thank Allison Martin for her skillful and prompt work in editing and help in preparing the manuscript. Sahar Amer, Rosamond Rodman, and Adam Knobler made helpful comments on the Introduction, though fault for any shortcomings lies with us. Additional thanks go to Elizabeth Castelli, who encouraged us to pursue this project, along with Amanda Johnson, Herta Pitman, and Emily Leithauser at Palgrave, for their enthusiasm, support, and patience. Finally, we wish to thank each other and the contributors for the rewarding experience of collaboration on this volume.

Introduction

Alexandra Cuffel and Brian Britt

Differences of identity are marked in multiple ways and thus must be studied in multiple ways. The use of certain categories of gender or ethnicity for the study of pre-modern cultures may be anachronistic, but as a provisional strategy, it may produce significant new insights. By collecting essays from historians, art historians, and scholars of literature and religion on a variety of pre-modern texts, this volume demonstrates how interdisciplinary approaches to several kinds of difference create new understandings of pre-modern constructions of difference.

Religion, Gender, and Culture in the Pre-Modern World compares shifting formulations of gender, interreligious and ethnic relations in the Near East, Europe, the Americas, and Africa from antiquity to the nineteenth century. This book addresses two fundamental questions that face scholars of pre-modern cultures. First, to what extent can contemporary identity categories of gender, ethnicity, and religion adequately address pre-modern contexts? Second, how will focused studies of pre-modern religious and gender difference relate to such widely used categories and theories? To address these questions this collection encompasses four areas in pre-modern history, literature, and religion: sexual identities and behaviors, especially same-sex love and cross-dressing; women and the embodied conceptualizations of "femininity" and "masculinity"; the role of sexuality, marriage, and gender in expressions of religious and ethnic difference; and how contacts between diverse peoples related to hybrid identities and new group boundaries. The essays collected here demonstrate close intersections of religious, ethnic, and gendered identities and show how these categories came to be worked out upon the body and its adornment. In diverse, culturally specific examples, these essays suggest that the body, especially its capacity for sexuality, often provided the basis or metaphor for boundaries between groups and was the focus of group anxieties about identity.

Diverse perspectives sharpen the concepts and methods of study. As essays by Sahar Amer, Brian Britt, Alexandra Cuffel, Adam Knobler, and

Irven Resnick and Kenneth Kitchell show, differences of gender and sexuality often relate directly to ethnic and religious differences. Yet constructing, maintaining, and crossing boundaries of difference take place in specific contexts of discourse and culture. Like Aristotle's definition of rhetoric as the use of available means of persuasion, discourses of identity difference depend on these particular circumstances. Religion, ethnicity, and gender, the perennial markers of identity difference, are used to perform similar kinds of cultural work. Rigorous studies of pre-modern difference might lie not within particular comparisons of gender or religious difference but, paradoxically, across them. In other words, meaningful comparisons may not be found at the conceptual level of notions of gender or ethnicity but at the level of how communities seize upon categories of difference at hand. By examining the cultural work of difference that various specific but disparate communities sought to accomplish, we hope that this collection will encourage other scholars to explore the intersections of gender, religion, and ethnicity across multiple cultures and to reflect on the similarities and differences that such comparisons reveal in their own theorizations of "otherness."

The book is divided into three main chronological sections: ancient, medieval, and early modern. The first section on ancient cultures contains three chapters, one on ancient Israelite curses against Canaanites and Gibeonites within the context of fears about intermarriage; the second dealing with the meanings of the contradictory literary and artistic depictions of nymphs in ancient Greece as simultaneously demure and sexually lascivious; and the third focusing on the mockery of old ideas of Roman masculinity and the conscious adoption of women's dress as part of the victorious warrior's identity.

Four chapters comprise the section on the Middle Ages: one exploring European Christian transformations of the legends of the female demon-beast, Lamia, as a way of polemicizing against Jews and heretics as simultaneously bestial and feminine; a second examining same-sex love between women in parallel examples from medieval French and Arabic literature; a third analyzing conversion and sexual reorientation versus death of Christian warrior women in Muslim and Arabic epics; and a fourth on the role of the hunter as a bridge between not only the natural animal world and humans, but also between men and women in the epic traditions of Mali and Guinea.

The final section on the early modern period begins with an examination of conversion and intermarriage between Sephardi Jews and Africans in Suriname despite Spanish and Portuguese legislation against miscegenation from the seventeenth to the nineteenth centuries. The second looks at the transformation of the feather as an article of male clothing to one belonging to female attire, and the ways in which conflicts surrounding "feathered clothing" reflected medical and social debates about male and female power and nature in Tudor-Stuart England. The third examines the naked and clothed breast in European discussions of feminine nature as applied to sixteenth century Brazilian and nineteenth century Polynesian women and their use of or resistance to "civilizing" and erotic shaping of their bodies, and the final chapter suggests new avenues of research regarding the impact of medieval canon law on marriage in initial colonial encounters and legislation dealing with polygamy, consanguinity, and miscegenation.

Interest in inter-religious and intercultural relations in the pre-modern world has increased exponentially over the past two to three decades, as has fascination with the history of pre-modern gender. While scholars have examined the intersection between gender and intercultural relations in the pre-modern periods, noting, for example, the parallels between religious minorities and women, books in this area have tended to be focused geographically.[1] Others have examined specifically how religious or ethnic minorities became associated with one gender or another, usually women, or how attitudes toward and experiences of religious minorities (or majorities) differed depending on gender, though again, these have gravitated toward a very specific geographic and chronological focus.[2] More recent books, such as Sharon Farmer and Carol Braun Pasternack's *Gender and Difference in the Middle Ages* and Leslie Brubaker and Julia Smith's *Gender in the Early Medieval World 300–900* (both collections), attempt to address gender across a variety of cultures, especially during the Middle Ages.[3] Likewise, scholars studying issues in inter-religious or cross-cultural relations continue to push toward a more comparative scope.[4] Yet despite the rapid growth in studies of pre-modern religion, ethnicity, and gender, and the impulse toward cross-cultural comparisons, few collections bring these areas together and examine their intersections over time. This collection gives readers the opportunity to compare divergent cultural and historical contexts.

By using contemporary categories of analysis in the study of distant historical periods, this volume engages in a "comparative" method. Jonathan Z. Smith, one of the most original and influential figures in comparative religion, explains comparison in terms of "similarities and differences, and with respect to some category, question, theory, or model of interest to the study of religion."[5] "The aim of such as comparison," suggests Smith, "is the redescription of the exempla (at the very least, each in terms of the other) and a rectification of the academic categories in relation to which they have been imagined."[6] Applying categories of gender, ethnicity, and sexuality to pre-modern cultural contexts, the essays collected here participate in the two-way interaction between exempla and categories described by Smith. The studies demonstrate the need to attend closely to historical and cultural "exampla" without the heavy imposition of theoretical categories.

Sexual Behaviors and Identities

A generation ago, Michel Foucault and others cast doubt on the availability of contemporary categories to the study of ancient and pre-modern societies. His three-part *History of Sexuality* not only delineated such crucial discourses as "arts of living" and the "care of the self" but also provided models and methods for the combined analysis of knowledge, power, and sexuality that have animated work all across the humanities and social sciences focusing on modern and pre-modern topics.[7] The question of whether modern understandings of sexual and gender categories can be applied to pre-modern contexts has elicited particularly intense debates among pre-modernists. To cite one dramatic case, the modern scientific notion of perversion prompts the philosopher and Foucault scholar Arnold Davidson to ask: "Were there any perverts before the later part of the nineteenth century? Strange as it may sound, the answer to this question is, *no*."[8]

Homosexuality and the question of a homosexual identity or culture have been another hotly contested issue. Foucault and scholars who have followed his lead carefully distinguish between those who performed homosexual acts as opposed to those who possessed a "homosexual" culture or identity.[9] Others have been willing to explore questions of an identifiable "group" or groups based in part on sexual preference or partners and other aspects of dress and behavior during pre-modern eras.[10] More commonly, scholars exploring varieties of same-sex love during pre-modern periods have passed beyond this particular debate to complicate such behaviors or identities as culturally specific and very often other than a simple binary of homo- or heterosexual. For example, Khaled al-Rouayheb has demonstrated that in the early modern Islamic world sexual roles could change from "passive" to "active" among men as they grew older, the two roles could be occupied simultaneously by a man or youth with different male partners and/or with his wife.[11] Scholars examining cross-dressing among men in both medieval Western Europe and the Near East have discovered that while men sometimes willing adopted a female or feminized identity, such identity could but did not necessarily entail sexual desire or intercourse with other men.[12] Yet in the midst of this exciting and carefully nuanced study of pre-modern male same-sex love and transgendered behaviors, much less work has been done on same-sex love between pre-modern women, as Sahar Amer points out in her contribution to this collection.[13] Judith Brown and Bernadette Brooten stand out as important exceptions; however, same-sex love between pre-modern women remains a relatively poorly studied subject.[14] In the current book, the chapters by Sahar Amer and Alexandra Cuffel take a step toward filling this gap. Their contributions are especially valuable since they address portrayals of same-sex love between women in the Islamic world, which has been even less explored than in the Western world.[15] Furthermore, Amer argues that some of the medieval French depictions or insinuations of sexual relations between women derived from Arabic ones, and that Western authors muted these tales, reflecting greater discomfort with such relationships than that which existed in the Middle East. Cuffel's findings that sex between women served as a satisfactory "stepping stone" to the more laudable heterosexual marriage just as Christianity was a "stepping stone" to Islam bolsters the impression that in the Middle Ages same-sex love between women was acceptable in some circles in the Islamic world. Such assertions fly in the face of popular perceptions that the Islamic world was more conservative regarding sexuality in general and in the treatment of women in particular.

Conceptualizing Gender

The ways in which pre-modern peoples could shift their own or a particular group's real and symbolic gendered identity though changing their clothing, hair, or even physiology have captured the attention of classicists, medievalists, and early modernists alike. Following the work of scholars such as Mary Douglas and Joan Scott, scholars have been acutely aware that the body and gender frequently serve to mark nonsexual social, political, religious, and ethnic anxieties and hierarchies.[16] Cross-dressing, particularly among women, has received particular attention from scholars who seek to understand the ways in which women's actions either allowed them to lay claim to a higher (masculine) identity, or served to condemn them.[17] Within the context of medieval studies, focus has tended to be on ways in which women subverted religious hierarchies by dressing as men.[18] Within the field of Islamic studies, this emphasis on the religious context of cross-dressing is less strong; however, the number of studies of cross-dressing women in the Islamic world are also relatively few.[19] Because they deal with women's adoption of masculine military garb and activities, Amer's chapter, and, to a lesser extent, Cuffel's, add significantly to the understanding of cross-dressing in the medieval Near East and Europe and provide new contexts for studying better known cross-dressing warriors like Joan of Arc.

Cross-dressing men in the pre-modern world have been studied less extensively. Caroline Walker Bynum has demonstrated that monks and abbots in Western Europe frequently took on a feminine identity in imitation of a "motherly" Jesus.[20] Ruth Karras has examined the case of a male prostitute who took on a female persona while Everett Rowson has explored "effeminate" men as a social group in the early Islamic world.[21] Eunuchs, albeit through their genital lack rather than through a change of clothing, have emerged as a kind of third gender in the Byzantine and medieval Islamic world.[22] Within the field of classics, scholars have demonstrated that men were negatively feminized by being associated with a passive role in male-male sexual liaisons.[23] Carlin Barton's contribution to this collection is that much more startling, therefore, for she discovers that Roman men regularly adopted feminine or feminized dress, hair, and behaviors as a way of expressing power and subverting old Roman ideals of masculinity. Her work challenges the model of masculinity being a constant ideal and opens new avenues of research in the field of gender within classical studies which has been primarily focused on sexuality.

Likewise, Catherine Howey's chapter on the shifting meanings of feathers in early modern England adds to our understanding of cross-dressing among men and women in the pre-modern world. In her case, she connects elite women's choice to don an initially masculine item of clothing, the feather, with leisure, fashion, international trade, consumption and perceptions of foreign peoples, in particular peoples of the New World. This approach is a departure from many studies of pre-modern cross-dressing which have traditionally focused solely on its meanings of a particular local culture's concepts of gender and sexuality, rather than understanding it in the contexts of commercial relations and cross-cultural encounters.

Beyond cross-dressing per se, studies of how condemned sexual behaviors and gender identities served negatively to mark particular men or ethnic groups in the classical, late antique, medieval and early modern periods, have abounded.[24] These phenomena and other usages of gender of ancient Near East have been far less well studied as an analytic category. Most studies have focused on women's roles and activities, attitudes toward them, or the existence and meanings of goddesses.[25] An important exception to this trend is the work of Howard Eilberg-Schwarz; nevertheless, much research on the ways in which gender was used as a tool to create hierarchies remains to be done.[26] Brian Britt's chapter takes a step toward this goal, for he shows how cursing in the foundational narratives of the ancient Israelites served to create genealogical and religious boundaries between peoples, namely between the Israelites and the Canaanites and the Gibeonites. Sexuality and gender play key roles in these curses. In the story of Noah, Ham, and Canaan, the curse is prompted by Ham's inappropriate sexual gaze on the nakedness of his father which in turn marks future generations not only for servitude, but for sexual immorality as well.[27] Effeminate gender roles mark another rival group, the Gibeonites. These curses, rooted in gendered bodies, served to differentiate Israelites from these "others" as a defense against aggression as well as a justification for it. Britt thus underscores the possibilities for understanding the biblical text in new ways by applying questions of gender, sexuality, and bodily meanings common in other fields of research to the fields of ancient Near Eastern or Biblical studies.

Sex, Marriage, and Difference

Marriage, divorce, and rape law and practice have long been a staple for social historians, regardless of their chronological focus.[28] Literary scholars and art historians have also begun to analyze representations of rape as reflections of the gender values of specific cultures and expressions of domination and hierarchy in the pre-modern world.[29] Edward Said was instrumental in underscoring Western assumptions about Muslim sexuality during the early modern and modern eras, and this field of inquiry has blossomed since his work and expanded into all areas of colonial, and indeed, precolonial encounter.[30]

Issues of miscegenation, that is, marriage or sex across ethnic and, in pre-modern contexts, religious boundaries have received increased attention in a variety of disciplines and chronological foci. For example, Eilberg-Schwartz has applied anthropological methodologies to get at the ways animal symbolism reflected ancient Israelite anxieties about interreligious and interethnic mixing in the Hebrew Bible.[31] David Nirenberg has used accounts and laws against sexual encounters between Christians, Jews, and Muslims to raise broader questions about the meaning and development of interreligious relations during the Middle Ages as a whole.[32]

Marriage law, rape, the sexualization of the other, and miscegenation have come together in very powerful and often politicized ways within the context of early modern European and later, U.S. expansion, conquest and enslavement or domination of non-European peoples.[33] Scholars focusing on the pre-modern world also grapple with these topics, yet those working in one chronological area are frequently unaware of the theories and findings of those in others; pre-modernists have often employed postcolonial theory to good effect, though modernists are often unaware of the research on earlier periods.[34] What is lacking in both cases is a sense of the continuum: how did law and attitudes on marriage and sexual behavior from the ancient and medieval periods affect those of the early modern and modern? In the current collection James Muldoon's study raises precisely this problem, indicating that early modern and modern law and issues surrounding marriage were very much informed by medieval canon law. He then goes on to explore the practical impact of such early influences on colonial encounter. He suggests new paths of research in which colonial formation and laws regarding the number of spouses and their religion should be understood both in their medieval contexts and also in terms of the ways in which they eroded local economies and political and familial structures. These laws also prevented or strongly discouraged certain types of accommodations, such as interethnic or interreligious marriage.

Aviva Ben-Ur presents us with a case study of such accommodations, namely intermarriage and communal inclusion among Jews in Suriname and their African slaves or servants. Her chapter serves to complicate and enrich our understandings of relations between Afro- and Euro-origin peoples during the early modern and modern eras, for she focuses on an understudied region of the pre-modern world. Her work is especially significant because she analyzes Jewish rather than Christian slave owners and the ways in which their marriage patterns and sexual interactions with their slaves and freedmen and women differed from those of Christian Portuguese and Spanish communities. Her research also adds to the recent, growing scholarship on Black-Jewish relations in pre-modern contexts.[35]

Moving from actual sex and marriage to the realm of imagination, Adam Knobler's contribution on the shifting portrayals of Brazilian and Polynesian women's breasts demonstrates that the New World itself was sometimes identified with a woman's breast. Furthermore, Western efforts to imagine and shape the breasts of Brazilian and Polynesian women simultaneously reflected their efforts to "shape" or civilize these regions into their own image, and their own concerns about European women's behavior and standards of beauty. In her chapter, Ben-Ur found similar patterns in Euro-Jewish evaluations of Afro-Caribbean breasts; these breasts often served as an object of beauty and a basis for critiquing the appearance Jewish women of European origin. Thus the other's body, especially the woman's body, served as a template or mirror against which Europeans sought to define themselves. These two chapters add to our understanding of how the body comes to symbolize social identity and anxiety within geographically disparate regions, a question initially raised by Mary Douglas. They also expand upon the growing scholarship on the sexualization of the other.

In these essays, sex, marriage, and gender serve as staples in defining, and, sometimes, defying boundaries between peoples. When no clear boundaries exist, or those boundaries are challenged in uncomfortable ways, cultures frequently create stories in which they are reinforced violently through raping, or devouring. Both Ben-Ur and Cuffel explore willing and coerced sex and marriage, as expressions of religious or ethnic domination as well as being reflections of the sexual or gender ideologies of specific cultures. In the Arabic epics and frame narratives explored by Cuffel, when willing shifts in sexuality, and thus, in turn, religious affiliation, fail, rape becomes the ultimate tool of conquest and appropriation. In this case, violent sexuality, when practiced by the desirable religious group, is laudable since it leads to (unexpected) sexual satisfaction on the part of the Christian woman which is mirrored by her religious satisfaction in Islam after she has been forcibly incorporated into it.

By contrast, in Irven Resnick and Kenneth Kitchell's chapter, "'Sweepings of Lamia': Transformations of the Myths of Lilith and Lamia," violence and sexuality signify danger since the seductions of Lamia/Lilith usually end in Lamia/Lilith's violent, literal consumption of the human lover. In the late antique and medieval Judeo-Christian context, connections between Jews, Lamia, and related poisonous creatures helped to mark the Jews as a threat to Christian society and make sexual encounter with Jews seem repugnant and perilous. Stephen Belcher's "Hunters and Boundaries in Mande Cultures" shows how tales of violence, in this case the tragic end of love affairs or marriages between hunters and their animal-human spouses, likewise serve to police boundaries between ethnicities, people of differing social status, and between the natural and human world. These tales often also serve as origin narratives to the hunter society, a group where hierarchies based on age, genealogy, or vocation disintegrated; however, the melding of human and animal worlds is implicitly approved, or at least, rendered ambiguous. These two works make a significant contribution to the exploration of how sexualization and gender become means for creating or breaking boundaries. Because relatively little has been done in this area for pre-modern Africa, Belcher's work is especially important.[36] The two chapters also exemplify the growing interest in animals as cultural signifiers, whether in the realms of difference/ "otherness," gender or some other aspect of society. Some researchers, such as Fabre-Vasses, have explored the tensions between real human interactions with particular animals and the mythologies attached to these animals.[37] Scholars of medieval and early modern Europe have been doing very fruitful explorations of the assigned meanings of monsters and other animals.[38] In particular, Debra Hassig, working on medieval bestiaries, has demonstrated the importance of animals as symbols of otherness and sexuality.[39]

When sexuality defines difference, it is often tinged with violence. At other times, as with the nymphs discussed by Knoblauch in "Promiscuous or Proper? Nymphs as Female Role Models in Ancient Greece," what appears to be violence is more symbolic than real. Nevertheless, its ritualized inclusion seems necessary to mark the transition from one status to another, in this case from maiden to married woman, and from one source of dominance to another, that is, from father to husband. In the French romance *Yde et Olive*, examined by Sahar Amer in her contribution to this collection, violence—"screams and fighting"—becomes a marker for heterosexual encounters in contrast to love between women.[40] These examples, especially Knoblauch's chapter, force us to reconsider the meanings of rape outside of its literal equation with violent, coerced intercourse.

Hybrid Identities, Group Boundaries

Real or imagined hybridity—whether in the form of a half-woman, half-beast demon such as Lamia/Lilith, satyrs, or the more subtle hybridity of the feather-donning nobility and upper classes of Tudor-Stuart England—frequently served as a powerful indicator of sexual, gendered, ethnic, social, or religious liminality. Postcolonial theorists such as Homi Bhabha have made "hybridity" into an analytical category for understanding encounters and accommodations between peoples.[41] Pre-modernists from various fields have likewise examined literal depictions of hybridity, often between the animal and human realms, for their symbolic indications about cultural boundaries.[42] That various kinds of hybridity serve as indications of liminality, cultural tension, or resistance is intriguing. More curious, however, is why liminality is sought and celebrated in some instances, is a site of fear and condemnation in others, and is neutral in yet other instances. At what point is mixing celebrated or tolerated, when is it condemned, and why? These are questions that will continue to exercise scholars of intercultural and interreligious relations long in the future, but several of the chapters in this collection serve as exempla of these processes in different pre-modern milieux.

Ben-Ur demonstrates that marriage laws and sexual encounters between Caribbean Jews and their African-origin slaves reflected wider patterns of social dominance. What is striking is the degree to which the Jews willingly made certain slaves and their descendents free members of the Jewish community thus creating a kind of "half space" in which some people could be Jewish free members of the congregation and eligible marriage partners for Euro-origin Jews, yet not of equal status to their former masters. Yet over time access to even this status became more restricted. Muldoon likewise finds anxiety and ambivalence on the part of Christian travelers, theologians, and lawyers regarding differing marriage practices of those they hoped to convert, with some being willing to consider certain forms of accommodations and not others. These accommodations and the partial state of belonging granted to Afro-Jews form a kind of hybrid identity—being neither truly a member of their previous groups nor entirely liked or accepted by the new. The chapters also raise the question of when and why are intermarriage and foreign customs judged acceptable or not, and what causes such attitudes to change?

Similar questions of what becomes tolerable and why arise in studies of cross-dressing, hybridity, body-type, and adornment. In nearly all the examples explored in this collection, cross-dressing or otherwise hybrid identities serve to challenge and explore boundaries of class and sexual or gender propriety. Amer effectively demonstrates that in the Old French tradition, Yde's cross-dressing and even miraculous transformation from a woman into a man challenged social hierarchies, since Yde had to "dress down" in her role as a soldier, and challenged gender and sexual norms by her marriage and dallying with her/his wife, Olive, yet at the same time upheld them. (Olive upholds the patriarchal hierarchy by deferring to her "husband" Yde, even though she knows Yde is a woman, plus Yde's transformation into a man and siring a son allows the resolution of noble dynastic and inheritance concerns). Both Amer and Cuffel show that Arabic accounts of same-sex love or marriages between women also ultimately affirmed dominant, male concerns and ideals, however, these narratives provide more space and tolerance for same-sex relationships and feminine power than their Western counterparts. That space springs from the hybrid identity created by the women warriors and would-be husbands in French and Arabic accounts as they adopt (or are miraculously bestowed) male clothing, genitalia, and roles, yet remain, paradoxically, women.

Carlin Barton, in her "Hercules in a Skirt," demonstrates how cross-dressing among Roman conquerors and military leaders mocked the revered ideal of the "hard" Roman man, by taking up a weak "effeminate" or "enslaved" identity. Yet in donning feminine or "effeminate" garb, these individuals also reaffirmed their masculine strength (and thus the Roman ideal) before onlookers, since such cross-dressing, and thus "crossed" identity could only be undertaken from a position of strength. Similarly, Howey points out that in early modern England wearing feathers often in combination with symbol-laden bird emblems presented contradictory messages of virtue and godly devotion simultaneously with vanity and sinfulness. Women who chose this adornment likewise challenged gender expectations since heretofore the feather had been exclusively part of the male wardrobe. Eventually the adoption of the feather into feminine attire succeeded in completely undermining gender definitions and became a site of considerable social anxiety since feathers remained "masculinized" while women wore them, yet they were too "feminized" for men. As a result, wearing feathers ultimately made men as well as women cross not merely into the dress and identity of the other, but into a mixed identity that discomfited preachers and medical writers alike. Likewise, in Knobler's piece, while Europeans tried to imagine or force Brazilian and Polynesian women into their notions of physical beauty and clothed propriety, ultimately European and American imaginings of and actions toward these women remained paradoxical: simultaneously "civilized" and clothed, and sexualized and naked.

In Mande society another kind of "crossing" occurred, this time not through clothing but by individuals who passed between definitions of animal and human. Belcher demonstrates that in Mandean literature, especially folk literature and hunter's narratives, hunters and their associations come into being through the hunter's marriage or other type of encounter with a woman who is both beast and human. Both the relationship and the hunters themselves challenged the boundaries between human and animal, revered elder and the young, and smith and noble. Again the message is mixed since the animal-woman is frequently killed and eaten by her husband in her animal state (suggesting a condemnation of the relationship) yet her husband is also the hero who goes on to form a potentially subversive identity and a set of followers for himself.

Like the magical animal-women of African epics, the nymphs and satyrs of Knoblauch's essay occupy a "half-way" status between the supernatural and the human. Nymphs serve as guides to new social roles, however in this case they serve to maintain traditional social order rather than subvert and transform it. In Resnick and Kitchell's chapter on the Christian transformations of Lamia/Lilith Jews rather than women are associated with a kind of animal-human, and in this instance, hermaphrodite identity. The results, unlike that of the African examples, are anything but ambiguous. Linking the Jews with this monster marked them as bodily other, but in this case not a desirable or fascinating other but a hideous and dangerous one. The potential monstrosity of animal identity is mirrored in Muslim portrayals of Christian princesses, for one finds monstrous, bestial characterizations as well as positive, beautiful ones within the same work. Resnick, Kitchell, Cuffel and other scholars examining medieval creations of otherness correlate "ugliness" and "beauty" to the degree of threat a group is perceived as posing, or the group or individual's potential to be successfully absorbed by the dominant.[43]

Like the behaviors and characters they describe, the diverse narratives analyzed by the authors in this collection are "liminal" in that they occupy a border space, both confirming and subverting norms, not merely about gender but about social hierarchies and identities. All play upon anxieties and ambiguities about the body's appearance, whether in dress or actual physical form, and demonstrate that physical appearance and sexualized imagery frequently signify far more than concerns over individual sexual or gendered behavior. Rather they become a template or language for creating, defining, and disrupting boundaries of ethnicity and religion, along with gender.

While previous scholars have also explored this phenomenon,[44] what these essays underscore is that diverse communities and cultures use the body, sexuality, and gender to address similar concerns through drastically different approaches. Thus we join recent cautionary voices that emphasize the importance of a nuanced and culturally specific approach. For example

David Nirenberg, in his study of communal violence among Jews, Christians, and Muslims in medieval Iberia, strongly warns against generalizations from one specific cultural moment to another.[45] Similarly, Meier Sternberg challenges the notion of ethnic and sexual stereotypes in the work of Sander Gilman. Sternberg's chief complaint is that Gilman tends to universalize human patterns of stereotyping to the point where they become "metastereotypes" promoted by scholars who act as "mythmakers."[46] Sternberg's warning here reflects a perennial tension between scholars who emphasize the dynamic and specific nature of their subjects and those who aim to generalize and theorize on the basis of empirical evidence. Yet in the same work, Sternberg himself offers a highly conceptual account of Hebrew ethnicity, one in which the protean "Ḥebrewgram" designates foreignness and describes complex patterns of group identity representation in the Bible.

These studies show that a common emphasis on physical appearance and sexualized bodies to group identities can be seen in a wide variety of pre-modern contexts, and that the identity categories of sexuality, ethnicity, and religion are deeply intertwined. Each of the studies shows how changes in group boundaries and definitions in terms of religion, gender, and ethnicity express cultural anxiety. Insofar as some of these changes demonstrate the impermanence of religious, gender, and ethnic categories, it is our hope that they may also challenge more settled interpretations of the function and interrelationships among these forms of identity. The studies also indicate the value of uncovering the historical links and transformations between cultural communities. All of the regions examined in this collection were connected to one another, and we believe future research on group identity will benefit from more direct engagement with cultural interactions.[47]

Notes

1. David Nirenberg, "Conversion, Sex, and Segregation: Jews and Christians in Medieval Spain," *American Historical Review* 107.4 (2002): 1065–93; Susan B. Edington and Sarah Lambert, eds., *Gendering the Crusades* (New York: Columbia University Press, 2001); Lynn Tarte Ramey, *Christian, Saracen and Genre in Medieval French Literature* (New York: Routledge, 2001); Susan Einbinder, "Jewish Women Martyrs: Changing Models of Representation," *Exemplaria* 12.1 (2000): 105–27; Carole Hillenbrand, *The Crusades: Islamic Perspectives* (New York: Routledge, 2000); Josiah Blackmore and Gregory Hutcheson, eds., *Queer Iberia: Sexualities, Cultures and Crossings from the Middle Ages to the Renaissance* (Durham, NC: Duke University Press, 1999); Jacqueline de Weever, *Sheba's Daughters: Whitening and Demonizing Saracen Women in*

Medieval French Epic (New York: Garland, 1998); R. I. Moore, *Formation of a Persecuting Society, Power and Deviance in Western Europe 950–1250* (Oxford/New York: Blackwell Press, 1987); John Boswell, *Christianity, Social Tolerance, and Homosexuality: Gay People in Western Europe from the Beginning of the Christian Era to the Fourteenth Century* (Chicago: University of Chicago Press, 1980); William Chester Jordan, "Jews on Top: Women and the Availability of Consumption Loans in Northern France in the Mid-Thirteenth Century," *Journal of Jewish Studies* 29 (1978): 39–56.

2. Irven Resnick, "Medieval Roots of the Myth of Jewish Male Menses," *Harvard Theological Review* 93.3 (2000): 241–63; Willis Johnson, "The Myth of Jewish Male Menses," *Journal of Medieval History* 24 (1998): 273–95; Klaus Hödl, *Die Pathologisierung des jüdischen Körpers: Antisemitismus, Geschlecht und Medizin im Fin de Siècle* (Vienna: Picus Verlag, 1997); Ross Shepard Kraemer, "The Other as Woman: An Aspect of Polemic Among Pagans, Jews, and Christians in the Greco-Roman World," in Lawrence J. Silberstein and Robert L. Cohn, eds., *The Other in Jewish Thought and History: Constructions of Jewish Culture and Identity*, New Perspectives on Jewish Studies (New York: New York University Press, 1994); Anna Sapir Abulafia, "Bodies in the Jewish-Christian Debate," in Sarah Kay and Miri Rubin, eds., *Framing Medieval Bodies* (Manchester/New York: Manchester University Press, 1994), 123–37; Elliot Wolfson, "Woman—The Feminine as Other in Theosophic Kabbalah: Some Philosophical Observations on the Divine Androgyne," in Silberstein and Cohn, eds., *The Other in Jewish Thought and History*.

3. Sharon Farmer and Carol Braun Pasternack, eds., *Gender and Difference in the Middle Ages* (Minneapolis: University of Minnesota Press, 2003); Leslie Brubaker and Julia Smith, eds., *Gender in the Early Medieval World 300–900* (Cambridge/New York: Cambridge University Press, 2004).

4. Nancy Bisaha, *Creating East and West: Renaissance Humanists and the Turks* (Philadelphia: University of Pennsylvania Press, 2004); Lucy Pick, *Conflict and Coexistence: Archbishop Rodrigo and the Muslims and Jews in Medieval Spain* (Ann Arbor: University of Michigan Press, 2004); Elisheva Baumgarten, *Mothers and Children: Jewish Family Life in Medieval Europe* (Princeton: Princeton University Press, 2004); Kenneth Mills and Anthony Grafton, eds., *Conversion: Old Worlds and New* (Rochester, NY: Rochester University Press, 2003); J. Meri, *The Cult of Saints Among Muslims and Jews in Medieval Syria* (Oxford/New York: Oxford University Press, 2002); Avigdor Levi, ed., *Jews, Turks, Ottomans, a Shared History Fifteenth Through the Twentieth Centuries* (Syracuse, NY: Syracuse University Press, 2002); Michael Signer and John van Engen, eds., *Jews and Christians in the Twelfth-Century Europe* (Notre Dame, IN: University of Notre Dame Press, 2001); Nora Berend, *At the Gate of Christendom: Jews, Muslims and "Pagans" in Medieval Hungary c. 1100–c. 1300* (Cambridge/New York: Cambridge University Press, 2001); Mark Meyerson and Edward English, eds., *Christians, Muslims and Jews in Medieval and Early Modern Spain* (Notre Dame, IN: University of Notre Dame Press, 1999); Daniel Boyarin, *Dying for God: Martyrdom and the Making of Christianity and Judaism* (Stanford: Stanford University Press, 1999); David R Blanks, Michael Frassetto, eds., *Western Views*

of Islam in Medieval and Early Modern Europe (New York: St. Martin's Press, 1999); Sahar Amer, *Esope au féminin: Marie de France et la politique de l'interculturalité* (Amsterdam/Atlanta, GA: Rodopi, 1999); James Muldoon, ed., *Varieties of Conversion in the Middle Ages* (Gainsville, FL: University Press of Florida, 1997); "From Witness to Witchcraft: Jews and Judaism in Medieval Christian Thought," *Wolfenbütteler Mittelalter-Studien* 11 (Wiesbaden: Harrassowitz, 1996); Louise Mirrer, *Women, Jews, and Muslims in the Texts of Reconquest Castile* (Ann Arbor: University of Michigan Press, 1996); Ivan Marcus, *Rituals of Childhood: Jewish Acculturation in Medieval Europe* (New Haven, CT: Yale University Press, 1996); John Tolan, ed., *Medieval Christian Perceptions of Islam: A Book of Essays* (New York: Garland, 1996); Norman Roth, *Jews, Visigoths, and Muslims in Medieval Spain: Cooperation and Conflict* (Leiden/New York: Brill, 1994); Vivian Mann, Thomas Glick, and Jerrilynn Dodds, eds., *Convivencia: Jews, Christians, and Muslims in Medieval Spain* (New York: G. Braziller in association with the Jewish Museum, 1992); M. Gervers and R. J. Bikhazi, eds., *Conversion and Continuity: Indigenous Christian Communities in Islamic Lands, Eighth to Eighteenth Centuries* (Toronto: Pontifical Institute of Mediaeval Studies, 1990). The establishment of a number of journals such as *Medieval Encounters, Journal of World History* dedicated specifically to such comparative work likewise attest to this trend.

5. Jonathan Z. Smith, "Bible and Religion," in *Relating Religion: Essays in the Study of Religion* (Chicago: University of Chicago Press, 2004), 197–98.

6. Ibid., 198.

7. M. Foucault, *The History of Sexuality*, 3 vols. (New York: Pantheon Books, 1978).

8. Arnold Davidson, *The Emergence of Sexuality* (Harvard: Harvard University Press, 2001), 22.

9. Foucault, *History of Sexuality*, 1:43. Also see: David Halperin, *One Hundred Years of Homosexuality and Other Essays in Greek Love* (New York: Routeldge, 1990); David Halperin, John Winkler, and Froma Zeitlin, eds., *Before Homosexuality: The Construction of the Erotic Experience in the Ancient Greek World* (Princeton: Princeton University Press, 1990); A. Schmitt, "Different Approaches to Male/Male Sexuality/Eroticism from Morocco to Usbekistan," in A. Schmitt and J. Sofer, eds., *Sexuality and Eroticism among Males in Muslim Societies* (New York: Haworth Press, 1992); Mark Jordan, *The Invention of Sodomy in Christian Theology* (Chicago: University Press Books, 1997); Everett Rowson, "Two Homoerotic Narratives from Mamluk Literature: al-Ṣafadī's *Law'at al-shākī* and Ibn Dānyāl's *al-Mutayyam*," in J. W. Wright and E. Rowson, eds., *Homoeroticism in Classical Arabic Literature* (New York: Columbia University Press, 1997); Everett Rowson "The Categorization of Gender and Sexual Irregularity in Medieval Arabic Vice Lists," in Julia Epstein and Kristina Straub, eds., *Body Guards: The Cultural Politics of Gender Ambiguity* (New York: Routledge, 1991).

10. John Boswell, *Christianity, Social Tolerance, and Homosexuality: Gay People in Western Europe from the Beginning of the Christian Era to the Fourteenth Century* (Chicago: University of Chicago Press, 1980); John Boswell, *Same-Sex Unions*

in Premodern Europe (New York: Villard, 1994); Catherine Edwards, *The Politics of Immorality in Ancient Rome* (Cambridge: Cambridge University Press, 1993); Amy Richlin, "Not Before Homosexuality: The Materiality of the *Cinaedus* and the Roman Law against Love Between Men," *Journal of the History of Sexuality* 3 (1993): 523–73; Bernadette Brooten, *Love Between Women: Early Christian Responses to Female Homoeroticism* (Chicago: Chicago University Press, 1996); Carolyn Dinshaw, *Getting Medieval: Sexualities and Postmodern Communities* (Durham, NC: Duke University Press, 1999). On this debate as a whole see: Mathew Kuefler, *The Boswell Thesis: Essays on Christianity, Social Tolerance and Homosexuality* (Chicago/London: Chicago University Press, 2006).

11. Khaled el-Rouayheb, *Before Homosexuality in the Arab-Islamic World, 1500–1800* (Chicago/London: University of Chicago Press, 2005).

12. Nancy Partner, "No Sex, No Gender," *Speculum* 68.2 (1993): 419–43; Ruth Mazo Karras and David Lorenzo Boyd, " 'Ut cum muliere': A Male Transvestite Prostitute in Fourteenth-Century London," in L. O. Aranye Frandenburg and Carla Freccero, eds., *Premodern Sexualities* (New York: Routledge, 1995); Everett Rowson, "Gender Irregularity as Entertainment: Institutionalized Transvestism at the Caliphal Court in Medieval Baghdad" in Farmer and Pasternack, *Gender and Difference in the Middle Ages*, 45–72.

13. A great deal of work has been done on women's cross-dressing and transgendered behaviors, however. We address this literature in the following sections.

14. Judith Brown, *Immodest Acts: The Life of a Lesbian Nun in Renaissance Italy* (New York: Oxford University Press, 1986); Brooten, *Love Between Women*. Also see: Ann Matter, "Discourse of Desire: Sexuality and Christian Women's Visionary Narratives," *Journal of Homosexuality* 18 (1989–90): 119–31; Ann Matter, "My Sister, My Spouse: Woman Identified Women in Medieval Christianity," in *The Boswell Thesis*, 152–66; Judith Hallett, "Female Homoeroticism and the Denial of Roman Reality in Latin Literature," *Yale Journal of Criticism* 3 (1989): 209–27; Robert Padgug, "Lesbian Sexuality in Medieval and Early Modern Europe," in Martin Duberman, Martha Vicinus, and George Chauncy, eds., *Hidden From History: Reclaiming a Gay and Lesbian Past* (New York: New American Library, 1989); Valerie Traub "The (In)significance of 'Lesbian' Desire in Early Modern England," in Jonathan Goldberg, ed., *Queering the Renaissance* (Durham, NC: Duke University Press, 1994); Page DuBois, *Sappho is Burning* (Chicago: University of Chicago Press, 1995); Simon Gaunt, "Sobs and Sighs Between Women: The Homoerotics of Compassion in the Book of Margery Kempe," in Frandenburg and Freccero, *Premodern Sexualities*; Jacqueline Murray, "Twice Marginal and Twice Invisible: Lesbians in the Middle Ages," in Vern Bullough and James Brundage, eds., *A Handbook of Medieval Sexuality* (New York: Garland, 1996), 191–222; Jane McIntosh Snyder, *Lesbian Desire in the Lyrics of Sappho* (New York: Columbia University Press, 1997); Francesca Canadé Sautman and Pamela Sheingorn, eds., *Same Sex Love and Desire Among Women in the Middle Ages* (New York: Palgrave, 2001); Nancy Sorkin Rabinowitz and Lisa Auanger, eds., *Among Women: From the Homosocial to the Homoerotic in the Ancient World*

(Austin: University of Texas Press, 2002); Anna Klosowska, *Queer Love in the Middle Ages* (New York: Palgrave, 2005).

15. Among the few who devote an entire study to the subject are: Stephen O. Murray, "Woman-Woman Love in Islamic Societies," in Stephen O. Murray and Will Roscoe, eds., *Islamic Homosexualities: Culture, History, and Literature* (New York: New York University Press, 1997), 97–104; Fedwa Malti-Douglas, "Tribadism/Lesbianism and the Sexualized Body in Medieval Arabo-Islamic Narratives," in Sautman and Sheingorn, *Same Sex Love and Desire*, 123–41; Sahar Amer, "Lesbian Sex and the Military: From the Medieval Arabic Tradition to French Literature," in Sautman and Sheingorn, *Same Sex Love and Desire*, 179–98. Also see the forthcoming book by Sahar Amer on the subject. Other studies that have touched upon the issue include: Everett Rowson, "Categorization of Gender and Sexual Irregularity in Medieval Arabic Vice Lists"; Everett Rowson, "Gender Irregularity as Entertainment," and Everett Rowson, "The Effeminates of Early Medina," *Journal of the American Oriental Society* 3 (1991): 671–93; Remke Kruk, "Clipped Wings: Medieval Arabic Adaptations of the Amazon Myth," *Harvard Middle Eastern and Islamic Review* 1 and 2 (1994): 2:132–51; Remke Kruk, "Warrior Women in Arabic Popular Romance: Qannāṣa bint Muzāḥim and Other Valient Ladies," Part One *Journal of Arabic Literature* 24 (1993): 213–30; Part Two, *Journal of Arabic Literature* 25 (1994): 16–33.

16. Joan Wallach Scott, "Gender: A Useful Category of Historical Analysis," in *Gender and the Politics of History, Gender and Culture* (New York: Columbia University Press,1989), 28–50; Mary Douglas, *Implicit Meanings: Essays in Anthropology* (London/Boston: Routledge and Paul,1975); Mary Douglas, *Purity and Danger: An Analysis of the Concepts of Pollution and Taboo* (London: Routledge and K. Paul, 1966).

17. Caroline Walker Bynum, *Fragmentation and Redemption* (New York: Zone Books, 1992); Caroline Walker Bynum, *Holy Feast, Holy Fast: The Religious Significance of Food to Medieval Women* (Berkeley/Los Angeles: University of California Press, 1987); Khalifa Bennasser, "Gender and Sanctity in Early Byzantine Monasticism: A Study of the Phenomenon of Female Ascetics in Male Monastic Habit with a Translation of the Life of St. Matrona" (PhD dissertation, Rutgers, 1984); Vern and Bonnie Bullough, *Cross Dressing, Sex and Gender* (Philadelphia: University of Pennsylvania Press, 1993); Gillian Cloke, *This Female Man of God: Women and Spiritual Power in the Patristic Age, AD350–450* (New York: Routledge, 1995); Elizabeth Castelli, " 'I Will Make Mary Male': Pieties of the Body and Gender Transformation of Christian Women in Late Antiquity," in Epstein and Straub, *Body Guards*; Valerie Hotchkiss, *Clothes Make the Man: Female Cross-Dressing in Medieval Europe* (New York: Garland, 1996); J. L. Welch, "Cross-Dressing and Cross-Purposes: Gender Possibilities in the Acts of Thecla" in Sabrina Ramet, ed., *Gender Reversals and Gender Cultures: Anthropological and Historical Perspectives* (New York: Routledge, 1996); Roberta Davidson, "Cross-Dressing in Medieval Romance," in Lori Hope Lefkowitz, ed., *Textual Bodies: Changing Boundaries of Literary Representation* (Albany, NY: State University of New York Press, 1997);

Michelle Szkilnik, "The Grammar of the Sexes in Medieval French Romance," in Karen J. Taylor, ed., *Gender Transgressions: Crossing the Normative Barrier in Old French Literature* (New York: Garland, 1998), 61–88; Robert L. A. Clark, "A Heroine's Sexual Itinerary: Incest, Transvestism, and Same-Sex Marriage in Yde et Olive" in Taylor, *Gender Transgressions*; Erika Hess, *Literary Hybrids: Cross-Dressing, Shape Shifting and Indeterminacy in Medieval and Modern French Literature* (New York: Routledge, 2004); Penelope Johnson, "The Body of Gerardesca of Pisa Reclothed and Resexed," in Kuefler, *The Boswell Thesis*, 287–300.

18. Bennasser, "Gender and Sanctity in Early Byzantine Monasticism"; Paul Halsall, "Women's Bodies, Men's Souls: Sanctity and Gender in Byzantium" (PhD Thesis, Fordham University, 1999); Cloke, *This Female Man of God*; Welch, "Cross-Dressing and Cross-Purposes."

19. Rowson, "Gender Irregularity as Entertainment"; Rowson, "The Effeminates of Early Medina"; Remke Kruk, "The Bold and the Beautiful: Women and 'Fitna' in the *Sīrat Dhāt al-Himma:* The Story of Nūra" in Gavin R. G. Hambly, ed., *Women in the Medieval Islamic World* (New York: St. Martin's, 1998), 99–116; Remke Kruk, "Back to the Boudoir, Arabic Versions of the *Sīrat al-amīr Ḥamza*, Warrior Princesses and the *Sīra's* Literary Unity," *Amsterdamer Beträge zur älteren Germanistik* 48 (1997): 129–48; Kruk, "Clipped Wings"; Margaret Smith, *Rabi`a the Mystic & her Fellow-Saints in Islam: Being the Life and Teachings of Rabi`a al-`Adawiyya Al-Qaysiyya of Basra Together with Some Account of the Place of the Women Saints in Islam* (Cambridge/New York, Cambridge University Press, 1984).

20. Caroline Walker Bynum, *Jesus as Mother: Studies in the Spirituality of the High Middle Ages* (Berkeley: University of California Press, 1982).

21. Karras and Boyd, " 'Ut cum muliere': A Male Transvestite Prostitute in Fourteenth-Century London"; Rowson, "Gender Irregularity."

22. Liz James, ed., *Women, Men, and Eunuchs: Gender in Byzantium* (New York: Routledge, 1997); Kathryn Ringrose, "Living in the Shadows: Eunuchs and Gender in Byzantium," in Gilbert Herdt, ed., *Third Sex, Third Gender: Beyond Sexual Dimorphism in Culture and History* (New York: Zone Books, 1994), 85–110; Kathryn Ringrose, "Reconfiguring the Prophet Daniel: Gender, Sanctity and Castration in Byzantium," in Farmer and Pasternack, *Gender and Difference*, 73–106; Kathryn Ringrose, *The Perfect Servant: Eunuchs and the Social Construction of Gender in Byzantium* (Chicago: University of Chicago Press, 2003); Mathew Kuefler, *The Manly Eunuch: Masculinity, Gender Ambiguity and Christian Ideology in Late Antiquity* (Chicago: Chicago University Press, 2001); Shaun Tougher and Ra'anan Abusch, eds., *Eunuchs in Antiquity and Beyond* (London: Classical Press of Wales and Duckworth, 2002); Shaun Tougher, "Social Transformation, Gender Transformation? The Court Eunuch, 300–900" in Brubaker and Smith, *Gender in the Early Medieval World*; Shaun Tougher, "Holy Eunuchs!: Masculinity and Eunuch Saints in Byzantium" in P. H. Cullum and Katherine J. Lewis, eds., *Holiness and Masculinity in the Middle Ages* (Toronto: University of Toronto Press, 2005).

23. See especially Amy Richlin, *The Garden of Priapus: Sexuality and Aggression in Roman Humor* (New York: Oxford University Press, 1992).

24. Richlin, *The Garden of Priapus;* Michael Satlow, *Tasting the Dish: Rabbinic Rhetorics of Sexuality* (Atlanta: Scholars Press, 1995); Boswell, *Christianity, Social Tolerance, and Homosexuality;* Irven Resnick, "Medieval Roots of the Myth of Jewish Male Menses," *Harvard Theological Review* 93.3 (2000): 241–63; Mathew Kuefler, "Male Friendship and the Suspicion of Sodomy in Twelfth-Century France," in *Boswell Thesis,* 179–212; Ruth Mazzo Karras, "Knighthood, Compulsory Homosexuality and Sodomy," in Kuefler, *Boswell Thesis,* 273–86; Alan Bray, "Homosexuality and the Signs of Male Friendship in Elizabethan England," *History Workshop* (1990): 1–19; Hödl, *Die Pathologisierung des jüdischen Körpers;* el-Rouayheb, *Before Homosexuality in the Arab-Islamic World.*

25. Averil Cameron and Amélie Kuhrt, eds., *Images of Women in Antiquity* (Detroit: Wayne State University Press, 1983); Barbara Lesko, ed., *Women's Earliest Records: From Ancient Egypt and Western Asia: Proceedings of the Conference on Women in the Ancient Near East, Brown University, Providence, Rhode Island, November 5–7, 1987* (Atlanta, GA: Scholar's Press, 1989); Tikva Frymer-Kensky, *In the Wake of the Goddesses: Women, Culture and the Biblical Transformation of Pagan Myth* (New York/Toronto: The Free Press, 1992); Gay Robins, *Women in Ancient Egypt* (Cambridge, MA: Harvard University Press, 1993); Victor Harold Matthews and Bernard M Levinson, eds., *Gender and Law in the Hebrew Bible and the Ancient Near East* (Sheffield, UK: Sheffield Academic Press, 1998); Tikva Simone Frymer-Kensky, *Gender and Archeology,* ed. Rita Wright (Philadelphia: University of Pennsylvania Press, 1996); Rivka Harris, *Gender and Aging in Mesopotamia: The Gilgamish Epic and Other Ancient Literature* (Norman, OK: University of Oklohoma Press, 2000); Zainab Bahrani, *Women of Babylon: Gender and Representation in Mesopotamia* (New York: Routledge, 2001).

26. Howard Eilberg-Schwartz, *God's Phallus and Other Problems for Men and Monotheism* (Boston: Beacon Press, 1994); Howard Eilberg-Schwartz, *The Savage in Judaism: An Anthropology of Israelite Religion and Ancient Judaism* (Bloomington: Indiana University Press, 1990). Also see: Rabinowitz and Auanger, eds., *Among Women: From the Homosocial to the Homoerotic in the Ancient World.*

27. Interestingly for the point being explored here, later rabbinic Jewish retellings of the tale transform Ham's behavior into an act of sexual brutality—Ham's castration of Noah.

28. Angeliki Laiou, ed., *Consent and Coercion to Sex and Marriage in Ancient and Medieval Societies* (Washington, DC: Dumbarton Oaks, 1993); Susan Deacy, ed., *Rape in Antiquity* (London/Swansea: Duckworth in association with the Classical Press of Wales, 1997); Karen F. Pierce, *Violence and Society in the Early Medieval West,* ed. Guy Halsall (Rochester, NY: Boydell Press, 1998).

29. Kathryn Gravdal, *Ravishing Maidens: Writing Rape in Medieval French Literature and Law* (Philadelphia: University of Pennsylvania Press, 1991);

Anna Klosowska, ed., *Violence Against Women in Medieval Texts* (Gainsville: University Press of Florida, 1998); Diane Wolfthal, *Images of Rape: The "Heroic" Tradition and its Alternatives* (Cambridge/New York: Cambridge University Press, 1999); Jocelyn Catty, *Writing Rape, Writing Women in Early Modern England* (New York: St. Martin's Press, 1999); Elizabeth Robertson and Christine Rose, eds., *Representing Rape in Medieval and Early Modern literature* (New York: Palgrave, 2001).

30. Edward Said, *Orientalism* (New York: Pantheon Books: 1978); Anne McClintock, *Imperial Leather: Race, Gender, and the Colonial Contest* (New York: Routledge, 1995); Lenore Manderson and Margaret Jolly, eds., *Sites of Desires, Economies of Pleasure: Sexualities in Asia and the Pacific* (Chicago: University of Chicago Press, 1997); Jennifer Morgan, " 'Some Could Suckle Over Their Shoulder': Male Travelers, Female Bodies and the Gendering of Racial Ideology 1500–1700," *William and Mary Quarterly* 54.1 (1997): 167–92; Nancy Paxton, *Writing under the Raj, Gender, Race, and Rape in the British Colonial Imagination 1830–1947* (New Brunswick: Rutgers University Press, 1999); Dinshaw, *Getting Medieval; Postcolonial Middle Ages*, ed. Jeffery Jerome Cohen (New York: St. Martin's Press, 2000); Ann Laura Stoler, *Carnal Knowledge and Imperial Power, Race and the Intimate in Colonial Rule* (Berkeley: University of California Press, 2002); Ananya Jahanara Kabir and Deanne Williams, eds., *Postcolonial Approaches to the European Middle Ages, Translating Cultures* (New York: Cambridge University Press, 2005).

31. Eilberg-Schwartz, *The Savage in Judaism*.

32. David Nirenberg, "Conversion, Sex, and Segregation: Jews and Christians in Medieval Spain," *American Historical Review* 107.4 (2002): 1065–93.

33. Paxton, *Writing Under the Raj, Gender, Race, and Rape*; Stoler, *Carnal Knowledge*; Sandra Gunning, *Race, Rape and Lynching: The Red Record of American Literature 1890–1912* (New York: Oxford University Press, 1996); Martha Elizabeth Hodes, ed., *Sex, Love, Race: Crossing Boundaries in North American history* (New York: New York University Press, 1999); Werner Sollers, *Interracialism: Black-White Intermarriage in American History, Literature and Law* (Oxford/New York: Oxford University Press, 2000); Peter Wallenstein, *Tell the Court love my Wife, Race, Marriage and Law: An American History* (New York: Palgrave, 2002); Frank H. Wu, *Yellow: Race in America beyond Black and White* (New York: Basic Books, 2002); Lyn Thompson, "Remembering the Jews of Algeria—Miscegenation, Degeneration, and other Metropolitan Anxieties" and Georges Van Den Abbeele, "Love, Labor, and Race: Colonial Men and White Women in France during the Great War" both in Tyler Edward Stovall and Georges Van den Abbeele, eds., *French Civilization and its Discontents: Nationalism, Colonialism, Race* (Lanham: Lexington Books, 2003).

34. Dinshaw, *Getting Medieval*; Jeffery Cohen, *Postcolonial Middle Ages*; Kabir and Williams, *Postcolonial Approaches to the European Middle Ages*.

35. David Goldberg, *The Curse of Ham: Race and Slavery in Early Judaism, Christianity, and Islam* (Princeton/Oxford: Princeton University Press, 2003); Jonathan Schorsch, *Jews and Blacks in the Early Modern World* (Cambridge, UK: Cambridge University Press, 2004).

36. Exceptions include: Robert Collins, ed., *Problems in African History: The Precolonial Centuries*, 3rd updated edition (New York: Marcus Wiener, 2005); Susan Kingsley Kent, ed., *Gender in African Prehistory* (Walnut Creek, CA: AltaMira Press, 1998); Edna Bay, *The Wives of Leopards: Gender, Politics, and Culture in the Kingdom of Dahomey* (Charlottesville: University of Virginia Press, 1998); Tarikhu Farrar, "The Queen Mother, Matriarchy and the Question of Female Political Authority in Precolonial West African Monarchy," *Journal of Black Studies* 27.5 (1997): 579–97; Onaiwu W. Ogbomo, *When Men and Women Mattered: A History of the Gender Relations among the Owan of Nigeria* (Rochester, NY: Rochester University Press, 1997); Eugenia Herbert, *Iron, Gender and Power: Rituals of Transformation in African Societies* (Bloomington/Indianapolis: Indiana University Press, 1994); "Black Women in Antiquity," *Journal of African Civilizations* 6 (1988).

37. Cladine Fabre-Vasses, *The Singular Beast: Jews, Christians and the Pig* (New York: Columbia, 1997).

38. Timothy Jones and David Sprunger, eds., *Marvels, Monsters and Miracles: Studies in the Medieval and Early Modern Imaginations* (Kalamazoo, MI: Medieval Institute Publications, 2002); Debra Higgs Strickland, *Saracens, Demons, and Jews: Making Monsters in Medieval Art* (Princeton/Oxford: Princeton University Press, 2003); Laura Lunger Knoppers and Joan B. Landes, eds., *Monstrous Bodies, Political Monstrosities in Early Modern Europe* (Ithaca: Cornell University Press, 2004); Julie Crawford, *Marvelous Protestantism: Monstrous Births in Post Reformation England* (Baltimore: Johns Hopkins University Press, 2005).

39. Debra Hassig, ed., *The Medieval Bestiary in Art, Life, and Literature* (New York: Garland, 1998); Debra Hassig, *Medieval Bestiaries: Text, Image, and Ideology* (Cambridge/New York: Cambridge University Press, 1995.

40. As Amer points out however, martial images do characterize lesbian as well as heterosexual intercourse. See her chapter in this collection and, "Lesbian Sex and the Military: From the Medieval Arabic Tradition to French Literature," in *Same Sex Love and Desire among Women in the Middle Ages* (New York: Palgrave Press, 2001), 179–98.

41. Homi Bhabha, *The Location of Culture* (New York: Routledge, 1994).

42. See earlier paragraphs on animals.

43. Sara Lipton, *Images of Intolerance: The Representation of Jews and Judaism in the Bible moralisée*. The S. Mark Taper Foundation imprint in Jewish studies. (Berkeley: University of California Press, 1999); Lester K. Little, *Religious Poverty and the Profit Economy in Medieval Europe* (Ithaca: Cornell University Press, 1978); Ruth Melinkoff, *Antisemitic Hate Signs in Hebrew Illuminated Manuscripts from Medieval Germany* (Jerusalem: Center for Jewish Art, Hebrew University of Jerusalem,1999); Ruth Melinkoff, *Outcasts: Signs of Otherness in Northern European Art of the Late Middle Ages*, 2 vols. California Studies in the History of Art, 32 (Berkeley: University of California Press, 1993).

44. Joan Wallach Scott, "Gender: A Useful Category of Historical Analysis," in *Gender and the Politics of History: Gender and culture* (New York: Columbia University Press, 1989), 28–50; Mary Douglas, *Implicit Meanings: Essays in*

Anthropology (Routledge and Paul: London/Boston, 1975); Mary Douglas, *Purity and danger: An Analysis of the Concepts of Pollution and Taboo* (Routledge and K. Paul, London, 1966).

45. Nirenberg, *Communities of Violence: Persecution of Minorities in the Middle Ages* (Princeton: Princeton University Press, 1996).

46. Meier Sternberg, *Hebrews Between Cultures: Group Portraits and National Literature* (Bloomington: Indiana University Press, 1999), 171–81.

47. Belcher's discussion of African oral epics might seem the most geographically disassociated of the contributions, however, there are strong literary and historical ties between African and Arabic, and then from Arabic to Western epics. Also, some scholars have suggested that preaching and storytelling traditions among slave and free Africans and their descendants in the United States owe a substantial debt to the role of African griots. See: Michael A. Gomez, *Exchanging Our Country Marks: The Transformation of African Identities in the Colonial and the Antebellum South* (Chapel Hill: University of North Carolina Press, 1997), 280.

I

———————————————

Ancient Cultures

Chapter 1

Ethnic Curses as "Last Resort of the Weak" in Genesis 9:18–28 and Joshua 9:22–27

Brian Britt

Introduction

Biblical curses appear in a wide range of biblical texts and contexts. Scholars have typically classified curses as a vestige of magical, pre-Israelite culture. A different approach is taken in recent studies by Jeff Anderson and Paul Keim, which attend to the social contexts and functions of biblical curses, including the enforcement of norms and social order, the ratification of treaties, and explanations for evil and suffering.[1] This chapter considers another social function of curses noted by Anderson: their use as what anthropologist James Scott calls a "last resort of the weak."[2] For people who are victimized or deprived of self-determination and sufficient means of material existence, power can still be exercised in symbolic form, through curses. Defined for present purposes as the use of words to invoke harm upon another through supernatural means, curses by weak parties upon stronger ones can counteract the imbalance of power in such relationships.

A theoretical context for this approach appears in Scott's characterization of certain speech acts and other symbolic expression as "everyday resistance." Even when the material life of one group is tightly controlled by another, Scott argues that in hundreds of subtle ways, oppressed people are able to resist the worldview of their oppressors even as they suffer great material hardships. Scott argues that oppressed people, following "hidden transcripts" that affirm their identity and dignity, demonstrate the capacity to think and act independently of their oppressors, even when they are prevented from overthrowing them.[3] Known sometimes as the "curse of the poor," which Max Weber believed to be a source of fear in the ancient world, curses by weak people against their stronger opponents may be socially effective in galvanizing weak groups and frightening their powerful opponents.[4] The dynamics of power in these curses are typically expressed in terms of gender and ethnicity.

This chapter applies Scott's notion of "everyday resistance" to biblical curses against opposing ethnic groups: the Canaanites and Gibeonites. The identity of each group remains a puzzle for scholarship, one that demands a reconsideration of the category of "ethnicity" itself. Both of the texts I consider here—Gen. 9 and Josh. 9—provide the first biblical mention of the ethnic groups they curse; naming and cursing are thus simultaneous for the biblical canon. As neighbors and rivals, both groups represent a clear threat to Israelite power, particularly in terms of inter-marriage, and these curses seek to justify the struggle against them and to express symbolic resistance in light of Israelite vulnerability. But power relationships change, and in canonical context, curses of the weak against the strong can become their opposite, justifying oppression by the strong against the weak. I will explore this problem by taking up Nietzsche's diagnosis of the Christian and Jewish *ressentiment*, the "slave morality" that celebrates weakness, as the result of just such a reversal. Ethnic curses are thus highly volatile and socially efficacious: at one moment the "last resort of the weak," at another instruments of social oppression. As such, biblical curses contain the hermeneutical flexibility to accommodate changing times and thus provide a model for biblical tradition without radical indeterminacy of meaning.

According to Jeff Anderson, curses can apply to cases where the legal system failed to ensure justice and as a deterrent to those who those who might wish to harm the poor and needy. In addition to such texts as Prov. 30:10 and Eccl. 7:21, Anderson cites the "beggar's curse" of popular folklore; Keith Thomas's study of early modern England; Ronald Reminick's study of the evil eye; and Max Weber's notion that the curse of the poor was "the weapon of democracy."[5] As an expression of symbolic power, writes Anderson, "[s]uch curses also served as a substitute for political action," as a way to seek revenge or even to avert war. Anderson cites Judg. 9 and the curse of Shimei in 2 Sam. 16 as examples in which survivors of a defeated family seek to curse their oppressors.[6]

Two Ethnic Curses

Two biblical curses consign ethnic groups to servitude: the curse on Canaan (Gen. 9:26) and the curse on Gibeon (Josh. 9:23). The servitude of both groups is attested in Josh. (9:23 and 16:10, 17:12; cf. Judg. 1:29–30) but neither ethnic group plays a prominent role in the prophets or the books of Samuel and Kings. In the first case, a sexually charged failure of filial respect is loosely tied to the punishment of Ham, "father of Canaan" (9:18, 22): Canaan is curses as the "servant of servants" to his brothers (v. 25). Ham's sin is ambiguous, but for later biblical tradition it was understood to be a sexual crime, thus linking ethnic difference with sexuality.[7] In the second case, a ruse of the Gibeonites leads Joshua to make a pact with them without seeking divine counsel (9:14). Both cases follow etiological form, explaining how the ethnic rivalries arose; in the first, the action of an individual (Ham) justifies the fate of his son and a people, Canaan; in the second, the deception behind the pact leads Joshua to curse the Gibeonites. Taken at face value, the curses suggest a direct link between ancient and contemporary realities. But such a correspondence is not easy to establish. The "conquest" model of the Israelite settlement of Canaan depicted in Joshua does not reflect the findings of archaeologists and historians of the period; there is no consensus among historians on the emergence of Israel in Canaan and the relationship between this process and the biblical text.[8] As such, these curses may not so much describe undisputed reality as some etiological stories do ("how the tiger got its stripes," or "why the sky is blue") as form part of a group history or mythology. In fact, the Deuteronomistic history (e.g., Josh.10, 2 Sam. 21) generally regards Gibeon as relatively powerful, and closely tied to the cultic life of Israel (e.g., 2 Sam. 6, 1 Kgs. 3, 1 Chron. 16), despite the assertion in Josh. 9 that the Gibeonites are cursed to be servile water-carriers and hewers of wood.

Joseph Blenkinsopp considers the treaty of Josh. 9 to be generally consistent with historical accounts and literary traditions of the period, but he notes the problems with any attempt to date the treaty.[9] More importantly, Blenkinsopp observes that the prospect of one Israelite group prevailing over a powerful adversary like Gibeon strains credibility, and that the treaty oath customarily sworn by the weaker party is here sworn by Israel.[10] The treaty, Blenkinsopp concludes, suggests an early attempt by a weak Israelite party to align with a stronger local one, as part of a larger pattern of peaceful settlement (as opposed to conquest). Whether the curse reflects the reverse of historical reality, it is clear that the Gibeonites stand apart from other conquered peoples in Joshua, that they are included in the covenant (Deut. 29:10), and that they are powerful enough to demand the death of

Saul's offspring when the treaty is violated (2 Sam. 21). The Gibeonites are an ambiguous, problematic ethnic group.

The curse of Canaan in Gen. 9 is far less clear than the curse of Gibeon. At the conclusion of the flood story, the actions of the three sons of Noah predict their legacies to the major ethnic groups descending from them. Long before the biblical narrative presents the Israelite settlement of Canaan, an ambiguous sexual sin justifies the subjugation of Canaan by the descendants of Shem. But like the case of Gibeon, the historical evidence for such domination is sketchy; the biblical accounts from Judges to 1 Kings cast doubt on the bold hierarchy proposed in the curse of Canaan.

Who were the Canaanites and Gibeonites? Easy answers are not forthcoming. The Gibeonites are merely those who live in Gibeon, which we are told is a "great city" (Josh. 9:3, 10:2). Both terms refer to geographic areas that are presumably the home of these peoples. Canaan, though, refers to a relatively large area, ranging from the whole of Transjordan (Josh. 14:1 and Num. 13:2, Deut. 32:49) to a significant portion within it: "all the regions of the Philistines, and all those of the Geshurites (from the Shihor, which is east of Egypt, northward to the boundary of Edron; it is reckoned as Canaanite . . .)" (Josh. 13:2). "Canaanite" would thus seem to describe a larger or more generic group of people than "Gibeonite," which though difficult to fix with precision, refers to a particular city-state and its people (Josh. 10). Neither group appears to be as distinct from Israel as the category of ethnicity might suggest. I return to the question of ethnicity later in this chapter.

The Social and Historical Context of Curses

In their earliest historical context, the curses against Gibeon and Canaan thus reflect the intention or wish of a weaker party to subdue a stronger one, if only in verbal and religious terms. Putting aside the problems of historicity, I approach the curses as literary and sociological phenomena, not as magical forces but as powerful uses of language nevertheless. With Paul Keim, I see biblical curses as a crucial indicator of group power and interactions.[11] As a curse by the weak on the strong, these curses fall into the larger category of "weapons of the weak." By wishing evil or subjugation on its enemies, Israel resorts to one of the few weapons available to the weak.

Ancient curses, and curses in general, can be highly ritualized or relatively spontaneous. Treaties and royal inscriptions conventionally include curses as a way to protect and seal the power of powerful authorities (see e.g., Deut. 28). Less ritualized curses can simply perform the role of imprecations and maledictions, spontaneously conveying the passion of an individual like

Shimei in 2 Sam. 16. Ritualized curses are more typical of kings, priests, and other ruling authorities, while spontaneous curses tend to be the domain of common people.

The curses on Gibeon and Canaan are more spontaneous than ritualized. The question may illuminate whether they represent power or evidence of relative weakness. Both cases occur in the heat of the moment—Noah's nakedness and Joshua's anger toward Gibeon. Both curses follow unexpected loss, even humiliation; in the case of Noah, the humiliation has clear sexual overtones, while for Joshua the curse emerges from a ruse that replaces force with cunning in a way that is anomalous for warrior culture (9:4).[12]

The curses on Canaan and Gibeon may represent revised accounts of a time when Israel was threatened by these other groups and used "weapons of the weak" against them. Any event related in the Primary History has at least two historical contexts: the time of the event and the time of its writing. Compressing the results of historical research, we can propose two phases: one in which Israel was too weak to challenge rival groups, and a second, later phase when Israel was able to gain sufficient power to exercise autonomy in a significant territorial area; such power might even include victory over Gibeon and Canaan, if not their complete subordination. By this account, the curse of the powerless in the first phase would be seen as fulfilled in the second phase. At the point when this national story or history is created and circulated, the victory of the weak over the strong takes on ideological meaning: the facts of history confirm specific religious and political values. Gibeonites and Canaanites are named as distinct ethnic groups, and the curses on them are depicted as fulfilled. This process of canonization makes this biblical story authoritative and normative.

A third hypothetical phase, when the gains of monarchy and territory have been lost, can be added to the first two. Thus the initial phase of weakness, in which the curse may represent more of a wish than a reality, has counterparts in the third phase after Israel is exiled and once again subordinated by other groups. With the benefit of hindsight, biblical authors condense and explain traditions of the remembered past. The study of this process can usefully be described as what Jan Assmann calls "mnemohistory," the history of memory.[13] Unlike traditional history, concerned mainly with evaluating claims about historicity and evidence, mnemohistory proposes to examine the process whereby memory is recorded, changed, and handed down. In the case of ancient Israel, mnemohistory describes many operations of biblical authors, such as rearranging, condensing, and reversing traditions. In the case of ethnic curses, it may even incorporate the memory of the "hidden transcripts" of resistance: the written declaration of Canaanite or Gibeonite servitude may echo a much earlier and less formal expression of resentment against strong rivals.

Mnemohistory would characterize the curses as the combination of a memory of past struggle with later victories and defeats. Later group differences are projected onto the past and hence justified by atavistic curses that create and enforce group boundaries. After the weakness of the early, settlement period, the Israelites begin to write their national history from the vantage point of victory and prosperity: rival peoples no longer threaten their existence. But the primary history is not only a celebration of Israelite triumph; it is also a sharp indictment of the repeated failures of Israelite kings and people to keep the covenant. Among their failings none is as profound as improper liaisons with foreigners and their gods.

Completed under the yoke of exile, the Deuteronomistic history combines the triumph of a successful monarchy with the crushing defeat of the Babylonian conquest. In this way, the formation of the national history contains moments of triumph and stability (most likely under Josiah) as well as moments of disaster, after the destruction of Jerusalem. This double focus gives two meanings to the curses, which, like curses in general, can redound upon those who utter them. The good fortune of conquering Canaan and the Gibeonites can swiftly be undone in case of Israelite faithlessness. For Israel, ethnic curses contain a seed of self-criticism and potential punishment.

Curses and Culture: Nietzsche

One of the first to analyze the layering of these "phases" in biblical history was Friedrich Nietzsche. For Nietzsche, the Bible provides an unnatural rationalization of history from the standpoint of the priestly class. This history follows a decline from the Kingdom, when "Yahweh was the expression of their consciousness of power, of their delight in themselves" to a period after the destruction of Israel in which the priesthood "made of it a stupid salvation—mechanism of guilt towards Yahweh and punishment, piety towards Yaweh and reward."[14] This priestly religion becomes the basis for what Nietzsche regards as the unnatural decadence and *ressentiment* of Christian morality. The doctrine of a transcendent god is, for Nietzsche, an act of "revenge" on Israel's enemies: "The *one* god and the *one* Son of God: both products of *ressentiment*."[15] At the heart of this transformation, for Nietzsche, was scripture itself, in the form of the Deuterononomic code whose discovery is reported in 2 Kgs. 22: "[A] great literary forgery becomes necessary, a 'sacred book' is discovered—it is made public with all hieratic pomp, with days of repentance and with lamentation over the long years of 'sinfulness.' "[16]

Nietzsche's characterization of Judaism and Christianity is highly problematic, with its simplistic, flawed analysis and polemical rhetoric, but it recognizes that biblical tradition emerges from historical loss. The doctrines of sin, transcendent God, and the exaltation of the weak represent a brilliant but unnatural response to defeat. The subsequent rise of Christianity as a dominant power encodes this morality of weakness and *ressentiment* on a mass scale. A crucial dimension of this process is that symbolic elements of scripture and religious teaching constitute genuine power. Nietzsche's analysis of Christian and Jewish morality as a subtle form of aggression, a kind of power for the powerless, closely parallels the notion of curses as a weapon of the weak. In this sense, the religious worldviews of Christianity and Judaism function like massive curses. (In fact, Nietzsche concludes his entire analysis of Christianity and Judaism in *The Anti-Christ* with a curse: "I call Christianity the *one* great curse, the *one* great intrinsic depravity, the *one* great instinct for revenge for which no expedient is sufficiently poisonous, secret, subterranean, *petty*[.] I call it the *one* immortal blemish of mankind.")[17] Words, including curses, express real power for Nietzsche; the driving force of this *ressentiment* culture is the Bible itself.

These reflections take us far from the curses on Canaan and Gibeon, participating in the kind of "genealogy" that often generates more confusion than insight. The line connecting biblical curses through biblical tradition does not, in my mind, lead inevitably to the state of affairs described by Nietzsche. What Nietzsche provides, however, is a serious attempt to establish continuity between ancient Israel and modern Europe; his is one of the few philosophical accounts to take religious tradition and religious speech seriously, so much so that he makes religion and religious speech (cursing) central to his work. Like Sigmund Freud and Jan Assmann after him, Nietzsche acknowledges symbolic representations along with "history" *per se*; as a representation, a layered record of memory, the Bible becomes a primary source for analysis rather than a flawed account of history.[18] In addition, Nietzsche's application of *ressentiment* seeks to explain one of the most striking qualities of ancient Israel: the claim to covenant with a superior deity despite a history of only modest political and economic success.

The phase before Israel's ascent to a territorial power may in fact provide a kind of model and mirror for a phase after which that power had been lost. To apply Assmann's notion of mnemohistory, we could say that the memory of early Israelite resentment toward the Canaanites and Gibeonites returns in subsequent periods when Israelite domination of these groups was either a reality or a norm to which they wished to return. Noted perhaps as victories from the time of conquest, the subordination of the Canaanites and Gibeonites likely provided reassurance of Israelite power in later times. By the time of the exile and return, the curses would constitute a kind of normative or ideological wish that embodied some of the characteristics Nietzsche meant by *ressentiment*.

In terms of biblical tradition, which elaborately intertwines historical strands, the initial Israelite hostility to foreigners could furnish later generations, in moments of victory as well as defeat, with the memory of curses. At times of Israelite prosperity and success, such curses, retrojected onto the past, would constitute a crucial element of a national history in which weak ancestors foretold success. Later, after bitter exile and loss, the curses against Canaan and Gibeon could redound on Israel as rash words uttered without consulting Yhwh (see 9:14), or as conditional curses that function when Israel follows the covenant. Curses against Gibeon and Canaan also anticipate the florid oracles against the nations in prophetic discourse: Israel may be defeated now, but the day will come when the nations are once again brought low.

Genesis 9

The curse of Ham is difficult to attach to specific historical events, but understanding its rhetorical and literary significance requires a general sense of its origins. As a story of second beginnings, the Flood narrative combines primordial myth with a concern to explain the status of the nations issuing from Noah. From the retrospective standpoint of conflict between Israel and Canaan, the story offers a chance to ground that conflict in mythical terms. The most obvious problem with the curse is why Canaan, one of Ham's four sons, is cursed when it is Ham who sins. The text appears to strain the ancient myth to justify a specifically anti-Canaanite position. What begins as a modest account of Noah as the father of local peoples takes on a much broader significance in light of the table of nations (usually attributed to the Priestly source) that follows in Gen. 10.

What are the details of the curse? "And he (Noah) said, 'Cursed be Canaan, slave of slaves will he be to his brothers.' And he said, 'Blessed be Yhwh, God of Shem, let Canaan be a slave to him. May God enlarge Japheth, may he sleep in the tents of Shem, and may Canaan be a slave to them'" (Gen. 9: 25–26). Recent studies have emphasized the corrosive potential of this text, from its well-known use to justify the enslavement of Africans to the more general reinforcement of ethnic rivalries and violence.[19] Like the curse on the Gibeonites, the curse on Canaan comes from an angry Israelite leader. Whether it represents a position of strength or weakness is impossible to decide with certainty, since there are phases of both in the Primary History. There is very little in subsequent biblical texts to suggest that Canaan was understood to be destined to *perpetual* slavery, and as David Aaron shows, the early rabbis focused on the curse as punishment for a moral (sexual) transgression; modern conceptions of race have little to do with the text and its early exegesis.[20]

Still, the text sends a clear message that Canaan is the slave of Shem and Japheth, and subsequent conflicts with "Canaanites," who may be a specific ethnic group or any inhabitants of the land of Canaan, clearly underlie the text. Ham's transgression of looking upon his father's nakedness may indicate a sexual offense or a more general failure of filial piety, but it strongly contrasts the behavior of his brothers, and it arouses the anger of his father Noah. With a single act of improper looking, Ham seals the fate of his son Canaan and the people after him. Crossing the boundary of sexual propriety within the family leads to exclusion from the family. There is a kind of poetic justice in the curse insofar as Shem and Japheth act as servants toward their father, covering his nakedness. Canaan, son of Ham, must now become a servant to these brothers because of the failure to behave as a servant.

According to Meir Sternberg, Gen. 9 marks a "dividing line" in biblical history between ethnic groups. Ham's unfilial, sexually immoral behavior anticipates the immorality of all Hamite peoples, including Egyptians as well as Canaanites.[21] The designation "Canaanites," like "Hebrews" in Sternberg's account, becomes a deliberate by-word rooted more in scriptural rivalries than in ethnographic taxonomies:

> To make the hated adversaries hateful, the Bible . . . overturns the name's standard group attribute (merchant class and/or Phoenician habitation) into ethnicity, so as to taint the archenemy with Noah's curse upon their putative eponymous ancestor, Canaan son of Ham, who violated his father's nakedness . . . No wonder he anticipates (or inspires) his offspring, the latter-day Sodomites.[22]

Translating a general description into an ethnic term, the biblical narrative mixes past and present, judgment with history. The in-family nature of the curse on Canaan may also be revealing in light of the linguistic and cultural similarities of Israelites and Canaanites. As I suggest in the discussion of ethnicity below, the curse of Canaan may betray a familiarity between the two peoples on a level more literal than is usually considered.

Joshua 9

The curse on the Gibeonites represents part of a treaty that assigns them the role of water-carriers and hewers of wood for the temple (v. 23). The judgment comes in the wake of the ruse with which the Gibeonites convince the Israelites that they were stronger than they really were. By securing an oath of protection from the Israelites, the Gibeonites avoid the annihilation meted out to other residents of Canaan. Thus one kind of powerful, binding speech (oath) leads Joshua to issue another (curse). The "curse" here, as Herbert Brichto notes, is more of a "decree" than an "imprecation," since it enacts a ban on the Gibeonites rather than a wish or prayer for harm against them.[23] Like the rest of Josh. 1–12, the conquest of the Gibeonites depicts glorious victory for Israel over the inhabitants of Canaan, but in this case the usual annihilation under the rule of ritualized dedication for destruction(חרם) is avoided.

As Joseph Blenkinsopp notes, the treaty with Gibeon is puzzling in a number of ways. Gibeon, we are told in 10:2, is a "great city" full of mighty men. The treaty oath, which is usually sworn by the weaker party, is sworn by the supposed victor, Israel. Comparing the episode to the treaty with Shechem in Gen. 34, Blenkinsopp suggests that early Israelite settlers sought the treaty with the more powerful Gibeon, whom they may later have conquered.[24] If Blenkinsopp is correct, then the curse assigned to Gibeon is part of a retrospective account of the Israelite settlement that reverses the power relationship from a strong Gibeon and weak Israel to a weak Gibeon and strong Israel. Such a curse is consistent with the idea of curses as a "last resort of the weak."

Gender plays as much a role in the curse on Gibeon as sexuality does in the curse on Canaan. According to Robert Gordon, to consign the Gibeonites to be hewers of wood and drawers of water is an example of an "effeminacy curse."[25] Citing numerous other ancient Near Eastern examples, Gordon argues that the Gibeonites' tasks are traditionally associated with women. He cites the Ugaritic *Legend of King Karet*, which specifically describes women in the roles of wood-cutters and drawers of water on the way to meet warriors returning from battle. Gordon associates Josh. 9 with a tradition of effeminacy curses used to taunt, threaten, or subordinate rival men, especially in the context of military conflict.

As an effeminacy curse, the curse on the Gibeonites performs the patriarchal maneuver of defining ethnic difference in terms of gender. Gender, in turn, becomes a trope to contrast the powerful (masculine) Israelites to the subordinate, feminized Gibeonites. The fact that the Gibeonites have served in this servile role "until this day" (v. 27) offers the reader evidence that the effeminacy curse is binding. But there is something oddly unconvincing about this curse; if the biblical text inverts the reality of Gibeon's power over Israel, then the effeminacy curse may be a "last resort of the weak," a verbal act of resistance against power. To depict the invincible Gibeonites as feminized servants would thus constitute an act of cultural resistance. In Josh. 9 as in Gen. 9, ethnic dominance is expressed through gender dominance, and the "effeminacy curse" against the Gibeonites may have a distant counterpart in the curse on Ham/Canaan.

But how ethnically distinct were the Gibeonites? Gibeon is closely related to the family of Saul, a fact the Deuteronomistic history appears to minimize by avoiding any mention of Gibeon during the period of Judges and Saul.[26] Yet Saul and his family may have Gibeonite origins, and it is possible that he tried to establish Gibeon as a religious and political center.[27] If so, the distinction between Israelite and Gibeonite may have much more to do with political or religious differences than any genuinely distinct history of a people or "ethnic" group. As Blenkinsopp indicates, Gibeon's importance involves cultic tradition as well as political and military strength. Frequent reference is made to Gibeon as a well-known place, even a place for sacrifice (e.g., 1 Kgs. 3:4). The text of Josh. 9 itself appears to be composite: different terms describe the Israelite parties to the treaty, and there is evidence of Deuteronomistic editing; there is no consensus, however, on what this editing implies for biblical history.[28]

Peter Kearney observes some striking similarities between Gen. 3 and Josh. 9. Both stories report the ability of a clever (עָרוּם) party to trick the central characters (Eve, Joshua) into unwise actions. In both stories, deception leads to a "curse on the deceiver."[29] According to Kearney, the curse of Josh. 9 reinforces the Deuteronomistic warning against treaties with foreign groups. Two Deuteronomistic texts, Deut. 29 and 1 Kgs. 8, make direct allusions to the treaty with Gibeon as a dangerous infidelity.[30] In Deut. 29, suggests Kearney, the treaty with Gibeon emerges as a paradigmatic case of unwarranted traffic with foreigners. Kearney finds further evidence of a "deception motif" in stories of treaties with foreigners in the narrative of 2 Kgs. 20, where a Babylonian delegation arrives at the court of Hezekiah.[31] Kearney also links Josh. 9–10 and 2 Kgs. 20, which depict the danger of making treaties with foreigners, as the only two texts in the Bible describing sun miracles.

Conflicts in and around Gibeon during the Babylonian and early Persian periods may help explain the anti-Gibeonite biases of the Deuteronomistic History. Synthesizing archaeological data from the area, Diana Edelman proposes that if Gibeon was closely tied to the house of Saul, the return of exiles during the Persian period could have revived hopes for the restoration of Gibeon as a religious and political capital. The prevailing returnees, who favored the house of David and Jerusalem over Saul and Gibeon, wove their anti-Gibeonite views into the history, minimizing pro-Gibeonite and pro-Saulide claims. By Edelman's account, then, much of what the Bible says about Gibeon may be traced to the polemics of the Persian period, though she admits that the evidence here is inconclusive.[32] Much more likely would be a scenario in which an ancient tradition of Israelite weakness vis-à-vis Gibeon has been revived to serve a latter-day situation. The complex rivalry between Israel and Gibeon has its roots in the shadowy period of the settlement, and, like the motif of the Egyptian Moses of Assmann's mnemohistory, it reappeared frequently throughout Israelite tradition.

Ethnicity, Gender, and Curses

What is ethnicity in the Bible? The question raises significant historical and conceptual difficulties. Biblical ways of naming groups rarely find exact corroboration in contemporary texts, and it is not always clear how such group designations are made. As Niels Peter Lemche observes in his study of the Canaanites, "[W]e today possess very definite ideas about the identity of peoples and nations which accord well with the division of our world into nation-states. In the ancient world . . . no such nation-states existed and no nationalistic ideology had yet arisen."[33] Lemche's comment reflects one position in current debates among biblical scholars on the category of ethnicity. The debate concerns at least two separate questions: whether the modern category of ethnicity can apply to the ancient world, and whether group designations like "Israel," "Hebrews," and "Canaanites" do in fact refer to historical groups. On the second question, Israel Finkelstein and others claim that the Israelites were originally Canaanites, and he points out that excavations show little difference between early Israelite and surrounding cultures, with the exception that Israelite sites have no pork bones.[34] Does this mean that Israel was not an ethnic group? It depends on what one means by ethnicity. In a paper disputing those who label Israelite culture a lifestyle rather than an ethnicity, William Dever argues that "ethnicity *is* lifestyle."[35]

What is certain is that ethnicity cannot be taken as a universal category or that particular group designations are self-evident. "Gibeonite" and "Canaanite" refer sometimes to people in particular places and at others to specific groups. The terms are even more sharply defined in the context of conflict, as in the case of Judg. 1:1 and Gen. 9 for the Canaanites and 2 Sam. 21 and Josh. 9 for the Gibeonites. The notions of group identity and election in Israelite religion produced contradictory views of other groups: envious admiration, unlikely self-confidence; simultaneous impulses (borne out in the mixture of attitudes in Joshua and Judges) toward annihilation, annexation, and coexistence. At the heart of such distinctions are gendered curses and prohibitions on marriage and procreation outside the group defined in terms of ethnicity. This mixture of attitudes reflects a religious ideology that claims unique access to a supreme deity who sometimes punishes Israel by means of more powerful enemies.

The curses on Canaan and Gibeon betray rivalries with formidable enemies. Neither curse reflects an unchanging state of affairs in which Israel is master and the Canaanites and Gibeonites are slaves. Within the context of a historically layered canon, the curses hold the balance of power in suspension. In this sense, the curses resemble the aporetic curse on the Amalekites (Exod. 17), in which Moses is directed to write down the command to forget the Amalekites for all generations. The meaning of the curse depends on historical conditions. The curse on an enemy can reflect a position of weakness from which victory seems fanciful or a genuine rivalry in which the curse relates to a struggle for power.

The linguistic flexibility of ethnic terms and curses calls for new models of biblical ethnicity. In a study that combines archaeology with studies of cultural ideas of tradition and language, Elizabeth Bloch-Smith suggests new ways of understanding Israelite ethnicity. Taking the "meaningful boundaries" and "tell-tale" approaches to ethnicity together, she argues that "collective memory" and biblical texts themselves should serve as guides to understanding Israelite ethnicity. Such an approach offers a new way of thinking about the relationship between biblical text and biblical archaeology: "Biblical texts confer significance on archaeologically attested traits; archaeology supplies a date and a context for specific features preserved in redacted texts . . . Israel should be defined on its own terms (as filtered through later generations) rather than as a modern scholarly construct."[36]

Bloch-Smith thus shifts the formulation of ethnicity from contemporary to ancient sources. Setting aside whether it is possible to speak in any transcultural or neutral sense about ethnicity, this approach asks how ancient Israel defines and understands what we call ethnicity, and it permits Bloch-Smith to offer a solution to the puzzling difference between the Philistine and Canaanite archaeological records. While both ethnic groups are defined as rivals, archaeology has found no salient differences between "Israelite" and "Canaanite" or "Gibeonite" discoveries in the area.[37]

In the case of the Philistines, writes Bloch-Smith, biblical texts match archaeology fairly closely; the differences between the groups marked in the Bible can be seen in the material record. In fact, Israelite ethnicity may have evolved through alliances made against the Philistines.[38] But biblical texts on Canaanites don't match archaeological records, either because the past was reconstructed or because the differences between Israelites and Canaanites concerned religion more than other practices or attributes.[39] If the latter is the case, then it becomes difficult to distinguish religion from ethnicity; ethnicity becomes a way of reifying religious differences between two groups who share most other cultural practices in common. By this account, the curse on Ham and Canaan may reflect the sense in which moral and religious difference can produce ethnic difference *within a family*. Ethnic distinctions must then be understood primarily in terms of "collective memory": "The later biblical 'collective memory,' which regarded kinship, cult, and territory as primordial unifying factors, simplified, perhaps obscured, and may even have superseded the true unifying features of the Israelite *ethnos* in the twelfth to eleventh centuries BCE."[40]

Bloch-Smith's notion of collective memory resembles Assmann's notion of "mnemohistory." For the Gibeonites and Canaanites, the question becomes one of how the biblical accounts reflect the context of their composition and the context of the period to which it refers. The problem is also basic to Blenkinsopp's treatment of Gibeon, which, by its suggestive link between the house of Saul and Gibeon, complicates any attempt to distinguish Gibeon from Israel in traditional "ethnic" terms ordinarily construed. If it is the case that biblical ethnicity—at least in the case of Gibeon and Canaan—emerges more from political and religious conflict than from a prior sense of separate identities as people, then the curses against these groups reinforce or even help create ideas of group difference not clearly visible from archaeological data. Ethnic curses, in other words, become a means to distinguish one group from another, to define and maintain the boundaries between Israel and Canaanites or Gibeonites. As the biblical narratives and archaeological work about both groups attests, these boundaries were in fact difficult to maintain, because they had so much in common. This difficulty, I suggest, is attested by the emphatic curses on Gibeon and Canaan themselves.

Ethnic curses, then, produce and reproduce troubled boundaries between Israel and others. The relative strength and weakness of Israel and others cannot be known with certainty, but the inherent ambiguity of curses allows them to adopt to reversals of power relations. If the notion of group difference emerges less out of separate group history and practice than from disputes and rivalries within groups, it follows at least that such boundaries are not inevitable; the transformation of curses as a resort of the weak into a justification for subordination of these groups at moments of strength is not, therefore, justifiable.

In "What is a People?" Giorgio Agamben suggests that "the concept of people always already contains within itself the fundamental biopolitical fracture," a split between "naked life (*people*) and political existence (*People*)."[41] In terms of Bloch-Smith's suggestion, this split may refer to the development of *ethnic* difference out of *religious* difference. The tendency to *naturalize* differences between selves and others, which Agamben associates with Hellenistic influences on Western culture, may also exist in ancient Israel, whose collective memory increasingly reifies Canaanites and

Gibeonites. While Agamben does not deal with biblical curses in particular, his observations about "people" become particularly valuable in a context where the Bible becomes an authoritative text for powerful groups who engage in Hellenistic interpretation. The fluidity of group boundaries and power dynamics tends to harden under such conditions, leading to notions of ethnicity quite remote from the world of Genesis or Joshua.

For many different uses and contexts, curses represent a set of basic themes on which tradition or mnemohistory can perform variations. Early conditions in which strong rivals were defined and cursed by the weaker Israelites influenced later biblical expressions and attitudes toward Canaanites and Gibeonites. In the end, it is impossible to sift the layers of "memory" and "history" in either Gen. 9 or Josh. 9. But what can be said with confidence is that group *difference* becomes a problem that ethnic curses seem designed, retroactively, to solve.

As several studies of ancient Near Eastern curses show, some curses were used to reinforce the power of the sovereign in protecting an inscription or sealing a treaty, but in other cases there were simple maledictions.[42] Curses seem to be a perennial and protean phenomenon; they can be spontaneous or ritualized, useful for the weak and the powerful. What is compelling about biblical curses is how their protean nature follows the contours of history and postbiblical tradition.

Galatians 3

The problems of biblical curse and ethnicity converge in Paul's designation in Galatians of those who are under the law as a curse. Here Paul appropriates the biblical tradition of cursing another group by making curses themselves the sign of division between groups. Instead of cursing Jewish upholders of the law, Paul's text, citing Deut. 27:26, defines the law itself as a curse, thereby distinguishing two groups primarily on the basis of doctrine rather than ethnicity:

Therefore, the men of faith are blessed together with Abraham the believer. By contrast, those who are men of works of [the] Law are under a curse. For it is written, "Cursed is everyone who does not stay with everything that is written in the book of the Law, to do it." It is, then, obvious that nobody is justified before God by Law, because "The righteous shall live by faith." Also, the Law is not by faith, but "he who does them shall live by them." Christ has redeemed us from the curse of the Law by becoming a curse for us, for it is written, "cursed is everyone who hangs on a tree." (Gal. 3:9–13)[43]

Norman H. Young argues that Paul elaborates here on the biblical curse on those who fail to observe all of the law. In effect, Paul inverts the curse against group members who transgress into a curse against an entire group. For John Gager, the curse applies to Gentiles whose devotion to Christ Jesus leads them to observe Jewish law, not to Jews themselves.[44] The question of what implications the curse has for Jews remains open, but despite all attempts to temper it, the text plainly pronounces a curse on "others" based on religion, and this curse takes the form of an ethnic curse, since in Gal. 3, religious difference takes the form of ethnic identity markers, even in scholarly arguments to the contrary, such as the following: "Paul agrees with the Judaizers that those who belong to the Sinai covenant are obliged to fulfill all its demands. . . . Since those of faith are outside Sinai's jurisdictions, Paul's failure to circumcise his Gentile converts does not place them under the curse of the law."[45]

Paul's text cannot fairly be judged an ethnic curse, if "ethnic" refers to one's group identity solely by birth. In context, it represents the voice of one subgroup against another, and it makes detailed use of Jewish texts to do so. Like the curses on Gibeon or Canaan, the curse of Gal. 3 may reflect the attempt to establish boundaries between groups that are hard to distinguish. But like ethnicity in ancient Israel, the notion of group identity may have more to do with religious orthodoxy than it does today. According to Denise Buell, early Christians made frequent use of ethnic distinctions in their self-identification, both "because religious practices were already associated with ethnicity in the early Roman empire," and also "because race was understood to be mutable, 'becoming Christian' could be depicted in ethnic terms."[46]

We know Paul is capable of issuing curses freely against his doctrinal adversaries (Gal. 1:8–9). And the text does clearly delineate two different groups, one of whom Paul characterizes at times as Jews. Subsequent readings of the text drew upon its potency for distinguishing among groups. Luther's commentary claims that "the papacy is cursed" and "[T]hese [spiritual and temporal] blessings the justiciaries and law-workers of all ages, as the Jews, Papists, Sectaries, and such like, do confound and mingle together."[47]

With Luther's reception of Paul's text, biblical interpretation transfers a curse *within* Judaism to a curse *on* Judaism, or to a widely known version of it. At least two reversals occur in the text, and they follow two passages from Deuteronomy on cursing and the law (27:15–26) and the curse on anyone hung on a tree (21:23). The first reversal shifts from a covenant curse admonishing the fulfillment of the law to a curse on those who regard the law as primary. The second reversal shifts from those who are cursed for hanging on a tree to the notion of the crucified Jesus as a curse. With Paul's text we have traveled far from the ancient Israelite curses as covenant/treaty elements or invective against enemies to curses as a byproduct of theological identity and sacrificial soteriology. With reversals that more closely approximate Nietzsche's *ressentiment* than anything in the Hebrew Bible, the logic of ethnic cursing is now directed against the people of Israel themselves. It would appear that Paul makes an "ethnic" curse out of a doctrinal dispute, but as the discussion of ethnicity in ancient Israel suggests, such may also have been the case for Canaanites and Gibeonites.

Current notions of ethnicity may, in the end, have little to offer our understanding of particular biblical texts and traditions. If group difference can be produced and mobilized out of religious controversy, Christianity may be as much or as little an ethnic designation as the distinction between Israelites and Canaanites, despite Paul's universalistic rhetoric. Such a view would support Jon Levenson's suggestion that Paul's ideology is less universalistic than that of the "Judaizers" he opposes.[48]

Conclusion

Because they take so many forms and their meaning depends so much on context, the study of biblical curses frustrates attempts to be precise. Yet that does not make them indeterminate—indeed, the texts' interpretations have fallen within clear, sometimes deadly, parameters. This chapter has argued that ethnic curses against Canaan and Gibeon likely alternated between phases when they represented a resort of the weak to times when they reflected the subordination of others by a relatively strong Israel. In both of these phases and throughout the process of "canonization," these ethnic curses reinforced group identity by defining and maintaining boundaries between groups. In light of the archaeological evidence, the biblical curses suggest the impulse to differentiate groups that were uncomfortably similar to each other. Sometimes weaker, sometimes stronger, the people of Israel resisted identification with their neighbors through curses. In doing so, these ethnic curses may have helped create and develop ancient notions of ethnicity in which differences were produced from religious disputes within groups.

As it turns out, the Gibeonites and Canaanites (as thus named) do not bedevil the Israelites after the formation of the monarchy nearly as much as the Assyrians, Babylonians, and others. Nor does their servitude figure prominently beyond the texts that announce it (with the exception of Josh. 16:10, 17:12, and Judg. 1:29–30 in the case of the Canaanites). Canaan and Gibeon are, however, important *places* in biblical history, and the people who live there must be identified vis-à-vis Israelite identity. The ethnic curses against the Canaanites and Gibeonites represent the first and defining appearance of these peoples in the Primary History. To curse was to name, and to name was to stake claims of identity and difference, especially for the purpose of deciding questions about marriage and procreation. And while these curses put Gibeonites and Canaanites on the moral and religious map of ancient Israel, they displayed a remarkable capacity to change meaning from times when Israel had the power to subordinate them to times of weakness when they could only wish to do so.

From the perspective of mnemohistory, we can say little about the historical substrate of these ethnic curses. The archaeological and biblical evidence that the Gibeonites and Canaanites were culturally similar to Israel suggests that the curses helped create rather than simply reflect ethnic difference, particularly differences of religious practice. By the time the Primary History (from Gen. to 2 Kings) took shape, these ethnic rivalries had apparently subsided, leaving a residue of conflict that now had more to do with Israelite identity than strife with these groups. The memory of ethnic rivalry could provide solace in defeat or vindication in the defeat of others, but in either case it reinforced the separation of "us" from "them." After the Babylonian destruction and exile, ethnic curses would once again reflect the voice of the weak against the strong, finding echoes in prophetic oracles against the nations and, more indirectly, in attitudes toward powerful empires in the Diaspora novels of Esther and Daniel. Later, when biblical tradition became normative for the Roman Empire and the West, this exaltation of the weak would lead Nietzsche to formulate the ethic of *ressentiment* in which the strong exert a kind of tyranny by wearing the mantle of the weak.

If contemporary ideas of morality exalt the pride of weak or defeated people, then they may have roots in such biblical texts as the ethnic curses against Canaan and Gibeon. Despite the clear difference between modern morality and ancient curses, the two share a common biblical tradition that includes the demarcation of ethnic groups through conflict and curse, a tradition that continues in the New Testament. What is more, these curses display a remarkable flexibility of meaning (within parameters—not in a radically relative sense) even in ancient Israel, and by accommodating reversals of power relations, these curses represent one model for the operations of biblical tradition itself. If biblical tradition is rich and subtle enough to contain the "hidden transcripts" embedded in ethnic curses, then contemporary understandings of ethnicity and power may have more in common with the ancient texts than meets the eye. Unlike Freud, who argues that tradition involves the repression and return of particular events and contents, and unlike others who might argue that all interpretations of a text are equally valid and possible, this model of tradition suggests that the ethnic curses of Gen. 9 and Josh. 9, encoded in the kind of retrospective mnemo-history described by Assmann, provide a sufficiently coherent account of the past to support identity claims in times of strength and weakness alike.

Ethnic curses in the Bible have been understood to underscore boundaries between distinct groups, but the curses on Ham/Canaan and Gibeon appear rather to establish such boundaries between groups that may otherwise be hard to distinguish from each other. In this way, the category of ethnicity is something more like the category of "religious affiliation" than "race," which would help explain Buell's analysis of "Christian" as an ethnic term. Drawing heavily from discourses of gender and inscribed symbolically on the bodies of others, ethnic curses may thus function mainly to create and remember identities and assert power (real or imagined). It may be impossible to unravel the social and historical uses of ethnic curses in the Bible, but the biblical text combines discourses of ethnicity, power, and gender in ways that scholars have only begun to analyze.

Notes

1. Jeff S. Anderson, "The Social Function of Curses in the Hebrew Bible," *ZAW* 110 (1998): 223–37; Paul Arden Keim, "When Sanctions Fail: The Social Function of Curse in Ancient Israel" (PhD Dissertation, Harvard University, 1992). An earlier version of this chapter was presented to the Bible and Cultural Studies Section, Society of Biblical Literature annual meeting, Atlanta, November 2003. My thanks to Alexandra Cuffel for comments on a draft of this chapter.
2. James C. Scott, *Weapons of the Weak: Everyday Forms of Peasant Resistance* (New Haven: Yale University Press, 1986).
3. James C. Scott, *Domination and the Arts of Resistance: Hidden Transcripts* (New Haven: Yale University Press, 1990), 14.
4. Max Weber, *Ancient Judaism,* trans. Hans H. Gerth and Don Martindale (Glencoe: Free Press, 1952), 256–57.
5. Anderson, "The Social Function of Curses in the Hebrew Bible," 231–32.
6. Ibid., 232–33.
7. Thus argues Jacob Milgrom for the sexual prohibitions of Leviticus 18, *Leviticus 17–22* (New York: Doubleday, 2000), 1519.
8. See, e.g., Baruch Halpern, *The Emergence of Israel in Canaan* (Chico, CA: Scholars Press, 1983), and Hershal Shanks, William G. Dever, Baruch Halpern, and P. Kyle McCarter, *The Rise of Ancient Israel* (Washington, DC: Biblical Archaeology Society, 1992).
9. Joseph Blenkinsopp, *Gibeon and Israel: The Role of Gibeon and the Gibeonites in the Political and Religious History of Early Israel* (Cambridge: Cambridge University Press, 1972), 38–39.
10. Ibid., 40.

11. Keim, *When Sanctions Fail.*
12. Susan Niditch, *War in the Hebrew Bible: A Study in the Ethics of Violence* (New York: Oxford University Press, 1993), 106–22.
13. Jan Assmann, *Moses the Egyptian* (Cambridge: Harvard University Press, 1998), 14–20.
14. Nietzsche, *The Anti-Christ*, in *Twilight of the Idols and The Anti-Christ*, trans. R. J. Hollingdale (New York: Penguin, 1990), 147, 149.
15. Nietzsche, *The Anti-Christ*, 165.
16. Ibid., 150. Nietzsche read works by such biblical scholars as Julius Wellhausen; see Thomas H. Brobjer, "Nietzsche's Reading and Private Library, 1885–1889," *Journal of the History of Ideas* 58 (1997): 663–80.
17. Nietzsche, *The Anti-Christ*, 199.
18. See Tim Murphy, *Nietzsche, Metaphor, Religion* (Albany: State University of New York Press, 2001) and James C. O'Flaherty, Timothy F. Sellner, and Robert M. Helm, eds., *Studies in Nietzsche and the Judaeo-Christian Tradition* (Chapel Hill: University of North Carolina Press, 1985).
19. David M. Goldenberg, *The Curse of Ham: Race and Slavery in Early Judaism, Christianity, and Islam* (Princeton: Princeton University Press, 2003); Stephen Haynes, *Noah's Curse: The Biblical Justification of American Slavery* (Oxford: Oxford University Press, 2002).
20. David H. Aaron, "Early Rabbinic Exegesis on Noah's Son Ham and the So-Called 'Hamitic Myth,' " *JAAR* 53 (1995): 721–59.
21. Meir Sternberg, *Hebrews Between Cultures: Group Portraits and National Literature* (Bloomington: Indiana University Press, 1998), 109–12.
22. Ibid., 15.
23. Herbert Chanan Brichto, *The Problem of "Curse" in the Hebrew Bible*, Journal of Biblical Literature Monograph Series 13 (Philadelphia: Society of Biblical Literature, 1968), 89. Brichto notes throughout his study that different terms and meanings for "curse" appear in the Bible.
24. Blenkinsopp, *Gibeon and Israel*, 39–40.
25. Robert Gordon, "Gibeonite Ruse and Israelite Curse in Joshua 9," in A. D. H. Mayes and R. B. Salters, eds., *Covenant as Context: Essays in Honor of E. W. Nicholson* (Oxford: Oxford University Press, 2003), 180 [163–90].
26. Blenkinsopp, *Gibeon and Israel*, 2.
27. Ibid., 60–68. If the family of Saul is associated with the Gibeonites, then the childlessness of Michal (2 Sam. 6:23) may reflect another anti-Gibeonite episode; thanks to Alex Cuffel for this observation.
28. Blenkinsopp, *Gibeon and Israel*, 32–33.
29. Peter Kearney, "The Role of the Gibeonites in the Deuteronomic History," *CBQ* 35 (1973): 12.
30. Ibid., 1–19.
31. Ibid., 8.
32. Diana Edelman, "Gibeon and the Gibeonites Revisited," in Oded Lipschits and Joseph Blenkinsopp, eds., *Judah and the Judeans in the Neo-Babylonian Period* (Winona Lake, IN: Eisenbrauns: 2003), 164–65 [153–67].

33. Lemche, *The Canaanites and their Land* JSOT Supp 110 (Sheffield: Sheffield Academic Press, 1991), 52.
34. Israel Finkelstein and Neil Asher Silberman, *The Bible Unearthed: Archaeology's New Vision of Ancient Israel and the Origin of its Sacred Texts* (New York: Free Press, 2001), 118–19.
35. William Dever, "Ethnicity and Archaeology," Society for Biblical Literature Annual Meeting, November 19, 2005. See also Dever's polemical essay, "The Western Cultural Tradition is at Risk," *Biblical Archaeology Review* (March–April 2006): 26, 76.
36. Elizabeth Bloch-Smith, "Israelite Ethnicity in Iron I: Archaeology Preserves what is Remembered and what is Forgotten in Israel's History," *Journal of Biblical Literature* 122 (2003): 412 [401–25].
37. Ibid., 410–11.
38. Ibid., 421.
39. Ibid., 425.
40. Ibid., 421.
41. Giorgio Agamben, *Means Without End: Notes on Politics*, trans. Vincenzo Binetti and Cesare Casarino (Minneapolis: University of Minnesota Press, 2000), 32.
42. See Delbert Hillers, *Treaty-Curses and the Old Testament Prophets*, Biblica et Orientalia 16 (Rome: Pontifical Biblical Institute, 1964), 24; Jerrold S. Cooper, *The Curse of Agade* (Baltimore: Johns Hopkins, 1983), 61–63; and Kevin J. Cathcart, "The Curses in Old Aramaic Inscriptions," in Kevin Cathcart and Michael Maher, eds., *Targumic and Cognate Studies* JSOT Supp 230 (Sheffield, 1996), 140–52.
43. Hans Dieter Betz, *Galatians* (Philadelphia: Fortress Press, 1979), 137.
44. John Gager, *Reinventing Paul* (Oxford: Oxford University Press, 2000), 89.
45. Norman H. Young, "Who's Cursed—And Why" *JBL* 117 (1998): 92 [79–92].
46. Denise Buell, *Why This New Race* (New York: Columbia University Press, 2005), 473.
47. Martin Luther, *A Commentary on St. Paul's Epistle to the Galatians* (London: James Clarke and Co., 1961), 242–43.
48. Jon Levenson, *The Death and Resurrection of the Beloved Son* (New Haven: Yale University Press, 1993), 215–18.

Chapter 2

Promiscuous or Proper? Nymphs as Female Role Models in Ancient Greece

Ann-Marie Knoblauch

Introduction

It is a tricky business attempting to classify women in the ancient Greek world. On the one hand, Greek historical sources nearly ignore them altogether, while literary sources (such as epics and tragedies) provide a few well-established types: the devoted wife (Penelope), the unbalanced foreigner (Medea), the promiscuous and deceitful goddesses (Calypso, Circe, Aphrodite), and the treacherous and deadly monsters (Medusa, Sirens), to name a few. Much less frequently mentioned (and perhaps less interesting) are the mortal females who lived appropriate lives within the physical and social confines of the ancient Greek world. These are the women who lived mostly in seclusion in their family home until, probably around the age of sixteen to eighteen, they married and made the important transition from girl to woman, wife and mother.

Despite the near-silence in textual sources on this transition in a girl's life, it was undoubtedly one of the most (if not the most) important times of her life, one marked not only by celebration, but also anxiety. The young girl's nervousness is easy enough to understand: she was leaving the only home and companions she had ever known, and she was moving into a household with strangers (including in-laws) where she would be required to assume a new role.[1] Furthermore, the young woman's nervousness was no doubt exacerbated by the impending sexual relationship with her husband. It stands to reason that within such life-altering times, mythological characters could serve as role models and help ease the anxiety. In ancient Greece, the role models were *numfai* [nymphs], a class of semidivine mythological characters found in every corner of the Greek world. Mortal girls at this stage were also called nymphs, and they looked to their mythological counterparts for guidance through this anxious and exciting time in their lives. The mythological nymphs are considered to be positive role models for these girls because of their general character of modesty, generosity, and strength, as well as their piety and devotion to the gods they serve.

The term *numfe* [nymph] has a range of meanings in ancient Greece. In the mortal sense, nymph refers to a young girl who has already reached puberty but is not yet married.[2] In this context, *numfe* is often translated as "maiden." Sexuality enters the picture of the mortal nymph as a potentiality more than a reality, as most women who identify as nymphs are virgins. This does not mean that they are not sexual, as in many ways they are at the physical peak of their sexual readiness, but it is an unexplored sexuality.

Mythological nymphs present a slightly different picture. They can be both generic and specific: we know the names of virtually hundreds of nymphs from Greek mythology, and many more go unnamed. Nymphs inhabit (and oversee) untamed places like woods, rivers, and caves and become part of the local history in virtually every region of Greece. Their characters typically reflect the spirit of the geographical features they encompass (water, mountains, woods), although they are usually calm and modest both in appearance in the visual arts and in their demeanor as reflected in literary sources. As semidivine creatures, nymphs bridge the world between the gods and mortals. They are mentioned in association with the more powerful Olympian gods (especially Artemis, Aphrodite, Hermes, and Dionysos), while they are themselves the objects of cult worship by mortals.[3] Another indication of their status between mortals and gods, and of special interest to us here, is the ease with which they partner sexually with both groups, as well as members of their own semidivine group.

Mythological nymphs are appropriate role models for their mortal counterparts as they share many of the same characteristics, yet at the same time they seem to differ rather drastically in their attitudes toward sex. Mythological nymphs are not bound to the same social mores as mortal Greek women. They can actively pursue members of the opposite sex and they are far from modest when it comes to their relations with their sexual partners. The very fact that mythological nymphs openly and willingly partner with males sets them apart from their virginal mortal counterparts, and furthermore places them in a unique category of females in the ancient Greek world: those who are actively (and sometimes aggressively) sexual. How can such females be appropriate role models for modest, maturing young women preparing for their lives as wives and mothers?

In this paper I am interested in examining the relationship between the mortal nymphs and their mythological counterparts and role models, particularly in terms of the ways in which each group approaches its sexuality. Why (and how) did mythological nymphs maintain a prominent position in the Greek mythological mindset, particularly for young women? The answer to this question lies in part, I believe, in a perceived association between the two groups. Mortal nymphs and mythological nymphs are very similar in terms of their sexual allure, but only in the often-distorted world of mythology is the sexuality of the nymph permitted to extend to action rather than just potentiality. Furthermore, I argue that the mythological nymphs are allowed to be sexually different (perhaps even deviant) because of their otherness and their marginality between the worlds of gods and humans. They are committed to the rules and mores of neither group, and so can act independently of both. Such a position makes the nymphs both aberrant and alluring to a Greek male, and accessible in a way that goddesses and other sexualized females from mythology are not. Understanding the sexual mores of the mythological world in general, and the nymphs more specifically, further refines the meaning of these creatures for mortal young women.

Sex and Power in Greek Mythology

Greek mythology is peopled with a distinct hierarchy of characters including gods, semidivine creatures, and mortals. All of these characters engage in sex, both among their own group and up and down the hierarchical ladder. This makes sex in Greek mythology often about power, particularly when the partnering involves different levels of the hierarchy of characters. An unwilling partner, whether male or female, is often not in a position to reject the advances because he or she is on a lower level of the hierarchy. In other words, gods pursue heroes and/or semidivine female nymphs and mortals (some examples include Calypso and Odysseus, Aphrodite and Anchises, Apollo and Daphne, Zeus and Io, Zeus and Aegina) and semidivine characters pursue mortals (Thetis and Peleus). The objects of such pursuits therefore are disempowered by their lower status in the hierarchy of gods and mortals.

In recent discussions of sex by force or coercion in antiquity, emphasis has rightly been placed on the hierarchical relationship between the two characters involved. Gods who force themselves on humans, for example, are less culpable (if at all) than humans who do the same to other humans, to the point where the god's action is not considered coercion at all, but rather "seduction."[4] Even if the woman (or, more seldom, man) resists or objects to the advances of the god, more often than not the victim usually gives in or gives up. The momentary discomfort is often ignored or overlooked in favor of the long-term benefits of the union, ideally the birth of a hero. The consummation between Zeus and Alkmene, parents of the hero Herakles, serves as an example.[5] Beautiful Alkmene had been married to Amphitryon but she refused to consummate the union until he successfully did away with one of her foes. While her husband carried out her wishes, Zeus came to Alkmene in the form of Amphitryon and the god spent three days in bed with her. When her husband returned home after having completed the task and realized the deception, his first reaction was to punish her by burning her on a pyre, but Zeus intervened and Amphitryon forgave her. We are never told how Alkmene reacted when she found out she had been tricked into sleeping with Zeus, or sentenced to death for a deception done to her. Likely such issues were never raised for two reasons. First, the Greeks perceived the victim was not Alkmene but her husband who had something stolen from him, and second, the result of the union of Zeus and Alkmene, Herakles, was such a blessing to humans that the issue of whether the attraction between his parents was mutual was inconsequential. Although Alkmene was to be punished because she had inadvertently slept with Zeus, a young girl hearing this story might identify with the young bride who resists the advances of her husband. For such a girl, the lesson to be learned is an obvious one.

Coerced sex is not only instigated by men. The goddess Aphrodite lusts after the Trojan hero Anchises, and disguises herself as a mortal woman and arrives at Anchises' door. He is suspicious of her heavenly aura, but she convinces him she is a mortal. She tells Anchises how she came to him: "there were many of us dancing, brides and marriageable girls, and a vast crowd ringed us about." (*Homeric Hymn to Aphrodite*, lines 117–120).[6] At that point, the god Hermes snatched her from the dancers and told her she was to be Anchises' wife. Apparently this abduction is a plausible scenario to Anchises, because he seduces her. Because he believes she is a mortal, he is able to dominate the encounter. She only reveals her true identity afterwards, and, ashamed that she lusted for a mortal, she forces (the now terrified) Anchises to agree to lie about the union, which will produce the hero Aeneas. Aphrodite allows Anchises to tell people he slept with a nymph of Mount Ida, an appropriate partner and parent to the Trojan royal house. This episode is interesting because it explains the (perceived) sexual relationship among gods, mortals, and nymphs. A god can only sleep with a mortal if disguised, and knowing that Aeneas will require some kind of plausible parentage, she allows the mortal father to tell people he has slept with a nymph—definitely a step up for the mortal, and a win-win situation for both.

The example of Alkmene and Aphrodite are two of many examples that illustrate the intricacies of deception, coercion, and subterfuge in sexual relationships between gods, heroes and mortals. Aphrodite, concerned for her reputation, offers her victim a plausible and flattering story that will raise his own stock amongst the Trojans and insure his silence: he can acknowledge that he slept with a nymph—that he slept up.[7] In the case of Alkmene, Zeus feels neither the need to be embarrassed by his attraction nor shows any concern for the difficult position in which he has placed Alkmene with her husband.

The dynamics change when nymphs are involved in the encounter. In many ways they are the most interesting because they can both pursue and be pursued; they can be empowered or disempowered by the encounter, depending on the partner. Semidivine nymphs are pursued by gods, to whom they submit, and they pursue mortals, who submit to them. Nymphs are frequently pursued by Zeus, and the result of the sexual interaction is typically a hero. Aegina, the eponymous nymph of the island in the Saronic Gulf not far from Athens, was abducted by Zeus. It was the result of this union that eventually brought forth the heroes Achilles and Patroklos.[8] Likewise Hylas, a member of the Argonautica team, is lost when a water nymph, struck by his beauty, pulls him into the water and makes him her husband when he is filling water jars.[9]

Nymphs also have sexual encounters with "their own kind," that is to say, semidivine males. This particular relationship is interesting and especially revealing in a discussion of sexual behavior of nymphs because the relationship between these two sexual partners, both on the same ladder of the hierarchy, does not have the built-in power imbalance that exists with god/nymph or nymph/mortal partnering. In order to understand sexual behavior among the nymphs, and whether such promiscuity is acceptable to women looking to the nymphs as their mythological role models, it is necessary to understand how the nymph responds to sexual activity with her mythological counterpart.

Satyrs and Nymphs: Consensual or Nonconsensual Sex?

The semidivine males that nymphs most frequently partner up with are satyrs, mythological creatures who live on the fringes of the human world, who bear physical qualities of both man and beast, usually goat or horse. The satyr's most familiar qualities are an appreciation of wine, dancing, music and frolicking, and an active pursuit of sexual gratification. These traits make the satyr in some sense a symbol of fertility, particularly the fertility of the natural world. The satyr is neither man, god, nor beast, but bridges all of these worlds, possessing positive and negative qualities of each. The satyr is the most familiar and loyal member of the entourage of Dionysos, god of wine and fertility.

Satyrs, like nymphs, are ubiquitous creatures in the Greek mythological landscape, but unlike many nymphs they enjoy (or suffer from) a certain anonymity.[10] The two appear as partners: dancing, frolicking, and chasing one another on countless painted Athenian vases from the archaic and classical periods. When satyrs appear with nymphs, sexual activity is frequently implied, but never are the two shown engaging in intercourse.[11] At times, however, the satyr grasps the female nymph in his arms while she throws up her arms and leans away from him, or she runs from him. Her gesture makes her appear powerless, leading to the interpretation that 1) the nymph is being taken against her will and 2) sex is inevitable. If correct, then it is another example of the imbalance and power hierarchy of sexual encounters, much like the god-mortal relationships discussed earlier. While it is safe to say that such scenes imply sex, it is less likely (and less logical) that the female is being taken against her will. In spite of the visual depictions in which she is shown without any freedom of movement, I argue that the nymph is not a victim, but a willing and acquiescing participant in a (staged) abduction intended to highlight the ultra-masculine and ultra-feminine qualities of the participants. Such scenes are intended (among other things) to reflect the same kind of apprehension that a young woman felt as she prepared for marriage. The transition to marriage was the most important transition in a young girl's life, one she approached with nervous anticipation. The successful union of the satyr and the nymph serves as a model of what young girls should aspire to.

Satyr and nymph sexual encounters should be treated separately from other mythological episodes because they are mythological peers, but also for another reason. With most stories of coerced sex and abduction, the characters are named and familiar. We know their histories and their backgrounds (Helen, Persephone, Io and Cassandra, to name a few well known victims from mythology). We may have some information regarding motivations, and the results of the unions. With satyrs and nymphs we have none of those things. Scenes of satyrs clasping nymphs are completely anonymous, and we know nothing of their offspring (with the exception of occasional depictions of anonymous baby satyrs). This suggests that it is not so much the individuals that are important in these scenes, what matters is the *type* of characters involved (satyrs and nymphs) and the *activity* (sex).

The placement of scenes featuring nymphs and satyrs support their role as universal, positive symbols of the natural union.

One of the most interesting depictions of the satyr/nymph union (identified by inscription) appears on a black figure volute krater produced in Athens around 570 BC, known as the François Vase. This vessel offers an early representation of a satyr and nymph scene, identified by inscription.[12] The François Vase is a unique monument from the early sixth century BC, a 66 cm tall vessel produced in Athens on which were painted six horizontal figural registers that run around the vase. Together, the registers depict a virtual encyclopedia of mythological episodes that centers on the wedding of Peleus and Thetis which wraps around the entire vase along the main horizontal register at the shoulder. Other registers on the François Vase include popular myths of archaic Greece: the Calydonian Boar Hunt, Theseus landing on the shores of Delos with the youths and maidens of Athens, and the ambush of Troilos at the Fountainhouse, among others. The painted scenes echoed themes of poems and would have been used to illustrate contemporary poems that would have been sung at Greek symposia, and it has been suggested that such an elaborate vessel would have been commissioned on the occasion of a wedding.[13] Below the main register of the wedding of Peleus and Thetis is the Return of Hephaistos to Olympos, another common myth depicted on archaic pottery in Athens. It is in the context of the Return of Hephaistos that the satyr and nymph appear together on the François Vase.[14]

Hephaistos, son of Hera, was conceived and born without male assistance. Lame at birth, he was banished by Hera by being hurled off Mount Olympos. He landed on the island of Lemnos, where he learned the skills of metalworking and forging. To avenge his exile he crafted a magic throne for his mother, which would bind her with invisible fetters. His trickery worked, and the Olympians debated how to bring Hephaistos back to Olympos, the only way to undo the magic of the throne and restore order to the mountain. After much deliberation (and at least one failed attempt by Ares), Dionysos was sent to convince the bitter Hephaistos to return. To accomplish this task, Dionysos made Hephaistos drunk, and only while intoxicated did the god allow himself to be led back to Olympos where he would undo his trickery. Hera was released, Dionysos was made one of the twelve Olympians (in one version) and Hephaistos was given Aphrodite for his bride (in another). In visual depictions of the episode on archaic vases we are often shown the drunken lame god riding on the back of an ass and accompanied by the god Dionysos. Occasionally, an entourage, including satyrs and nymphs, follows behind.

The breadth and detail that is characteristic of the François Vase in general is also found in the depiction of the Return of Hephaistos, where the typical components of Dionysos leading Hephaistos on an ass are accompanied by a full entourage including three ithyphallic, half-horse, half-man figures, labeled SILENOI (an early alternative name for satyrs). Directly behind Hephaisos, the first satyr struggles under the weight of a full wineskin. Behind him a second satyr plays the double flutes, or auloi. Behind this satyr a third satyr, only partially preserved, clasps a female in his arms. Behind this group three females (labeled NUFAI) walk calmly behind the satyr clasping the female.

There are two points worth making about the nymphs and satyrs found in this scene. Firstly, the components that characterize the general episode of the Return of Hepahistos are drunkenness and a sense of relief. The return of the god marks the restoration of peace to Mount Olympos, and the entourage of nymphs and satyrs, when they are included in the scene, are celebratory, not anxious. For this reason, the satyr grasping the nymph is not abducting her, nor does her rape her. These are satyrs and nymphs, fulfilling their appropriate mythological roles. Secondly, the nymphs who appear on the vase behind the satyrs and satyr and nymph couple (of which only the lower part survives) appear calm, as if part of a procession. There is no sense of agitation whatsoever, and they cheerfully follow behind the satyr clasping the nymph.

In addition to the group of vases produced in Athens during the archaic period, there are two other visual monuments on which are depicted a satyr grasping a nymph in his arms in an "abduction" composition. Both date back to the second half of the sixth century BC, and both are quite distinct from the painted vases. These monuments are a sculpted relief on the head-dress worn by a caryatid holding up the Siphnian Treasury at Delphi, and staters, a type silver coin minted by the island of Thasos in the Northern Aegean. These monuments support the interpretation that the satyr/nymph sexual relationship is not aggressive, but progressive.

The richly decorated treasury erected at the Panhellenic sanctuary at Delphi by the Siphnians shortly before 525 BC includes two caryatid figures which support the entablature.[15] One caryatid is fairly well preserved, and on her polos (a tall cylindrical hat) is an intriguing, albeit fragmentary, sculpted relief. On the backside, three satyrs and two females dance and frolic. One satyr holds his hands to his mouth, probably playing a pair of flutes, while a second dances beside him. A third satyr grasps a female in his arms. Beside this group a second female moves toward the front of the relief, looking backwards as she advances. Recently a fragment discovered in a stone wall near Delphi has been inserted into the front of the polos. Although poorly preserved, the new piece introduces a second scene. A female figure stands before an indefinable low mass, probably a table. At least one other figure stands facing this woman on the opposite side of the table.

Behind this group one can vaguely make out the outline of a tall pillar with a rounded projection on the left side; the right side is completely illegible.[16]

Assuming all sides of the polos are part of a connected scene, there seems to be some kind of open-air ritual taking place, at which satyrs and females are present. On the front, females make offerings at an altar, and on the back, there is a scene of dancing. Themelis, in his publication of this new fragment,[17] convincingly argues that the worship of Dionysos (in the form of a pillar statue behind an altar) is taking place here. Given the festive scene of the dancing creatures on the back and the females calmly sacrificing on the front, it seems unlikely that the satyr abducts the nymph here or that she is an unwilling partner to his advances. As on the François Vase, the two here unite as creatures (and forces) of nature. They are part of an episode that underscores the complementary qualities of the nymph and satyr.

The Siphnian Treasury is distinct from the painted vases of Attica because of its context as a state monument. This treasury was erected in a sanctuary accessible to all groups and intended to 1) reflect positively back on the island of Siphnos and 2) be accessible to a non-Siphnian visitor to the Panhellenic sanctuary at Delphi.[18] Delphi was located on the slopes of Mount Parnassos, sacred to Dionysos, and there are several ancient sources that refer to the nymphs who lived there. Possibly the scene on the polos may be set on the slopes of Parnassos, and perhaps the nymphs were the local denizens of the mountain, who had an important cult in their own right and one with which any viewer would be familiar.[19] Like the François Vase, the nymph/satyr partnering in this context is about the fruitful union of the two semidivine creatures who inhabit the rugged slopes of Mount Parnassos, not an abduction or forcible sexual encounter.

A third monument (or class of monuments) also belongs firmly to the realm of public monuments. These are coins minted by the island of Thasos in the Northern Aegean depicting a satyr holding a female figure in his arms. This scene appears on the earliest issues produced in the second half of the sixth century BC and continuing for well over a hundred years.[20] The earliest satyr issues depict a robust and muscular satyr facing right clutching a nymph in his arms. The female's right arm is upraised between herself and the satyr, terminating in a forked hand. The scene is often described as the abduction of a "resisting female," because the lively positioning of her arms is read as an attempt to escape. Later issues of the same series dating to the later fifth and early fourth century BC depict the same pair but with a notably different tenor to their relationship. Now the right arm of the female, instead of being upraised between the two figures, reaches behind the satyr's neck. On some examples her right hand is even visible behind his head, sometimes grasping his neck, but more often extending behind his head or shoulders.[21]

One argument against interpreting this motif as an abduction lies in the appropriateness of such an episode on a coin, where, as on the Siphnian Treasury, one would expect to find the type of image or symbol that would reflect positively back on the city responsible for the monument. A second argument lies in the continuation of this type over time and how it changes. It seems unlikely that after a hundred years of attempted seduction, the initially unwilling partner eventually succumbs to the ardor of the satyr. It is much more likely that on the archaic coins and in the classical coins of Thasos we have the same action taking place, but while the style and composition of the archaic coins highlight the energy and wildness of the two, the classical coins promote a more humanized representation of the same story.

In the case of the satyr and the nymph he often held in his arms, the evidence points to a consensual relationship that highlights the positive individual natures of each. These two semidivine creatures are complementary forces in the natural world, and depictions of their union highlight these natures.

The François Vase, the Siphnian Treasury, and the coins of Thasos are useful monuments through which to understand the motivations of the satyrs clasping the nymphs, because they show the activity in a broader context, or at least on monuments that would, by definition, assume a positive reflection of the union of these two forces of nature (a vessel to celebrate a marriage, a Panhellenic sanctuary, and coins). The images of satyrs clasping or chasing nymphs are staged encounters between the ultra-masculine and ultra-feminine that are intended to highlight the benefits of each on a natural level (as symbols of earth and water), on a mythological level, and on a mortal level where the relationship between satyrs and nymphs, like so many mythological relationships, was seen as an extreme version of mortal behavior.

Nymphs, Abduction, and Marriage

We have established that what looks like an abduction between satyrs and nymphs might not actually be so. If the satyr physically overpowers the nymph it is more of an indication of his physical strength and masculinity rather than an indication of forced sex. Yet in spite of the fact that the nymph acquiesces, there is still an element of anxiety in these scenes. It is hard to ignore her arm thrown up between them. This type of anxiety, I suggest, is similar to what is experienced by young women preparing for marriage in ancient Greece. There is evidence that young girls were chosen (or "taken") by their new husbands in socially sanctioned rituals that were akin to abductions, which had mythological parallels.[22] There was an ambivalence felt by these girls: on the one hand they were leaving a sheltered and familiar life in the family home, on the other hand they were fulfilling the societal expectations that they would become wives and mothers.

Literary sources suggest that young women convened and trained for participation in choral groups that would perform songs and circular dances with other young women as part of the preparation for marriage. Such dances were for the purpose of presenting these young women to the male community. In many cases this was the first (and only) time in a woman's life that she would be displayed so publicly. What is known of the custom comes primarily from fragmentary poetry that was apparently sung by such girls called *partheneia* ("virgin-songs" or "maiden's songs").[23] The poems speak like advertisements for the young women, referring to physical attributes such as their golden hair, lovely ankles, beautiful voices, and good breeding. One fragment by the lyric poet Alkman compares one of the girls to a champion racehorse:

. . . she herself appears
To stand out as supreme, just as if one
Were to set among grazing herds a horse
Of sturdy build, a prize-winning champion with clattering
    Hooves,
One of those winged steeds in dreams. . . .

. . . but the hair
Of my cousin Hagesichora has a bloom upon it
As of pure gold,
And her silvery face—
Why do I tell you openly?
Here she is, Hagesichora!
But she who is second to Agido in beauty. (FR1)[24]

The poems also refer to mythological choruses that inspire them, choruses of nymphs who dance for gods, often Artemis (the goddess who watches over young women during their transition to married life). We recall that Aphrodite invented a similar group to convince Anchises she was mortal (and participated in typical mortal activities). The training for a participation in such a choral group was a unique and positive time in a girl's life, when she interacted for the first time with other women of her own age outside of her family. Texts also suggest an ambivalence to the experience. In addition to the *partheneia* fragments, several poems by Sappho called *epithalamia* ("wedding songs") refer to what seems to be similar choral groups who performed at weddings, probably the weddings of one of their members. The Sappho poems, mostly fragmentary, underscore the friendship that developed among the girls and the bittersweet feelings when one left the group for marriage. In one fragment, Sappho reminds the groom of his good luck:

Happy bridegroom, for the marriage you prayed for
Is taking place, and you have the girl you prayed for. . . .
"Your shape is graceful, your eyes. . . .
Sweet as honey, love streams over your beautiful face
. . . .Aphrodite has honored you greatly." (Fr. 112)[25]

In another the girls express their sadness of leaving behind their childhood (and especially their virginity):

Virginity, virginity, where have you gone, deserting me?
Never again shall I come to you, never again shall I come. (Fr. 114)[26]

Only older married women could look back at this time of their life wistfully as a time of happy memories when they shared the companionship of other women. In the tragedy *Iphigenia in Tauris* by Euripides, the chorus of women, reminiscing about their youth, recall their own participation in such choral groups:

. . . my house, my roof, my room,
From which I used to go . . .
And take my place
In the bright company,
Give them my hands and circle round and dance
And always try to be the loveliest,
Under my mother's gaze,
In my unrivalled radiance of attire
And in the motion of my hands and feet,
While my embroidered veil
I would hold closely round me as I danced
And bowed and hid my cheek
Under the shadow of my clustering curls. (lines 1141–51)[27]

This description of premarital dancing suggests a chaperoned circle dance of young women dressed in their finest. (From the text it is not obvious whether the chaperone is a deity or the dancer's literal mother.) Such choral groups as described in the *partheneia, epithalamia* as well as *Iphigenia in Tauris* have mythological prototypes, many of which underscore non-normative behavior and reflecting the anxiety felt by a society needing to protect and at the same time expose a vulnerable group of women. In the

Homeric Hymn to Demeter (lines 1–11), Persephone is dancing in a field, picking flowers with a group of Oceanides (a group of specialized nymphs) when she is taken to be the bride of Hades. In the hymn, Zeus sanctions the abduction, in spite of the grief it causes for her mother Demeter. Bruce Lincoln argues that Zeus' complicity in the abduction reflects his role as Persephone's "social parent," that is, the one who arranges her marriage and the transfer of his daughter to her new husband. Hades acts properly because he undertakes the difficult task of transforming the nymph from a child to a woman.[28] Persephone's journey is reenacted in social rituals in ancient Greece in which young women are secluded and the transition occurs. Persephone loses her virginity in the underworld, an ill-defined place from which she should not be able to return, neither physically nor mentally.[29]

Christiane Sourvinou-Inwood introduces archaeological evidence that supports Lincoln's theory. In a sanctuary to Persephone at Locri Epizephyrii in South Italy, several molded terracotta relief plaques have been found on which are depicted scenes of abduction of young girls. These plaques would have been dedicated at the sanctuary to Persephone. Sourvinou-Inwood identifies two types of scenes: on one type the clearly bearded Hades carries Persephone in a winged chariot, the second (with many more examples) features a young beardless abductor, naked except for a cloak in a chariot. The abducted maidens in the reliefs often carry in their hand objects associated with Persephone: a cock, a ball, a basket with fruit or flowers. Sometimes the girl appears to willingly accept her situation, sometimes she has a look of fear on her face but is otherwise acquiescent. Sourvinou-Inwood suggests the young abductor plaques are not mythological, but refer instead to ideal representations of marriage rituals, where fear and abduction are part of the ritual. The fear on the faces of these girls is not real, but pretended as part of a ritual element of marriage.[30]

Conclusions

The "abduction" of nymphs by satyrs reflects about the same level of threat as the "abduction" of young women by their future husbands, in other words, a very small one. There is anxiety involved with both scenarios. Young girls are anxious about their new role in life, which includes sexuality among many other things. The images of the "resisting" nymphs reflect and offer sympathy to young girls in this situation, but as we see in the Locrian plaques the nervousness might be staged and the ultimate result is positive. Nymphs are very appropriate role models for young girls not *in spite of* their sexuality but I would argue *because* of it. They can sympathize with the girls while at the same time offer proof of the positive outcome of both mythological and mortal unions. The nymph who willingly submits to the satyr bridges the divide between modesty and promiscuity, much the same way a young girl both fears and desires marriage. Not only is the nymph an appropriate role model for young girls, but they are the *only* role models for mortal maidens who are at a unique and transitional stage in their life. The period of courtship and marriage is one of the few times when a woman would be exposed to the broader community; nymphs have endured (and enjoyed) such exposure throughout time without losing their femininity or their modesty. How does the nymph manage to balance these worlds? Once again we can return to the nymphs' hierarchical position between mortals and gods. No other type of female has the flexibility to adopt, as appropriate, the behavior and mores of either group to suit the context.

Notes

1. For a recent discussion, see Helen Foley, "Mothers and Daughters" in Jenifer Neils, ed., *Coming of Age in Ancient Greece* (New Haven: Yale University Press, 2003), 112–37, esp. 122–35.
2. The word nymph can also refer to a newly married woman before the birth of her first child.
3. Jennifer Larson offers a recent, thorough, and excellent overview of nymphs in the Greek world. See Larson, *Greek Nymphs* (New York: Oxford University Press, 2001), esp. 91–120, for the relationship between nymphs and Olympian gods. The worship of nymphs by mortals is most evident in nympholepsy, or the divinatory powers often ascribed to nymphs. See Larson *Greek Nymphs*, 11–20.
4. As Mary Lefkowitz puts it, "in the case of myths involving the unions of gods or goddesses with mortal men and women, we should talk about abduction or seduction rather than rape, because the gods see to it that the experience, however transient, is pleasant for mortals. Moreover, the consequences of these unions are usually glorious for the families of the mortals involved, despite and even because of the suffering that individual members of the family may undergo" (M. Lefkowitz, "Seduction and Rape in Greek Myth," in Angeliki E. Laiou, ed., *Consent and Coercion to Sex and Marriage in Ancient and Medieval Societies* (Washington, DC: Dumbarton Oaks Research Library and Collection, 1993), 17 [17–37].
5. Textual sources about the Alkmene myth appear as early as Homer (*Iliad* 14.323–324), where Zeus mentions his affair with Alkmene to Hera. Other early sources provide other details, including Hesiod's *Ehoiai* (Hes fr 195 MW).

6. Martin West, *Homeric Hymns, Homeric Apocrypha, Lives of Homer* (Cambridge: Harvard University Press, 2003). This episode serves as the featured story of the hymn.
7. It should come as no surprise that Anchises eventually reveals the divine mother of Aeneas, and he is punished accordingly.
8. Larson, *Greek Nymphs*, 38.
9. Apollonios, *Argonautica* 1. 1228–39.
10. In spite of their frequent appearance, very few satyrs are known by name, and only two, Silenos and Marsyas, are associated with a specific mythological narrative. Occasionally satyrs are labeled on Greek vases, but typically the names are puns associated with sexual activity or drinking.
11. Satyrs are by far the most frequent mythological character depicted on the tens of thousands painted vases produced in Athens between the years 600 and 400 BC. See Guy Hedreen, *Silens in Attic Black-Figure Vase-Painting: Myth and Performance* (Ann Arbor: University of Michigan Press 1992). Greek vase painters did not shy away from sexually explicit scenes on vases, and it is interesting that nymphs never fall into that group. Unlike foreigners, female entertainers, and prostitutes, it is inappropriate to show nymphs in a sexually explicit context.
12. Florence 4209. Mauro Christophani, Maria Grazia Marzi et al. provide a full photographic documentation of the vase. Mauro Christophani, Maria Grazia Marzi, eds., *Materiali per servire alla storia del Vaso François, Bollettino d'Arte* Seria speciale 1. 1981.
13. Martin Robertson, *A History of Greek Art* (London: Cambridge University Press, 1975), 126.
14. More specifically on the myth of the Return of Hepahistos on the François Vase see Thomas H. Carpenter, *Art and Myth in Ancient Greece* (London: Thames and Hudson 1991), 7–21; Carpenter, *Dionysian Imagery in Fifth-Century Athens* (Oxford: Clarendon Press, 1997); and Hedreen, *Silens in Attic Black-Figure Vase-Painting*, 13–30.
15. G. Daux and E. Hansen, *Le trésor de Siphnos, Fouilles de Delphes II* (Paris: Diffusion, De Boccard, 1987).
16. For illustrations of the polos and the new fragment see P. G. Themelis, "The Cult Scene on the Polos of the Siphnian Karyatid at Delphi" in Robin Hägg, ed., *The Iconography of Greek Cult in the Archaic and Classical Periods* (Athens: Centre d'etude de la religion grecque antique, 1992), 49–72.
17. Ibid.
18. For a discussion of public media versus private media in ancient art, see K. W. Arafat, "State of the Art—Art of the State: Sexual Violence and Politics in Late Archaic and Early Classical Vase-Painting," in S. Deacy and K. F. Pierce, eds., *Rape in Antiquity: Sexual Violence in the Greek and Roman Worlds* (London: Duckworth, 1997), 97–121 esp. 97–99.
19. J. Larson, "The Corycian Nymphs and the Bee Maidens of the Homeric Hymn to Hermes," *Greek, Roman and Byzantine Studies* 36 (1995): 341–57; C. M. Edwards, "Greek Votive Reliefs to Pan and the Nymphs" (PhD Dissertation, New York University, 1985), 13; Jeremy McInerney, "Parnassos, Delphi and the Thyiades," *Greek, Roman and Byzantine Studies* 38 (1997): 263–83.

20. The coins of Thasos were first organized by LeRider: Georges Daux, ed., *Guide de Thasos* (Paris: E. de Boccard, 1968), 185–191. More recently, work by Olivier Picard has refined the organization and contributed to our understanding of the iconography: Olivier Picard, "Monnaies et gravure monétaire à Thasos à la fin du Ve Siècle" *Philia epe eis Georgion E. Mylonan, dia ta 60 ete tou anaskaphikou tou ergou , B* (Athens: En Athenais Archaiologike Hetaireia, 1987), 150–63; Olivier Picard, "La Diffusion du classicisme par les monnaies en Thrace, à la fin du Ve et au début du IVe siècle" *12th International Congress of Archaeology*, 1983 vol. B1 (Athens: Hypourgeio Politismou kai Epistemon, 1988), 180–85; and Olivier Picard, "The Coinage of Thasos" *Nomismatika Chronika* 9 (1990): 23–27.

21. For illustrations of the Thasian coins see Colin Kraay, *Greek Coins* (New York: H.M. Abrams, 1966) pls 140 (early) and 141 (late).

22. See Claude Calame, *Choruses of Young Women in Ancient Greece* (New York: Rowman & Littlefield, 2001), 89–206 and especially 91–92 for the mythological paradigm of abduction and marriage.

23. Calame is the most through source for these types of songs, known best from fragments by Alkman.

24. Andrew Miller, *Greek Lyric* (Cambridge: Hackett Publishing Company, 1996).

25. Lyn Hatherly Wilson, *Sappho's Bittersweet Songs* (New York: Routledge, 1996).

26. Ibid.

27. David Grene and Richmond Lattimore, eds., *Euripides II, The Complete Greek Tragedies Iphigeneia in Tauris*, trans. Witter Brynner (Chicago: University of Chicago Press, 1969), 170.

28. Bruce Lincoln, "The Rape of Persephone: A Greek Scenario of Women's Initiation," *Harvard Theological Review* 72 (1979): 223–35, esp. 226–27.

29. That she is allowed to return to her mother for six months of the year, of course, is the nonnormative mythological slant.

30. Christiane Sourvinou-Inwood, "The Young Abductor of the Locrian Pinakes," *Bulletin of the Institute of Classical Studies* 20 (1973):12–21, esp.14–17, with illustrations of both types.

Chapter 3

Hercules in a Skirt, or the Feminization of Victory during the Roman Civil Wars and Early Empire

Carlin Barton

Ipsa suas vires odit Romana iuventus.
The young men of Rome hate their manliness.

(*Petronius*, Satyricon *120.84*)

In the ninth book of Ovid's *Heroides*, the rude and conquering Hercules—having filled the earth with the romance of his trials, the "hard man" annealed by adversity, responsible for the peace of the world and the safety of the seas—ends his heroic career in jewels and a turban, a Maeonian girdle and Sidonian gown, holding a wool basket and a spindle. Vapidly he sits and spins, the once grave victor dressed like a wanton and a girl. The Tyrian Omphale, the queen to whom he has surrendered himself, dons the skin of the Nemean lion and raises the club that once slew monsters. Adorned with those brutal signs of struggle the queen regards herself in the mirror. She has conquered the conqueror; hers is the new dispensation. The woman in the lion's skin is both the completion and the inversion of the old order.

But in the eyes of the rejected wife, Deiianira, the transvestite Hercules is a shame—to her, to his father Jupiter, and to his former adversaries.

With his sly commentary on the virile victor, composed in the New Golden Age of Augustus, the Roman master of paradox provides a pattern for the "gender equivocations" of the civil war period and the first century of the monarchy, a period in which the *durus homo* (the "hard man") becomes the object of a sometimes bitter running joke.

Martial's Galla, having exhausted a stable of flaccid fairies (*cinaedi*) with their long hair and combed-out beards, attempts to find a "real man."[1] Alas for Galla: she might seek out the man continually expatiating on the virtues of the Curii and the Fabii, a shaggy man, a fierce, hard, and rustic man. She will indeed find such a man, Martial warns, but he won't be what she anticipated. "It's difficult," he says, "to marry a 'real man.' "[2]

Occasionally one can find a man, according to Juvenal, who has not succumbed to the fashion to depilate his entire body, a taciturn man whose bristling arms and chest promise a dangerous spirit, an *anima atrox*. No one except his physician, grinning while cutting into swollen piles, knows by our hero's shaven ass that he is a passive homosexual. "There is no faithfulness in appearance," the satirist complains. "What street does not abound in severe-looking debauchees?"[3] Far worse than the conspicuous inverts, for Juvenal, are the men who attack them "in the language of Hercules" while wiggling their bottoms.[4] "I want," he says, "to flee beyond the land of the Sarmatians and the icy ocean whenever I hear those Bacchantes—who feign being Curii—talk about morals."[5]

Martial's Maternus, "an admirer of severe clothing, clad in Baetic wool and grey, considers those dressed in scarlet not to be men, and declares amethyst robes the clothes of women. Although he praises natural colors and is always seen in somber hues, cerise are his morals. He will ask you why I suspect that he is a 'soft man' (*vir mollis*).[6] The answer: 'We bathe together.' "[7]

Every Roman could read the traditional signs of the "soft" man in the dressing of his hair, the folds and color of his cloak, his gait, his gestures, his speech, his company, his dinner parties.[8] ("Corrupt" appearance could not, as in our world, disguise the "pure" soul).[9] According to Seneca, "a man's disposition (*ingenium*) cannot possibly be of one sort and his *animus* another. If his soul be *sanus, compositus, gravis, temperans*, his *ingenium* will also be *siccum* and *sobrium*. When his soul is vitiated (*vitiatus*) his *ingenium* also is contaminated (*adflatur*). Do you not see that if a man's soul is enfeebled, his limbs drag and his feet move sluggishly?—that if his spirit is *effeminatus*, the softness appears in his very gait?"[10]

Allowing for the exaggerations of the satirists, there seem to have been, in the late Republic and early Empire, an increasing number of Romans who disdained to conform to the rigors of Roman etiquette, like Maecenas, or Augustus's friend Sallustius Crispus who preferred a life of luxury to the rank of senator.[11] Despising their manliness, such men deport themselves carelessly—like male prostitutes: singing, dancing, playing the buffoon, ministering slavishly to the women. To paraphrase Seneca: They pluck or pattern their beards, or they closely shave their upper lip, while allowing the rest of their facial hair to grow; they wear cloaks of improper colors or transparent togas. They do nothing that could escape notice; on the contrary, they endeavor to incite and attract attention; they invite censure—so long as it makes them conspicuous. "This," according to Seneca, "was the style of Maecenas and all the others who err, not by hazard, but knowingly and willingly."[12] Seneca singles out Maecenas, Augustus's Etruscan "arbiter of elegance," as the embodiment of the style of speech and dress and behavior that he finds most inverted.[13] But Maecenas, the foreigner who held court in Rome like a second Cleopatra, was only the most conspicuous of those who deliberately scorned the demands of Roman "manliness."

Juvenal laments the topsy-turvy world in which all the traditionally positive categories and names—including that of warrior hero—have been suborned: "We call someone's dwarf 'Atlas,' a black slave 'Swan,' a diminutive and deformed wench 'Europa.' Lazy curs scabbed with mange, that lick the edge of the lamp now dry, will get the name of 'Leopard,' 'Tiger,' 'Lion,' or whatever other beast there is on earth that roars with fiercer throat. Therefore take care and fear lest it is upon the same principle that you are given the name [of the victorious generals] 'Creticus' or 'Camerinus.' "[14] The Romans have become so accustomed to this paradox that some Romans had only to see an ascetic or hear him talk of the "traditions of our ancestors" (*mos maiorum*) to detect the hypocrite.

We are wont to associate restraint with impotence, and freedom with virility. The heroes of our popular culture tend to be unbridled and ecstatic—lonely rebels indulging in violence without limits. But for the Romans, restraint and license, gravity and levity, hardness and softness operated within a physics that is, at least in part, alien to us; they carried valances that are different than those we would place on them.

Warrior societies without a strongly centralized peacekeeping force tend to be characterized by highly formalized behavior. Containing the vendetta—the principal threat to the continued existence of such a society— requires carefully restrained and ritualized action, particularly on the part of the great chieftains. This inhibition is the *gravitas* of the Roman lord. It implies a threat, a power to harm that is being contained or carefully handled (just as in colloquial English the "heavy" is "someone to be reckoned with," or a "weighty" matter is a matter that could have dangerous consequences). This gravity of the dangerous man, the "hard man" was manifested in carefully standardized patterns of speech and action that acted as a deterrent to internal violence by suppressing equivocal behavior.[15] *Gravitas*, as exceptional self-control, was the basis of the Roman idea of *fides* (faithfulnes, predictability), the cement of all contractual relations, the bond of society.[16] *Fides* and *gravitas* were consistently attributed by the

Romans to their heroes, "hard men" like Mucius Scaevola, Cincinnatus, Curius Dentatus, Fabricius, Regulus and others.

René Girard remarks on the reluctance of "primitive man" to engage in non-ritualized games or contests: "In a society where every action or gesture may have irreparable consequences it is not surprising that the members should display a 'noble gravity' of bearing besides which our own demeanor appears ridiculous."[17] A breach of etiquette was an act of belligerence and invitation to violence. To willfully transgress the elaborate and predictable patterns of decorum was to declare oneself alienated from the *res publica* and to issue a challenge to its continuity.

Gravitas was to be contrasted with *levitas*, the *durus* with the *mollis*: certain people, like Greeks—or women—who offer no threat, and who are not engaged in "weighty" matters, were characterized by lightness and softness: buoyancy, fickleness, and variety of expression. The lower one was on the social scale, the more inconsistency and individuality one could indulge in. It was for the slaves and prostitutes, the corybants and the *cinaedi* to dance, to make extravagant gestures, to wear strange clothing. The courtesan could break her oath, for she had no "face."

The abrogation of the severe and standardized behaviors of Roman etiquette was the symptom and signal of "the war of all against all."[18] Idiosyncrasy, peculiarity, signaled the rule of violence. When we hear that Caesar "dressed funny," we think only that he was a stylish eccentric. When we hear that the followers of Catiline wore outlandish clothes, it does not have the apocalyptic tones to our ears that it would have to a Roman.[19] The robe of many colors belonged to the man unleashing the vendetta, the man without *fides*.

At the height of their power, the proud confederacy of warrior chieftains that had conquered the Mediterranean lost its sovereignty to the first in a line of "soft men": Julius Caesar. The Julius Caesar who conquered the conquerors was the culmination and the negation of the Roman warrior code with its model of the *vir gravis*.

After Caesar's victory, Cicero was asked why he had chosen the wrong side in the civil war. His reply: "The way he wore his toga took me in." Caesar, Macrobius explains, wore his toga in the manner of the "soft ones," trailing a loose flap as he walked. So unlikely a conqueror was this fop that Sulla seems a prophet when he said to Pompey, "I bid you beware of that ill-girt lad."[20]

Peevish and fretful about his person, Caesar "not only diligently sheered his head and shaved his face," according to Suetonius, "but even caused his body hair to be plucked out by the roots, a practice for which some persons chided him. Moreover, he bore with unease his deformity of baldness. . . . They say that he was conspicuous for his dress, wearing the broadly-striped toga with fringes about the wrists, always worn rather loosely. Hence Sulla's frequent admonition to his fellow aristocrats: 'beware the boy who is ill-girded.' "[21] Caesar the fop, or the *cinaedus*, as Catullus (57) branded him, was a singularly sinister character, falling into the same category as the parricide and the adulterer, the arsonist and the assassin.[22]

A pair of Elegies to Maecenas illuminate the attraction and repulsion the Romans felt for the dichotomies of sexual identity and their relationship to civil war in this period: Maecenas was a very soft man. He was also a very powerful man, served as Augustus's agent and sometimes acted as a viceroy. The anonymous author of these tributes to Maecenas admits the extreme and luxurious lifestyle of his patron. Indeed, he defends it—on the model of Hercules relaxing after his victories by playing a woman and a slave to Omphale, or on the model of Jupiter, who, having successfully tackled the giants, rests in anticipation of the ministrations of his catamite Ganymede.[23] "All things," he says, "beseem the victor at the conclusion of war" (*Omnia victores Marte sedente decent*).[24] "So it goes: the victor is allowed to love, to hold dominion in the shade, to sleep on perfumed rose-petals: it is for the vanquished to plough, to reap; fear lords it over him; never must he learn to stretch his limbs on the blanket-covered ground."[25] Maecenas, like Hercules, can "play"—even at being enslaved and emasculated—because he is the victorious warrior.[26] It is for the defeated and humiliated to toil, to be grave and restrained.[27]

The Augustan historian Livy tells the legend of the Gallic king Brennus who, having offered to lift the siege of the Capitol and ransom the starving Romans besieged there in 386BCE, used weights heavier than the standard. When the Romans complained, he threw his sword onto the already excessive weights, with the words "*Vae victis!*" ("Woe to the defeated!").[28] Standards apply only to the defeated. Inversely, as Pyrrhus explains to Agammemnon in Seneca's Troades: "To the victor is permitted whatever pleases him" (*Quodcumque libuit facere victori licet*).[29]

As a result of the civil wars, the association of *levitas* (and *mollitia*) with victory had as its complement the equation of *gravitas* (and *fides* and *duritia*) with defeat and humiliation. The Roman people were reduced to subjects of an autocrat and the roles that traditionally constrained and signaled the power of the warlords were now also the shackles of the enslaved. Those who would proclaim their freedom now had to do it with behavior traditionally associated with servility and femininity.[30]

The orator Hortensius, like Julius Caesar, was accused of dressing with excessive care. He was also reproached for appearing like an actor and using histrionic gestures (actors coming from the lowest classes). When his opponent in court, Torquatus, "a man with a rather rustic and inelegant nature" (*subagresti homo ingenio et infestivo*) likened him to the dancing girl

Dionysia, Hortensius is said to have responded in a voice at once soft and low: "I would rather be Dionysia—yes Dionysia—than you, Torquatus, knowing nothing of the Muses, of Aphrodite or of Dionysus" (*voce molli atque demissa Hortensius "Dionysia," inquit, "Dionysia malo equidem esse quam tu, Torquate, amousos, anaphroditos, aprosdionusos*").[31]

Seneca compares the torment of the lovesick Maecenas trying to sleep on his bed of down to the agony of the tortured Roman hero Regulus upon the cross. But while Regulus submits to the cruelty of the hostile Carthaginian, Maecenas submits to the dominion of his beloved Terentia. According to Seneca, "If there should be one bold enough to say that he would rather have been born a Maecenas than a Regulus, the fellow, although he may not admit it, would rather have been born a Terentia!"[32] Maecenas suffers like Regulus—even more than Regulus. But to desire to suffer like Maecenas is to desire to be a woman.[33]

The model of the *vir gravis* remained—potent and stigmatized, like the preserved titles and forms of the aristocratic Republic that now both honored and mocked their bearers.[34]

Augustus's victory over Antony—as advertised by Augustus—delivered Rome from the impending tyranny of an Omphale-Cleopatra.[35] In the propaganda that attempted to relieve Augustus of the onus of fratricide, the civil war that finally brought down the ancient confederacy of chieftains was styled as a war against a foreign woman—an inappropriate and unequal opponent.[36] But the message sent out by Augustus was an ambiguous one: "The very god of Actium struck the lyre with an ivory quill after the bugles of victory were hushed. He [Apollo] was lately a warrior to prevent a woman from having Rome as a marriage gift for her foul lewdness."[37]

After the brassy trumpets of Augustus's triumph over the luxurious Eastern Queen—the ambitious and wanton Cleopatra—were stilled, the victor's new tune was in a softer mode. The author of both elegies repeatedly emphasizes Augustus's connection to Maecenas and the former's blessing of the latter. The prince himself, through his connection to Apollo and the establishment of Greek games with musical contests, is linked with the Hellenizers who were in turn associated with the luxury and sexual inversion that Augustus's "restoration" of the ancient mores might seem to thwart. Indeed Augustus's "restoration" can be interpreted as an all-out frontal attack on the ancient code whose every symbol it employed. As Ronald Syme points out, "Augustus may be associated with moral reform, but he is also associated with Maecenas, with the unspeakable Vedius Pollio, and with Julia and Julia's daughter."[38] One could argue that with the empowerment of the delicate Augustus and the dainty Maecenas, Omphale had not lost but won.[39] There were, as Suetonius indicates, those who felt that "a *cinaedus* now ruled the world with his middle finger."[40]

The establishment of the monarchy was experienced both as the end and culmination of civil war, and as the conclusion and continuation of a Saturnalia that had gotten out of hand. With the elevation of Augustus, moreover, came the permanent installation of a centralized police force in the city of Rome and the suppression of the vendetta as a principle of equilibrium and guarantee of *fides*. Now everyone was relieved of the necessity of *gravitas*. In the besieged, the garrisoned city of Rome both the "heavy" and the "light" were equally weightless. The Roman male, liberated from rigid masculine sex roles, delighted in the freedom of playing a slave and a woman. Simultaneously, the Roman male, like Ovid's Hercules, deprived of power and emasculated, suffered an insult to be avenged—by Deiianira—on himself.

Notes

I would like to thank Professor Richard C. Trexler, editor of *Gender Rhetorics* (Binghamton, NY: Center for Medieval & Early Renaissance Studies, 1994), for permission to republish my article (with minor changes and additions) in this collection. Unless otherwise attributed, translations are my own.

1. For an extensive discussion of the *cinaedus* see Amy Richlin, "Not Before Homosexuality: The Materiality of the *Cinaedus* and the Roman Law against Love Between Men," *Journal of the History of Sexuality* 3.4 (1993): 523–73, esp. 530–34.
2. *quaere aliquem Curios semper Fabiosque loquentem,/ hirsutum et dura rusticitate trucem:/ invenies: sed habet tristis quoque turba cinaedos:/ difficile est vero nubere, Galla, viro* (Martial 7.58). Compare Martial 1.24: "Do you see, Decianus, that man with hair uncombed, whose gloomy sternness even you fear, who speaks of the Curii and those liberators, the Camilli? Don't credit his appearance: he became a wife yesterday." *Aspicis incomptis illum, Deciane, capillis,/ cuius et ipse times triste supercilium,/ qui loquitur Curios adsertoresque Camillos?/ Nolito fronti credere: nupsit heri.* Cf. 2.36, 2.54, 6.56, 9.27, 9.47, 12.42; cf. *Anthologia Palatina* 11.155, 157; Amy Richlin, *The Garden of Priapus* (New Haven: Yale University Press, 1983), 138–39.
3. "Do you castigate dirty things while you are yourself the most notorious ditch (*fossa*) among the Socratic *cinaedi*? Indeed, hairy limbs and the hard bristles that cover your arms give promise of a fierce spirit: but it is from a smooth ass that the chuckling physician cuts your swollen piles. Their words are few; their desire is for silence, and they cut their hair shorter than their eyebrows." *Frontis nulla fides, quis enim non vicus abundat/ tristibus obscaenis? Castigas turpia, cum sis/ inter Socraticos notissima fossa cinaedos?/ Hispida membra quidem et durae per bracchia saetae/ promittunt atrocem animum, sed podice levi/caeduntur tumidae medico ridente mariscae./ Rarus sermo illis et magna libido tacendi/ atque supercilio brevior coma* (Juvenal 2.8–15). See all of Juvenal 2.1–63.

4. *Sed peiores, qui talia verbis Herculis invadunt et de virtute locuti clunem agitant* (Juvenal 2.19).

5. *Ultra Sauromatas fugere hinc libet et glacialem/ Oceanum, quotiens aliquid de moribus audent/ qui Curios simulant et Bacchanalia vivunt* (Juvenal 2.1–3).

6. For a discussion of *mollitia* see Catherine Edwards, *The Politics of Immorality in Ancient Rome* (Cambridge: Cambridge University Press, 1993).

7. "His gaze never lifts, but observing the sodomites with devouring eyes, he regards their pricks with lips that cannot rest." *Amator ille tristium lacernarum/ et baeticatus atque leucophaeatus,/ qui coccinatos non putat viros esse/ amethystinasque mulierum vocat vestes,/ nativa laudet, habeat et licet semper/ fuscos colores, galbinos habet mores./ Rogabit unde suspicer virum mollem:/ una lavamur. Aspicit nihil sursum,/ sed spectat oculis devorantibus draucos/ nec otiosis mentulas videt labris* (Martial 1.96).

8. Romans were suspicious of variation in dress. Scipio Aemilianus is reported to have reproached Publius Sulpicius Galba, accusing him of being a *homo delicatus* and *chirodotus* (wearing a long-sleeved tunic) (Aulus Gellius, *Noctes Atticae* 6.12.4–5). Compare 6.12.5: "The man who perfumes himself daily and adorns himself before a mirror, whose eyebrows are shaved, who strolls about with his beard plucked and thighs shaved, who at banquets, though a young man, has reclined with his lover in a long-sleeved tunic on the inner side of the couch, who is fond not only of wine but of men—does anyone doubt that he does what *cinaedi* commonly do?" *Verba sunt haec Scipionis: "Nam qui cotidie unguentatus adversum speculum ornetur, cuius supercilia radantur, qui barba vulsa feminibusque subvulsis ambulet, qui in conviviis adulescentulus cum amatore, cum chirodota tunica interior accubuerit, qui non modo vinosus, sed virosus quoque sit, eumne quisquam dubitet, quin idem fecerit quod cinaedi facere solent?"* For other signs of softness see Seneca, *Naturales quaestiones* 7.31.2–3.

9. Physical and moral traits are consistently linked in Roman thought. See Elizabeth Cornelia Evans, "Roman Descriptions of Personal Appearance in History and Biography," *Harvard Studies in Classical Philology* 46 (1935): 43–84; Maud W. Gleason, "The Semiotics of Gender: Physiognomy and Self-Fashioning in the Second Century C.E.," in David M. Halperin, John J. Winkler, and Froma I. Zeitlin, eds., *Before Sexuality; The Construction of Erotic Experience in the Ancient Greek World* (Princeton: Princeton University Press, 1990), 389–415.

10. *Si ille effeminatus est, ipso incessu adparer mollitiam?* (*Epistulae* 114.3). The looseness of Maecenas's speech is reflected in his attire (*Epistulae* 114.4, 6).

11. Tacitus, *Annales* 3.30. See also Seneca, *Naturales quaestiones* 7.31.2–3. The Augustan poet Propertius proudly renounces the title pater and the spawning of soldiers; he acknowledges no commander save Cynthia (2.7).

12. *Epistulae* 114.21.

13. His style was that of an intoxicated man (*ebrius*)(*Epistulae* 114.4–8).

14. Juvenal 8.32–38. Just as short hair and laconic speech are no longer sure signs of the real man, so also a long beard and a cloak, traditionally the signs of the ascetic philosopher have been suborned by the libertine (Martial 1.24; 9.48; Juvenal 2.3ff; Aulus Gellius, *Noctes Atticae* 9.2; 13.8.4–5; 15.2; 17.19). See Amy Richlin, *The Garden of Priapus*, 136.

15. For *gravitas* and *levitas* in Roman thought see Georges Dumézil, "*Maiestas* et *gravitas*; de quelques diffrences entre les Romains et les austronsians," *Revue de Philologie* 3.25 (1951): 7–28; H. Wagenvoort, "*Gravitas* and *Maiestas*," in *Roman Dynamism* (Oxford: Oxford Blackwell, 1947), 104–27; and Wagenvoort, "*Gravitas et Maiestas*," *Mnemosyne* 5 (1952): 287–306; Carlin Barton, *Roman Honor* (Berkeley: University of California Press, 2001), 36n11, 61, 68, 226. For similar contrasts between "heaviness" and "lightness" in other cultures see Hu Hsien-chin, "The Chinese Concepts of Face," in Douglas G. Haring, ed., *Personal Character and Cultural Milieu* (Syracuse, NY: Syracuse University Press, 1958), 367–86, esp. 369, 371; and Pierre Bourdieu, "The Sentiment of Honour in Kabyle Society," in J. G. Peristiany, ed., *Honour and Shame; The Values of Mediterranean Society* (Chicago: University of Chicago Press, 1966), 193–241, esp. 210–11.

16. So, the remorseless grey pin-striped suit of the advocate signals to the potential employer or client that he or she knows the rules of the game and is willing to abide by them. Standardized dress and behavior inspires their "faith."

17. René Girard, *Violence and the Sacred*, trans. Patrick Gregory (Baltimore: Johns Hopkins University Press, 1977), chap. 1, esp. 19–27, 30–31, cf. 81. Our informal casual behavior today is largely a result of the state's monopoly of violence. Where that monopoly breaks down, the importance of well-established rules of etiquette reasserts itself—as in urban street gangs, or in negotiations between hostile nations.

18. To bring an end to civil war it was essential, according to Horace, to end unbridled freedom and to restore the severe self-discipline of the soldier (*Carmina* 3.24.27ff).

19. See, for example, Cicero's description of the odd dress and grooming of the followers of the revolutionary Catiline (*In Catilinam* 2.22–23); Richlin, "Not Before Homosexuality" 541–42; Richlin, *The Garden of Priapus*, 100, 222.

20. *In Caesarem quoque mordacitas Ciceronis dentes suos strinxit. Nam primum post victoriam Caesaris interrogatus cur in electione partis errasset, respondit: "Praecinctura me decepit," jocatus in Caesarem, qui ita toga praecingebatur ut trahendo laciniam velut mollis incederet, adeo ut Sulla tamquam providus dixerit Pompeio: "Cave tibi illum puerum male praecinctum"* (2.3.9). For *discinctus* ("loose-belted") as a synonym for *cinaedus* see *Persius* 3.31, 4.21; Seneca, *Epistulae* 92.35, 114.4.6; Suetonius, *Caligula*, 52; Richlin, "Not Before Homosexuality," 531, 542 n.45.

21. *Circa corporis curam morosior, ut non solum tonderetur diligenter ac raderetur, sed velleretur etiam, ut quidem exprobraverunt, calvitii vero deformitatem iniquissime ferret. . . . Etiam cultu notabilem ferunt: usum enim lato clavo ad manus fimbriato nec umquam aliter quam <ut> super eum cingeretur, et quidem fluxiore cinctura; unde emanasse Sullae dictum optimates saepius admonentis, ut male praecinctum puerum caverent* (*Divus Julius* 45.2–3).

22. Vices tended to be interchangeable and concatenated in this period. Caesar the *cinaedus* is Caesar the womanizer (*Catullus* 57). "Sallust [having joined Caesar's camp after his expulsion from the senate in 49BCE] was one of that throng into which, as into a whirlpool, every vice had poured. Whatever shameless and lewd characters, parricides, despisers of religion, and debtors, were to be found in the

city, in the municipal towns, the colonies, and throughout Italy,—the most abandoned and infamous, fitted for camp only by the extravagance of their vices, and their eagerness to overturn the state, had sunk there as into the waters of an ocean." (*Eius enim partis erat Sallustius, quo tamquam in unam voraginem coetus omnium vitiorum excesserat: quidquid impudicorum, cilonum, parricidarum, sacrilegorum, deditorum fuit in urbe, municipiis, coloniis, Italia tota, sicut in fretis subsederant, nominis perditi ac notissimi, nulla in parte castris apti nisi licentia vitiorum et cupiditate rerum novarum* [Pseudo-Cicero, *In Sallustium* 6]). Notice the idea, expressed in the metaphor of the ocean, or streams and rivulets running into the sea, of indiscriminate mixture; this camp was a hodge-podge of every category of vice. Compare Pseudo-Sallust on Caesar and the "fast set": "men whose lives were polluted with disgrace and licentiousness flocked to your camp, inspired by the evil reports of the malicious, with the hope of seizing the Republic. They openly threatened all who remained neutral with murder, rapine, and all that delights a corrupted soul." *Per idem tempus maledictis ineiquorum occupandae rei publicae in spem adducti homines, quibus omnia probro ac luxuria polluta erant, concurrere in castra tua et aperte quieteis mortem rapinas, postremo omnia quae corrupto animo lubebat, minitari* (*Epistulae ad Caesarem* 1.2.5 [ed. Kurfess]).

23. Ibid., 1.87–92.
24. Ibid., 1.50.
25. Ibid., 1.93–96.
26. The author emphasizes Maecenas's military career. *Quam nunc ille tener, tam gravis hostis erat* (44). Even the critical Seneca admits that Maecenas had a nature both great and virile but that his successes "ungirded" him. (*Habuit enim ingenium et grande et virile nisi illud secunda discinxissent* [*Epistulae* 92.35].) Juvenal's Laronia rails against the "unnatural acts" and "effeminacies" of men "protected by the closelyjoined shields of the phalanx." *Sed illos/ defendit numerus/ iunctaeque umbone phalanges* (2.36–46). This indulgence did not extend to Valerius Maximus's centurian (6.1.10); Richlin, "Not Before Homosexuality," 543–44.
27. Victory released Antony, the scion of Hercules, "from laws like Solon's for the regulation of conception" (Plutarch, *Antonius* 60.3). The victorious Caesar hoped for multiple wives and Augustus's position allowed him to appropriate Livia, the pregnant wife of another man, with impunity. The examples could be multiplied indefinitely.
28. Livy 5.48.9.
29. Seneca, *Troades* 335, cf. 333: "There is no law which spares the captive or forbids his punishment." *Lex nulla capto parcit aut poenam impedit.* (For this sentiment compare Plautus, *Pseudolus* 5.2.19). Just as the hairy man might be exposed as a pathetic homosexual, the *cinaedus* might be revealed to be the virile adulterer, shaming the husband. According to Macrobius (*Saturnalia* 2.4.12) Maecenas was both effeminate and the seducer of unfaithful wives. See E. Courtney, "*Vivat ludatque cinaedus,*" *Mnemosyne* 15 (1962): 262–66; Edwards, *The Politics of Immorality*, 83 and n. 71.

30. The Roman love poets and their pride in enslavement are the result of the tendencies discussed in this paper. See Jasper Griffith, "Propertius and Anthony," *Journal of Roman Studies* 47 (1977): 17–26. Antony, the defeated enemy, enslaved first to Fulvia and then to Cleopatra, was the perfect model for Maecenas.

31. Aulus Gellius, *Noctes Atticae* 1.5.2–3.

32. *De providentia* 3.9–11.

33. *Non usque eo in possessionem generis humani vitia venerunt, ut dubium sit an electione fati data plures nasci Reguli quam Maecenates velint; aut si quis fuerit, qui audeat dicere Maecenatem se quam Regulum nasci maluisse, idem iste, tacet licet, nasci Terentiam maluit!*

34. So Augustus's friend Sallustius Crispus, who preferred a life of luxury to the rank of senator yet surpassed in power many who had won consulships and triumphs (*Tacitus Annales* 3.30). Compare the *praetextati mores* that the warlike youth from Armenia will take away with him from Rome in Juvenal 170. See Richlin, "Not Before Homosexuality," 28.

35. See Natalie Kampen, "Omphale and the Instability of Gender" in Kampen ed., *Sexuality in Ancient Art* (Cambridge: Cambridge University Press, 1996), 233–46, for a discussion (with illustrations) of the negative political associations of the Omphale in the civil war period (and the radical changes in associations that these mythic figures underwent in the second and third centuries of the Empire).

36. For Cleopatra as the unequal opponent see Carlin Barton, *The Sorrows of the Ancient Romans* (Princeton: Princeton University Press, 1983), 183, 185. The more "unworthy" the opposition, the more "unequal" the person brought into competition, the more the opponent appears as a ludicrous or obscene mimic. See also Propertius, 3.11. 29–55.

37. *Actius ipse lyram plectro percussit eburno,/ postquam victrices conticuere tubae./ Hic modo miles erat, ne posset femina Romam/ dotalem stupri turpis habere sui (Elegiae ad Maecenatem 1.51).*

38. Ronald Syme, *The Roman Revolution* (Oxford: Oxford University Press, 1939), 452. See also 443–58, 460–61 for Augustus's reforms and the skepticism with which they were greeted. "It was observed with malicious glee that neither of the consuls who gave their names to the Lex Papia Popaea had wife or child" [Dio 56.10.3] (452).

39. For accusations of effeminacy leveled at Augustus see Suetonius Augustus 68. For his attempts to present himself simultaneously as the hard man and the libertine see Judith P. Hallett, "*Perusinae Glandes* and the Changing Image of Augustus" *American Journal of Ancient History* 2 (1977): 151–71.

40. Suetonius, *Augustus 68: sed et populus quondam universus ludorum die et accepit in contumeliam eius et adsensu maximo conprobavit versum in scaena pronuntiatum de gallo Matris deum tympanizante: videsne, ut cinaedus orbem digito temperat?*

II

Medieval Cultures

Chapter 4

"The Sweepings of Lamia": Transformations of the Myths of Lilith and Lamia

Irven M. Resnick and Kenneth F. Kitchell Jr.

Christian religious polemics have often employed animal imagery to denigrate the Jewish "other." John Chrysostom (ca. 347–407) compared Jews to pigs and goats because of their wanton habits,[1] to stallions because of their lustfulness,[2] to dogs,[3] to hyenas,[4] and, generally, to wild beasts only fit for killing.[5] By contrast, members of the Church are gentle lambs or sheep guided by the Good Shepherd, who alone can protect his flock from the predatory habits of this beastly enemy. Although the violence of John Chrysostom's metaphors may surpass that of other Christian polemicists, his imagery is quite typical. However, as one evaluates such animal images in anti-Jewish religious polemics, the modern reader must not overlook classificatory distinctions that were fundamental to the medieval reader.

Animals could be classified under a variety of rubrics. Especially once thirteenth-century scholars rediscovered Aristotle's biological treatises, animals would be categorized according to their various means of reproduction; according to their anatomical differences; according to their diverse means of locomotion; according to their habitats; according to whether they were wild or domesticated, and so on. Whereas this taxonomy rooted in ancient philosophy provided one means of grouping different animals and their attributes or properties, another model was available from the Bible, wherein animals are clearly separated into three major genuses: creatures of the land, of the water, and of the air (cf. Gen. 1:20–25). These three animal genuses will be subsumed under two broader rubrics: clean and unclean (cf. Lev. 11).

These two rubrics—clean and unclean—are in one sense exhaustive, covering all the animals created by God. Yet in another way these categories extend even beyond created nature, and force one also to take into consideration a third group, a true *tertium quid*: hybrid or monstrous beasts which transgress the boundaries of the natural order. The hybrid and the monster are not necessarily one and the same. For example, in the medieval bestiary tradition the mule is a hybrid that comes from a horse and an ass, created by human intervention and experiment in cross-breeding. According to the twelfth-century *Book of Beasts*, "Anas himself, the son of a great-grandchild of Esau, was the first man to cause herds of horses to be covered by asses in the desert—so that thence this new kind of animal [the mule] might be born from many of them, against nature."[6] Other examples of "adulterous mixture" have resulted from human industry, creating true hybrids. Precisely because the hybrid mixture is "against nature," it falls under the category of the unclean.[7]

Monsters are unclean as well, but typically they are not viewed as the product of human intervention or experiments in cross-breeding, but as the result of some flaw in nature—for example, a flaw in the material employed in generation.[8] Precisely because they are permitted but not willed by the Creator, and because they represent a falling away from Nature, they too must be classified among unclean animals.

One should not be surprised at the frequency with which Jews are compared to unclean animals in nature—like dogs and pigs—since biblical purity laws amply demonstrate that such animals, either when consumed or from contact with their carcasses, are obstacles to holiness.[9] For Rabanus Maurus, the Jew and the pig are closely related both because of the latter's uncleanness and because of its attributes, that is, its wantonness and gluttony.[10] Bruno of Segni (d. 1123), in a fascinating allegorical exegesis, suggests that in truth Christians are like clean, ruminant animals because they—and not the Jews—twice digest the text of Scripture, locating in it the spiritual and not merely the literal sense.[11] This image finds an echo in Hermann of Cologne's (ca. 1107–81) account of his conversion from Judaism to Christianity. Since Jews, he laments, have been content only with a literal interpretation of Scripture, they are like beasts of burden, whereas Christians, using reason, refresh themselves with a spiritual understanding. Animals that do not chew the cud are unclean, whereas after having adopted Christianity Hermann "transferred to the stomach of memory for frequent rumination" whatever edifying lessons he learned from the Bishop of Munster.[12]

As Christians would identify themselves with the clean animals of Scripture, so too these animal images suggested that contact with Jews is contact with uncleanness. As Christian theology allegorized biblical purity laws, uncleanness came to represent moral danger. At the same time, these animal images were useful instruments that implied the Jews' intellectual (and not merely moral) shortcomings. Such animal imagery was easily transferred to medieval art and iconography. Although the *Judensau* motif is perhaps best known,[13] at times Jews are also depicted in association with other animals with a suspect or threatening nature: cats,[14] owls,[15] and scorpions.[16]

John Chrysostom had acknowledged that although the Jews' behavior made them *like* the animals mentioned, they had not been transformed into animals in their essential nature.[17] They remain for him human beings, though of the worst sort. Some modern historians, however, suggest that by the twelfth century in the Latin world, the failure of philosophical polemics to persuade Jews of the error of their views had led some Christian polemicists to infer that perhaps Jews were more than simply *like* animals: in their very nature, in reality, they *are* beasts, or, perhaps, part-beast, which is demonstrated no more clearly than by the fact that for them reason seems to have no sway. Recently, Odo of Tournai's *Disputation with the Jew, Leo, Concerning the Advent of Christ, the Son of God* (*Disputatio contra Judaeum Leonem nomine de adventu Christi filii Dei*)[18] has been seen as preparing the way for later twelfth-century polemicists like Peter the Venerable, whose *Against the Inveterate Stubbornness of the Jews* could only explain the Jews' rejection of Christianity by insisting that they had lost the capacity to reason and, as such, were more bestial than human.[19]

With such a shift, metaphor became reality. In one way, this shift occurred as a result of centuries-old polemical traditions; in another way, it was perhaps a "reasonable" conclusion reached by those who had begun to despair of the success of rational polemics. Here, however, we would like to examine another animal image employed in anti-Jewish exegesis and polemic—an image that associates Jews not merely with unclean animals but instead with those hybrid creatures, quasi-beasts, or monsters that arose as accidents of nature.

It has been argued that for the Middle Ages, the defining quality of a monster is to be found especially in its violation of the boundaries that ought to separate animal from human. Thus, Charles Stewart has remarked, "Typically, monstrosity involves a combination of animal and human features . . . Importantly, monstrosity involves more than just form. It entails an affront to the moral order."[20] As a flaw appearing in the order of nature, the monster is on the most superficial level an affront to the good order of creation. But more than this, a monster unites in itself a more perfect with an inferior species and typically displays the characteristics of its inferior nature. In this way, the monster is an affront to the ontological order as well.

Besides this, a monster is not only a flawed nature that displays the imperfection of its matter;[21] a monster is, most often, also a creature that withdraws from moral standards and *acts* monstrously, offending our sense of order.

Medieval observers understood too that monsters exist, but *ought not* to exist. They are liminal objects that present a perplexing paradox. As Timothy Beal notes, "Monsters are in the world but not of the world. They are paradoxical personifications of *otherness within sameness.* That is, they are threatening figures of anomaly within the well-established and accepted order of things. They represent the outside that has gotten inside, the beyond-the-pale that, much to our horror, has gotten into the pale."[22] One response to the monstrous presence, which has violated nature's good design, is demonization.

Beal's description of monsters as "paradoxical personifications of *otherness within sameness . . .* threatening figures of anomaly within the well-established and accepted order of things . . . the beyond-the-pale that, much to our horror, has gotten into the pale" could equally well describe the Jew in medieval society. One should not be surprised, then, to discover Jews assimilated to monstrous creatures in medieval tradition.[23] An example is the Lamia, a monster of uncertain and sometimes contradictory attributes, who, despite her classical antecedents, comes to symbolize the Jews in medieval texts. For medieval Christendom, the Lamia is dangerous, sexually ambivalent, part-human and part-beast. Straddling the secure taxonomies of the natural world, the Lamia threatens it with disorder, just as she threatens all human moral values.[24] The development of this complex and cross-culturally contaminated description is the result of centuries of cultural interplay. By tracing the development of the Lamia legend in classical and medieval sources, we intend here to shed some light on the way in which this monstrous creature began as a cultural symbol for the Greeks, helping them define and reinforce several aspects of their social fabric, became confused by biblical exegetes with a preexistent Jewish bogey, and emerged, ironically, to serve theological and political purposes designed to demonize medieval Jews, heretics, and others.

Lamia According to Ancient and Classical Sources

Now this story has not been made up for some child, in order to make it less wild and more controllable, but rather for those with greater and more thoroughgoing thoughtlessness than this.

Dio Chrysostom, Discourse[25]

The Latin *Lamia* is certainly a direct transliteration of the Greek λάμια. The ultimate origin of the Greek name, however, is a matter of controversy.

Some have sought its roots in ancient Mesopotamian demonology;[26] others, however, have defended Lamia's Greek rather than Oriental origins, deriving the word λάμια from the same root as Greek words for "gullet"(λαιμός, less commonly λάμος), a reference to the Lamia's voracious, consuming, and devouring nature.[27]

Lamia appears frequently in Greek mythology and folklore and, based on her early appearance in the literature (as early as Stesichorus—sixth century BCE) and on her widespread citations throughout antiquity, we can be assured both of her antiquity and popularity. As her history is pieced together from various sources, Lamia is said to be a female or hermaphroditic demon who lives in caves and ventures forth to devour children or young men she has seduced. She has an ugly face and removable eyes, is distinctly foul smelling, has unwashed testicles, farts when caught, and has large pendulous breasts.[28] In some sources, Lamia was the daughter of a Libyan king who was seduced by Zeus and bore him several children. When Hera discovered her consort's infidelity, she sought out Lamia's children by Zeus and murdered them. Thus deprived of maternal joys, Lamia saw to it that others would feel the same grief and began to devour children, even snatching them from the womb itself.[29] Her grief transformed utterly her appearance, so that her face reflected the bestial savagery in her heart. Presumably, like her fellow demons Empusa, Gorgo, and Mormo, she was commonly invoked to convince wayward youngsters of the wisdom of behaving well.[30]

We have one further source for the role Lamia played in her earliest manifestations, for several images of demons are preserved on Greek vases which, despite the cautions raised by Boardman, are almost certainly either Lamia herself or some similar monster. In either case they give us some insights into which of the Lamia's many subsequent attributes were most important to early Greeks. Two of the vases, both Attic black figures, date from ca. 500 BCE or slightly thereafter. In the first, the monster confronts a sphinx. She is depicted as hairy, with prominent breasts and enormous talons—all salient characteristics of Lamia. The other shows a grotesque scene in which a naked woman, bound to a palm tree, is being tortured by satyrs. She has enormous breasts, a sagging belly, and, on close inspection, two prominent fangs. The Satyrs pull out her tongue with tongs and burn her genital area from below. Boardman claimed that the kneeling satyr "scorch[es] her pubic hair," but Halm-Tisserant[31] had previously pointed out that incised lines on this portion of the damaged vase show that the figure had an erect phallus. As already noted, Aristophanes endows Lamia with testicles. The phallus surely points us to Lamia, and the palm tree, like the Sphinx in the previous vase, puts the scene in Libya, her favorite haunt.

A third vase is in the comic Kabirion style and shows a stunted man running from a hairy monster with prominent breasts and even more prominent talons.[32] While we would dearly love to have an inscribed picture of Lamia, or to be aware of a literary source from which these scenes may have come, two facts are probably secure—Lamia and child-killing demons like her were well-established in the high period of Greek culture and her lively iconography betokens an equally lively presence either in oral narrative or, most likely, in comic productions.[33]

These features were soon invoked for the moralizing needs of the philosophers, and later authors. As late as the fifteenth century, the author of a treatise entitled "Lamia" remarked that fabulous tales—even old wives' tales like the stories of Lamia—are sometimes the beginning of or a tool of philosophy.[34] Scobie has noted an often overlooked tale told by Dio Chrysostom (ca. 40–15 CE) which, while not using the term Lamia, is clearly a Lamia tale.[35] Dio stresses that the tale is not "made up for a child, to make it less wild and unmanageable" but is a real story that can be put to good philosophic use. The tale is set in Libya, a favorite setting for the Lamia.[36] The creatures were said to be a type of θηρίον, or beast, and were beautiful women from the waist up who used their breasts to fill sailors with a desire for intercourse with them. Yet once on shore, the sailors were eaten simultaneously by the creature's upper and lower half, the latter being serpent-like and ending in a serpent's head.[37] It should be noted that these creatures lived in caves, and smelled terribly.

A closer description of the Lamia would be hard to find, yet her purposes have changed remarkably. Johnston has argued persuasively that the Lamia and her kind were originally creatures that helped to define negatively what a female in early Greek society should actually be: She should mate with, and not kill, young men and should produce, not devour, children.[38] This makes excellent sense for a culture which so regulated and controlled its female population. Yet here we see that Dio, writing a minimum of six centuries after the Lamia's first appearance, has begun one of many modifications in the Lamia. He has taken it over as a model, he says, for teaching us about our desires and appetites—what appears at first as attractive and seductive ends in ruin and corruption. A later sophistic writer, Flavius Philostratus (born ca. 170 CE), writes in much the same vein when he discusses the Lamia bested by the wonder worker Apollonius of Tyre. In his *Life of Apollonius* Philostratus tells us that the lamiae's powers of seduction were great for they, and related demons, "are lascivious creatures, and their passion is for making love and especially for the flesh of young men. They use the pleasures of sex as a decoy for those on whom they wish to dine."[39]

Apuleius, a third sophist, who wrote slightly earlier than Philostratus, also has an intriguing Lamia tale, but Apuleius is more prone to indulge his love of the wondrous and the magical than to point out directly the moral lessons of his tale.[40] His bawdy tale of Lucius, who turns into an ass through an overly active curiosity, begins with a fairly lengthy story concerning a young man, ironically named Socrates, who was seduced by an "old but relatively attractive" woman named Meroe.[41] "Inflamed by lust" she brings him to her bed and keeps him a virtual hostage. Socrates claims she is a witch who uses her wiles to force any man she desires to fall in love with her and who has changed many of her enemies and former lovers into animals.[42] At last free of her, but broken in body and spirit, Socrates meets an old friend who rescues him and brings him to an inn. Here, however, Meroe and her sister Panthia burst in the doors at night. Meroe stabs Socrates in the neck, drains his blood into a bottle, pulls his heart out through his throat and inserts a sponge to stop up the wound. They then squat over the friend, urinate on him copiously with an especially foul smelling urine, and depart. It is at this stage that Apuleius calls the sisters "lamiae."[43]

The next morning Socrates is miraculously still alive, though clearly enervated. Only when they are once more on the road and Socrates tries to take a drink at a stream does the sponge fall out and Socrates dies. The story is well told and appropriately frightening. Meroe is a type of humanized Lamia, for she and her sister display many of the traits of Lamia such as lusting after young men, a foul smell, and vampirism, but they have been reduced from the status of demon to that of witch, a subject which greatly interested Apulcius. Such is the change that during his recounting of the famous Cupid and Psyche tale, Apuleius can have Cupid call Psyche's sisters *illae lamiae*, with the approximate meaning of "those bitches."

Before moving on to Lamia's later manifestations, there remains one further Greek example of Lamia, for Aristotle seems to mention her twice. In *Nicomachean Ethics* 1148b, describing how some basic natures can become perverse and almost bestial, he uses as an example "the woman who, so they say, tears open pregnant women and devours their children." This would seem clearly to be Lamia who, in this instance, is seen more as a deranged female (e.g. at the start of her story) than as the subsequent monster.[44] Later, Aristotle tells us that there is a shark called the Lamia, and from Oppian we get further evidence of its fierceness and voraciousness.[45] It is noteworthy that the she-demon Lamia had so entered the classical framework of references that she could be used by transference for a real, natural object that participated in lamian attributes. One need only look to English terms such as "Devil Fish" to recognize the tendency.

By comparison with the Greeks, the Romans mention Lamia infrequently. Varro knew of Euripides' *Lamia*, Horace briefly mentions her, and Apuleius was quite taken with her. But interest in the Lamia as a monster for didactic use is renewed principally among Christian authors whose view of the Lamia represents an aggregate drawn from Greek and Jewish traditions adapted to their own needs. An example is offered by the text of the first Vatican Mythographer, dated to perhaps between 875 and 1075 CE:[46]

> Crotopus was a king of the Argives whose daughter was violated by Apollo. Whereupon the indignant father killed his daughter because she was a Vestal priestess and had to preserve her virginity forever. As revenge, Apollo sent a horrible monster which a certain very courageous youth, Coroebus, slew. Statius describes this very well in his history. This monster was named Lamia, for *lamiae* are the furrows of fields filled with foul corruption or the whirlpools of rivers, whence this most ferocious beast is known as Lamia.[47]

In fact, Statius' story of Crotopus and Coroebus makes no mention of Lamia, but the story is clearly the one to which the mythographer refers.[48] Crotopus's virgin daughter, Cynthia, does indeed have an affair with Apollo, resulting in the birth of a child. Shamed and afraid of her father's disapproval, Cynthia left her infant son in a sheep pen for shepherds to raise. Later, wild dogs seized the child and killed it. When she learned of her son's fate, Cynthia at last disclosed to her father the source of her greatest grief, whereupon Crotopus put his daughter to death for her amorous transgression. To avenge her death Apollo does indeed send an unnamed monster with distinctive lamian characteristics who was conceived beneath the river Acheron in the foul lair of the Furies.[49] She has the face and the breast of a woman, but has a serpent rising from her forehead. She displays lamian behavior as well, for she steals into bed chambers at night and snatches nursing infants away from their mothers' breasts, devouring them. After the monster has terrorized the Argive countryside, Coroebus and his followers finally slay her.

Whether Statius actually had Lamia in mind or not is immaterial. What is important is that later commentators were prone to interpret such passages in lamian terms, putting her to the uses they saw fit.

Jewish Contributions to Lamia

And Lilith will find repose there and find a place of rest.

Isa. 34:14

ἐκει ἀνπαύσονται ὀνοκένταυροι, εὑρον γαρ ἀνάπαυσιν
There the ass-centaurs will take their rest, for they have found their rest . . .

Isa. 34:14 (LXX)

ibi cubavit Lamia et invenit sibi requiem.
There the Lamia lay down and found her rest.

Isa. 34:14 (Vulg.)

In Isa. 34, the Hebrew prophet presents an apocalyptic scenario in which Edom is chastised by the Lord on the "Day of Yahweh," a time when its land and rivers are turned to smoking pitch, becoming a wasteland, a habitat fit only for wild dogs, wildcats, jackals, satyrs, and for the demon "Lilith."[50]

Moving from the Hebrew text to the Greek Septuagint (LXX), however, we find that the "ass-centaur" has replaced Lilith. When Isa. 34:14 was translated centuries later by Symmachus,[51] the cast of characters has again changed dramatically and the Hebrew "Lilith" and the LXX's "ass-centaur" appear as Lamia, and Lamia was then carried on in Symmachus's Greek translation, in the *Vetus latina*,[52] and in Jerome's Latin Vulgate, which in turn preserved "Lamia" for later Latin readers. This fact is obscured by modern English versions in which Lilith-Lamia is rendered as "night hag," "night monster," or "night fairy," and in others still as a "screech owl."[53]

How is it that Lilith in the Hebrew text of Isa. 34:14 is rendered by Symmachus's Greek text and by the Latin Vulgate as Lamia? It is our contention that certain traits or characteristics shared in common by Lilith and Lamia encouraged Latin and Greek translators to make this equation.

As early as the seventh century BCE an incantation appears on a Syrian tablet designed to protect women during childbirth by chasing away Lilith. Later rabbinic sources add to the tradition of Lilith, often attributing to her characteristics she shares with the Lamia. In the Talmudic period, Lilith was identified as Adam's first wife.[54] When Adam wished to have intercourse with her in the "missionary" position, Lilith refused to lie beneath him because, both having been created from the dust of the earth, they should be equal, and one should not lie above the other. When Adam attempted to force himself on her, she uttered the magic name of God and flew off to the desert around the Red Sea, where she gave birth to numerous demons. When God ordered her to desist, she agreed only on the condition that she should have power over newborns—males until the eighth day (the day when male infants are circumcised) and females until the twentieth day.[55] Again, Lilith threatens newborns much as Lamia may snatch them away and devour them and, as in Greek legends, she dwells in deserted regions.

Despite her refusal to obey Adam, Lilith returns to him after the expulsion from Eden and has intercourse with him against his will. As penance, Adam promised to refrain from intercourse with Eve for one-hundred thirty years. But he could not control involuntary nocturnal emissions, caused by female spirits who coupled with him and who then gave birth to demons and *lilim* (masc. pl. of Lilith). Patai finds additional information in Aramaic incantation texts which, though they date from 600 CE and later, probably reflect popular beliefs from an earlier period. In these texts, Lilith appears, like Lamia, as a ghostly paramour. Female Liliths join with men at night and male *lilim* join with women.[56] But, jealous of their human mate's progeny, they are wont to suck their blood and strangle them. According to one medieval Jewish narrative, Elijah once encountered Lilith. When he asked her where she was going, she replied "I am on my way to drink the blood and eat the flesh of young children."[57] *Numbers Rabbah* also notes that Lilith may, when finding no others, even turn upon her own children.[58] Lilith was a special danger to women during childbirth, menstruation, and before defloration. As a result, both mother and infant had to be protected from Lilith with special incantations and amulets. These beliefs persisted, for in medieval Jewish mystical texts the Adam-Lilith myth expanded. Not only are nocturnal emissions a sign that a man has been visited by Lilith, but Lilith may also seduce men when they are in a waking state. When she succeeds, she is transformed from a beautiful seductress to a cruel fury, and kills her victim.[59]

Female demons were commonly held to threaten and feed upon children.[60] Lilith's characteristics, as seen earlier, allow for her equation with the Greek Lamia. Early modern Christian authors also note the persistence of the Lilith-Lamia myth in European Jewish communities. Johannes Buxtorf the Elder (1564–1629), author of the *Synagoga Judaica*, remarks that when a Jewish woman is pregnant and birth approaches, she takes a piece of chalk and draws a circle around her bed, on all the walls, and above the door, where she inscribes in Hebrew characters: Adam, Eve, away with Lilith! For his Christian readers, Buxtorf explains that Lilith is that one who appears in Isa. 34:14, and is translated sometimes in Latin texts as *strige*, that is, a screech owl—or as *Lamia*. Lamia he describes as an animal or nocturnal specter presenting the face of a woman, although in reality it is a demon (*empusa*) accustomed to kill or steal away male infants before they are circumcised.[61]

Jewish and Greek mythology is brought together, then, through a Greek translation of Isa. 34:14 that results in the identification of Lamia and Lilith. Having viewed the history of both creatures, one may understand how this happened. They shared very similar appearances, dwelled in deserted areas and were perceived to be a threat to the unborn or newborns. Each seems to describe, if in a negative fashion, a paradigm for what a proper woman's role should be. For Jewish tradition, "Lilith . . . is the negative side, as the rabbis saw it, of woman. Lilith is assertive, seductive, and ultimately destructive; Eve is passive, faithful, and supportive."[62] Lamia served the same purpose in Greek tales. Both Lamia and Lilith possess unclean sexual connotations and often suck the blood from their human progeny or lovers. The blending of the two traditions would have important consequences over time, for while the Lamia of Greek antiquity might be dismissed as a pagan phantasm, the status of the biblical Lilith-Lamia had the voice of authority behind it and had to be taken into account by biblical exegetes.

Lamia as Allegory among Christian Biblical Commentators

Lamia is the devil or demons, as in Jeremiah . . . Likewise, Lamia stands for a heretic or a hypocrite, as Isaiah says.

Rabanus Maurus, De Universo 8.2
(PL 111:226B)

In the Lamia the duplicity of the Jews and the fabrications of hypocrites are expressed.

Rabanus Maurus, Commentaria in Jeremiam 20.4
(PL 111:1249B–C)

Lamia has a human face but a bestial body. This is the flesh; this is the internal enemy.

Hugh of St. Victor Miscellanea 6.85
(PL 177:852B)

The substitution of Lamia for Lilith in Latin translations of Isa. 34:14 resulted both in curious exegetical strategies among Christian interpreters and in the near complete disappearance of Lilith from Christian tradition. Although Isa. 34 describes the destruction that God will bring to Edom, Jews and Christians understood Edom quite differently. For Jews, "Edom" can signify any number of Israel's adversaries.[63] Thus, Isa. 34 may be interpreted as a vision of the Lord's vengeance to be wrought against all of Israel's enemies. For many Jewish exegetes, at least from the fourth century CE, Edom had come to symbolize Rome itself, and therefore the text of Isa. 34 promised the destruction of the increasingly hostile Christianized Roman empire.[64] This interpretation was certainly known to Jerome, who died 420 CE and who remarks that the Jews (*Hebraei*) contend that Isaiah's prophecy of devastation refers to the destruction of the Roman empire, just as some Christian interpreters view the beast of the Book of Revelations, understood "literally" (*iuxta litteram*), as a prophecy of Rome's destruction (cf. Rev. 13:1ff).[65]

For Christian interpreters, however, Edom does not designate Rome or foretell the destruction of the Christianized empire. Rather, in its polemics with Judaism, the Church identified itself with the younger Jacob/Israel, while the older Esau/Edom symbolized the Jews, who had lost the blessing not only of their father Isaac but of God the Father. Consequently, Jerome's *Commentarii in Isaiam,* in a remarkable tour de force, treats the destruction brought to Edom not only as a figure for the devastation of the historical

Jerusalem—in ruins following the disastrous wars of 66–72 CE and 132–135 CE—but also as a sign of divine wrath poured forth against (and not in defense of) the Jews themselves.[66] The various demons Isaiah said dwelled in Edom, for example, the ass-centaur (*onocentaurus*) and Lilith-Lamia, refer, tropologically, to the Jews themselves or to various demonic phantasms sent to pursue and punish them in the ruins of Jerusalem. John Cassian, a contemporary of Jerome who died after 430 CE, explains that Isaiah did not give the names of animals to these various demons by accident—calling them sirens, *lamiae*, ostriches, hedgehogs, dragons, scorpions, and others—but because the names truly reflect the wild and savage nature of the demons signified by them.[67] Although the Jews, claims Jerome, would treat Isaiah's description of devastation and Edom's possession by wild beasts as having a (perhaps future) historical reference, for Jerome and other Christian interpreters the presence of Lamia and the other demons in Edom and nearby Jerusalem symbolizes the present condition of the Jews, who incurred the judgment of the Lord, were exiled from the Holy City, and now live in desolation like wild beasts.[68]

The only other passage in the Vulgate in which Lamia appears is Lam. 4:3: "But even the *lamiae* have bared the breast and nursed their whelps."[69] Both this passage and Isa. 34:14 became important for the transmission of the Lamia myth to Western literature. However, neither Lamia nor Lilith appears in the Hebrew text or Greek translation of Lam. 4:3. How, then, did Lamia appear in the Vulgate versions of this passage? The Hebrew text of Lam. 4:3 is not without its problems. It reads "*Tanin* draw out the breast as they suckle their young ones." *Tanin* would normally refer to serpents or dragons, and sometimes to a primordial water monster or dragon. This, however, presents a problem to a potential commentator, for these creatures are not mammals and could not therefore nurse their young.

One solution to the problem was provided by Jewish commentators who noted a marked similarity between *tanin* and the pl. form *tanim*.[70] The *tan* (pl. *tanim*) is a wild canine (probably a jackal; cf. Jer. 51:37 and Isa. 34:13). Since Lam. 4 follows a lengthy description of the desolation that has befallen Jerusalem at the hands of the Babylonians, it would be unremarkable to see jackals (*tanim*) suckling their whelps where previously princes of Judah and priests of the Temple had walked. Consequently, although the written Hebrew text provides *tanin*, it is emended for public reading to *tanim*. This equation is reflected too in Origen's *Hexapla*, in which the Heb. *tanin* of Lam. 4:3 is rendered in Latin as *canes feri*.[71] Jewish exegetes who emended the text were employing a common solution, for this is not an infrequent phenomenon. There are between 1000–1500 instances in the Hebrew Bible in which the written text is vocalized differently in public reading, the best known involving the vocalization of the tetragrammaton, but extensive lists of other instances exist.[72]

This emendation was not adopted by the translators of the LXX who, by using *drakon*, preserve the sense of the original Hebrew text. Nonetheless, later rabbinic commentators seem to have become aware of a linkage between a wild dog and the Greek λαιμός, from which lamia may be derived. In tractate Shabbat of the Babylonian Talmud, R. Abba said in the name of the third-century R. Simeon ben Lakish that in Greek a dog is called *lamos*, while the editor's note suggests λαιμός as a possibility.[73] Perhaps, then, after the codification of the LXX, an equation of the Hebrew for wild dog or jackal and the Greek lamia had become accepted and understood.

For the Christianized society of the later Roman Empire, there is no single lamian characteristic that justifies the identification of the biblical Lamia with its classical antecedents. Jerome is quite aware that Lamia finds her origin in the vain imaginings of pagan poets.[74] Yet he does not dismiss the biblical Lamia as the invention of poets. It remains the composite, hybrid, or monstrous nature of the older Lamia-Lilith that enables him and others to identify Jews and heretics with Lamia. Her voracious, poisonous, predatory, sexually ambivalent, infant-killing, and theriomorphic nature—part woman and part animal—lies beneath his inclination to equate Lamia with the Jews. As descendants of the inhabitants of Jerusalem, Jews are corrupted at their mother's (Lamia's) breast with poisonous milk and, consequently, they speak "poisoned" words against the Lord, Jesus.[75] As such, they are a danger to the "true" children of Israel, that is, the Church, for they exist outside of it and contradict its teachings. In this way, *lamiae* (i.e. Jews) "poison" the young with seductive doctrines and, spiritually, kill them.

This reading is reiterated by later medieval commentators, although with the addition of other elements of the Lamia myth. For example, Rabanus Maurus (d. 856 CE) identifies the Lamia as a creature having a human face but a beast's body. This composite Lamia becomes a type for heretics and Jews, who, says Rabanus Maurus, display a human face and claim that they serve God.[76] In reality their hearts are of a bestial character and they are far removed from the love of God. They "bare their breasts" when they preach their error abroad, and they "nourish their whelps" when they introduce others to their impiety.[77] Similarly for Haymo of Halberstadt, commenting on Isaiah 34 the Lamia is a monster having the face and body of a woman, but the hooves of a horse.[78] For Beatus Liebanensis Lamia has a human face but a tail like a dragon.[79] In her partial theriomorphism she represents Jews and heretics, and when she "bares her breasts" she publicly preaches her error, nourishing her "young" on impiety. Her form accords with that of the great beast in the Book of Revelations that "spoke like a dragon (Rev. 13:11)." In contrast to Lamia's poisoned milk, Christian exegetes commonly cited the nourishing milk of mother Church, whose twin breasts signify the Old and New Testaments. It is the "breasts" of the Church or of the Virgin Mary, and not of Lamia—that is, Jews or heretics—which Solomon describes as "beautiful" (see Song of Songs 4:10).[80]

This identification of the Jews with Lamia is strengthened by the next verse in Lam. 4:3 (Vulg.): "The daughter of my people is cruel like an ostrich (*struthio*) in the desert." Like Lamia, the ostrich is understood to refer to Jews and to hypocrites. This identification of the *struthio* with the Jews is accomplished by a reading of Job 39:16, where the ostrich is an animal that, failing to incubate her own eggs, treats her young (*filii*) carelessly and is hardened toward them (*duratur*) as if they were not her own. Similarly, according to Rabanus Maurus's *Commentaria in Jeremiam*, the Jews were hardened (*indurata*) toward the apostles, who were sons of this same people.[81] The proximity of *Lamia* and *struthio* in Lam. 4:3 assured that both would be understood as references to the Jews. At the same time, the ostrich's disregard for her eggs is linked to Lamia in another way. Isaac of Stella (1110/20–ca. 1169 CE) explains that any mother forgetful of and without compassion for her progeny is more cruel, more inhuman and bestial than the Furies, since "even the *lamiae* have bared the breast . . . (Lam. 4:3)."[82] Whereas Lam. 4:3 indicates that Lamia nourished at least her own young, the *struthio* threatens every positive image of the nourishing mother. She is crueler and more inhuman than the Furies. She is a mother who is not a mother, having carelessly abandoned her young. She is the Jew writ large.

For Paschasius Radbertus (d. ca. 860 CE) too the composite character of the Lamia is an allusion to the cruel nature of the scribes and Pharisees who offer the teat of perverse doctrine to the children of the synagogue. In his *Expositio in lamentationes* he attempts to support this allegorical interpretation with a false etymology derived from Isidore of Seville, linking *Lamia* to *lanio* (to "tear," "rend," or "butcher").[83] The Pharisees do not bare their breasts in order to provide nourishment to the sons of the synagogue; rather, like the ostrich, they abandon their young. They "tear apart" (*lanio*) the people of God with their perverse doctrine. Paschasius adds that just as Lamia is clearly known in ancient myths (*in fabulis*) to be more cruel than all other beasts, so also the Pharisees are the most cruel of beasts, like the ostrich who as soon as she lays her eggs deserts them and cares so little for them that she fails to incubate them.[84] In the same way, the perversity of the Jews is such that the Jews do nothing less than rend and tear the people away from God, keeping them from eternal life. Although he acknowledges that according to some natural scientists (*physici*) the ostrich does at least bury her eggs in the warm sand so that the sun may incubate them, Paschasius Radbertus contends that the doctors of the law do not show even this measure of concern for their "young."

Rupert of Deutz, who died ca. 1129–30 CE, employs this same false etymology to suggest that the Jews have not only abandoned their young like the ostrich but have actually butchered them,[85] as they butchered Jesus on the Cross, saying, "His blood be upon us and upon our children . . . (Matt. 27:25)."[86] Perhaps Rupert here recalls the response of some Jews to the violence of the first crusade: rather than surrender their children to forced baptism, in ritual fashion they killed them—as well as themselves— as they would slaughter an animal according to the dietary laws or *kashrut*.[87] Although Lamia is a monstrous creature, Rupert adds, it displays neverthe-less a natural affection for its young when it bares its breast. But the "daughter of my people" (Lam. 4:3), the Jews, is crueler than even the monstrous Lamia.

A further confusion led Christian exegetes to identify Lamia with the Furies. Jerome had insisted that Lamia is the Hebrew Lilith (cf. Isa. 34:14), because for the Jews Lilith-Lamia is one of the Furies, known antiphrasti-cally as the *Parcae* because they spare (*parcant*) no one.[88] In the same way, the Jews and hypocrites spare no one with their sacrilegious blasphemy— not the prophets and especially not the Church, the daughter of the people of Israel. This equation of Lamia with the Furies is transmitted from Jerome to Paschasius Radbertus, Isaac of Stella, and others.[89]

The lasciviousness associated with Lilith-Lamia also reappears in this medieval amalgam. According to Hincmar of Rheims (d. 882 CE), unsus-pecting men may copulate with *lamiae* (i.e., female spirits), just as women may be ravished by spirits that assume the appearance of those men whose love they desire.[90] Equally disconcerting, then, is that the power of *lamiae* to adopt various human guises blurs the boundaries not only between the human and the animal but also between the demonic and the human. According to Peter Damian (278) (d. 1072 CE) sexual promiscuity or sex-ual perversion prepares one as a dwelling place for unclean spirits, nymphs, *lamiae*, and sirens.[91] It should not be surprising that for medieval Christianity unrestrained sexual desire—a symbol of the Fall—becomes the gateway between the human world and the demonic realm through which Lamia enters.

Lamia among the Natural Philosophers

The Lamia . . . is a large and very cruel animal . . . called lidit *in Hebrew, and the Jews think that it was one of the Furies, which are called the* Parcae, *because they spare (*parcant*) nothing.*

Thomas of Cantimpré, De natura rerum 4.56

> *Lamiae . . . are said to be types of monkeys, and they are said to have the head of a maiden, the body of a pig, the feet of a horse, and, as the historians relate, they are very cruel.*
>
> Albert the Great, Super Threnos 4.3

Gervais of Tilbury (ca. 1150–1220), who composed his *Otia imperialia* between 1210–14 for the instruction and entertainment of the excommunicate emperor Otto IV, records a number of popular folktales and legends of the Lamia. Precisely because it does not invoke the biblical evidence, this text seems a good place to begin a discussion of the "secular" medieval Lamia. Gervais remarks again that some say that *lamiae* are women who enter houses at night, snatch infants from their cribs, and attack sleeping persons.[92] Others treat *lamiae* as dragons that assume human form to snatch lactating women from the riverbanks in order to nurse their own offspring, or to feed on men. However, Gervais also acknowledges another account, which he attributes to natural philosophers (*physici*), for whom *lamiae* are nocturnal phantasms that have the power to torment sleeping persons, owing to the coarseness of their humoral complexion, and seem able to drink human blood and to move infants from one place to another.[93] Gervais's nod to the *physici* is another indication, however, that as the influx of ancient knowledge grew ever greater, it became increasingly important to give an account of *lamiae* that restored them, in some measure, to the natural world.

Michael Scot, the early thirteenth-century translator of Aristotle's *Historia animalium*, mentions Lamia only in passing, and associates her with other monstrous creatures like the minotaur or hippocentaur.[94] But Lamia's problematic and elastic properties are perhaps best illustrated in the work of the premier natural philosopher of Christendom, Albert the Great (d. 1280 CE) and his disciple, Thomas of Cantimpré. Albert discusses the Lamia in two places in his monumental *De animalibus*. In the first, in the context of a discussion of marine animals based on his reading of Aristotle, he refers to the Lamia:

> Further, the one that is called *malakye* in Greek, as well as the *agrali*, fishing frog and the *lamyae*, are also in the sea, and they all copulate by mounting as we have related. This has also been seen by a number of different people and it is through their tales that this is believed to be so. The *lamiae* have women's faces, or so many have said.[95]

This sea creature, however, later will be identified with a nocturnal land animal when the Lamia receives its own entry in Albert's catalogue of beasts:

> LAMIA. The Lamia is a large, very cruel animal which comes out of the woods at night, enters gardens and breaks trees, scattering them about. For it

has strong arms suited for every sort of act. When men come upon it, according to Aristotle, it fights with them and wounds them with its bite. One who has been wounded, however, is not healed from its bite until it hears the voice of the same animal roaring. This animal delights in living in deserted, ruined places. It has something of a woman's shape to its face and is quite devoted to its young when it nurses them. Some say, however, that there are some *lamiae* in Chaldea of the same size which are domesticated and which are rich in milk.[96]

The Lamia, then, provides an interesting challenge for Albert the natural scientist. It is clear that several of the "old" lamian traits are here, for these versions of Lamia variously bite, fiercely attack the human world from abodes in the wilderness, and have a mixed female and animal shape. Yet they also give milk and are devoted to their young. He even has echoes of Aristotle's shark. All these traits have been met earlier, but in this context Albert will not resort to allegory. He is trying rather to act as a proper natural scientist and his first instinct is to treat the various types of Lamia presented to him much as Aristotle would have done—by fitting them into understandable *taxa* which give sense to the natural world.

Yet Albert was both a natural scientist and biblical exegete. As the latter he could readily resort to an allegorical interpretation of Lamia when appropriate and equate Lamia and the devil.[97] Likewise, Albert suggests in his commentary on Lam. 4:3 that *lamiae* are a kind of monkey with the head of a maiden, a pig-like body, and a horse's hooves. He adds that historians (*historiographi*) report that it is the cruelest of all beasts and especially enjoys ripping fetuses from the wombs of pregnant women to eat them. "This signifies the prelates of both synagogue and Church, who mutilate the concepts of the Church in its womb and devour them while they nurse their patrons on to sin."[98] Note also Albert's pun, since the *conceptos* ripped from the womb can equally be rendered as "fetuses" or "concepts." Elsewhere he cites a medieval Greek commentator on Aristotle, the elusive Michael of Ephesus, for the claim that *lamiae* live in Lydia [*sic*] and cut open the bellies of pregnant women to eat the fetuses.[99] Here too Albert, in his guise as an exegete, adds "So too are some people who devour those who are still tender in their faith, not granting any concession to their infirmities, but rather spending the viscera of the poor on their own pleasures."[100]

Albert's identification of quite disparate candidates for the name Lamia parallels what one finds in the work of a contemporary and disciple from whom he borrowed a great deal, namely Thomas of Cantimpré (*De natura rerum* 4.56):

The Lamia, as the *Liber rerum* says, is a large, very cruel animal. It comes out of the woods at night, enters gardens and breaks trees, scattering the branches about. For it has strong arms suited for every sort of act. When men approach it in order to stop it, it fights with them and wounds them with its bite. Its bite is marvelous beyond all measure, however, just as Aristotle reports. One who has been wounded by the Lamia's teeth is not healed from its bite until it hears the voice of the same animal roaring. . . . We do not know if these are the *lamie* about which Jeremiah says in *Lamentations* (4.3) "The *lamie* have bared their breasts and have nursed their young" . . . Yet this can well be believed according to the gloss on this passage in Lamentations, because the gloss says that this beast is very ferocious yet offers its breasts to the young seeking them and nurses its progeny. This animal is called the *lidit* in Hebrew and the Jews think it was one of the Furies, which were called the *Parcae*, since they spare (*parcant*) no one. I have heard from someone that *lamie* are beasts in the Orient in the vicinity of those areas which contain the Tower of Babel in the field of Sennaar. And these beasts are larger than goats and are replete with milk. They are domesticated by humans, are led to pasture and are useful because of their abundant milk . . .[101]

This passage is very similar to one in the work of Vincent of Beauvais.[102] It is well to remember that Vincent had been a student in Paris, and entered the newly recognized Dominican order ca. 1220. All three—Thomas, Vincent, and Albert—provide information on the Lamia which recalls her ancient, classical origins as well as her biblical roots. Yet each also strives to enter into the new Aristotelianism by accounting for the Lamia within "scientific" *taxa*, be it that of monkeys, sharks, or goats. The results are not universally successful by modern standards, but we are quite far from using the Lamia merely to frighten children, chastise clerics, or stigmatize Jews. These other uses of course persist. For example, Angelo Poliziano (d. 1494) reports that his grandmother used to frighten him as a boy with stories of *lamiae* who dwell in solitary places and devour crying children.[103] The effort to "naturalize" Lamia, to restore her to the natural world, appears all the more impressive for the persistence of these other fabulous accounts.

Conclusion

The Lamia has not fallen from the contemporary imagination. Her name lives in Greece today where, at least until recently the sudden death of a child was referred to with the proverbial "Lamia has strangled the child."[104] Perhaps ironically, things have come back to the point from which they began, for the Lamia is fairly devoid of metaphorical or allegorical allusions in Greek folklore. She is once more a symbol of deformity and slovenliness, so much so that "the sweepings of Lamia," is proverbial for untidiness. Her tendency to devour young men reemerged in Greek folktales, although she can be fooled into sparing them if they treat her with respect.[105] That Lamia still lived in caves is demonstrated by the fact that a Lamia supposedly lived in a cave near to the village of Kephalovryso in Aetolia. The Lamia-shark has even endured, for later Greeks have a Lamia of the sea, a sort of dangerous mermaid. Still, when all is said, despite the fact that a land Lamia was supposedly shot in Attica and measured three fathoms in length, Lawson concludes that the *lamiae* "occupy a place in popular belief such as she held of old . . . bogeys which frighten none but children."[106]

In her article on the Lamia, Johnston writes most insightfully that, "Demons are clay with which people mold images of their fears and anxieties." She claims correctly that "a society marginalizes that which is undesirable by labeling it demonic and then further marginalizes the demonic by attaching to it other marginal traits such as bimorphism."[107] Although Johnston is largely interested in the lessons Lamia had to teach the Greek world about the role of the female, the present survey has in many ways corroborated her account. Certainly, the allegorical equation of Lamia with Jews and heretics was meant to transfer to them her monstrous, theriomorphic nature and to suggest in them the absence of normal human—and especially maternal—instincts. This equation may also recall medieval narratives, circulating from the twelfth century, that accused Jews of ritual cannibalism and convicted them both of drinking the blood of Christian infants and of sexual predation.

Lamia's enduring and lively presence is attested from Stesichorus to modern times. Her basic attributes of dangerous, sexual predation and her role as a threat to children have amazingly remained recognizable over the centuries despite the accretions of qualities drawn from diverse sources and from the desires of those who have used her to frighten children, teach moral lessons, sermonize about Church abuses, engage in religious polemic, or help reestablish the natural sciences in the consciousness of the West. Demons are indeed our clay. But it is the basic human desire to mold that clay and to make it conform to our needs, desires, and interests, that so intrigues us.

Notes

We wish to express our gratitude to the Center for Hellenic Studies, the American Academy at Rome, and the Oxford Centre for Hebrew and Jewish Studies, whose directors, resources, and staff contributed greatly to the completion of this article.

1. *Homily* 1.4.1. The *Homilies* can be found in *Patrologia Graeca* 48: 843–942.
2. *Homily* 4.6.3.

3. *Homily* 1.2.1, and quoting Phil. 3: 2.
4. *Homily* 1.3.1. The association of Jews and the hyena becomes common in the medieval bestiary since, as the hyena was alleged to dig up buried corpses, so too Jews were said to give themselves over to dead idols. See T. H. White, ed., *The Book of Beasts* (New York: Dover Publications, 1984), 31. For the *Physiologus*, the hyena was also a beast that alternated its sex: "At one time it becomes male, at another a female, and it is unclean because it has two natures. . . . Thus double-minded men are compared to the brute. . . . The sons of Israel are like this animal." See *Physiologus*, trans. Michael J. Curley (Austin and London: University of Texas Press, 1979), 53. For the frequency with which Jews were compared to hyenas, see especially Debra Hassig, *Medieval Bestiaries: Text, Image, Ideology* (Cambridge: Cambridge University Press, 1995), ch. 13; 145–55.
5. *Homily* 1.2.4; 1.2.6.
6. White, *Book of Beasts*, 89.
7. *Physiologus*, 53. Cf. Albert the Great, *Quaestiones super de animalibus* 16.19, ed. Ephrem Filthaut, in *Opera omnia* 12 (Münster: Aschendorff, 1955).
8. Cf. Albertus Magnus, *De animalibus* 18.1.6.46–54, ed. Hermann Stadler, Beiträge zur Geschichte der Philosophie des Mittelalters, 16 (Münster: Aschendorff, 1920). For English translation, see *Albertus Magnus* On Animals: *A Medieval Summa Zoologica*, 2 vols., trans. Kenneth F. Kitchell Jr. and Irven Michael Resnick (Baltimore and London: Johns Hopkins University Press, 1999), 2: 1303–07.
9. On the relationship between the laws of *kashrut* and the notion of impurity in Judaism, see the helpful study of Hyam Maccoby, *Ritual and Morality: The Ritual Purity System and its Place in Judaism* (Cambridge: Cambridge University Press, 1999), ch. 6.
10. Rabanus Maurus, *De universo* (PL 111: 206D).
11. Bruno of Segni, *Expositio in Leviticum*, 11: "Ruminare quid est, nisi sanctam Scripturam diligenter investigare et cordis sensu minutissime frangere, et ad spiritualem intelligentiam diutissime volvendo perducere? Judaei ergo neque ungulam dividunt, neque ruminant, quoniam neque utrumque Testamentum recipiunt, neque quod suscipiant ruminando spiritualiter intelligunt; litteram enim solam et integram deglutientes, nihil aliud quam litteram sapiunt." PL 164: 414C. See also his *Expositio in Genesim*, 24, PL 164: 201D-202A.
12. Hermann of Cologne, *A Short Account of his Own Conversion*, in *Conversion and Text: the Cases of Augustine of Hippo, Herman-Judah, and Constantine Tsatsos*, trans. Karl F. Morrison (Charlottesville, VA: University of Virginia Press, 1992), 79.
13. For the *Judensau* and its appearances in medieval iconography, see Isaiah Shachar, *The Judensau: A Medieval Anti-Jewish Motif and its History* (London: The Warburg Institute, 1974). For a fascinating ethno-anthropological study, see Claudine Fabre-Vassas, *La Bête singulière: les Juifs, les chrétiens, le cochon* (Paris: Editions Gallimard, 1994), available in translation as *The Singular Beast: Jews, Christians, and the Pig*, trans. Carol Volk (New York: Columbia University Press, 1997).
14. See Sara Lipton, *Images of Intolerance. The Representation of Jews and Judaism in the* Bible moralisée (Berkeley: University of California Press, 1999), ch. 4.

15. Again, the *Book of Beasts* (134) reports that "Owls are symbolical to the Jews, who repulse our Saviour when he comes to redeem them . . . [because] They value darkness more than light." Cf. *Physiologus*, 11. See also Mariko Miyazaki, "Misercord Owls and Medieval Anti-Semitism," in Debra Hassig, ed., *The Mark of the Beast: The Medieval Bestiary in Art, Life, and Literature* (New York and London: Garland Publishing, Inc., 1999): 23–50.

16. Shachar, *The Judensau*, 1.

17. *Homily* 4.6.3.

18. For a study and translation of this text, see Odo of Tournai, *On Original Sin* and *A Disputation with the Jew, Leo, Concerning the Advent of Christ, the Son of God: Two Theological Treatises*, trans. Irven M. Resnick (Philadelphia: University of Pennsylvania Press, 1994). For the view that Odo helped pave the way for the conclusion that Jews suffer an intrinsic irrationality, like brute beasts, see Jeremy Cohen, *Living Letters of the Law* (Berkeley: University of California Press, 1999), 191; and Anna Sapir-Abulafia, "Christian Imagery of Jews in the Twelfth Century: A look at Odo of Cambrai and Guibert of Nogent," *Theoretisches Geschiedenis* 16(1989): 383–91.

19. See Peter the Venerable, *Adversus Judeorum inveteratam duritiem*, ed. Yvonne Friedman, CC CM 58 (Turnhout: Brepols, 1985), 57–58. For a consideration of this text, see Anna Sapir Abulafia's "Twelfth-Century Renaissance Theology and the Jews," in Jeremy Cohen, ed., *From Witness to Witchcraft: Jews and Judaism in Medieval Christian Thought*, Wolfenbütteler Mittelalter-Studien, 11 (Wiesbaden: Harrassowitz Verlag, 1996), 135–37; and her *Christians and Jews in the Twelfth-Century Renaissance* (London and New York: Routledge, 1995), 115–17.

20. Charles Stewart, *Demons and the Devil: Moral Imagination in Modern Greek Culture* (Princeton, NJ: Princeton University Press, 1991), 180.

21. For a formal definition of a "monster" as a flawed nature resulting from a shortcoming in the matter on which its efficient cause must operate, see Albert the Great's *Quaestiones super de animalibus*, 18.5–6.

22. Timothy Beal, *Religion and its Monsters* (New York, London: Routledge, 2002), 4.

23. For a treatment of medieval depictions of Jews and the monstrous races, see Debra Higgs Strickland, *Saracens, Demons, & Jews* (Princeton: Princeton University Press, 2003), ch. 3.

24. For a discussion of ambivalent or heightened sexuality as a mark of the monstrous, see too Debra Hassig, "Sex in the Bestiaries," in *The Mark of the Beast: The Medieval Bestiary in Art, Life, and Literature* (New York and London: Garland Publishing, Inc., 1999), 71–98.

25. Dio Chrysostom, *Discourse* 5.16. The Greek text may be found in *Dio Chrysostom*, 5 vols., trans. J. W. Cohoon (Cambridge, MA: Harvard University Press, 1931), 1: 242. Translations are our own.

26. David R. West, "Gello and Lamia. Two Hellenic Daemons of Semitic Origin," *Internationales Jahrbuch für die Altertumskunde Syrien-Palästinas* 23 (1992): 366.

27. Such is the opinion of the scholia to Aristophanes' *Vespae* 1035 as printed in F. Dübner, *Scholia Graeca in Aristophanem* (Paris: Firmin-Didot, 1877), 158, but omitted for brevity in W. J. W. Koster, *Scholia in Vespas; Pacem; Aves et Lysistratam: Fasc. 1, Continens scholia vetera et recentiora in Aristophanis Vespas*

(Groningen: Bouma, 1978), 165. For a later version, see Faustinus Arevalus's notes to Isidore of Seville's *Etymologiarum sive Originum libri XX*, at PL 82: 922B, n. 102. There he argues that the Greek *lamia* may be derived from *laimos*, Lat. *ingluvies*, suggesting again a crop, a gaping maw, and a voracious quality. These, and other theories of the Greek etymology of λαμία are discussed by Sarah Iles Johnston, "Defining the Dreadful: Remarks on the Greek Child-Killing Demon," in Marvin Meyer and Paul Mirecki, eds., *Ancient Magic and Ritual Power* (Leiden: E.J. Brill, 1995), 380; Èmil Boisacq, *Dictionnaire étymologique de la langue grec*, 3rd ed. (Paris: Klincksieck, 1938), 553–54, s.v. λαμός); Hjalmar Frisk, *Griechisches etymologisches Wörterbuch* (Heidelberg: Winter, 1961), 80, s.v. λαμυρός); and Pierre Chantraine, *Dictionnaire étymologique de la langue grec. Histoire des mots* (Paris: Klincksieck, 1968), s.v. λαμυρός.

28. The earliest recounting of the story, as opposed to a mere reference, is in the scholia to Aristophanes *Pax* 758, readily found in D. Holwerda, *Scholia in Vespas; Pacem; Aves et Lysistratam. Fasc. II, Continens scholia vetera et recentiora in Aristophanis Pacem* (Groningen: Bouma, 1982), 118–19. Another cohesive version is that of Diodorus Siculus *Library* 20.41.1–6, who wrote under Caesar and Augustus. But he may be following the lost works of the historian Duris who lived ca. 340–260 BCE. Cf. Felix Jacoby, *Die Fragmente der griechischen Historiker*, 3 vols. (Berlin: Weidmann, 1923–58), 76 F 17. Diodorus also cites a lost play of Euripides. Less accessible sources for these stories are found in scholia to Aristophanes and in lesser known authors from antiquity. For full citations, see H. W. Stoll, "Lamia" in *Ausführliches Lexikon der griechischen und römischen Mythologie*, vol. 2.2, ed. W. H. Roscher (Hildesheim: Olms, 1965; reprint 1894–97) 1818–21; Emily Vermeule, "Herakles Brings a Tribute," in Urusla Höckmann and Natje Krug, eds., *Festschrift für Frank Brommer* (Mainz: Philipp von Zabern, 1977), 295–301; and Johnston, "Defining the Dreadful," 367–68.

29. Horace, *Ars poetica*, 340. See the notes of C. D. Brink, *Horace on Poetry: The Ars Poetica* (Cambridge: Cambridge University Press, 1971), 356–57. As Horace is citing this as the sort of thing that should not be shown on the stage, it may be that he has deliberately phrased his statement to reflect, not an actual belief, but an extreme to which an unscrupulous playwright might go. Pausanias 10.12.1, writing in Greek, but in Roman times, records the odd variant that the original Sibyl was the daughter of Zeus and Lamia. See *Pausanias, Description of Greece*, 5 vols., trans. W. H. S. Jones (Cambridge, MA: Harvard University Press, 1935), 4: 431. Frazer makes a strong case for her nationality being Libyan. See *Pausanias's Description of Greece*, 2nd ed., 6 vols., trans. James Frazer (London: Macmillan and Co., 1993), 5: 288. Clement of Alexandria seems to preserve the same tale. See *Clement of Alexandria* Stromateis *Books One to Three*, 1.70.1, trans. John Ferguson (Washington, DC: Catholic University of America Press, 1991), 75.

30. She was still so used as late as Lucian, *Philopseudes* 2; Diodorus Siculus 20.41; and Strabo, *Geography* 1.2.8. Porphyry, commenting on Horace, *Ars Poetica* 340, states "haec ad infantes terrendos solet nominari." Cf. Johnston, "Defining the Dreadful," 365–69.

31. Monique Halm-Tisserant, "Folklore et Superstition en Grèce Classique: Lamia Torturée?" *Kernos* 2 (1989): 76 and pl. I.a-b.

32. These vases are discussed and dates and bibliography are offered by John Boardman, "Lamia," in *Lexicon Iconographicum Mythologiae Classicae* (Zurich: Artemis Verlag, 1992) 6.1: 188–89, with plates 6.2: 90–91, and Monique Halm-Tisserant, "Folklore et Superstition," 67–82. Vermeule, "Herakles Brings a Tribute," offers one or two other possible illustrations of Lamia. Cf. Johnston, "Defining the Dreadful," 372–73.

33. Monique Halm-Tisserant, "Folklore et Superstition," 77–79.

34. See the *Lamia* of Angelus Politianus, in *Opera omnia*, 3 vols., ed. Ida Maçer (Torino: Bottega d'Erasmo, 1971), 1: 451.

35. Alex Scobie, "Some Folktales in Graeco-Roman and Far Eastern Sources," *Philologus* 121(1977): 7–10. The tale forms the entire body of Dio Chrysostom's fifth discourse. Since Dio's creature is ultimately exterminated by Herakles and is compared closely to a sphinx, it should be added to the testimonia so masterfully treated by Vermeule, "Herakles Brings a Tribute," note 6.

36. Vermeule, "Herakles Brings a Tribute," 297, claims that Euripides may have been responsible for the location of the Lamia tale in Libya.

37. Dio Chrysostom, *Discourse* 5.12, 240.

38. Johnston, "Defining the Dreadful," 366–67.

39. *Life of Apollonius* 4.25.

40. For Apuleius' status as a philosopher, see James Tatum, *Apuleius and the Golden Ass* (Ithaca: Cornell University Press, 1979), 122–34.

41. Apuleius, *Metamorphoses* 1:1–17. Cf. David Leinweber, "Witchcraft and Lamiae in 'The Golden Ass,' " *Folklore* 105 (1994): 77–82.

42. Apuleius, *Metamorphoses* 1: 8.

43. Ibid., 1:17.

44. Rackham translates the phrase as "the creature in human form," and considers that this may well be Lamia. See *Nicomachean Ethics*, trans. H. Rackham (Cambridge, MA: Harvard University Press, 1968), 400. René Gauthier and Jean Yves Jolif quote an anonymous commentator who definitely equated this reference with Lamia. See *L'Éthique à Nicomaque* (Louvain: Publications universitaires de Louvain, 1959), 2: 627. John Burnet cites Fritzsche as in favor of the equation but calls it "very doubtful." See John Burnet, ed., *The Ethics of Aristotle* (London: Methuen, 1990), 311. The fact remains that the Greek seems to indicate a single individual who routinely (present tense) performs this crime. A single action of an anonymous female does not seem to make sense.

45. Aristotle, *Historia Animalium* 540b17; cf. Pliny, *Historia Naturalis* 9.40.78. The *lamna* of Oppian *Halieutica* 1.370f. is surely the same creature and its ferociousness and tendency to bite are clear; see D'Arcy Thompson, *A Glossary of Greek Fishes* (London: Oxford University Press, 1947), 144.

46. Nevio Zorzetti and Jacques Berlioz, *Le premier mythographe du Vatican* (Paris: Les belles lettres, 1995), xi–xii.

47. "Crotopus rex fuit Argivorum cuius filiam Apollo vitiavit, quod pater indignans filiam interemit quia Vestae sacerdos fuit et in virginitate semper perdurare debuit. In cuius ultione Apollo horribile monstrum misit quod Cor ebus iuuenis quidam fortissimus occidit. Et hanc historiam Statius decentissime scribit. Ipsum enim monstrum Lamia vocabatur, Lamiae sunt enim fossae

camporum proluviis plene uel uoragines fluminum, unde ipsa ferocissima bestia Lamia dicebatur." Zorzetti and Berlioz, *Le premier mythographe du Vatican*, 93.

48. Statius, *Thebaid* 1.554ff, in *Statius. Silvae-Thebaid I–IV*, 2 vols., trans. J. H. Mozley (London: William Heinemann Ltd., 1928), 1: 382–85.

49. Statius, *Thebaid* 1.597–99, 384.

50. The origin and meaning of the name "Lilith" at Isa. 34:14 is much debated. See for example, Vincent Tanghe, "Lilit in Edom (Jes, 5–15)," *Ephemerides theologicae Lovanienses* 69.1(1993): 125–33; G. R. Driver, "Lilith," *Palestine Exploration Quarterly* 91 (1959): 55–57.

51. Patristic sources are in disagreement over the identity of Symmachus, who likely worked about the end of the second or beginning of the third century. According to Epiphanius, Symmachus was a Samaritan who later became a convert to Judaism. Eusebius regarded Symmachus as a member of the Ebionite community, and therefore as a sort of half-Christian, as does Jerome. For a discussion of the divergent views on the identity of Symmachus, see August Bludau, *Die Schriftsfälschungen der Häretiker. Ein Beitrag zur Testkritik der Bibel*, in *Neutestamentliche Abhandlungen*, 11.5, ed. M. Meinertz (Münster: Ashcendorff, 1925), 14–16.

52. See Roger Gryson, ed., "Esaias," *Vetus latina, die Reste der altlateinischen Bibel* 12.1 (Freiburg: Herder, 1987–93), 709.

53. See James Hastings, *A Dictionary of the Bible*, 5 vols. (Peabody, MA: Hendrickson Publishers, 1988), 3: 122. For the owl as a frequent companion of witches in antiquity, and for witches turning themselves into owls, see Alex Scobie, "Strigiform Witches in Roman and Other Cultures," *Fabula* 19 (1978): 74–101. On the *strix* itself and its changes through time, see Samuel Grant Oliphant, "The Story of the Strix: Ancient," *TAPA* 44 (1913): 133–49, and "The Story of the Strix: Isidorus and the Glossographers," *TAPA* 45 (1914): 49–63.

54. See Walter Krebs, "Lilith—Adams erste Frau," *Zeitschrift für Religions-und Geistesgeschichte* 27.2 (1975): 141–52.

55. This myth may also be found fully elaborated in the *Alphabet of Ben Sira*, a Hebrew biblical commentary written between the seventh and tenth century CE, and also translated into Latin. For a discussion of rabbinic and talmudic sources for the Lilith legend, see also A. M. Killen, "La légende de Lilith," *Revue de littérature comparée* 12 (1932): 277–311.

56. According to Robert Graves and Raphael Patai, *Hebrew Myths: The Book of Genesis* (New York: Doubleday, 1989), 68, in the *Targum Yerushalmi*, the priestly benediction of Num. 6:26 becomes "The Lord bless thee in all thy doings, and preserve thee from the Lilim."

57. Gershom G. Scholem, *Jewish Gnosticism, Merkabah Mysticism, and Talmudic Tradition* (New York: Jewish Theological Seminary, 1965), 73.

58. *Midrash Rabbah: Numbers*, 16.25, 2 vols., trans. Judah J. Slotki (London: Soncino Press, 1983), 2: 694.

59. Raphael Patai, *The Hebrew Goddess*, 3rd edition (Detroit: Wayne State University Press, 1990), 233.

60. See *The Chronicle of Ahimaaz*, 12a, trans. Marcus Salzman, Columbia University Oriental Studies, 18 (New York: AMS Press, Inc., 1966), 81.

61. Johannes Buxtorf, *Synagoga Judaica* (Basel: E. König, 1680; reprint Hildesheim; New York: G. Olms, 1989), 81 and 85.

62. Howard Schwartz, "Jewish Tales of the Supernatural," *Judaism* 36 (1987): 343. Precisely because Lilith represents a socially constructed negative image of the female, she has become in modern times a symbol of feminist liberation in interpretation and literature. See Michèle Bitton, "Lilith ou la première Ève: un mythe Juif Tardif," *Archives de sciences sociale des religions* 71 (1990): 113–36.

63. Cf. 2. Kgs. 8:13–14 and 14:7, where David defeats the Edomites in the "Valley of Salt."

64. On the identification of Rome and Edom, see Jacob Neusner, *Judaism in the Matrix of Christianity* (Philadelphia: Fortress Press, 1986), 73–87. Thus, Isa. 34:14 was understood to mean that when the Lord will lay waste to Rome, Lilith will dwell there in repose. See for example *Zohar* 3, 19a, in *The Wisdom of the Zohar*, 3 vols., trans. David Goldstein, (Oxford: Oxford University Press, 1989), 2: 540.

65. "Hebraei, ut supra diximus, haec de romano imperio prophetata contendunt, et in ultionem sion, uastitatem quondam regni potentissimi praedicari, quod iuxta litteram plerique nostrorum etiam in apocalypsi ioannis scriptum putant." Jerome, *Commentarii in Isaiam* 10.34.8, CC SL 73, ed. M. Adriaen (Turnholt: Brepols, 1963), 421.

66. Ibid.

67. John Cassian, *Collationes*, 7.3.2, ed. M. Petschenig, CSEL 13 (Vienna: 1886), 212.

68. "Haec iuxta hebraicum et explanationem historicam dicta sint. Ceterum qui tropologicam sequuntur, expulso populo iudaeorum sub bestiarum et portentorum nominibus, idololatras et variis superstitionibus seruientes in hierusalem habitaturos esse confirmant; et hos esse onocrotalos et hericios, ibin et coruum, dracones et struthiones et onocentauros, et daemonia et pilosos et lamiam (quae hebraice dicitur lilith; et a solo symmacho translata est Lamia, quam quidam hebraeorum ἐριυυν id est furiam, suspicantur)." Jerome, *Commentarii in Isaiam* 10.34.8, 422.

69. "Sed et lamiae nudaverunt mammam, lactaverunt catulos suos . . ." Lam. 4:3 (Vulg.)

70. For a discussion of Lam. 4:3 see Marc Epstein, " 'If Lions Could Carve Stones . . .': Medieval Jewry and the Allegorization of the Animal Kingdom. A Textual and Iconographic Study" (PhD dissertation, Yale University, 1992; Ann Arbor, MI: University of Michigan, 1993), 250–51 and 298–99. *Tanin* taken as a primordial water dragon helps to explain the New English Bible translation of this passage: "Even whales uncover the teat." One should compare this to Gen. 1:21 where *taninim* is usually translated "sea-monster"; Deut. 32:33, where it is a poisonous serpent; and Jer. 51:34 where *tanin* is a dragon (Vulg. *draco*).

71. See *Origenis Hexaplorum, quae supersunt: sive veterum interpretum graecorum in totum Vetus Testamentum fragmenta*, 2 vols., ed. Frederick Field (Oxford: Clarendon Press, 1875) 2: 758.

72. See Harry M. Orlinsky, "The Origin of the Kethib-Qere System: A New Approach," *Supplements to Vetus Testamentum* 7 (1959): 184–92; W. Emery Barnes,

"Ancient Corrections in the Text of the Old Testament (*Tikkun Sopherim*)," *Journal of Theological Studies* 1(1900): 387–414; Dominique Barthélemy, "Les Tiqqunê Sopherim et la critique textuelle de l'Ancient Testament," *Supplements to Vetus Testamentum* 9 (1963): 285–304; Saul Lieberman, *Hellenism in Jewish Palestine* (New York: Jewish Theological Seminary, 1962), 25ff; and William McKane, "Observations on the Tikkûnê Sôperîm," in Matthew Black and William Smalley, eds., *On Language, Culture, and Religion: In Honor of Eugene A. Nida* (The Hague; Paris: Mouton, 1974), 53–77.

73. B. T. Shabbat 63a-b. For the editor's footnote, see *Hebrew-English Edition of the Babylonian Talmud: Shabbat*, trans. R. Dr. H. Freedman (London/Jerusalem: the Soncino Press, 1987). Our thanks to Professor Joshua Schwartz of Bar-Ilan University for drawing our attention to this passage.

74. "Onocentauri, et pilosi, et Lamia, quae gentilium fabulae et poetarum figmenta discribunt." Jerome, *Commentarii in Isaiam* 10.35.1, 424.

75. See Paulinus of Aquileia [d. 802], *Contra Felicem Urgellitanum* 3.10 (PL 99: 442Df).

76. Rabanus Maurus, *Commentaria in Jeremiam* 20.4 (PL 111:1249C)

77. Cf. Gregory the Great, *Moralia* 19.18. 9–10, 27 (PL 76: 116A), *Moralia* 23.29.36, 53 (PL 76: 707f), and *Moralia* 33.29; Herveus of Bourgdieu, *Commentaria in Isaiam* 5.34.15 (PL 181: 329A).

78. Haymo of Halberstadt, *Commentaria in Isaiam*, 34 (PL 116: 893C).

79. Beatus Liebanensis and Eterius Exomensis, *Adversus Elipandum libri duo*, 2.15, ed. B. Löfstedt, CC CM 59 (Turnholt: Brepols, 1984), 114.

80. See Gilbert of Hoyland, *Sermones in Canticum Salomonis* 30.9 (PL 184:160); and, John of Ford, *Super extremam partem Cantici canticorum sermones cxx*, 111.9, eds. E. Mikkers and H. Costello, CC CM 18 (Turnholt: Brepols, 1970), 755. Contrast this image of *Lamia* with the portrait of the Virgin presented in the popular *alma mater redemptoris*.

81. Rabanus Maurus, *Commentaria in Jeremiam* 20.4 (PL 111: 1249C).

82. Isaac of Stella, *Sermones*, 40.5, ed. A. Hoste and G. Raciti, *Sources Chrétiennes* 339 (Paris:Les éditions du cerf, 1987), 14.

83. Paschasius Radbertus, *Expositio in lamentationes Hieremiae, libri quinqui*, 4.3, ed. B. Paulus, CC CM 85 (Turnholt: Brepols, 1988), 252. Cf. Isidore of Seville, *Etymologiarum sive Originum libri XX*, 8.11.101, 2 vols., ed. W. M. Lindsay (Oxford: Clarendon Press, 1911).

84. *Expositio in lamentationes*, 4.3, 253.

85. Rupert of Deutz, *De Trinitate et operibus eius, in Jeremiam Prophetam*, 1.83 (PL 167: 1414A–B).

86. Cf. his *Commentaria in Job* 29.13 (PL 168: 1090B). For a similar gloss on Lam. 4:3, see Vincent of Beauvais, *Speculum naturale* 19.65 (Douai: 1624; reprint Graz: Akademische Druck und Verlaganstalt, 1964–65), 1418.

87. For translations of Hebrew chronicles of the First Crusade, which describe the practice of *kiddush ha-Shem* or self-martyrdom, see the Appendix to Robert Chazan, *European Jewry and the First Crusade* (Berkeley: University of California Press, 1996). For interpretation see also Jeremy Cohen, *Sanctifying*

the Name of God: Jewish Martyrs and Jewish Memories of the First Crusade (Philadelphia: University of Pennsylvania Press, 2004).

88. For the claim that the *Parcae* are so called by antiphrasis, see Jerome, *Epist.* 50.2 (PL 22: 474); *Commentarius in librum nominum Hebraeorum* (PL 23: 1515C–D); Augustine, *Contra Mendacium* 1.10.24 (PL 40: 534); Eugippius, *Thesaurus*, 191 (PL 62: 846D); Isidore of Seville, *Etymologiae* 1.37.24, Rabanus Maurus, *Enarrationes in librum Numerorum* 4.8 (PL 108: 821A); John Scotus Eriugena, *De praedestinatione*, 15.7 (PL 122: 415C); and Rupert of Deutz, *De Trinitate et operibus eius, in Numeros Commentariorum*, 2.31 (PL 167: 915A).

89. Jerome, *Commentarii in Isaiam* 10.35.1, 422; Paschasius Radbertus, *In Lamentationes Jeremiae*, 4 (PL 120: 1205B); Isaac of Stella, *Sermones*, 40.5.

90. Hincmar of Rheims, *De divortio Lotharii Regis et Theutbergae Reginae*, ed. Letha Böhringer, *MGH: Concilia*, 4.1 (Hanover: Hahn, 1992), 206: "Quidam autem a lamiis sive genichialibus feminis debilitati, quaedam etiam feminae a dusiis in specie virorum, quorum amore ardebant, concubitum pertulisse inventae sunt."

91. "Venite itaque, audite me, scorta, prostibula savia, volutabra porcorum pinguium, cubilia spirituum inmundorum, nimphae, sirenae, lamiae, dianae, et si quid adhuc portenti, si quid prodigii reperitur, nomini vestro competere iudicetur." Peter Damian, *Epistula* 112, in *Die Briefe des Petrus Damiani*, ed. Kurt Reindel, *MGH: Die Briefe der deutschen Kaiserzeit* 4, 3 (Munich: 1983–93), 278. Note too that sirens were depicted in the Middle Ages as part woman, part fish, fowl, or horse. Beryl Rowland states that the siren also seduced men and adds that "A Hellenic relief of a winged and bird-footed woman sitting astride a sleeping traveller shows the fundamental conception of the siren as *incuba*." *Birds with Human Souls* (Knoxville, TN: University of Tennessee Press, 1978), 155. Cf. John Pollard, *Birds in Greek Life and Myth* (London: Thames and Hudson, 1977), 188–91.

92. "lamiae dicuntur esse mulieres, quae noctu domos penetrant, infantes ex cunis extrahunt, et nonnunquam dormientes affligunt." *Otia imperialia* 3.85, 38. Cf. John of Salisbury, *Polycraticus* 2.17 (PL 199: 436), where the *lamiae* are still treated as demonic phantasms said to be capable of devouring the limbs of infants.

93. *Otia imperialia* 3.86, 39–40.

94. Michael Scot, *Liber phisionomiae*, 20. We have used the Venice edition (1477). The *Liber phisionomiae* constitutes the third book of his tripartite *Liber introductorius*, and follows after the *Liber quattuor distinctionum* and *Liber particularis*.

95. Albert the Great, *De animalibus*, 5.1.2.15, vol. 1: 414. The animals' names in this passage are based, if corruptly, on Albert's source for this passage—Aristotle's *Historia Animalium* 540b18f.

96. Albert the Great, *De animalibus*, 22.2.1.112(64), vol. 2: 1409.

97. Albert the Great, *Sermo de tempore*, 62.1, in *Opera omnia*, ed. A. Borgnet (Paris: L. Vives, 1891), 13: 243.

98. Albert the Great, *Super Threnos*, 4.3, in *Opera omnia*, ed. A. Borgnet (Paris: L. Vives, 1893), 18: 317.

99. Michael accurately recalls many of the features of the ancient Greek Lamia when, in his commentary on Aristotle's *Nicomachean Ethics*, he remarks: "Lamia was a certain woman of Pontus who, because she had lost her children, ate the young of other women" and he later accurately identifies Lamia as a certain ruler of Libya who devoured embryos ripped from the womb. See *Eustratii et Michaelis et anonyma In Ethica Nicomachea Commentaria, Commentaria in Aristotelem Graeca*, ed. Gustavus Heylbut (Berlin: Reimer, 1892), 20: 427, 547. Michael's biography is obscure and his dates uncertain. He likely lived before 1100 and was a member of the circle of Anna Kommene in Constantinople, where he was instrumental in Aristotle's revival. He completed commentaries to Aristotle's *Generation of Animals, Nicomachean Ethics, Politics, Rhetoric, Sophistical Refutations*, and *Metaphysics*. See "Michael Ephesus," *The Oxford Dictionary of Byzantium* (New York, Oxford: Oxford University Press, 1991), 2: 1369.

100. Albert the Great, *Super Threnos* 2.21, 288.

101. *Liber de natura rerum*, 4.56, ed. H. Boese (Berlin: De Gruyter, 1973). "Sennaar" is the place name referring to Mesopotamia in Gen. 10:10 and 11:3 (Heb. Shinar; Sennaar in the LXX). According to Gen. 11:1–9 it is indeed on the plain of Shinar/Sennaar that the tower of Babel was constructed. For a discussion of Thomas's passage and its roots in medieval folk traditions, see Claude Lecouteux, "Lamia-holzmuowa-holzfrowe-Lamich," *Euphorion* 3 (1981): 360–65. Despite the odd properties of this beast (it has strong arms, for example) a late fifteenth century illustrated text of Thomas of Cantimpre's *De natura rerum* (fol. 19va) shows the lamia very much like a wild dog. This, and the reference to Lam. 4:3 may be responsible for the translator's error, rendering lamia as jackal. See Thomas of Cantimpré, *De natura rerum (Lib. IV–XII): Tacuinum Sanitatis*, codice C–67 (fols. 2v–116r) de la Biblioteca Universitaria de Granada, commentarios a la edición facsimil, 2 vols., ed. Luis García Ballester (Granada: Universidad de Granada, 1974). Volume 1 contains a long historical introduction, followed by Charles Talbot's English translation (251–326); vol. 2 contains a facsimile edition, with 611 illustrations.

102. Vincent of Beauvais, *Speculum naturale*, 19.65, 1418.

103. "Mihi quidem etiam puerulo avia narrabat, esse aliquas in solitudinibus Lamias, quae plorantes glutirent pueros. Maxima tunc mihi formido Lamia erat, maximum terriculum." Angelus Politianus, *Lamia*, 451.

104. John Lawson, *Modern Greek Folklore and Ancient Greek Religion: A Study in Survivals* (New Hyde Park: University Books, 1964), 162–76.

105. R. M. Dawkins, *More Greek Folktales* (Oxford: Clarendon Press, 1955), 63–64.

106. John Lawson, *Modern Greek Folklore*, 176.

107. Johnston, "Defining the Dreadful," 371, 381; cf. 361–63.

Chapter 5

Cross-Dressing and Female Same-Sex Marriage in Medieval French and Arabic Literatures

Sahar Amer

The presuppositions we make about sexed bodies . . . are suddenly and significantly upset by those examples that fail to comply with the categories that naturalize and stabilize that field of bodies for us within the terms of cultural conventions. Hence, the strange, the incoherent, that which falls "outside," gives us a way of understanding the taken-for-granted world of sexual categorization as a constructed one, indeed, as one that might be constructed differently.

Butler, Gender Trouble, 110

The title of Jacqueline Murray's essay "Twice Marginal and Twice Invisible," in Bullough and Brundage's *Handbook of Medieval Sexuality* is revealing of the status of the medieval lesbian in contemporary scholarship.[1] In this essay, Jacqueline Murray decries the fact that the medieval Western lesbian has been regularly elided in most literary criticism first under the rubric "homosexual" in mainstream woman history, and under the rubric "woman" in studies of medieval homosexuality which have focused almost exclusively on male homosexuality. She observes: "Of all groups within medieval society lesbians are the most marginalized and least visible" (191).

My research indicates that one fundamental reason why lesbians as a category of analysis or as evidence of a certain textual (or social) reality have been occulted is the fact that much of medieval French literary writings continues to be read in isolation from the cultural context of interaction, seduction and anxiety between the Arab-Islamicate world and Western Christian Europe.[2] Steven Kruger has tellingly pointed out that, "medieval thinking about the sexuality of Christians is crucially different from, and yet intimately intertwined with medieval constructions of the sexuality of . . . Muslims."[3] It is this idea of sexual, textual and cultural interconnections that I would like to explore further here. I propose to read several Old French texts through the lens of medieval Arabic literature in order to uncover a discourse on female same-sex desire in French that has remained thus far unnoticed. I will explore in particular the ways in which the Arabic homoerotic tradition was adapted and rewritten by medieval French Christian writers and the extent to which much of medieval French literary writings can be read in terms of hybridization and cross-fertilization. We will see that just as the Middle Ages can no longer be viewed as a monocultural, monolithic historical era, Western sexuality, contrary to the beliefs of many, is not reducible to heterosexuality or heterosexism. The question that I will pose here is therefore not only where is the lesbian, but also even more specifically, can the literary expression of lesbian desire and lesbian love in medieval French literature claim an Arabic literary genealogy?

Before examining specific medieval French and Arabic texts describing lesbian practices, a few words must be said of the challenges posed by cross-cultural research, especially when dealing with representations of sexuality (homosexuality, lesbianism) in the East and the West. One of these challenges has to do with the audience's contemporary presuppositions of the relations between France and the Arab-Islamicate world in the Middle Ages. Until today, these presuppositions continue to be shaped and informed by implicit (and explicit) Orientalist fantasies. In addition, the contemporary Western audience's own understanding of sexuality (homosexuality and lesbianism) still affects the ways medieval cross-cultural sexuality studies are apprehended. Much research has recently been conducted on the vast differences in the ways in which sexuality studies (and thus also homosexuality and lesbianism) are understood by French and U.S. scholars. These differences have important implications for gay and lesbian studies as a field of scholarship: While they have by now become part of U.S. universities and scholarly publications, gay and lesbian studies still remain greatly marginalized in the French academic system, as Dominique Fisher and Lawrence Schehr have recently argued in their *Articulations of Difference*.[4] There is still no tenure track or established chair in this field or in sexuality studies in the French university and there is still no equivalent to "queer studies" in the French academe. The U.S. and French understanding of their sexuality is determined by their own national affiliation, a situation that has been coined as the "national-sexual" by Mireille Rosello.[5]

The "national-sexual" affects not only the ways each culture perceives the other (the way the French perceive the United States and vice versa), but also the ways in which each of them perceives Middle Eastern and Islamicate sexualities. France, much more than the United States, has had a long history of interaction with the Middle East and Islamicate world. This Franco/Christian-Arab/Islamicate history extends beyond the medieval encounters I am interested in; it was sustained (under very different political and ideological configurations) in the history of France's imperialist interests in North Africa throughout the nineteenth century and manifests itself today through the tense relations with its Maghrebian immigrant population since the 1970s. France's long and complex history of interaction with the Muslim and Arab world renders the cross-cultural investigation into France's past and particularly the recovery of its possible Arabic literary lineage an especially sensitive topic for some Western audience.

France (and the West generally) thus has a great deal at stake in cross-cultural research, particularly one that compares its own textual culture with the literary production of the Arab world. One possible outcome of such an investigation is the destabilization of current power and intellectual relations. The crux of the problem lies in the West's (both the United States and France) contemporary discursive self-presentation as secular, sexually liberated, and firmly positioned in the first world. This perspective is of course opposed to the contemporary assumption of Muslim and Arab women as an always already constituted coherent, stable category of sexually oppressed, sociopolitically subordinated objects, victims of an all-powerful patriarchal, legal, and religious system regardless of class, or of marginal and resistant modes of experiences. Such a definition of the West and of Muslim-Arab women locks all analysis into binary structures: Muslim women versus Muslim men and the Arab-Islamicate world versus the West. It also ends up "colonizing" once more Arab-Muslim women and freezes them into a structurally unequal first/third world relation.[6] Ultimately, the plurality of their (literary) experiences, their historical agency, and their resistant literary modes of sexual expression are effaced and replaced by cultural (and homophobia-induced) amnesia both in the West and in the Arab-Islamicate world today. This is to say that cross-cultural gender and sexuality research is not a neutral field of inquiry. Like any discipline, it does not produce objective knowledge, but raises fundamental political and ethical questions.[7]

*   *   *

I have shown elsewhere that in comparison to the explicitness and the great number of details that characterize the descriptions of lesbian sexual practices in the Arabic tradition, very few French medieval literary texts discuss lesbianism or lesbian sexuality *explicitly*.[8] Much more frequently, the medieval French literary tradition addresses the question of homosexuality and lesbianism via cross-dressing, a phenomenon that Michèle Perret has dubbed second-degree homosexuality.[9]

Instances of cross-dressing are abundant in both the French and Arabic traditions. Joan of Arc may be the most famous Western historical female cross-dresser, and the French tradition of miracle plays and the hagiographic literature are replete with female to male cross-dressers.[10] In addition, the hero(ine) of several thirteenth- and fourteenth- century French romances is a woman disguised as a knight (examples include *Le Roman de Silence*, the story of Blanchandine in *Tristan de Nanteuil*, or the story of Grisandole in *L'Estoire de Merlin*).[11] Similarly, the Arabic epic tradition offers countless examples of women warriors and amazons (Princess 'Ain al-Hayat in *Qissat Firuz Shah*, the characters of Queen al-Rabab, al-Gayda', Gamra and Nitra in the *Romance of 'Antar*, Al-Samta'and Aluf in *Dhat al-Himma*, Princess Turban in *Hamza al-Bahlawan*, and the female community in the *Romance of Sayf*).[12] Furthermore, the eighth century poetry by Abu Nuwas (763–814) develops an entire genre (*ghulamiyyat*) where the beloved is a woman dressed as a man. All these texts (French and Arabic) certainly invite an exploration and an interrogation of gender relations and hierarchy through the proliferation of the ambiguous situations they describe. In most of them however, homosexuality may indeed be considered to function "in the second degree" (to use the phrase coined by Michèle Perret,) in the sense that it is always only suggested, never truly actualized or addressed directly.

What is of greater interest to me here is a special category of French and Arabic texts that combine female cross-dressing with same-sex marriage, texts where the cross-dressed woman ends up marrying another woman. This particular combination (cross-dressing and female same-sex marriage) occurs in a small corpus of Old French texts, most notably in the story of *Yde et Olive*, which is one of the mid-thirteenth century continuations of the epic poem *Huon de Bordeaux*,[13] its late fourteenth-century dramatic adaptation known as the *Miracle de la fille d'un roy*,[14] and its fifteenth-century French prose version written for three nobles at the court of Charles VII in 1454 (interestingly, in the midst of Joan of Arc's rehabilitation) and printed in the early sixteenth century as part of *Les prouesses et faictz du trespreux noble et vaillant Huon de Bordeaulx* (166v–178r).[15] Because of space limitations, I will address here the Yde and Olive stories only in their verse epic and dramatic renditions, and will compare them to what I consider to be their main Arabic literary and cultural model, one of the tales from *One Thousand and One Nights* known as the story of Kamar al-Zaman and the Princess Boudour. A close reading of the lesbian interlude in the French and Arabic traditions demonstrates the extent to which the French story is heir to the Arabic framed tale, taking as its source of inspiration the names of the main characters, the general storyline, and the combination of cross-dressing and same-sex marriage. We will also see how, all the while borrowing multiple thematic features from the Arabic version of the story, French narrators have endeavored to transform it, censor parts of it and replace it with other elements that are revealing of the vast differences in attitudes toward female same-sex unions in these two cultural traditions.

It must be emphasized from the outset that the changes that the lesbian story undergoes from the Arabic to the French tradition cannot be explained away as generic differences between the *Thousand and One Nights* and *Yde et Olive* or the requirements of the framed oral (popular) narrative tradition as opposed to the (written) epic. Recent scholarship has indeed pointed to the fact that texts such as the *Huon de Bordeaux* cycle are inter-disciplinary productions, a crossing between the epic and romance genres, that they were equally enjoyed by men and women and circulated freely in popular and courtly contexts. Similarly, the *Thousand and One Nights* enjoyed a much wider circulation than has been admitted traditionally and were the basis of multiple rewritings in divergent genres both in the Arab-Islamicate world and the West since the Middle Ages. This interdisciplinary, intergeneric reconsideration of medieval Arabic and European writings is especially fruitful to the type of cross-cultural work proposed here since it allows a more productive discussion of texts often thought to be generic opposites. The differences uncovered between the Arabic and French tradi-tion on lesbianism that will be discussed further therefore go beyond genre and extend to deeper cultural thinking about sexuality, gender, and normative behavioral expectations.

I will begin by briefly summarizing the two French texts, which despite some key differences to which I will return later, tell a very similar story. Yde's parents, king and queen of Aragon, after many prayers to God and the Virgin Mary, finally conceive a daughter named Yde in the epic (Ysabel in the miracle play). Yde's mother dies in childbirth and the father, grieving still some fifteen years later, decides to marry his own daughter since she alone among all women resembles her mother perfectly. Yde, horrified at this incestuous plan,[16] runs away dressed as man, and adopts the name of Ydé, in order to avoid being recognized. The text then recounts the various adventures and challenges that the cross-dressed Ydé/Ysabel faces and over-comes, the details of which differ somewhat in the epic and the play. The cross-dressed heroine finally arrives in Rome where s/he successfully leads the king's army against the Spaniards who attacked his lands (in the play, Ysabel arrives in Greece where she fights the Turks and the Saracens on behalf of the emperor of Constantinople). After one year, king Oton of Rome decides to compensate Ydé by making her/him his heir and marrying her to his daughter (Olive) who, we are told, loves the cross-dressed knight. Ydé/Ysabel laments her fate but seeing no alternative, puts herself in God's hands. The wedding is celebrated. While Ysabel confesses her true sex to her wife on their wedding night, Ydé feigns at first an illness, but fifteen days later, not finding any other pretext, confides her true identity to Olive who promises to keep her secret. Their conversation is overheard however (it is witnessed by a monk placed there as an observer of their wedding night by the emperor of Constantinople in the miracle play), and both women are denounced to the king. In order to ascertain the truth of this revelation and before rushing to burn them both at the stake as his advisors recommend, the king sends for the two women and orders a ritual bath in which Ydé must bathe naked. At this point in the epic, an angel descends from heaven and announces that God has transformed Ydé into a man. The angel also predicts the king's imminent death, and the birth of Croissant, the son of Ydé and Olive.

In the play, the ending is a bit more convoluted: God Himself (who had already personally intervened on various occasions earlier in the text on behalf of Ysabel) sends Saint Michael, disguised as a White Stag, to divert the witnesses of the bath. The angel reassures Ysabel about disrobing for the bath, revealing to her that God will reward her faith in Him with a penis. The king, seeing that Ysabel indeed had the requisite male sexual organs, blesses the union of the couple and would have rushed to punish the monk who had revealed him the same-sex marriage, had it not been for the timely and combined intervention of God and the Virgin Mary. Ysabel's sexual transformation is not permanent in the miracle play however since the story ends with Ysabel's return to her former biological sex, and with the double wedding of Ysabel to the emperor of Constantinople and of the emperor's daughter to Ysabel's father.

Several critics have noted the obvious interrogation of gender roles and of sexual identities that these texts invite.[17] Evidently, the Yde and Olive stories destabilize the foundation of heteronormativity and challenge the notion of a stable binary sexuality. This goal is not achieved through cross-dressing alone, but by adding one transgression to another: Cross-dressing, same-sex marriage, and transsexual (transgender) transformation. The impact of each of these disruptive elements is greatly intensified by their simultaneous presence in the text, and is a manifestation of what Marjorie Garber, in her *Vested Interests: Cross-Dressing and Cultural Anxiety*, has dubbed "the third term," which is not a term, much less a "sex," but rather "a mode of articulation, a way of describing a space of possibility. Three puts into question the idea of one of identity, self-sufficiency, self-knowledge."[18]

I will add that this text also disrupts social norms and class hierarchy, both of which were being closely regulated by medieval sumptuary laws.[19] In *Yde et Olive*, with each gender/sexual transgression, a space for subversion and an interrogation both of social class and of heteronormativity, of stable definitional social, sexual, and gender categories is implicitly opened. When Yde (Ysabel) decides to cross-dress in order to escape her father's incestuous desires and plans, she introduces a "category crisis," thus exposing "a failure of definitional distinction."[20] By cross-dressing and leaving, Yde must put aside both her gender and her social standing as the daughter of a king. Henceforth, she is often described as hungry; she associates with lower socioeconomic classes (the thieves in particular) and works as a servant for a German soldier. Cross-dressing is evidently located at the juncture of class and gender. As Yde transgresses against one set of boundaries (by adopting male garb), she transgresses against her socioeconomic class as well, and thus "calls into question the inviolability of both."[21] She hence reconfigures social and sexual identities previously conceived as stable and unchallengeable.

Yet, these spaces that invite an interrogation of gender roles and of socio-sexual identities end up being only a temporary interlude within the economy of the text, as the cross-dressed woman remains ultimately subordinated to traditional gender hierarchy and the upholding of heteronormativity (and social relations as we will see).[22] As a matter of fact, even though the Yde and Olive epic describes a same-sex union, that is a disruption of the "normalcy" of heterosexual marriage,[23] and despite the mental transgressive "residue" that the text may leave in the mind of the audience,[24] binary heterosexual relations are upheld and validated in the end.

Before going any further, let me point out that the interpretation of the French text that I am proposing here is a result of my cross-cultural approach and my comparative intertextual analysis of the Arabic and French renditions of the same story. In other words, while it is indeed true that the French Yde and Olive story describes a subversive (homo)sexual relation and undermines the notion that heterosexuality is the only form of permissible textual sexual encounter, my cross-cultural reading further demonstrates the limitations of such a reading. For once confronted to its Arabic model (which will be examined in detail further), the French story appears under a much more normative light. By allowing us to ask new questions or to ask old questions in new ways, cross-cultural scholarship thus inevitably forces us to adjust our analysis of one cultural discourse taken singly. This is not to say that the French Yde and Olive is not a subversive text *within its own* literary and historical context, or that cross-cultural research is equivalent to competitive cultural evaluation. Rather, cross-cultural research reveals the historical and ideological power structures that construct discursive representations of sexualities. It allows us to see the extent to which the French narrator(s) had to modify his source text to make it suitable to her/his audience. It also gives us a glimpse of what else could have been there in the French text, how else sexuality and homosexuality could have been described. Ultimately, such an investigation is valuable for the insight it affords us into the medieval creative (and censoring) process more generally.

Back to the French text and to its ultimately normative stance toward alternative sexuality (or more precisely, its *more* normative stance compared to the Arabic version of the story as we will see further). At first sight, the greater normativity of the French Yde and Olive seems to be achieved through the heavy emphasis on religious concerns. Not surprisingly, religious sentiment is prevalent in the miracle play, but it is also already ubiquitous in the epic (which in itself may explain why the *Yde et Olive* epic would have been rewritten one century later as a miracle play; it already contained many of its elements). Yde and Ysabel's most prominent characteristic is undoubtedly their steadfastness in the face of adversity and their firm religious attitude. Each time the female character faces an evil situation (the father's incestuous desires, the thieves, the war, even marriage with another woman), mention is regularly made of her religious determination against all adversities. In the epic, we are told that when Yde sees she cannot escape the same-sex marriage imposed upon her:

Nostre Seignour a sovent reclamé:	She called often onto our Lord
"Glorious Dix, qui mains en Trinité,	"Glorious God, who lives in Trinity,
De ceste lasse cor vous prengne pités,	Take pity on this weary body/heart,
Cui il convient par force marïer."	Who has to get married by force."
	(vv. 7105–08)[25]

At first reading, the adverb "par force" in line 7108 appears to highlight the overall heterosexual paradigm that underlies the entire epic: Yde is forced into this marriage; she is forced into an alternative sexual relation; she is forced into actions she herself decries. The narrator seems to insist on the fact that were she allowed to choose, Yde would *not* intentionally engage in the relationship that s/he is about to describe. The epic maintains nevertheless an overall ambiguity over the status of lesbianism. In line 7104 above, the term "cor" meaning both heart *and* body leads the reader to question Yde's emotional stance: Is Yde really forced into marriage with Olive as the adverb "par force" suggests? Or is she having erotic feelings toward her soon-to-be-wedded wife and is seeking God's succor because she knows that her body ("cor") might well follow her heart ("cor") and yield to the erotic attraction?[26] The recourse to the religious motif in the epic might therefore be interpreted as a means to highlight, rather than to eliminate, the subversive sexual element.[27] Let us not forget that in medieval literature (both in the West and in Islam), erotic expression occurs in the midst of the most spiritually charged discursive moments. Nevertheless, despite the ambiguity of the religious, the epic reverts to the normative: Yde's prayers always lead her to the same conclusion, namely complete submission to God and blind acceptance of His mysterious plans:

J'espouserai la fille au couronné, I will marry the daughter of the king
Si face Dix de moi sa volenté Let God accomplish His Will with me.
(vv. 7128–29)

The infinite faith placed in God by Yde and Ysabel leads directly, at least it would seem, to direct divine intervention in their affairs, and justifies their continuous appeal to Him and thanksgiving. The final miracle, at the moment of the transsexual transformation, comes to be perceived as nothing but another divine intervention, expected by now in the narrative economy of the text (albeit more significant since it involves the actual crossing from one sex to the other). The concluding divine reward in both texts, in the form of the penis, annihilates any remaining thoughts about homoeroticism from the narrative, removes all possible gender ambiguity and firmly establishes the definitive victory of heteronormativity.

But the upholding of heteronormativity in the French tradition in comparison to the Arabic version which will be discussed further[28] is most evident in the details given (or withheld rather) at two key moments in the text: First in the description of the relation between the two women on their wedding night and second at the moment of the sexual transformation at the end. I will speak about these in turn.

In *Miracle de la fille d'un Roy*, the interlacing of the erotic and the religious abruptly comes to an end at the wedding night which splits resolutely both discourses and subordinates the sexual to the religious. After praying with Anne and after being reassured by St. Michael about the preservation of her honor (vv. 2472–85), Ysabel is comforted only temporarily. Distressed a few moments later, she turns to the Virgin Mary seeking guidance: "Doulce mére Dieu, que feray? [Sweet Mother of Jesus, what shall I do?]" (v. 2562). In addition, as though to preclude any sexually jeopardizing encounter with her newly wedded wife, and to avoid any potentially ambiguous and theologically compromising situation, Ysabel does not wait for fifteen days, like her homologue in the epic, to reveal the truth of her sex, but opts rather for immediate disclosure:

Dame, en vostre mercy me met.	Lady, I place myself in your mercy.
Pour le confort que m'avez fait,	For the comfort you showed me,
Vous vueil descouvrir tout mon fait	I want to reveal you my entire story
Et ce pour quoy j'ay tel annuy.	And the reason why I feel such trouble.
Sachiez conme vous femme suy,	Know that I am a woman like you,
Fille de roy et de royne.	Daughter of a king and a queen.
. . .	. . .
Et pour moy garder de diffam	And in order to protect myself from dishonor
Ne me sui point monstrée fame,	I did not show myself as a woman,
Mais conme homme m'ay maintenu,	But have dressed (acted/appeared) as a man,
Et Dieu m'a si bien soustenu	And God has helped me so much
Et donné de sa grace tant	And given me so much of his grace
Qu'en lieu n'ay esté combatant	That in no place have I fought
Don't je n'aye eu la victoire,	Where I was not successful.
Dont je ly rens loenge et gloire.	For this I give him thanks and glory.
Or savez conment il m'est, dame	Now you know what it is with me, my Dame,
Puis que je sui conme vous femme	That I am a woman, like you
Et que j'ai mamelles: tastez.	And that I have breasts: Feel them.
Pour Dieu mercy, . . .	Have mercy on me, for God's sake, . . .

(vv. 2581–2609)

Let us note how here again, gender and social class are linked, though they are now in an inverse relation to what we saw earlier: Ysabel's confession of her biological sex is intimately associated with the revelation of her high social status ("Sachiez conme vous femme suy/ Fille de roy et de royne."). This double exposure eliminates all suspense from the play, as the heroine is shielded henceforth from any possible sexual or carnal temptation. At this moment, and despite the preceding textual spaces devoted to cross-dressing, the text chooses the promotion of heteronormativity: Ysabel punctuates her entire confession by references to her infinite faith in God, her submission to His will, and her undeviating preoccupation with honor and reputation. Her proposition to her wife to touch her breasts ("mamelles") to ascertain the truth of the fact that her husband is in fact a woman (v. 2607) shifts the reader/ viewer's attention from the visual to the tactile and highlights the deceptive nature of sight.[29] Gender as established by sight is revealed no longer to be *historia*, but *fabula*, a lie, a discursive construction.

The move from seeing to touching in an attempt to reach some measure of "truth," of gender stability, is not taken up by the emperor's daughter. The proposition to touch the "mamelles" thus remains at the level of philosophical, intellectual subversion of gender construction; it is not permitted to become a potentially intimate moment between the spouses. The emperor's daughter's response is interesting in this respect:

De ce ne convient plus parler.	There is no need to speak further of this.
Or vous mettez hors de soussi,	Put yourself at ease,
Car tout ce que m'avez dit cy	Because everything you have told me here
Je vous promet bien celeray,	I promise you to conceal,
Et tel honneur vous porteray	And I will show you such honor
Con doit faire a son mari femme.	As a woman must show her husband
En touz cas, ce vous jur par m'ame,	In all matters, I swear this upon my soul,
Ne ne vous aray ja mains chier.	Nor will I ever hold you less dear.

(vv. 2612–19)[30]

Robert Clark has interpreted these lines as an endorsement of severely condemned forms of sexuality:[31] After all, the emperor's daughter indicates that biological sex does not matter and that she is ready to uphold the sacrament of marriage despite the new information provided. I would argue instead that the emperor's daughter's response maintains the ideology of phallocentrism and heterosexuality.[32] The promise to continue to "honor" Ysabel as she would have, had Ysabel indeed been a man, maintains the emperor's daughter in a subordinate position not only in relation to biological masculinity, but more importantly here to any socially constructed or outward manifestation of masculinity.

In the Yde and Olive epic however, one senses the narrator's struggle between conformity to religious and social norms and the titillating temptation to describe the sexual proximity (if not promiscuity) of two women in bed.[33] In the epic, the same-sex union is not devoid of sexual content. First, and despite her understandable distress, we are told that Yde begins by securely locking the door ("la cambre a bien veroullié et fermee," v. 7164). She then pretends to be ill, thus incapable of consummating their marriage that night. As Yde tells Olive of her sickness, she accompanies her words with hugs: "With these words, Olive was hugged [A ices mos fu Olive accollee (v. 7171)]." The verb "accollee" (to hug) is repeated again twice in that same scene; the next time, by Olive. Let us note here that it is Olive, and not Yde, who pleads to have their wedding consummation put off for fifteen days after all the guests have left, saying that she is looking forward to "doing more" later; for now, she will be satisfied with kisses and with being "accolee":

Fors du basier bien voel estre accolee,	Besides kissing, I don't mind hugs
Mais de l'amour c'on dist qui est privee	But as to the love that is said to be intimate
Vous requier jou que soie deportee.	I request to be exempt from it.

(vv. 7185–88)

Yde agrees happily, and the narrator adds that the two women kiss and hug: "They kissed and hugged each other [Dont ont l'un l'autre baisie et accollee. (v. 7190)]." Although nothing in the epic specifies the kind of kiss or hug exchanged between the two women (sisterly, compassionate, respect, etc.), the acts of "baisier" and "accoler" that are evoked nevertheless invite erotic and sexual readings that are entirely absent from the miracle play.[34] Diane Watt has gone so far as to suggest that these verbs may well denote sexual intercourse between the two characters.[35] Without going as far, it remains important to recognize the sexual connotations of these signifiers for, though limited and probably euphemistic, they appear to have disturbed some (medieval) scribes or readers. The next two lines of the epic are partly (purposely?) effaced and are supplied by other manuscript readings:

En cele nuit n'i [ot] cri ne mellee.	That night, there were no screams or fights
La nu[I]s passa, si revint la journee.	The night ended, and the day shone.

(vv. 7191–92)

The silence that the text maintains over the details of the wedding night of the female couple speaks eloquently of the efforts made to keep the sexual and the titillating representation of lesbianism bracketed. The homoerotic is however not entirely silenced as seen with the repetition of "accollee."[36] The homoerotic is evident also in the demonstrative "*That night*" in the preceding quote, as though the narrator was pointing to the lack of violence of the lesbian wedding night in which there were no screams or fights, in contrast to the heterosexual wedding night in which there may have been screams and fights. The (possibly) (un)consummated love making of Yde and Olive is highlighted finally in the use of battle metaphors ("cri ne mellee"). These metaphors are further evidence of the implicit sexual (military) language used to portray lesbian relations in the Middle Ages, as I demonstrated elsewhere.[37] Moreover, when King Oton asks his daughter about her wedding night, Olive's answer is conveniently ambiguous:

"Fille," fait il, "comment iés mariee?"   "Daughter," He said, "How was
                                                       your wedding night?"
"Sire," dist ele, "ensi com moi agree."   "Sire," She said, "the way I like
                                                       it; or the way it pleases me."
                                                             (vv. 7198–99)

But ultimately, Yde (just like Ysabel one century later) reveals her biological sex to Olive in the midst of apologies and prayers for mercy.[38] The affective transgressive dimension that had been present, however timidly, is banned henceforth altogether from the text. The text appropriates the cross-dresser as female, and erases completely the "third term" that had been introduced earlier into the epic. This recuperative gesture is present in Olive's initial reaction to the revelation:

Olive l'ot, s'en fu espoëntee.   Olive listened, she was horrified.
                                              (v. 7216)

Olive's distress has been greatly de-emphasized by critics.[39] Yet, it echoes the Deuteronomic injunction against transvestism (Deut. 22:5), and reveals social anxiety about the dissolution of boundaries. Yde's cross-dressing that was threatening because it blurred or obliterated legible gender distinctions is henceforth annihilated by Olive's reaction. Olive's normative voice utterly silences the transgressive preceding section and signals the return to sanctioned sexual and grammatical categories;[40] it is indeed important to note, with Jacqueline de Weever, that the grammatical gender instability that had been prevalent thus far in the text ceases at this point.[41] The restoration of the normative is heralded in the epic by the threat of capital punishment (vv. 7251–52), which under the *lex foedissimam* (edict of Roman law) of 1400 was indeed the classic penalty for lesbians.[42] It is accompanied by the appearance of an angel who reveals God's personal intervention in Yde's affairs, and her timely sexual transformation into a man (vv. 7261–72); and perhaps even more importantly by the angel's announcement that Yde and Olive successfully conceive a son named Croissant, that very night: "On this day, Croissant was conceived" ["Et en cel jour fu Croissans engenrés," v. 7283].

Clearly, not only does Yde receive a penis to reward her for her unswerving belief in God and her submission to his will, but it is a well functioning one too, we are swiftly reassured, as evident in the efficiency with which the conception of the child occurs. The angel's statement is not simply a premonition; it is a speech act. Revelation of the miracle is accompanied by its accomplishment. Croissant's conception is all the more significant that it takes narrative precedence over any information the audience may have hoped for over Yde's successful sexual transformation. The transsexual miracle is far less amazing than it may appear at first sight however, for according to Western Galenic medical theories, it was believed that women's sexual organs were identical to men's, except they were inverted (the vagina was thought to be an inverted penis).[43] However, from the perspective of the audience of the epic or drama, most of whom were probably *not* familiar with pre-modern theories of medicine, it can be argued that an explicit depiction of the transsexual transformation was expected. Such a description, in contrast to its Ovidian textual precursor,[44] is absent however from all the stories that have preserved the Yde and Olive tale. We do not see the growth of the penis on Yde's body, and this is unexpected in the narrative economy of the epic, where the narrator had not shied away from elaborately describing Yde's female body (vv. 6503–21). We do not hear Yde's reaction to the unexpected "gift"of the penis. Is she shocked? Relieved? Surprised at least? Did she even want to be a man? The question of gender identity is subsumed under that of sex; it is unproblematized as though it did not matter, or rather as if it was expected that Yde of course would have wanted to be a man if given a choice. After all, according to the theological and scientific teachings of the time, if given a choice, any woman would have wanted to be a man. In *Yde et Olive*, perhaps precisely because it is an epic, thus concerned primarily with the question of lineage and foregrounding issues of marriage and procreation, there is a lingering presumption that male is better, that to wish to be a man (however inexplicitly or unconsciously since Yde never verbalizes such a longing), is perfectly "normal" and, culturally speaking, perfectly logical. Obviously, these assumptions undermine whatever disruption of, and challenge to, easy notions of binarism that transvestism may have invited at first reading. Underlying this assumption of male supremacy, women are scapegoated. The challenge or threat posed by cross-dressing is henceforth contained, as the epic moves unproblematically to the continuation of the Huon de Bordeaux family line. Diane Watt points out the advantages of such a narrative resolution in the context of an epic and for the male characters; in effect, such a resolution "provides not just Oton but also Florent [Yde's father] with a direct male descendant and thus enables the transmission of both their property according to the rules of patrilineage."[45] For the female characters however, gender construction and the possibility of alternative sexualities are scapegoated. The symbolic function of "transvestism *as* a powerful agent of destabilization and change, the sign of the *un*groundedness of identities on which social structures and hierarchies depend" is conveniently set aside, and subordinated to genealogy and social heteronormativity.[46]

Finally, it is important to note the narrative construction of the epic and the way the story of Croissant is embedded within two stories both dealing with *Yde et Olive* (known as *Yde et Olive I* and *Yde et Olive II*). This choice of ending the first part of *Yde et Olive* precisely at the moment of the sexual transformation and to return to that story only about 400 hundred lines later is significant because it points to the narrator's effort to divert the audience's attention from sexuality to social normativity and sexual legitimacy. Just as the narrative had moved swiftly over the momentarily erotic behavior of the newlyweds, we note that immediately following Yde's successful and rewarding sexual transformation, the reader's attention is displaced from this sexual transformation onto lineage and the successful continuation of the Huon de Bordeaux family line. The very space that could have been used by the audience to imagine the specifics of the sexual transformation (the erotic encounter between Olive and the now officially transsexual Yde) is replaced by a story that emphasizes family lineage and thus heteronormativity. And yet, one could have easily imagined a narrative that binds the two sections of the Yde and Olive stories before turning to their son. This order would have probably been more expected in the context of an epic cycle where narrative development is typically chronological and historically linear. During the Croissant episode, the transsexual Yde disappears from the text, and to some extent perhaps also from the reader's mind, and remains invisible until her lineage has been firmly established. In fact when s/he returns in *Yde et Olive II*, Yde has now fathered four sons and three daughters.[47] The displacement from the axis of sex and gender to that of lineage and social continuity reflects an anxiety over genealogy, fatherhood, and patriarchy. At the end of the epic, one fully measures the extent to which transvestism has been in fact only a temporary interlude within the economy of the text, and the extent to which questions over gender ambiguity have been displaced onto a sociopolitical axis.

In the miracle play, the reestablishment of the heterosexual status quo is manifest in the final double marriage that ends the play: Ysabel marries the emperor of Constantinople, while the emperor's daughter marries Ysabel's father. More than ever, it becomes evident that the erasure of gender and sociocultural distinctions that had initiated the entire play was temporary; at the end, the audience returns to the safety of the religiously sanctioned happy heterosexual union.[48] The end of the miracle play supports Michelle Szkilnik's theory that by the end of the fourteenth century, transsexual transformation is no longer allowed to remain permanent. All possible gender ambiguity is effaced both from the textual remains, as well as from the audience's imagination.

Yde and Olive and the Matter of Araby

But it is especially in comparison to the Arabic literary tradition on cross-dressing and female same-sex marriage that the extent of the heteronormativity of the medieval French texts can be fully apprehended. The comparative cross-cultural approach, in effect, allows us to grasp nuances in each text that remain hidden whenever one cultural discourse is examined alone, or is divorced from its multicultural context. While it is difficult, if not impossible, to trace the precise Arabic literary genealogy of *Yde et Olive*,[49] it appears undeniable that the "author(s)" of the French epic was familiar with the Arabic tradition on homosexuality, as well as with a great number of the stories contained in the *One Thousand and One Nights* (also known as *Arabian Nights*). In fact, the entire *Huon de Bordeaux* cycle seems heavily indebted to the Arabic storytelling tradition of *One Thousand and One Nights* which was known in the West at least as early as the first quarter of the twelfth century with Petrus Alfonsi's *Disciplina Clericalis* (1120s). Francesca Canadé Sautman has observed that the place/people names and the geographic location of the epic all point to a Southern (therefore Arabic and/or Islamicate) influence. She writes: "[M]any clusters around the same-sex change are centered in Spain and Italy, which is consonant with the mention of Aragon, Castille, and Barcelona in *Yde and Olive* and the use of the Southern name Olive."[50]

The names of the main characters in the French Yde and Olive weave an intertext with the tales of the *Arabian Nights*; the presence of this intertext suggests a narrative and geographical proximity and invite a comparative reading of these two textual traditions.[51] Let us begin by examining the name of Yde and Olive's first son, Croissant, whose story had interrupted the epic at the moment of the sexual transformation as we saw earlier. The first name Croissant (meaning "moon crescent") is very unusual in French;[52] it is, however, quite common in Arabic and can be found with great regularity throughout the Arabic literary tradition. In the *One Thousand and One Nights*, "Moon" (with its multiple synonyms and variations) is an androgynous name and is given with equal frequency to male and female characters. In the famous story that begins on the 170th night, "Story of Kamar al-Zaman and the Princess Boudour,"[53] which is the story best known for its depiction of lesbianism and which I will discuss in detail in a moment, both heroes' names evoke the moon: Kamar al-Zaman means "the moon of the century" while Boudour means "the moon of moons." This androgynous semantic field associated with the moon is again present in the tenth century *Encyclopedia of Pleasure* written by Ibn Nasr al-Katib, which is one of the earliest erotic treatises in Arabic. This text goes one step further and compares the vulva to a full moon.[54] It may thus be possible to argue that in Arabic literature, the name "Moon" was used at times as a symbolic code word for (homo)eroticism, or at least for androgyny. The choice of naming Yde and Olive's son "Croissant" in the French epic thus assumes significance.[55]

A second important intertext between the French and Arabic tales is the name of the female character Olive. Once again, the name "Olive" is unusual in French literary history. In the Arabic tale, even though we do not encounter the name "Olive" per se, the title characters are reunited at the end through a scene that involves the sale of olives. The reference to olives/Olive in these texts may not be coincidental, and may be associated with cross-dressing and androgyny more generally.

A third and final example of intertextual resonances between the two traditions is that of the name of Yde which is also highly unusual in the French medieval literary tradition. It is evocative however of the name of the first lesbian known to the Arabs according to al-Katib's *Encyclopedia of Pleasure*, Hind Bint al-Khuss al-Iyadiyyah.[56] The name "Iyadiyyah" (the final two syllables "iyyah" represent a diminutive suffix in Arabic) could have become Yde in French. Certainly, taken separately, each of these three name paralles discussed here (Croissant, Olive, and Yde) cannot be considered conclusive evidence of direct links between *Yde and Olive* and the tale of Kamar al-Zaman and the Princess Boudour. However, taken together, the selection of these Arabic names by the French narrators point to an Arabic literary/ cultural model and justify our comparative reading of the stories and of the representation of gender fluidity therein.

I would like to turn now to the story of Kamar al-Zaman and the Princess Boudour, which I believe constitutes one of the main, heretofore unacknowledged, models of the French Yde and Olive tales. In the remainder of this chapter, rather than examining the textual parallels, I will focus on the great differences in attitudes toward homosexuality, cross-dressing, and female same-sex marriage that separate the medieval French and Arabic literary traditions. I will begin by summarizing the second part of the Arabic tale—that is the section that deals directly with the topics of interest here, cross-dressing and same-sex marriage. After a great resistance to marriage, Kamar al-Zaman and Boudour eventually do get married through the intervention of magic and the active participation of Jinnis. But once married, they are separated again. In order to find her husband and to protect herself, Boudour cross-dresses as a man and because of her great resemblance to her lost husband, takes on his name, Kamar al-Zaman. She arrives at the Isle of Ebony where King Arnanos abdicates in her favor and forces her to marry his daughter, "the most virgin of the island" named Hayyat al-Nefous or the Life of Souls. Kamar al-Zaman is finally discovered through a scene that involves olives; Boudour reveals the truth to King Arnanos, and all ends seemingly in the most heteronormative, and polygamous way: Boudour is reunited to Kamar al-Zaman, abdicates in his favor, and in addition gives him Hayyat al-Nefous as a second wife. And the three of them live happily ever after.

In contrast to the function of cross-dressing in the French narratives of Yde and Olive, cross-dressing in *Alf layla wa layla* does not introduce a "category crisis." In fact, even after she adopts male clothing and her husband's name, Boudour continues to occupy the same social position as she did earlier in the tale, that of the offspring of a king.[57] The stability in Boudour's social identity means that this character will not need to prove herself a worthy knight, or accomplish extraordinary deeds in order to recover a social standing lost to cross-dressing, as Yde does. It also means that cross-dressing in *The Story of Kamar al-Zaman and the Princess Boudour* is not a transgressive social act, as it will become in the process of translation into French. Rather, in the Arabic text, cross-dressing functions as a key narrative strategy that permits the storyteller to focus very directly and explicitly on the erotic, if not sexual, ambiguities to which encounters with a cross-dressed heroine necessarily elicit.

The Wedding Night in *The Story of Kamar al-Zaman and the Princess Boudour*

In contrast to the French miracle play in which Ysabel reveals her true sex to her wife immediately in order to avoid any sexually jeopardizing encounter, and to the French verse epic where the wedding night is spent feigning illness in order to avoid (lesbian) sex between Yde and Olive, the Arabic tale focuses from the outset on the two young women's sexual relation. This is how their wedding night is depicted:

ثم ادخلوا حياة النفوس ابنة الملك على بدور ابنة الملك الغيور و ردوا عليهما الباب و اوقدوا لهما الشموع و الفوانيس و فرشوا لهما الفراش الحرير فدخلت بدور الى حياة النفوس.

They [the servants] made Hayat al-Nefous enter into the room where Boudour, daughter of king Ghouyour, was [sitting], and they closed the door on them. They lit candles and lights for them and spread their bed with silk [sheets]. Boudour entered into Hayat al-Nefous.[58]

The explicitness of the sexual encounter between the two girls is not evident in the English translation, for it rests on the use of the Arabic verb "dakhala"

(دخل to enter) twice in the preceding quote, first with the preposition "ala" على ("they made Hayat al-Nefous enter into the room where Boudour was") and then with the preposition "ila" الى ("Boudour entered into Hayat al-Nefous"). What must first be noted is the fact that the verb "dakhala"—meaning to enter, to penetrate—does not require the use of any preposition. The fact that the redactor chose to add not one, but two different prepositions with this verb must therefore make us pause.[59] In its first occurrence with the preposition "ala," the audience is led to understand that Boudour is already in the room into which Hayat al-Nefous is led. The second use of the verb "dakhala" with "ila" comes therefore as a surprise since such a combination can only mean (1) to penetrate into a physical space, or (2) to penetrate sexually, or to have intercourse. In the context of this scene, only the second meaning of "dakhala ila" is possible, leading us to conclude that Boudour and Hayat al-Nefous's initial encounter is utterly sexual.

While the redactor of the fourteenth-century Syrian manuscript of *Alf layla wa layla* does not further depict the lesbian wedding night, the power of such nondescription ought not to be overlooked. For it is indeed in its very "indescribability" that the impact of lesbian sexuality lies, and "its availability for cultural inscription and appropriation."[60] In the oral performance of the tale of *Kamar al-Zaman and the Princess Boudour*, the sexual encounter between Hayat al-Nefous and Boudour is likely to have been one of those key moments that would have invited further elaboration by the storyteller, or at the very least, stirred the imagination of the audience.[61] In contrast to the destiny of Yde and Olive's sexuality in the French thirteenth-century epic, which will be effaced by scribes or readers as we saw earlier, Boudour and Hayat al-Nefous's sexual relation will be expanded and amplified throughout the following centuries, leading to the detailed portrayal of lesbianism in Burton's English (1885–88) and Mardrus's French (1899–1904) translations.[62]

After their initial, overt sexual encounter, Boudour and Hayat al-Nefous spend the next two nights "kissing" and "caressing." This is how the redactor of the fourteenth-century Syrian manuscript depicts their intimacy:

جلست الى جانب حياة النفوس و قبلتها

(Boudour sat down next to Hayat al-Nefous and kissed her) (592).

On the following night, the redactor writes:

فرأت . . .حياة النفوس جالسة فجلست بجانبها و طقطقت عليها و قبلتها بين عينيها.

When [Boudour] saw Hayat al-Nefous sitting, she sat besides her, caressed her and kissed her between the eyes. (593)

The words "hugging" and "kissing" used in the Arabic tale evoke certainly the way Yde and Olive's encounter had been depicted by the Old French narrator of the verse epic as discussed earlier. We must note however that the meaning of these terms differs from their French counterparts in that in the Arabic erotic tradition, "kissing" and "hugging" have a specific and overtly sexual connotation. This is how "kissing" is defined in the *Encyclopedia of Pleasure*:

Kissing is a means by which sexual desire is aroused. . . . Kissing becomes more effective when it is accompanied by biting, pinching, sucking, sighing, and hugging. It is then that both the man and the woman burn with sexual desire simultaneously. . . . Kissing is the penis's messenger to the vulva. It is also said that kissing is an essential part of sexual union. . . . [K]issing, like lubrication, facilitates sexual union. . . . Coition without kissing is imperfect.[63]

Not only is kissing a metaphor for sexual union, but the placement of the kiss is also important to consider. Though uncommon in the Western tradition, the placement of the kiss on or between the eyes is recommended very specifically in the Arabic erotic tradition as a strategy to speed up a woman's orgasm.[64] Boudour's kiss between Hayat al-Nefous's eyes should thus be interpreted as an unambiguous reference to their foreplay, sexual relation, perhaps even orgasm. We are hence permitted to conclude that while the Arabic and French texts under consideration use the same semantic field and linguistic terms (kissing, hugging) to portray female same-sex relations, the Arabic text is anchored in a sociocultural context where such conduct holds a very precise sexual connotation. In this light, Boudour and Hayat al-Nefous's kisses, much more clearly than those between Yde and Olive, are to be interpreted as foreplay, sexual intimacy, if not intercourse.

It is on the third night that Boudour reveals her biological sex to her wedded wife. This scene is important because it represents the moment at which the French Yde and Olive narratives differ markedly from the Arabic tale that provided their main storyline. An investigation of the key differences between the two traditions reveals the extent to which medieval French narrators silenced some of the most daring homosexual features of the Arabic tale; it also exhibits the very divergent attitudes held by each of these traditions toward female homosexuality.

We must note from the outset that Boudour's revelation is not made by an apologetic or repenting cross-dresser as was the case with Yde/Ide in the French epic. It takes place instead in the midst of an erotic and sexually charged scene. This is how the scene is depicted in Mahdi's edition:

... قالت بكلام رقيق مؤنث و هو كلامها الحقيقى الغريزى و كشفت عن حالها
الى أن حكت لها ما جرى مع معشوقها زوجها قمر الزمان و اورتها فرجها وقالت لها
أنا امرأة ذات فرج و نهود.

[Boudour] spoke [to Hayat al-Nefous] in a soft, feminine voice, and this was her true, natural voice, and she unveiled the truth about her situation. . . . She told her what had happened to her and her beloved husband Kamar al-Zaman, and she showed her vulva and said to her [I am] a woman who has vulva and breasts. (595)

While in the *Miracle de la fille d'un roy*, Ysabel suggests that her wife touch her "mamelles" ("breasts") as proof that she is indeed a woman, the Arabic text goes farther in the proofs that Boudour is willing to give. As a matter of fact, Boudour does not simply *offer* to show her female sexual characteristics; she actually *shows* them. She does not just show her breasts; she also uncovers her vulva. In fact, she exhibits that first. The unveiling of Boudour's private parts is repeated twice in this scene, as though the redactor wished to highlight the sexual moment, as well as to encourage the audience's imagination concerning the implications of such a sexual exposition. As the text remains silent over Hayat al-Nefous's response to Boudour's stripping, the reader is permitted to conclude that she may not have been displeased by what she saw. Staging a female character who willingly (and titillatingly) uncovers her vulva and breasts thus becomes another step in the process of deepening the intimate contact between the two female spouses.

While in *Yde et Olive*, the revelation was overheard and rapidly divulged to the king, in the Arabic tale, Boudour's secret remains for the greater part of the tale known only to Hayat al-Nefous. The limited disclosure of Boudour's biological sex allows the sexual transgression by the two women to continue undisturbed. In fact, the greater permissiveness of the Arabic text (in comparison to the French narratives) toward lesbianism becomes even more pronounced in the scenes that *follow*, rather than precede, Boudour's revelation of her biological sex. Whereas in the Yde and Olive epics, the confession became the space of panic and the beginning of the return to heteronormativity, it is not accompanied by any anxiety about cross-dressing in the Arabic story, or about the lesbian sexuality that had taken place. There is no anxiety either about the necessity of maintaining visible, legible gender distinctions, or enforcing social hierarchy. There is no divinely ordained injunction against lesbianism to worry about, no impending capital punishment and, as we will see, no divine intervention to reestablish order in the midst of what must have appeared as sociocultural and moral chaos to the medieval West.

In fact, in the Arabic tale, Boudour's revelation gives rise to an alternative female space in which both women become equal, and hence enjoy mutual support and reciprocal intimacy. Boudour's revelation is met with mere surprise on the part of Hayat al-Nefous, not with "panic" or "pain": Hayat al-Nefous is "surprised at her story" (تعجبت) writes the redactor of the tale (595). More important perhaps, the revelation of Boudour's womanhood is also met with pleasure: Hayat al-Nefous "was pleased with the news" (فرحت بكشف حالها) (595). The fact that Boudour is a woman, not a man, puts Hayat al-Nefous more at ease. The presence of the cross-dresser in the Arabic text, rather than heightening anxiety as it did in the French tradition, opens up a space for dialogue between the two girls and ultimately increases their intimacy and pleasure. Immediately following the news about Boudour's biological sex, the redactor writes that both women "spoke, played, laughed, and slept" (تحدثوا و لعبوا و تضاحكوا و ناموا) (595). We must note here the grammatical construction of the Arabic verbs used in this description. For the first time in the homoerotic interlude of this tale, the redactor uses the reflexive form to express Boudour and Hayat al-Nefous's sexual play, laughter, conversation, and overall pleasure in each other's company. It is as though while Boudour performed a male role, the redactor was compelled to depict her in the conventionally male active position of kissing and caressing Hayat al-Nefous. After Boudour's revelation, however, Hayat al-Nefous becomes an equal partner in the relationship, both active giver and passive recipient of the same-sex intimacy. Some might argue that the very fact that Boudour's biological sex must remain a secret to everyone but Hayat al-Nefous and the reader indicates that medieval Arab-Islamicate society, just like French culture, did not condone lesbianism. If this is may be true at a social and legal level, it is not so at a narrative and discursive level. To the reader or listener, especially to the medieval lesbian in the audience, this tale must have provided a validation (albeit an imaginative one) for a way of life that differed radically from socially sanctioned sexual encounters.

Not only is Boudour and Hayat al-Nefous's intimacy highlighted *after* Boudour's revelation of her biological sex, but their marriage is finally consummated. Of course, it is not consummated in a heterosexual mode, but rather by destabilizing the association of heterosexual marriage with virginal blood. As a matter of fact, Hayat al-Nefous, in order to assuage her father's mounting concern over her prolonged virginity, stages her own defloration. She kills a chicken and spreads its blood over her own thighs and handkerchief. She also screams, repeating thereby the expected association of heterosexuality with violence and pain:

الى قريب الاذان فقامت حياة النفوس اخذت دجاجة و قلعت سراويلها و صرخت بعد أن ذبحتها و تلطخت بدمها و بلت منديلها. ثم أخفت الدجاجة و لبست سراويلها و نادت فدخلوا عليها أهلها.

Hayat al-Nefous woke up before the morning call to prayer. She took a chicken, took off her pants, screamed after killing it and spreading its blood over herself and her handkerchief. She then hid the chicken, put her pants back on and called. So her family entered the room. (596)

As Hayat al-Nefous expected, the stained handkerchief is taken by King Armanos and his wife (and society at large) to be definitive proof of the consummation of their daughter's marriage. The proud parents rush to exhibit the bloody cloth, without worrying about the provenance of the blood. Ironically, the very moment that the two lovers are portrayed as maintaining heteronormativity is also the very space where binary sexual relations are exposed and where the very notion of stable identities is challenged. Judith Butler's analysis of homosexual marriage is particularly pertinent to this discussion:

> The replication of this heterosexual tradition in a non-heterosexual context brings into relief the utterly constructed status of the so-called heterosexual original. Thus, gay is to straight *not* as copy is to original, but rather, as copy is to copy. The parodic repetition of the "original," . . . reveals the original to be nothing other than a parody of the *idea* of the natural and the original.[65]

In the Arabic tale, the exhibition of the bloody cloth in the context of a homosexual marriage reveals that heterosexuality is critiqued, denaturalized, animalized. After all, marriage is legitimized here not by the virginal blood of a bride, but by that of a lowly farm animal, the chicken. Meanwhile, Boudour and Hayat al-Nefous are allowed to continue their intimate lives with each other, inadvertently blessed this time by the entire social system.

The End of the Story: Homosexuality within Heterosexuality

In fact, nothing disturbs the lesbian relation—neither Hayat al-Nefous's sexual maturity, nor Boudour's revelation of her biological sex to her partner and to the reader. Whereas in the French epic, the revelation of Yde's sex is closely followed by the threat of capital punishment and by the divine miracle (the transsexual transformation), in the Arabic tale, the revelation contributes to the development of the intimate relationship between the two women. As a matter of fact, each night thereafter, Boudour and Hayat al-Nefous live in the same bliss, tending to their emotional, intimate relationship, while awaiting the eventual return of Kamar al-Zaman:

الى الليل تدخل الي حياة النفوس فيتحدثوا و تشكوا لها قلقها و شوقها الى معشوقها قمر الزمان.

At night, [Boudour] penetrated into Hayat al-Nefous. They spoke to each other and she told her about her worry and her love for Kamar al-Zaman. (596)

In this quote, the verb "dakhala" (to enter, to penetrate) is used again with the preposition "ila" that we discussed earlier, hence emphasizing the endurance of the sexual encounter between the two women, even after the revelation of Boudour's biological sex. Even though the lesbian relationship is presented here as an ersatz for heterosexual relations (the two women's intimacy occurs seemingly only *because* they are waiting for Kamar al-Zaman's return), it seems clear nevertheless that a space is opened up for alternative emotional, if not sexual, satisfaction. In the Arabic tale, lesbianism is allowed to exist, is fostered even, within a frame of heterosexuality, while in the French texts we examined earlier, lesbianism is placed at the other extreme of heterosexuality.

It is only when Boudour recognizes Kamar al-Zaman as the vendor of olives that the lesbian sexual relation comes to a halt. At first reading, the end of the Arabic tale may be seen as a return not only to the androcentric model of marriage (Kamar al-Zaman and Boudour are reunited), but also, and in keeping with the cultural background of *One Thousand and One Nights*, to polygamy: Hayat al-Nefous is given as second wife to Kamar al-Zaman. Moreover, the end of the text seems to herald the triumph of patriarchy since, once reunited with her husband, Boudour abdicates in favor of the "true" man of the story, Kamar al-Zaman. The ultimate triumph of patriarchy is further manifested in the fact that Hayat al-Nefous is never consulted about becoming a second wife. However, once again, heterosexuality in the Arabic text is only a temporary interlude as lesbianism is never conveniently bracketed, or completely and utterly contained and silenced. For when King Armanos asks Kamar al-Zaman to marry his daughter, Hayat al-Nefous, Boudour is the one who answers and this is what she says:

فقالت بدور و الله مثلي مثلها و ليلة لي و ليلة لها و اسكن أنا واياها في بيت واحد لاني تعودت عليها.

So Boudour replied: By God, for me like for her; a night for me and a night for her. And I will live together with her in one house because I have gotten used to her [literally: I have returned to her repeatedly]. (609)

While, on the surface, these lines suggest that Boudour generously accepts the sharing of her husband with Hayat al-Nefous, they also hint at the fact that the women's relationship is far from coming to a halt at the end of the tale. Even as she adheres to the basic legal principles of polygamy ("one night for me and one night for her"), Boudour introduces an important departure from its conventions when she states her desire to live in the same house as Hayat al-Nefous. Her use of the verb "ta'awwaddtu" (تعودت), which means both "to get used to" and "to return repeatedly to," reveals that the main reason for refusing the very common practice of the separation of households may well be her desire to continue "returning repeatedly to Hayat al-Nefous." Boudour's desire to continue sharing Hayat al-Nefous's house thus has significant implications for their same-sex relations. Not surprisingly, the survival of the lesbian relationship beyond the polygamous ending is the way Mardrus (the celebrated nineteenth-century French translator of *Alf layla wa layla*) will render the end of *The Story of Kamar al-Zaman and the Princess Boudour*:

Kamar al-Zaman governed his kingdom as perfectly as he contented his two wives, with whom he passed alternate evenings. Boudour and Hayat lived together in harmony, allowing the nights to their husband, but reserving the days for each other.[66]

Mardrus restates here explicitly what was depicted implicitly in the fourteenth-century Syrian manuscript that Mahdi edited. We must not disregard his translation out of hand, claiming it merely constitutes nineteenth-century Orientalist presuppositions, and in no way reflects medieval viewpoints.[67] Such an end is in fact quite consistent with the double meaning of "ta'awwaddtu" in the Syrian manuscript, and resonates very strongly with medieval Arabic erotic treatises which consider lesbianism as one form of sexual practice, alongside many others. The Arabic *Story of Kamar al-Zaman and the Princess Boudour*, in contrast to the French narratives of Yde and Olive, thus permits the survival of Boudour and Hayat al-Nefous's relationship, even as it places it within the parameters of heterosexuality and polygamy.[68] Whereas the French epic recuperates the cross-dressed Yde and silences the transgressive voice of the "third term," the Arabic tale does not interrupt the workings of this "third term," and allows a move toward a new structure where heterosexuality is viewed as only one possibility in a larger chain. The Arabic text thus, until the very end, permits border crossings, and reveals a complete and utter failure of definitional distinctions. One may say that while her French sister, because of her transsexual transformation, is forced ultimately to embrace heterosexuality, the Arabic lesbian, despite her heterosexual and polygamous marriage, is allowed to maintain her commitment and unfaltering faithfulness to her female partner.

Notes

1. Jacqueline Murray, "Twice Marginal and Twice Invisible," in Vern L. Bullough and James Brundage, eds., *The Handbook of Medieval Sexuality*. (New York: Garland, 1996), 191–222. With regard to pre-modern Europe, it is important to point out that my use of the word "lesbian" is not the same as what is often implied by it today. What I mean by "lesbian" in the Middle Ages is the emotional and sexual attachment between two women. It does not include the dimensions of political activism or engagement with which the modern notions of lesbianism and homosexuality are often connected, nor is it associated with the politics of gender identity.

2. The term Islamicate which I will use throughout this article was coined by Marshall G. S. Hodgson who defines it thus: " 'Islamicate' would refer not directly to the religion, Islam, itself, but to the social and cultural complex historically associated with Islam and the Muslims, both among Muslims themselves and even when found among non-Muslims." See his *The Venture of Islam: Conscience and History in a World Civilization* (Chicago: University of Chicago Press, 1974), 1:59. The advantage of this term is that it highlights the social and cultural dimensions over the religious. For reasons of variety, I will be using other terms (Arab, East, Orient, Middle East, etc.), even though I recognize the anachronism, limitations, and problems associated with each of these words. The same limitations apply to my use of the terms "West," "medieval France," or "medieval Europe."

3. Steven Kruger, "Conversion and Medieval Sexual, Religious, and Racial Categories," in Karma Lochrie, Peggy McCracken, and James A. Schultz, eds., *Constructing Medieval Sexuality* (Minneapolis: Minnesota University Press, 1997), 159.

4. D. Fisher and L. Schehr, eds., *Articulations of Difference: Gender Studies and Writing in French* (Stanford: Stanford University Press, 1997). See also Martine Antle and Dominique Fisher, eds., *The Rhetoric of the Other: Lesbian and Gay Strategies of Resistance in French and Francophone Contexts* (New Orleans: University Press of the South, 2002).

5. Mireille Rosello, "The National-Sexual: From the Fear of Ghettos to the Banalization of Queer Practices," in Fisher and Schehr, *Articulations of Difference*, 246–47.

6. This colonialist move has been aptly analyzed by Chandra Mohanty, in the context of Western feminists' "colonization" of third world women; see her "Under Western Eyes: Feminist Scholarship and Colonial Discourses," in *Feminist Review* 30 (Autumn 1988): 61–88. This paper extends many of Mohanty's conclusions on Western feminist and hegemonic discourses on "third-world women" to the particular case of medieval Arabic lesbianism and its reception by Western scholars.

7. The interconnections between knowledge and power and the political implications of the construction of truth and of disciplines have been analyzed by critics such as Foucault, Said, and Anouar Abdel Malek.

8. On the explicitness of the Arabic tradition, see my "Lesbian Sex and the Military: from the Arabic Tradition to French Literature," in F. Sautman and

P. Sheinghorn, eds., *Same-Sex Love and Desire among Women in the Middle Ages* (New York: Palgrave, 2001), 179–98. Similarly, in this article, I am interested only in explicit descriptions of lesbian sexual behavior, as opposed to what Judith Bennett has dubbed "lesbian-like," that is the proposition to study the social history of the lesbian in the Middle Ages by considering the lesbian as a larger category that would include all single women. See Judith Bennett, " 'Lesbian-Like' and the Social History of Lesbianisms," *Journal of the History of Sexuality* 9.1–2 (January–April 2000): 1–24.

9. Michèle Perret, "Travesties et transsexuelles: Yde, Silence, Grisandole, Blanchandine," *Romance Notes* 25.3 (1985): 328.

10. In Christianity, female cross-dressers (saints, real life or fictional characters) were viewed more positively than one might assume because such women thus demonstrated their desire to become men and attain a higher level of being. For a useful overview of cross-dressing, see Vern Bullough's chapter in *Handbook in Medieval Sexuality*, 223–42. For cross-dressing in hagiography, see John Anson, "The Female Transvestite in Early Monasticism," *Viator* 5.1 (1974): 1–32.

11. On cross-dressing in medieval French literature, see Michelle Szkilnik's "The Grammar of the Sexes in Medieval French Romance," in Karen J. Taylor, ed., *Gender Transgressions: Crossing the Normative Barrier in Old French Literature* (New York: Garland, 1998), 61–88. See also Valerie Hotchkiss, *Clothes Make the Man: Female Cross-Dressing in Medieval Europe* (New York: Garland, 1996); and Simon Gaunt, *Gender and Genre in Medieval French Literature* (Cambridge: Cambridge University Press, 1995).

12. Cf. M. C. Lyons, *The Arabic Epic: Heroic and Oral Story-Telling*, 3 vols. (Cambridge: Cambridge University Press, 1995). For an overview of women warriors in the Arabic tradition, see Driss Cherkaoui, *Le Roman de 'Antar: Perspective littéraire et historique* (Paris: Présence Africaine, 2000).

13. This romance is found in one single Turin Manuscript and includes the 5 *chansons* that make up the cycle: *La Chanson d'Esclarmonde, La Chanson de Clariet et Florent, La Chanson d'Yde et Olive, La Chanson de Croissant*, and *La Chanson de Godin*.

14. *The Miracles de Nostre Dame par personnages* is a collection of 40 plays, performed on a yearly basis in Paris from 1339–82 (except in the years of the urban insurrections of 1350s) by the Parisian goldsmiths' guild. They are preserved in only one luxury MS (Paris, BN, fr. 819–820) and have been edited by Gaston Paris and Ulysse Robert (Paris: Firmin et Didot, 1876). *The Miracle de la fille d'un roy* is in volume 7, 2–117.

15. The French prose text of Yde and Olive was translated into English prose in the first half of the sixteenth century by Sir John Bourchier (Lord Berners) and entitled *The Boke of Duke Huon of Burdeux*. This text was reprinted in 1570 and again in 1601; it has been edited by S. L. Lee in 1882–84 (London: N. Trübner), and reissued (New York: Kraus Reprint) in 1975 and 1981. Two additional French texts associate cross-dressing with female same-sex marriage: the mid fourteenth-century story of Blanchandine developed in the epic of *Tristan de Nanteuil*; and the story of Iphis in the fifteenth-century adaptation of Ovid, namely the *Ovide Moralisé*.

16. On the relation between the incest motif and later lesbian episode, see Diane Watt, "Read My Lips: Clippying and Kyssyng in the Early Sixteenth Century," in Livia, Anna, Kira Hall and Ed Finegan, eds., *Queerly Phrased: Language, Gender and Sexuality* (Oxford University Press, 1997), 167–77. On incest in the Middle Ages, see E. Archibald, *Incest and the Medieval Imagination* (Oxford University Press, 2001).

17. Diane Watt, "Behaving Like a Man? Incest, Lesbian Desire, and Gender Play in Yde et Olive," *Comparative Literature* 50.4 (1998): 265–85; Diane Watt, "Read my Lips"; Jacqueline de Weever, "The Lady, the Knight, and the Lover: Androgyny and Integration in La Chanson d'Yde et Olive," *Romanic Review* 81.4 (1991): 371–91; Nancy Vine Durling, "Rewriting Gender: Yde et Olive and Ovidian Myth," *Romance Languages Annual* 1 (1989): 256–62; Robert Clark, "A Heroine's Sexual Itinerary: Incest, Transvestism, and Same-Sex Marriage in Yde et Olive," in Karen J. Taylor, ed., *Gender Transgressions: Crossing the Normative Barrier in Old French Literature* (New York: Garland, 199), 889–905.

18. Marjorie Garber, *Vested Interests: Cross-Dressing and Cultural Anxiety* (New York: Routledge, 1992), 11.

19. This is the main point of Watt's important article "Behaving Like a Man?" My approach differs however from hers.

20. Garber, *Vested Interests*, 16.

21. Ibid., 32.

22. This is Perret's conclusion as well.

23. Judith Butler writes: "The replication of heterosexual constructs in non-heterosexual frames brings into relief the utterly constructed status of the so-called heterosexual original," in *Gender Trouble* (London: Routledge, 1990), 31.

24. This is Robert's Clark conclusion in "Queer Play: The Cultural Work of Crossdressing in Medieval Drama," *New Literary History* 28.2 (1997): 341. It is also Watt's overall conclusion in cited in both these articles.

25. All citations of the verse epic *Yde and Olive* are from the latest edition of the text, namely Barbara Anne Brewska's unpublished dissertation, "Esclarmonde, Clarisse et Florent, Yde et Olive I, Croissant, Yde et Olive II, Huon et les Geants: Sequel to Huon de Bordeaux" (Ph.D Vanderbilt, 1977). All translations are mine. An earlier edition of this text is that of Max Schweigel, *Esclarmonde, Clarisse et Florent, Yde et Olive: Dreifortsetsungen der chansun von Huon de Bordeaux, nach der einzigen Turiner handschrift* (Marburg: N.G. Elwert, 1889).

26. Watt's reading is more resolutely on the side of reciprocal erotic feelings between Yde and Olive. While I agree with the fact that this text develops female homoeroticism, my reading of the French story, informed by the comparative reading will be presented further, strongly "curtails the subversive possibilities of the story" (Watt, "Read My Lips," 173).

27. Interestingly, none of the critics who have analyzed the Yde and Olive stories address the religious emphasis in the texts.

28. Once again, I am not arguing for the absence of gender transgression in the French texts. Rather, I seek to qualify the *extent* of the transgressive element through cross-cultural research.

29. The deceptive nature of sight has by the thirteenth century become a *topos* in medieval literature. This *topos* was a logical development from the famous opposition between *historia* (sight, truth) and *fabula* (language, lie) developed by Cicero and popularized by Macrobius, Isidore of Seville, Willian of Conches, Bernardus Silvestris, Peter Abelard and Alan of Lille among many others.

30. Trans. by Clark, "Queer Play," 325.

31. Ibid., 326.

32. The normativity of the French miracle play will become more evident once compared both to the French epic and to the Arabic tradition, as I will show further.

33. This observation supports Skzilnik's assertion that earlier medieval texts are more at ease with gender ambiguity and fluidity than later ones.

34. It is important to note however that the verbs "baisier" and "accollee" in Old French literature can occur in nonsexual contexts as well.

35. Watt, "Read My Lips," 169.

36. The fifteenth-century prose version of the Yde and Olive story will be even more explicit of this eroticism, as Watt demonstrated with her comments on the use of the verb "taster" in her. "Behaving Like a Man?" 280.

37. See my "Lesbian Sex and the Military."

38. Contrary to Ysabel, Yde does not reveal her social class.

39. See Watt, "Behaving Like a Man?" 266 and 273.

40. It is important to remember that from the Church Fathers' point of view, transvestism was tolerated only as long as the woman remained cross-dressed and no one knew about the cross-dressing. On this subject, see Bullough's chapter on Cross Dressing in *Handbook of Medieval Sexuality*, 227–31 in particular.

41. De Weever, "The Lady, the Knight, and the Lover," 388.

42. Louis Crompton, "The Myth of Lesbian Impunity: Capital Laws from 1270 to 1791," *Journal of Homosexuality* 6 (1980–81): 11–25.

43. This has been particularly well articulated in Thomas Laqueur's *Making Sex: Body and Gender from the Greeks to Freud* (Boston: Harvard University Press, 1990).

44. Ovid's tale of Iphis and Ianthe (*Metamorphoses*, IX.786–90) spends a great deal of time describing the growth of the penis on Iphis's body. According to Watt, such a description is superfluous in the French epic since Yde's transformation (psychological and grammatical) had been anticipated earlier in the text ("Behaving Like a man?" 281).

45. Watt, "Behaving Like a Man?" 274.

46. Garber, *Vested Interests*, 223; emphasis in original.

47. It is interesting to note nevertheless that despite the effective transsexual transformation and the official triumph of heteronormativity, the name of the hero(ine) remains in the feminine form Yde, and not Ydé, as one might have expected.

48. The double marriage at the end of the play could theoretically at least be considered incestuous. On the relation between incest and female homoeroticism, see Watt, "Behaving Like a Man?"

49. The Arabic sources of *Yde and Olive* have to date never been pointed out. On the classical sources of the text and its relation to Ovid's tale of Iphis and Ianthe, see Nancy Vine Durling's "Rewriting Gender."

50. Sautman, "What Can They Possibly Do Together? Queer Epic Performances in *Tristan de Nanteuil*," in Sautman and Sheinghorn, *Same-Sex Love and Desire*, 209.

51. Although *Yde and Olive* is written in a Picard dialect (with some East Frankish and Walloon forms), thus associated with the North and the *Arabian Nights* would have entered France through the South (Spain or Italy), one can still speak of cultural encounters. There is indeed a growing body of evidence that documents commercial and religious links between Northern France and the Mediterranean since at least 1087. Michel Rouche, "L'Age des pirates et des saints (Ve-Xie siècles)," in A. Lottin, ed., *Histoire de Boulogne-sur-mer* (Lille: Presses Universitaires de Lille, 1983), 48.

52. Sautman points out that the name of Croissant appears "under another guise" in the contemporary *Baudoin de Sebourc*; unfortunately she does not specify how (226, n. 43).

53. This tale is one of the longest in the entire *Arabian Nights* cycle, covering 66 nights (from 170th to 236th) and also one of the eleven stories that made up the original nucleus of the tales. My research suggests that it would have circulated in medieval France either as an oral tradition, or in a written version that is lost today. See also the important parallels between this tale and Jean Renart's *Escoufle* which I discuss in a forthcoming work.

54. Ibn Nasr al-Katib, *The Encyclopedia of Pleasure*, ed. and trans. Khawam (Aleppo Publishing, 1977), 192. A modern Arabic edition of this text has been done by Khaled Atiyya in a series entitled "Arabic Literary History of Sexuality," with the publisher's name and date of publication (purposely?) blackened out; the entire text is printed on paper overlaid with prints of large red trees, making the reading challenging, possibly in order to evade easy recognition of the subject matter and censorship. The chapter on lesbianism is absent from the Arabic edition.

55. The choice of using an Arabic name in the context of the Christian West that we find in the epic *Yde et Olive* has a real life parallel: Let us not forget that Abelard and Heloise's son was named Astrolabe.

56. This character was nicknamed al-Zarqa' and would have lived in the pre-Islamicate era (*Encyclopedia of Pleasure*, 86, n. 100).

57. References to *The Story of Kamar al-Zaman and the Princess Boudour* come from Muhsin Mahdi's Arabic edition entitled *Kitab alf layla wa layla* [The Book of alf layla wa layla], 4 vols. (Leiden: Brill, 1984), 1:591. Mahdi's edition has been translated by Husain Haddawy, *The Arabian Nights*, 2 vols. (New York: Norton, 1995). However, Haddawy did not translate *The Story of Kamar al-Zaman and the Princess Boudour* as it appeared in Mahdi, but combined it with material from two key nineteenth-century printed editions, Calcutta II (1839–42) and Bulaq (1835). For this reason, I am providing my own translations of Mahdi's Arabic text.

58. Mahdi, *Kitab alf layla wa layla*, 592.

59. I am using the term "redactor" when speaking about the "authorship" of the *Arabian Nights* for reasons of convenience, as outlined by Andras Hamori, "A Comic Romance from the Thousand and One Nights: The Tale of Two Viziers," *Arabica* 30, no. 1 (1983): 38n1. The term "redactor" has been further developed by David Pinault who writes: "each redactor will doubtless have

benefited from the creativity of oral reciters who transmitted and embellished the given tale before it was committed to writing. . . . The term redactor indicates that person who stands at the end of this chain of oral and textual transmission, that person responsible for the shape in which the story reaches us in its final written form in a given manuscript or printed text." See his *Story-Telling Techniques in the Arabian Nights* (Leiden: Brill, 1992), 16.

60. Garber, "Chic of Araby," 229.

61. On oral performance as a privileged moment of creation, see Albert B. Lord, *The Singer of Tales* (Cambridge: Harvard University Press, 2000). While Lord focuses on Homer, his theoretical framework is helpful in understanding the complexity of the *Arabian Nights*, its oral existence in the Middle Ages, about which we have limited knowledge, and its written record.

62. Although Mardrus claims to have translated the Bulaq (1835) and Calcutta II (1839–42) editions of *Alf layla wa layla*, a close reading of his text and a comparison of his translation with both the Bulaq and the Calcutta II editions reveals that he added many details and scenes absent from these earlier renditions.

63. Ibn Nasr, *Encyclopedia of Pleasure*, 261–62.

64. Ibid., 235–36.

65. Judith Butler, *Gender Trouble: Feminism and the Subversion of Identity* (New York: Routledge, 1990), 31.

66. *One Thousand and One Nights*, ed. and trans. into French by Joseph Charles Mardrus; trans. into English by Pomys Mathers (n.p., Yugoslavia: Dorset Press, 1964), 2:67.

67. There is a tendency in contemporary scholarship (both in the East and the West) to consider Mahdi's Arabic edition of *Alf layla wa layla* as the most "authentic" version. However, we must not forget the fact that the manuscript he used is simply the sole surviving one in the Middle Ages and that other renditions of *Alf layla wa layla* most certainly existed, though they left no trace. We must also keep in mind the oral nature of this work which prohibits us from considering any of the surviving texts of the Arabian Nights as "definitive." On the relation between oral performance and the written text, see Lord, *The Singer of Tales*, especially chapter 6.

68. Some may argue that lesbianism is permitted in the Arabic tale precisely because of the cultural practice of the harem. Until today, however, the Western-held association of lesbianism with harem culture, though certainly possible because the harem is an all-female community, has still not been established definitively, and may reflect Western Orientalist fantasies rather than an Oriental reality.

Chapter 6

Reorienting Christian "Amazons": Women Warriors in Medieval Islamic Literature in the Context of the Crusades

Alexandra Cuffel

Introduction

Traditionally, scholars of the Middle Ages have not linked religious conversion with sexual orientation and/or practice. Nevertheless, in the Arabic epic *Sīrat Amīra Dhāt al-Himma*, and related passages from other epics and story collections such as *Alf laila wa laila* (*A Thousand and One Nights*), Christian warrior princesses regularly experience a two-tiered conversion: a religious one from Christianity to Islam, and a sexual one from loving other women to loving men. Islamicists have long recognized that cross-dressing women warriors were an important topos in Arabic literature, particularly in the oral epics, the origins or popularity of which often date from the crusading era.[1] Researchers have indicated in their summaries of these tales that many of these warriors were initially Christians, and the Dutch scholar Remke Kruk has noted that some of these epics contain "mildly lesbian scenes."[2] Yet, while recognizing the existence of these two themes, none have explored the intersection of these women's religion and their sexual orientation and ultimate fate within their historical context. In this article I argue that Christian women warriors in these texts and in more historically oriented chronicles served as important symbolic venues through whom Muslim men expressed their anxieties regarding Christian aggression and influence in the Holy Land. By portraying Christian women warriors as converting to both Islam and heterosexuality, Muslim authors asserted the ultimate and necessary victory of Islam and return to "right order," not only religiously but socially and sexually. In these tales, powerful Christian women who refuse to convert are both physically ugly and doomed to die.[3] The conjunction between Christian women's sexual and religious allure/repugnance and conversion/danger suggests that Muslim authors feared that through these women's desirability, Muslim men could be led astray religiously. Indeed, loss of control in the face of a Christian princess' beauty is a common theme.[4] These women's "incorrect" or incomplete sexuality in the form of lesbian behavior mirrors their "incorrect" or incomplete understanding of God. Just as Christianity was an intermediate step to Islam, so too was same-sex love between women a stage on the way to heterosexual love directed toward the Muslim, male hero.

Dating and the Problem of Epics as Historical/Cultural Sources

Before turning immediately to analyzing these narratives of Christian "amazons," it is necessary to comment about the dating of these texts, their relationship to one another, and attitudes toward women's participation in battle according to both the chronicle and epic literature. Many of the extant Arabic oral epics, such as *Sīrat 'Antar*, predate the coming of Islam, whereas others contain several strata of historical references. *Sīrat Amīra Dhāt al-Himma*, for example, seems to take place during the Umayyad period (661–750 CE) and then from the time of the early conflicts between Byzantium and the Abbasids during the eighth and ninth centuries CE, yet the text also refers to Franks and specific crusading kings.[5] Both early and later epics were extremely popular during the crusades and many were written down sometime between the fourteenth and sixteenth centuries CE, though they continue to be recited orally well into the modern period.[6] In their written form they contain many of the tell-tale repetitions of phrases and themes that characterize oral literature.[7] *'Alf laila wa laila* also possesses several chronological layers and some stories and themes appear in both *'Alf laila wa laila* and some of the epics.[8] In particular, for our purposes, the story of Ibrīza and Sharkān embedded in the tale of King 'Umar al-Nu'man in *'Alf laila wa laila* parallels some of the tales of Christian warrior women who convert for the love of a Muslim, male hero in *Dhāt al-Himma* very strongly, though *'Alf laila wa laila* also contains at least one story that exists in another epic, *Sīrat fāris al-Yaman al-malik Sayf ben Dhī Yazan*.[9]

Because of such multi-layered compositional histories, historians have had to approach these narratives with caution or abandon any effort to link the events described in the epics to actual events.[10] Scholars using Western Christian epic literature dealing with the crusades, such as the *Chanson d' Antioche* or the *Chanson de Jérusalem*, to ascertain the practices as well as the attitudes of the crusaders have faced similar problems.[11] Despite these difficulties, Carole Hillenbrand has argued for the importance of these Arabic epics as tools of popular propaganda against Christians during the crusades, and as windows into nonelite entertainment and Muslim attitudes.[12] Just as epics such as *Sīrat Amīra Dhāt al-Himma, Sīrat 'Antar, Sīrat fāris al-Yaman al-malik Sayf ben Dhī Yazan*, or *Sīrat Ḥamza* need to be seen simultaneously as having early or pre-Islamic origins yet also reflecting Muslim attitudes and tastes regarding jihād and encounters with Christians during the crusades and their aftermath, so too should their presentation of women's activities and sexuality be considered in light of concerns about women's behavior during Ayyubid and Mamluk rule of Egypt and the Levant (1169 CE–1517 CE).

Women, Exhortation, and War in Muslim Historical Chronicles and Epics

According to Muslim chroniclers as well as Arabic epics, both Muslim and Christian women participated in the crusades. Usāmah ibn Munqidh, writing about his experiences battling the Franks during the twelfth century in *Kitāb al-'Itibār*, includes a number of stories about Muslim women's assistance or participation in battling the Christians, and, occasionally, about Christian women's resistance to Muslims.[13] In his account only a few women actually take up arms directly.[14] With the exception of Funūn, an old servant woman of Usamah's father's, Muslim women in *Kitāb al-'Itibār*, who wish to kill Franks or Muslim men who have converted to Christianity or are otherwise aiding the Franks, enlist the aide of male neighbors or family.[15] An anonymous Frankish woman who succeeded in wounding a Muslim male warrior did so with the shard of a jar and was not armed as a soldier.[16] More commonly in *Kitāb al-'Itibār*, Muslim women act as advisors to their male relatives or as goads to battle when the men prove reluctant. For example, when Usāmah's cousin Shabīb sought to flee the oncoming Ismā 'īlis, the mother of one of his other cousins blocks his way, dressed in mail, a helmet, and carrying a sword and shield. Although she frightens him, they do not cross swords. Rather she upbraids him for leaving "your uncle's daughters and the women of your family to ravishers."[17] Thus, the woman's purpose in donning a warrior's garb was not to defend herself or other Muslims, but rather to shame her nephew into protecting her and the other women in his family.

In the epic literature women frequently spur the men around them to follow Islamic law and to go to battle for the sake of Islam or other good causes, much as in *Kitāb al-'Itibār*. For example in *Sīrat Baybars*, an epic praising the deeds of the Mamluk sultan, Baybars I (1223–77 CE), Khawājah 'Alī flees his debtors, only to be chided into facing his problems by his wife.[18] Fāṭima, the heroine of *Sīrat Dhāt al-Himma*, is constantly exhorting or scolding her son, 'Abd al-Wahhāb, and the other male warriors to do what is best for Islam rather than following their own desires, as well as advocating Islam to male and female unbelievers.[19] Yet Fāṭima and the other women of this *Sīrat* do not content themselves with mere advice. Instead, they are seasoned warriors in their own right. For example, in the encounter between Fāṭima and the Christian princess Qannāṣa and their respective (male) armies, Fāṭima embodies both the role of a superb warrior and a goad to men to fight on behalf of the faith:

> The princess Dhāt al-Himma . . . She surpassed in her deeds heavily built men, and she called out to them and attacked them, shouting, "By the religion of Muḥammad the Chosen, I am Fāṭima bint Mazlūm, it is not hidden!" The men followed her and they fought very bravely. They brought evil upon their enemies and prepared for them a terrible punishment.[20]

Fāṭima's warlike behavior serves as an example to the men who follow her, much like Shabīb's aunt in *Kitāb al-'Itibār*, and she guides men with words of encouragement and instruction. In the following pages Qannāṣa acts in a similar fashion as both a warrior and an advisor to her male fighters.[21] Yet here, Fāṭima and Qannāṣa are not only advisors and warriors, they are better fighters than most (if not all) men, a theme that runs throughout the *Sīrat*. Fāṭima's son, 'Abd al-Wahhāb, may be a warrior or even prince for Islam, however, the narrator designates Fāṭima as the "princess, pure fighter of holy wars."[22] Indeed she goes out to battle Qannāṣa for fear that this Christian will defeat 'Abd al-Wahhāb, much as she has done to other Muslim, male warriors. Thus, in this and many other stories in *Sīrat Dhāt al-Himma*, women become the *primary*, and most skillful martial defenders of their faith, rather than simply sources of encouragement, guidance, or even aide for correct male behavior.[23]

In other Muslim chronicles, Christian, rather than Muslim, women put on armor and fight as men, to the point of being indistinguishable from them until the women's clothes are removed.[24] While 'Imad al-Dīn (1125–1201 CE) describes Christian female soldiers in death or a state of defeat, in the account of Ibn Shaddad (1144–1234 CE), a Christian female archer successfully kills many Muslims before being killed herself.[25] Scholars examining the issue of Christian and Muslim women's participation in the crusades have warned about the potential rhetorical reasons for either ignoring their participation, or portraying it in a particular light.[26] Michael Evans has suggested that Christian accounts of women's participation served in part to underscore the humiliation of the Muslims via their manner of death, even as Usāmah ibn Munqidh portrayed Muslim women as trying to shame their menfolk into battle; male readers of the *Kitāb al-'Itibār* who showed similar hesitation would presumably feel likewise dishonored.[27] When describing Christian women dressed in armor and participating in battle, 'Imad al-Dīn adopts a respectful if surprised tone. Nevertheless his description of these Christian women's abandonment of "feminine" behavior and dress comes as part of the culmination of a much longer passage in which Christian women come to "help" the male crusaders by offering themselves as sexual partners as a kind of religious sacrifice. 'Imad al-Dīn denounces this behavior as sinful and even goes so far as to insinuate that the activity was like lizards crawling into the vaginas of prostitutes.[28] As a result, Christian women adopting the role of warriors serves in his text as yet another example of Christians' sexual perversity, a topos that was becoming increasingly widespread in Muslim depictions of Christian behavior during the crusades.[29] As Evans has indicated, Muslim and Christian writers always saw women's donning male attire and participating in war as "unnatural" behavior, even when they praised it.[30]

Warrior Women in the Arabic Epics

Given this context, how then should we understand the Arabic literary tradition of the cross-dressing Muslim and Christian women warriors? How should their sexuality, when it arises, be interpreted? *Sīrat Dhāt al-Himma* contains no hint that the author/compiler viewed women's martial activity or cross-dressing as inappropriate, no matter their faith. Rather, women are praised for their prowess. Other epics are more ambiguous or downright negative. There are many powerful women in *Sīrat Sayf ben Dhī Yazan*, however, as Kruk has indicated, the female army of the woman, Munyat al-Hudā, poses no serious threat to Sayf and his men. Instead, these women must put away their magical wings and become the dutiful spouses of Sayf's male followers.[31] Later, however, these women accompany their husbands and Sayf ibn Dhī Yazan on their next adventure, so their power is not entirely undermined.[32] Thus, in *Sīrat Sayf ibn Dhī Yazan*, women may maintain some of their abilities, but ultimately in the service of the male hero and his followers. In *Alf laila wa laila* neither Ibrīza nor her maidens' ability in wrestling nor beating Sharkān in chess prompt anything but praise and admiration.[33] However, she is not able to defend herself against King Umar al-Nu'mān, nor is she able to rally herself after the rape.[34] In this way Ibrīza is more like some of the women in *Sīrat Ḥamza* who sometimes lose or abandon their role as warriors upon marriage.[35] Such waning of women's power upon marriage is alien to *Sīrat Dhāt al-Himma*, as is the negative attitude toward women's martial activity that is expressed in *Sīrat Ḥamza*.[36] In *Sīrat Dhāt al-Himma*, Fāṭima herself is drugged and raped when she refuses her cousin's suit.[37] Though she has a child by this union, 'Abd al-Wahhāb, these events occur early in her life when she is just beginning to establish her military reputation; neither events discourage her from battle or make her submissive.[38]

Nevertheless, fighting women is not the same as fighting men, particularly in a mixed-sex battle. Early in the epic, the character Jundaba excuses his actions and turns the men of the princess al-Shamṭa against her by saying: "I did not kill the grey one (al-Shamṭa) except that it disgraced you and you are black and courageous [men] and you serve an old woman."[39] During the encounter with the Princess Qannāṣa, Fāṭima discourages 'Abd al-Wahhāb from battling her:

> My son, I will not let you go to this accursed woman, for if she defeats you it will be the most terrible disgrace, and if you defeat her it will bring you neither honor nor victory. I do not believe that you are safe from her evil or her cunning. Let me go out against her and fight her.[40]

Later on in the tale, Fāṭima addresses Qannāṣa herself: "But I will save him ('Abd al-Wahhāb) from apostasy, or I will protect him with my life and will meet in his place the mistresses of virgins, the owners of veils and necklaces!"[41]

Each of these passages implies that for a man to be led or defeated by a woman is somehow shameful. In the case of al-Shamṭa it is unclear whether the disgrace to her followers (according to Jundaba) derives from the fact that al-Shamṭa is a woman or that she is old, or both. Given that "bad" characters in these epics are often old, female, and ugly, al-Shamṭa's female gender probably worked in conjunction with her advanced age to form the basis of Jundaba's insult and justification.[42] The second passage is more clear; 'Abd al-Wahhāb's potential ignominy from defeat would be that much greater because his opponent was a woman, yet overcoming her would bring none of the acclaim normally derived from defeating an enemy. Fāṭima's mention of "veils and necklaces" of Qannāṣa and her followers emphasizes their feminine gender and points to this as the source of 'Abd al-Wahhāb's prospective shame. Despite the implied dishonor to men of female leadership or defeat in these passages, however, Fāṭima's comments about 'Abd al-Wahhāb "not being safe" from Qannāṣa and promises that she will "protect him with my life" also strongly suggest that Fāṭima offers herself as a replacement for her son because she fears he will be incapable of defeating the woman, whereas Fāṭima will stand a better chance against Qannāṣa. Thus, while *Sīrat Dhāt al-Himma* may retain hints of the derogatory associations with female warriors present in some of the other epics and related literature, they remain just that: hints. Even when emphasizing their feminine gender, in this text, Muslim and Christian "amazons" retain their cunning and martial power over and above that of their men.

Sexual Renunciation/Religious Perfection Versus Sexual/Religious Reorientation: Fāṭima and the Christian Princesses

So far in my discussion, there seems to be little difference between Christian and Muslim warrior women, especially in *Sīrat Dhāt al-Himma*. Attitudes toward women's involvement in battle vary from text to text, and sometimes authors of historical chronicles linked female cross-dressing and martial activity with Christianity as a form of religious criticism. In *Sīrat Dhāt al-Himma* what distinguishes the Muslim heroine, Fāṭima, from the Christian warrior women who eventually become Muslims, is her reason for scorning sexual contact with men. She repeatedly insists that she has no desire for any husband "except her sword."[43] Apart from being raped once by her husband, Ḥārith (the marriage was forced on her by the caliph), she does not engage in or desire any sexual activity throughout the rest of the epic. When encouraged to kill her infant son who is black because Ḥārith raped her and caused her to conceive their child while she was menstruating, she refuses, explaining:

There is no power and no strength save in the high, great God, beautiful whose image has indeed filled in darkness, and I am not afraid of the truth, and I am not alarmed and I do not kill my pure soul [resulting from] a valid

> marriage, a lenient contract, contracted by the Caliph of God, al-Mansur. . . .
> I am a woman who has occupied herself with something other than the
> world's enchantments, and I do not need anything in marriage or the like and
> that which I desire is the face of God most High.[44]

For Fāṭima, love of God and desire to do battle in his service leave no room for interest in men. Her extended description of God's qualities emphasizes her love and reverence for him, even as her insistence that she is uninterested not only in marriage, but in *anything* worldly signal her utter dedication to God. Her refusal to kill her son as described in the passage above is not based on motherly love, but on her piety and obedience to Islamic law; the child is the result of a marriage legal according to Islam and commanded by the spiritual, human head of Islam, the caliph. Fāṭima is, therefore, the consummate Muslim and *mujāhidah*, (female) jihād fighter, far more so than any male *mujāhid* in the epic, encumbered as they are by their passion for beautiful, often Christian women, personal jealousies, and political rivalries, not all of which serve the interests of Islam.

Christian women in *Sīrat Dhāt al-Himma* and related literature resemble Fāṭima in their abilities as warriors, their intelligence, and, often, their political power, beauty, external dedication to God, and disinterest in men. Nearly all the major and many of the minor Christian female characters in *Sīrat Dhāt al-Himma* are daughters of a king or queens in their own right and many belong to or are associated with a monastery. Al-Baṭṭāl finds Nūrā, one of the most powerful and troublesome of the Christian princesses, wrestling with her female companions in a monastery.[45] Zanānīr, another Christian princess, does not belong to a monastery herself, but she and her mother are introduced into the story while visiting Zanānīr's sister Ṣalbān, who does.[46] Both Ṣalbān and Zanānīr eventually marry Muslim men and are converted, although Ṣalbān is a fairly minor character.[47] Princess Alūf, like Nūrā, is found wrestling with her female companions and in the parallel story of Ibrīza in *'Alf laila wa laila* Ibrīza and her maidens are part of a monastery. In *Sīrat Dhāt al-Himma* Alūf and her ladies return with the Muslim male hero, Ṣaḥsāḥ, to Alūf's castle rather than a monastery, however the women's religious affiliation is emphasized by the crosses that they wear around their necks.[48] Even those Christian princesses who are not officially connected to a religious institution express strong devotion to their faith. For example, Iftuna not only does battle with Fāṭima, she goes to Fāṭima who is her prisoner to "preach the unity of God."[49] Association with a monastery, battles with the Muslims or the instigations of religious debates mark these women as representatives of Christianity, much as the numerous proclamations of Fāṭima's devotion to God and her status as a *mujāhidah* in *Sīrat Dhāt al-Himma* underscore her role as defender of Islam.

Also like Fāṭima these Christian princesses do not desire men. The focus of their love is not God, however, as in the case of Fāṭima, but other women. Of Nūrā, the narrator states, "And this princess loved women and hated men."[50] The text is more specific about Zanānīr. At one point she proclaims: "However, by the truth of the Messiah, I have no longing for men and my heart desires [none] except the ladies."[51] Alūf likewise rejects men and marriage in favor of women.[52] Later on we learn that Zanānīr had a particular female partner, Nahār:

And she (Zanānīr) had a servant girl, [s]he spoke to her, to Nahār, and Zanānīr would not drink with anyone except with her . . . [at] night she called the servant girl to her and they remained drinking, taking pleasure in and delighting [one another].[53]

Zanānīr's invocation of the Messiah emphasizes her Christianity. The juxtaposition of this invocation, however, to her statement of sexual preference implies a relationship between the two, or, at least, suggests that Zanānīr does not see her preference as inimical to her faith. Muslim men's discovery of these women and their female companions in a monastic context further strengthens the link between these women's choice of sexual partners and their religion. Indeed, Nūrā is described as loving women (as opposed to men) and loving her monastery within a single sentence.[54] In part, *Sīrat Amīra Dhāt al-Himma* and other texts' connection between Christianity and same-sex love between women needs to be seen as an extension of Muslim polemic targeting Christian sexual behavior as improper and a parody of Christian monastic vows of celibacy.[55] By contrast, Fāṭima is the perfect fulfillment of the ideal of sexual renunciation for the sake of religion since she desires God more than women or men.[56] She is also the better warrior on behalf of her faith, for often she and she alone can defeat these Christian women in battle.

Once the Christian warrior princesses convert, however, they are usually extremely devoted to their new religion, so much so that they threaten or kill their own families if their parents, siblings, or followers refuse to become Muslim.[57] For some both marriage to a Muslim man and conversion to his religion are linked through prophetic dreams, religious vows, or simply hearing the Qur'an recited by the man, as in the case of Zanānīr, daughter of Daghmus, who falls in love with al-Baṭṭāl's servant Safiy when she hears him reciting the Qur'an. Safiy promises to marry her if she will convert and assist the Muslims.[58] The other, more prominent Zanānīr of the story who eventually marries the Muslim hero Lu'lu', explains to her suitors and father, King Salbut, that the Messiah told her to marry the man who alone could outwrestle her or defeat her in battle.[59] Such instances suggest that both the heterosexual relationship with a Muslim man and conversion to Islam are predestined or at least guided by God.[60] These instances in combination with the strong religious imagery and actions surrounding the Christian "lesbian" princesses both before and after their change of partners and religion point to sexual and religious orientation being inextricably intertwined in *Sīrat Dhāt al-Himma* and related literature.

Voracious "Heterosexuals" and Ugly "Lesbians": Sexual Markings of the Unconvertable

Despite the tie between other forms of Muslim anti-Christian sexual polemic and tales of Christian "lesbians" in *Sīrat Dhāt al-Himma* and *'Alf laila wa laila*, these texts are usually very neutral in their descriptions of this behavior. The only clear condemnations appear in *'Alf laila wa laila*:

> The greatest of her (Dhāt al-Duwāhā's) meetings was at her son's Ḥardub, King of Rome on account the virginal slave girls, for she loved to have sex with them although she would delay her, she was in annihilation. And every slave girl pleased her; she would teach her wisdom and would press saffron upon her and cause her to swoon from an excess of sensual delight for some time. Toward whoever submitted to her she was charitable and she would take her child under her wing with (literally: "in") her. And whoever did not submit to her she would devise artful stratagems for her destruction. And in that situation she knew of Marjānah and Rīḥānah and the maidens of Ibrīzah trembled. And the princess Ibrīzah loathed the old woman and loathed that she slept with her because her body was coarser than a palm fiber brush and she was desiring sex with her with tyranny and instruction and Ibrīzah was becoming free from her toward wisdom and knowledge.[61]

The graphic descriptions of sexual activity coupled with indications that Dhāt al-Duwāhā's attentions were sometimes forced upon the young women and that Ibrīzah abhorred physical encounters with her, all suggest a negative attitude toward same-sex love between women on the part of the author. Yet as with the story of the warrior princess al-Shamṭa, several factors are at work here. Like al-Shamṭa, Dhāt al-Duwāhā is old, and more importantly she is an unrepentant enemy of Islam and therefore "unconvertible."

"Unconvertible" Christian women, such as Dhāt al-Duwāhā, stand in the strongest contrast to Fāṭima. In *Sīrat Dhāt al-Himma*, Bakhṭūs, the Christian queen of Georgia, is a fierce warrior, but she is also old and ugly.

Her sexual and gastronomical appetites—she has multiple male partners whom she kills if they fail to satisfy her sexually, and she eats a pig for breakfast and dinner—would have made her repugnant to Muslim readers or hearers of the epic since in Islam her libidinous conduct would be seen as promiscuous and highly inappropriate for a woman, and the pig is an unclean animal according to Muslim dietary law.[62] Her choice of multiple and frequent sexual partners likewise goes against Christian law and therefore implies a level of hypocrisy or impiety on the part of the Christians since she is one of their main political leaders. Bakhṭūs more than any of the other Christian female characters in *Sīrat Dhāt al-Himma* fits the stereotype of Christians, especially Christian women, indulging in sexual excess or improprieties common in Muslim writing. However, other "unconvertible" Christian women are made equally unappealing. Shuma, wife of Shumdaris, one of the arch enemies of Islam, has teeth like boar's tusks, suggesting that she is both ugly and unclean because of her similarity to a pig.[63] Dhāt al-Duwāhā, who, unlike the lovely Ibrīza, not only remains Christian but wreaks immense amounts of trouble for the Muslims in her roles as trickster and army advisor in *'Alf laila wa laila*, is depicted as ugly and animallike: "The hair on her torso stood up like the hair of a hedgehog. . . . she was like a hairless demon or a speckled snake."[64] This description contrasts sharply with the lush portrayal of the more physically and (as the story shows later) religiously desirable Ibrīza, whose body is likened to marble, crystal, and milk.[65] Dhāt al-Duwāhā is not even a very good warrior since Ibrīza beats her in a wrestling match, though ultimately Dhāt al-Duwāhā proves the more formidable and long-lived of the two. Thus, I would suggest that the negative depiction of Dhāt al-Duwāhā's sexual behavior and orientation, like her ugliness, serves to symbolize her status as a dangerous enemy of Islam as much or more than it reflects the author's disapproval of sexual relations between women. Unlike Ibrīzah and the other young Christian "lesbians" in *Sīrat Dhāt al-Himma*, Dhāt al-Duwāhā is portrayed as actively leading or bullying women into such sexual behavior, rather than it arising naturally out of lack of a "suitable" alternative. In this way she is more like Bakhṭūs, who sought out and coerced inappropriate sexual partners.

Ugliness and similarity to or association with despised animals such as pigs, snakes, or lizards is, therefore, a frequent indicator of unremitting feminine evil in these epic texts and even Muslim chronicles such as that of 'Imad al-Dīn. Feminine beauty like that of Ibrīza's, points to eventual, although not immediate, "goodness" in the form of acceptance of Islam.[66] One exception to this trend is the character of Maimuna in *Sīrat Dhāt al-Himma*. She is a rather ambiguous figure, for she, like many of the other Christian princesses in the *Sīrat* convert to Islam for the love of a Muslim male warrior, fights valiantly on the side of Islam after her conversion, yet, unlike other women in the epic, she reconverts to Christianity and becomes a major opponent of the Muslims. She, like many of her fellow princesses, states that she has no desire for men.[67] Later in the tale: "And God placed in her heart (Maimuna's) a strong, great love of the Amīra (Fāṭima) and she was in awe of her deed and the beauty of her fighting.[68] Such a comment could be a hint that Fāṭima, rather than 'Abd al-Wahhāb, had become the focus of Maimuna's desires, even as Maimuna's remark that she had no passion for men suggests that she preferred female sexual partners. However, the first remark was made to discourage the courtship of an unwanted male suitor, 'Anqush, who soon discovers that she loves an Arab man, 'Abd al-Wahhāb, and the second remark is immediately followed by her request that she be married to 'Abd al-Wahhāb. Thus, any allusions to a "lesbian" orientation are immediately countered by references to her ardor for 'Abd al-Wahhāb, a man. Indeed while other Christian princesses admire or even love Muslim men while they are still Christians, none pursue the object of their desire with Maimuna's degree of persistence. Maimuna does so even in the face of 'Abd al-Wahhāb's initial rejection.[69] Other Christian women occasionally assist the Muslim men who interest them, but remain difficult to attain as wives and converts.[70]

Maimuna is then more like the Georgian queen, Bakhṭūs, whose heterosexual desires are excessive and aggressive. That Maimuna is led by her passions, both maternal and especially sexual, is further revealed by her decision to abandon Islam first out loyalty to her Christian son, then out of passion for the Byzantine emperor, whom she later abandons in favor of another Christian man with greater skill as a warrior.[71] These choices reveal Maimuna as Fāṭima's opposite: where Fāṭima desires no marriage and no sexual intimacy of any kind, Maimuna has three husbands and does not even bother to divorce those she has before her passions drive her to the next one; Fāṭima's behavior toward her son is governed by Islamic law, whereas Maimuna is quick to join the Christian side on behalf of her son, even after he expresses mild interest in converting to Islam; Fāṭima serves as a spiritual and military leader of her people—even more than the caliph at times—in contrast to Maimuna who constantly shifts her religious loyalties. Ultimately, only one can defeat the other, and Fāṭima kills Maimuna in a battle that not only demonstrates Fāṭima's superiority as a warrior, but her greater spiritual knowledge as a receiver and interpreter of prophetic dreams.[72] Maimuna even compares poorly with other Christian princesses, for while she, like they, is willing to kill her father for the sake of her Muslim hero, she does so because her father thwarted her efforts to be united with 'Abd al-Wahhāb, not because her father would not convert to Islam.[73] While she may not be as grotesque as Bakhṭūs, Maimuna's pursuit of multiple male partners places her well within the common Muslim stereotypes of Christian women during the crusading period as licentious and sexually perverse. Her (hetero-) sexual promiscuity mirrors her religious promiscuity, however. Indeed, as with the "convertible" Christian princesses sexual choices symbolize religious ones and vice versa.

To Muslim hearers and readers, Maimuna's choice of multiple husbands would have made her far more repugnant than the other Christian women in the tale who, before their conversion to Islam, took pleasure in female partners. For at least some Muslim men, sexual intimacy between women was an acceptable and even laudatory precursor to or substitute for penetrative sex with a husband.[74] While, as Fedwa Malti-Douglas notes, in male-authored erotic texts, such as the thirteenth-century writer, Aḥmad al-Tīfāshī's *Nuzhat al-Albāb fīmā lā Yūjad fī Kitāb*, positive descriptions of sexual relations between women are placed lower in a hierarchical scale than those involving a penis, nevertheless the former are acceptable to certain men and served as preparation for heterosexual intercourse.[75] Aḥmad ibn Muḥummad Jurjānī, writing a couple of centuries earlier, created a similar hierarchy between women's same-sex love and heterosexual intercourse, though his own view of the subject is more difficult to ascertain.[76] Even in instances where the man is condemning women for having relations with one another, seeing them do so arouses him, suggesting that Muslim men did not find such acts repulsive, even when they felt obliged to censure them religiously.[77] For Muslim hearers/readers of *Sīrat Dhāt al-Himma* who shared al-Tīfāshī's outlook, the Christian princesses' sexual explorations with other women would served simultaneously to titillate male (and female) audience members and to mark these Christian women as sexually "unspoiled" yet "prepared" for male intercourse. This sexual state symbolizes their religious one: desirable, pure, and ready for conversion in contrast to women such as Maimuna or Bakhṭūs who have the "wrong" kind of sexual/religious relationship with men, or Dhāt al-Duwāhā who actively pushes other women into a "lesbian" relationship, even as she pushes the Christian armies and king against Islam.

Manly Women and the Apocalypse

Apocalyptic texts both from the Umayyad and Abbasid period and from the thirteenth to the sixteenth centuries of the common era—the same periods during which the early strata of *Sīrat Dhāt al-Himma* were being composed and becoming popular—provide a drastically different attitude toward same-sex love between women, and women's leadership. Women are also depicted in secular and religious roles normally reserved for men, something the apocalyptic authors feared greatly.[78] For example, the tenth-century Shi'i author Ibn Bābūwayh characterized the apocalyptic time as when "Women partnered their husbands in trade, focused on this world . . . the owners of vulvas rode upon the saddle, the woman resembled the man and the man the woman."[79] His approximate contemporary, al-Munādī made similar remarks, adding that women mounted the *minbar*, a place of public, religious authority.[80] Al-Kulaynī, also from this period, was more explicit in his concerns about improper sexual conduct, including cross-dressing and same-sex love, than these others:

> I saw sinfulness appear, and men were satisfied with men and women with women. . . . And I saw the boy offer what a woman offers and I saw women marrying women. . . . And I saw men fatten themselves for men and women for women, and I saw the man living from his buttocks and the woman living from her pudendum, I saw women entering the council like the men enter it . . . and I saw the man eat from the earnings [that] his wife [gained] from her whoredom . . . and I saw the woman subjugate her husband.[81]

Sixteenth-century authors, such as al-Muttaqi and al-Suyūtī, echoed similar concerns about the sexual behaviors which they felt foreshadowed the apocalypse. Al-Muttaqi lamented:

> And the man obeyed the woman . . . and men satisfied themselves with men and women with women . . . then from it (the last hour) a man shall marry a woman or his mother in her buttocks, and that is from what God and his Apostle forbade, and God and his Apostle detest it. And from it (the last hour) the man shall marry the man, and that is from what God and his Apostle forbade, and from it (the last hour) the woman shall marry the woman and that is from what God and his Apostle forbade and God and his Apostle detest it.[82]

In both of these passages anal intercourse, same-sex love on the part of both women and men, and sexual promiscuity in general are outlined as dangerous signs of God's immanent judgment. Added to women's sexual misbehavior is their acceptance of leadership roles, whether those consisted simply of taking an equal or leading role in business with her husband, mounting the pulpit and, presumably, preaching from it, or joining governmental councils. While all of these authors vociferously condemn same-sex love between women (and men) and women's equality or resemblance to men in appearance and behavior, the fact that they had to do so points to the commonality and acceptance of these practices by certain segments of or possibly the majority of the population as well as indicating other members' rejection of it.[83] I suggest that these apocalypses and the more positive portrayals of women engaging in "masculine" roles, loving other women, and cross-dressing in texts like *Sīrat Dhāt al-Himma* need to be seen in dialogue with one another, reflecting potentially contradictory or conflicting attitudes within the society.

Sex, War, and Conversion

These apocalyptic authors would have certainly disapproved of many of the behaviors and ideals espoused in *Sīrat Dhāt al-Himma* if for no other reason than Fāṭima commands the men around her. For these individuals, women rulers, warriors, or "lesbians" all served as signs of the disintegration of the proper, divine world order. These authors, and even those men who saw same-sex love between women as a harmless prelude or "training ground" for sex with a man, would have understood the Christian women's "conversion" to heterosexuality as an acceptance of the appropriate, "better" sexual order, even as most Muslims would have regarded Christian conversion to Islam as moving from an imperfect understanding of God to the true one.[84] Furthermore by depicting these Christian women as beautiful and powerful and allowing the women to *retain* their loveliness and martial and intellectual prowess after conversion, the authors/compilers of *Sīrat Dhāt al-Himma* portray the Muslims as successfully co-opting the very best of the Christian world for their own.[85] Muslim men have taken the most beautiful and puissant women away from the Christian side and sexually possessed them, while the Muslim army, the martial *jihād*, has gained the most fearsome warriors that the Christians could produce and turned them against the Byzantines. Other Arabic epics likewise portray the Muslim hero as conquering the hearts and kingdoms of their female opponents, however, as we have seen, these epics often require that the women become far more "tamed" than in *Sīrat Dhāt al-Himma*. As a result, the heroes lose the full benefit of these women's skills. Nevertheless, allowing the women to retain equal or greater power than the men around them also underscored the level of threat that these women and the religion they represented posed to Muslims.

In *Sīrat Dhāt al-Himma* and other epics, this link between military activity and sexual and religious orientation reflects both fear on the part of Muslims that their fellows would be lured to Christianity either for its own merits or for love of a woman, and the increasing equation between sex and war in medieval Arabic and European literature. Sahar Amer has demonstrated that in both medieval Arabic and French literature describing same-sex love, the language of sexual encounter is that of military battle. Lesbian sex is "hitting one shield against another," in contrast to using a "lance."[86] Not only was military imagery applied to sex, actual military activity was deeply sexualized. Muslim chroniclers of the crusades were especially fearful of Christians raping Muslim women.[87] Chroniclers extended the language of sexual violation of women to Jerusalem and its holy places, making the two equivalent. For example Ibn Taghribirdi, a fifteenth-century Muslim historian, quoted a poem in which the stealing (*salīb*) of women's virtue is equated with the Christians' primary religious symbol and their treatment of Muslims' holy places and objects by virtue of the similarity between the word *salīb* (plunder) and *ṣalīb* (cross); the two words differ only in the kind of "s" used:

> The sword is cutting and blood is spilt / How many Muslim men have become booty (*salīb*)/ And how many Muslim women's inviolability has been plundered (*salīb*)? / How many a mosque have they made into a church! / The cross (*ṣalīb*) has been set up in the *miḥrāb*. / The blood of the pig is suitable for it. / Qur'ans have been burned under the guise of incense.[88]

Christians likewise feared Muslim "rape" of Christian women and holy spaces and regularly depicted the Prophet Muḥammad as forcibly marrying the women of the peoples he conquered.[89] In all of these texts to have sex with someone was to conquer them and vice versa.

In the Arabic epics sex and war are intertwined in a number of ways. Wrestling, a kind of battle, signals sexual relations both between women, and between women and men. Princesses' sexual and religious conversions often begin with the Muslim male hero interrupting the young warrior woman as she engages in such mock battles with her female companions, or with simply a challenge to wrestle. Imbedded within these passages are comments about the warrior woman's sexual preference for other women; something that her match with the Muslim male hero is about to change.[90] Yet these "battles" have very real political consequences since the conversion of the princess also means aid and power for the Muslims. Thus, within a single moment the Christian woman and Muslim man "war" for gender, sexual, and political dominance. Often the woman's willingness to accept a suitor is contingent upon his ability to overcome her in these skirmishes; sexual access depends explicitly on military mastery. By implication gaining sexual access would likewise signify martial and political control. It is in this context that we should understand rape in *Sīrat Dhāt al-Himma*, a subject to which I will return.

Given these connections between sexual, religious, and political victory, Muslim men's frequent failure to win against these Christian women, at least initially, indicate a profound level of insecurity about Muslim men's success on all of these fronts in the face of their Christian opponents. While the composers of *Sīrat Dhāt al-Himma* were far more positive in their attitude toward female leadership than the authors of many contemporary apocalyptic texts, nevertheless, both sets of texts reflect the fear that the "right order" of scxual, religious, and political preference and dominance were in immanent danger of being overturned, if they had not been already. More specifically these texts point to Muslims' fear of being influenced or conquered by the Christians. In *Sīrat Dhāt al-Himma* apprehension about Christian influence or conquest is embodied by tales of Muslim men's actual or near conversion to Christianity under the influence of Christian "amazons."

One of the clues that conquest in combination with fear of conversion to Christianity are driving forces in *Sīrat Dhāt al-Himma* is that the Christian women convert to Islam at all. According to Islamic law, Muslim men were free to marry Jewish and Christian women, since both were "people of the book," although Muslim women were prohibited from marrying non-Muslims.[91] Christian women who had been captured in the course of resisting Islam were legal sexual partners either as slaves or wives, though ideally a Muslim man should not marry a Christian or Jewish slave woman.[92] Nevertheless, in *Sīrat Dhāt al-Himma*, the women are pushed toward conversion to Islam, even if during the early portion of their capture by the Muslims they are put up for auction or treated as slaves.[93] Beautiful Christian women who remain unconverted pose a temptation to Muslim men, as in the case of Abu Yukhlif who converts because the Christian princess Shamsa laughs at him and promises to marry him to one of her maidens if he will convert to Christianity. Later, when both are captured by the Muslim hero al-Baṭṭāl, she merely has to remove her clothing in front of him and Abu Yukhlif continues to aid the Christians against his former co-religionists, the Muslims.[94] Nūrā has a similar effect on the Muslim men who see her.[95] Saḥsāḥ, the suitor of the Christian princess Alūf, looses to her at wrestling and chess because he is dazzled by her beauty, and he forgets the difference between right and wrong. He is left to lament that he was tempted to stray from Islam, though in the end Alūf converts rather than he.[96] Lu'lu, the Muslim warrior who falls in love with the Christian princess Zanānīr, does not convert, but his friends fear that he might for Zanānīr's sake, and indeed he is the target of several attempts.[97]

Even more telling than these examples is one discussed earlier, namely the encounter between Fāṭima and Qannāsa. One of Fāṭima's primary motivations for battling Qannāsa instead of allowing 'Abd al-Wahhāb to do so was her fear that he might apostacize.[98] Calling Qannāsa the "owner of veils and necklaces" emphasized her femininity, however, the word "*maqān'a*," which Kruk translates as "veils," carries the potential of threat as well, since its root "*q-n-'a*" is also the root for "weapon." Thus Qannāṣa's weapon *is* her femininity, or at least one of her weapons, and therein lies the greatest threat to Muslim men and their faith. One of the reasons that Fāṭima is the best warrior in the epic is that she and only she, as a woman and as one completely uninterested in sex, can overcome these princesses and their charms. Given how closely sexual and political conquest were tied in medieval literature generally and in *Sīrat Dhāt al-Himma* specifically, however, these tales are not simply about the dangers of individual Muslims being lured by the sexual attractions of Christian women. Overpowering beauty that might cause (male) warriors to willingly join these Christian "amazons" symbolized the allure and martial threat of Christianity overall. The women had to convert willingly and retain their beauty and power because to do anything less would imply that Islam was inferior to Christianity. This drama is played out, however, in the language of sex and sexual orientation.

Interpreting Rape and Conversion

Not all Christian women in *Sīrat Dhāt al-Himma* underwent this "reorientation" willingly. Two women, Ṣalbān the nun, who is Zanānīr's sister, and Nūrā are captured and eventually raped by the Muslim men who have fallen in love with them. In the case of Ṣalbān, one Abu l-Hazahiz ties her up so that Sabk may "deflower" her. This experience prompts her to fall in love with Sabk and convert to Islam.[99] Al-Baṭṭāl, the trickster-hero of the epic and companion to 'Abd al-Wahhāb, attempts to rape or trick Nūrā into having sexual relations with him on several occasions and she beats him soundly each time until he fears to try to have intercourse with her, even once she has been forcibly married to him.[100] Only once Fāṭima intervenes, overcomes Nūrā one last time and ties her up, is al-Baṭṭāl able to "deflower" her. At that point Nūrā's "hate turns to love."[101]

In both instances the Muslim man has or requires assistance to be able to have sex with the Christian virgin. This need for aid underscores these women's physical power and potential danger to the men. Yet here as elsewhere in *Sīrat Dhāt al-Himma*, sex is not simply sex. Both women originally belonged to a monastery; Muslim (male) interference brought them out of that context. Of all the Christian warrior princesses Nūrā proffers the strongest resistance, and she is most like the apostate (from the Muslim perspective) Maimuna, for initially Nūrā only recites the confession of faith to allow herself some freedom in her choice of mates and to prevent herself being sold as a slave.[102] Thus Nūrā is simultaneously martially one of, if not the, most powerful of the Christian warriors; is so beautiful that she regularly causes chaos and loss of control among Muslim men; and she is potentially a false convert ready to be set loose within the ranks of Islam. These qualities make her extremely threatening to Muslim world order. Both Christian women, as representatives of their faith, needed to be "conquered." Fāṭima, as opposed to any Muslim man, provides the force necessary to rape/conquer Nūrā because Fāṭima is the most pure *mujāhidah* representing Islam.

These Christian princesses stand in stark contrast to Fāṭima in rape as in sexual orientation and conversion. Fāṭima's own rape was also a joint effort on the part of her husband and a servant.[103] The meaning is the same; she is too powerful to be overcome by a single man and a danger to him who would try. However, unlike the Christian women, she never presents a danger to Islam. More importantly, unlike these Christians, her "hatred" never turns to "love." Forced heterosexual encounter does not engender desire in Fāṭima for her male partner or any other kind of sexual act. Nor does it cause her to ally politically or religiously with those responsible. By depicting Ṣalbān and Nūrā as *enjoying* their rape in contrast to Fāṭima, the compilers/authors of *Sīrat Dhāt al-Himma* undermined the women's symbolic dedication to their own religion in the form of monastic vows, much as did portraying Christian women as sexually dallying with other female companions and then converting out of passion for a Muslim man.

Yet most of the rhetorical or polemical work that the rapes of Ṣalbān and Nūrā do: demonstrating Islam's ability to conquer Christianity and restore "correct" Muslim hierarchy and world order, undercutting these women's dedication to their religion and thus impugning Christianity itself, all of these could have been and usually were done by the regular topos of the Christian warrior woman's willing "reorientation" to a heterosexual relationship and to Islam, leaving the question: why rape? I would suggest that the key lies both in the military significance of intercourse and in the women's pleasure and conversion as a result of their violation. In reality, during the early expansion of Islam and then again during the Crusades, many of those defeated by Muslim forces remained loyal to their religion of origin and hostile to Islam. Ṣalbān and Nūrā's determined resistance to partnering with a Muslim male hero until the bitter end, yet ultimately rejoicing in their experience expressed Muslim hope or expectation that even those who opposed them most fiercely would ultimately recognize the superiority of their conquerors and their faith. Ṣalbān's name is particularly indicative of the symbolic nature of this sexual encounter, for without any distinguishing vowels it is the plural of "cross," indeed throughout this section of the *Sīrat* the Christians are referred to as *'abd al-ṣulbān* "servant of the crosses."[104] Thus, in her capture, rape and conversion, the Muslims are literally penetrating and transforming the cross, that is, Christianity.

Such a paradigm left no room in the hearers or readers' minds that Christianity might hold something to be cherished, or if it did, it could be, in the persons of these beautiful Christian women, absorbed into Islam. The indirect targeting of monasticism through Ṣalbān and Nūrā may reflect medieval Muslims' longstanding admiration and thus insecurity about monasticism or discomfort with the periodic destruction of monasteries during war.[105] In *Sīrat Dhāt al-Himma* passion for the *mujāhid* and what he represents overcomes celibacy and its religious tradition.

Whether sexual encounters are forced, are between two women, or are consensual between a man and a woman, what should be clear by now is that in *Sīrat Dhāt al-Himma* sex is intimately tied with religious conflict and changing identities, and that women's attire, sexuality, and behavior are at the center of the struggle between Christianity and Islam. While scholars have long noted that women's bodies can serve as symbolic sites to express issues of social or religious hierarchies, what makes *Sīrat Dhāt al-Himma* unusual is that women are both the heroes and the villains. Even men such as 'Abd al-Wahhāb and al-Baṭṭāl remain very firmly auxiliaries to the women warriors whom they love and who command and defeat them on a regular basis.

Given the symbolic meaning attached to sexuality in this epic, determining the degree to which the text reflects actual sexual practice, including sexual relations between women, or women's involvement or interest in war in the Islamic world is difficult. Nevertheless *Sīrat Dhāt al-Himma* demonstrates that some Muslims in the Middle Ages clearly *imagined* women adopting such powerful roles, and admired them for doing so. Abundant descriptions of same-sex love between women in other types of literature, such as the manuals by al-Tīfāshī and Jurjānī and the apocalyptic texts, however, strengthen the impression that such behavior went on, and that attitudes toward such relationships were mixed. Attitudes toward women who adopted manly roles, whether in religion or war seem to be equally ambiguous, or rather, polarized. We are left with a complex image of gender relations in the medieval Middle East.

Notes

1. Jean-Claude Garcin, "*Sīra/s* et Histoire," *Arabica*, 51 (2004): 33–53; Remke Kruk, "The Bold and the Beautiful: Women and 'Fitna' in the *Sīrat Dhāt al-Himma*: The Story of Nūra" in Gavin R. G. Hambly, ed., *Women in the Medieval Islamic World* (New York, 1998), 99–116; "Back to the Boudoir, Arabic Versions of the *Sīrat al-amīr Ḥamza*, Warrior Princesses and the *Sīra's* Literary

Unity," *Amsterdamer Beträge zur älteren Germanistik* 48 (1997): 129–48; "Clipped Wings: Medieval Arabic Adaptations of the Amazon Myth," *Harvard Middle Eastern and Islamic Review* 1–2 (1994) 2:132–51; "Warrior Women in Arabic Popular Romance: Qannāṣa bint Muzāḥim and Other Valient Ladies," Part One *Journal of Arabic Literature*, 24 (1993): 213–30; Part Two, *Journal of Arabic Literature* 25 (1994): 16–33; Wiebke Walter, "Das Bild der Frau in "Tausenuneinter Nacht" *Hallesche Beiträge der Orientalistik* 4 (1982): 69–91; M. C. Lyons, *The Arabian Epic: Heroic and Oral Story-Telling*, 3 vols. (Cambridge: Cambridge University Press, 1995), vol. 1. On the dating of these epics also see: "The Crusading Stratum in the Arabic Hero Cycles," in Maya Shatzmiller, ed., *Crusaders and Muslims in Twelfth-Century Syria* (Leiden/New York/Köln: Brill, 1993) 147–61; M. Canard, "Delhemma, épopée arabe des guerres arabo-byzantines," *Byzantion* 10 (1935): 283–300; M. Canard, "Les Expéditions des Arabes contre Constantinople dans l'histoire et dans la légende," *Journal Asiatique* 208 (1926): 61–121; Harry Norris' introduction to *The Adventures of Sayf Ben Dhi Yazan an Arabic Folktale*, trans. and summarized by Lena Jayyusi (Bloomington, IN: Indiana University Press, 1996), ix–xix.
2. Kruk, "Clipped Wings," esp. 142; Kruk, "Warrior Women in Arabic Popular Romance" Part One.
3. Such paired dichotomies in which foreign princesses who are willing to convert are beautiful in contrast to the ugly ones who are unwilling to do so also appear regularly in Christian epics. In these instances, however, it is Muslim princesses and queens who are converting to Christianity. On this subject see: Sharon Kinoshita, "Pagans are Wrong and Christians are Right: Alterity, Gender and Nation in the *Chanson de Roland*," *Journal of Medieval and Early Modern Studies* 31.1 (2001): 79–111; Lynn Tarte Ramey, "Role Models? Saracen Women in Medieval French Epic," *Romance Notes* 2 (2001): 131–41; Lynn Tarte Ramey, *Christian, Saracen and Genre in Medieval French Literature* (New York/London:Routledge, 2001), 35, 46–49; Jacqueline De Weever, *Sheba's Daughters: Whitening and Demonizing the Saracen Woman in Medieval French Epic* (New York/London: Garland Pub., 1998), xix, xxi–xxii, xxvi, 54–75, 96–100, 119.
4. *Sirat Amīra Dhāt al-Himma* (Cairo: al-Maktabah al-Husayniyah al-Misriyah, 1909) I.4.3, 8, 12; II.13.55; Lyons, *Arabian Epic*, 3, paragraphs 9–10 in 311–13, paragraph 47 in 347, paragraphs 54–55 in 354, 356, paragraphs 60–62 in 362–66, paragraph 72 in 376–77, paragraph 75 in 381–82; *Alf Laila wa Laila*, 2 vols. (Cairo: Dar al-Hilal, 1958); *The Book of the Thousand Nights and One Night*, 4 vols., trans. Powys Mathers (New York: St. Martin's Press, 1972); Kruk, "The Bold and the Beautiful."
5. Canard, "Delhemma, epopee arabe"; Canard, "Expéditions des Arabes contre Constantinople"; Kruk, "Back to the Boudoire"; Lyons, "Crusading Stratum"; Garcin, "Sira/s et histoire."
6. Canard, "Delhemma, epopee arabe"; Lyons, "Crusading Stratum"; Kruk, "Back to the Boudoire"; Norris, "Introduction," in *Sayf Ben Dhi Yazan*; Norris, "Western Travellers and Arab Story-Tellers of the Nineteenth Century. The Adventures of Abū Zayd al-Hilālī and al-Zīr al-Sālim as told by Shaykh Abū

Wundī of the 'Awāzim of Jordan," *Quaderni di Studi Arabi* 9 (1991): 183–92; Carole Hillenbrand, *The Crusades: Islamic Perspectives* (Edinburgh: Edinburgh University Press, 1999), 102–03, 230, 263–68, 273; Dwight Reynolds, *Heroic Poetry, Poetic Heroes: The Ethnography of Performance in an Arabic Oral Epic Tradition* (Ithaca: Cornell University Press, 1995).

7. Peter Heath, "Lord and Parry, *Sirat 'Antar*, Lions," *Edebiyat* New Series 2.1 and 2 (1988): 149–66.

8. Canard, "Expéditions des Arabes contre Constantinople"; Walter, "Das Bild der Frau"; V. Christides, "An Arabo-Byzantine Novel, 'Umar b. al-Nu'man compared with Digenes Akritas," *Byzantion: revue internationale des études byzantines*; More generally on this issue see: Robert Irwin, *The Arabian Nights: A Companion* (London/New York: I.B. Tauris, 2004): 1–8, 42–62.

9. Kruk, "Clipped Wings"; Irwin, *Arabian Nights*, 88–89.

10. Hillenbrand, *Crusades*, 263–67; Canard, "Expéditions des Arabes contre Constantinople"; Canard, "Delhemma, epopee arabe"; Canard, "Les Reine de Géorgie dans l'histoire et la légende Musulmanes," *Revue des Études Islamiques* 1 (1969): 3–20; Lyons, "Crusading Stratum"; Garcin, "*Sira/s* et Histoire"; Irwin, *Arabian Nights*, 5–6 argues concisely and coherently for just such a "historical" and cultural historical approach regarding *'Alf laila wa laila*, which he then proceeds to execute in chapters 4–8 (103–213) of his book.

11. See for example Susan Edginton's attempt to ascertain the nature of women's participation in the crusades using these two epics: Susan Edginton, " 'Son çou ore les fems qu jo voi la venire?' Women in the *Chanson d'Antioche*," Susan B. Edgington and Sarah Lambert, eds., in *Gendering the Crusades* (New York: Columbia University Press, 2002): 154–62.

12. Hillenbrand, *Crusades*, 263–67.

13. Usāmah ibn Munqidh, *Kitāb al-'Itibār*, ed. Philip Hitti (Princeton: Princeton University Press, 1930), 122–31; Usāmah ibn Munqidh, *An Arab-Syrian Gentleman and Warrior in the Period of the Crusades, Memoires of Usāmah ibn Munqidh*, trans. Philip Hitti (Princeton: Princeton University Press, 1987), 152–60. On the nature of this text and the tales contained therein see: Hillenbrand, *Crusades*, 259–62.

14. These include the mother of one Layth al-Dawlah Yaḥya, Funūn, the wife of 'Ali 'Abd ibn Abi al-Raydā, and an anonymous Frankish woman. Usāmah ibn Munqidh, *Kitāb al-'Itibār*, 123–24, 125, 127–29; Usāmah ibn Munqidh, *Arab-Syrian Gentleman*, 153, 154, 157–58.

15. Usāmah ibn Munqidh, *Kitāb al-'Itibār*, 124–25, 127–28; Usāmah ibn Munqidh, *Arab-Syrian Gentleman*, 154, 156–59.

16. Usāmah ibn Munqidh, *Kitāb al-'Itibār*, 128–29; Usāmah ibn Munqidh, *Arab-Syrian Gentleman*, 158.

17. تخلي بنات عمك و اهلك للحلاجين

Idem., *Kitāb al-'Itibār*, 124; Idem., *Arab-Syrian Gentleman*, 153. On the meaning of حلاجين—literally "cotton workers" see Ibid., 152n31. For other examples of women personally contributing aid and encouragement to men involved with jihad but not acting as warriors themselves see: Hillenbrand, *Crusades*, 223–24.

Also see Michael Evan's discussion of Usamah's rhetorical use of women in his narrative to shame men: Michael Evans, " 'Unfit to Bear Arms': The Gendering of Arms and Armour in Accounts of Women on Crusade," in Edgington and Lambert, *Gendering the Crusades*, 45–58.

18. Ḥasan Muḥammad Jawhar, ed., *Al-Ẓāhir Baybars*, 6 vols. (Egypt: Dar al-Maʿarif, 1967–68) 1:27–28; Georges Bohas and Jean-Patrick Guillaume, trans., *Roman de Baibars* 10 vols. (Paris: Éditions Sinbad, 1985), vol. 1 *Les enfances de Baïbars*, 50–52.

19. *Dhāt al-Himma*, II.11.55; Lyons, *Arabian Epic*, vol. 3, paragraphs 47, 60, 107, 112, 115, 117, 119, on 346, 362–63, 419, 426, 428, 432, 435 respectively. The story of Qannāṣa is translated in full by Remke Kruk. See her "Warrior Women" part 2, esp. 17, 21. Compare with the story of Aluf, a Christian princess who has converted to Islam. She rebukes Maslama, the son of the caliph for acting treacherously and breaking the covenant of God. *Dhāt al-Himma*, I.4. 27; Lyons, *Arabian Epic*, vol. 3, paragraph 9, on 312.

20. و كذلك الاميره ذات الاهمه قد زادت فى فعلها على الرجال الثقال و صاحت فيهم و حملت عليهم و نادت يا

لدين محمد المصطفى أنا فاطمه بنت مظلوم بلا خفاء و تبعتها الرجال و أجادوا معها فى الحرب والقتال و

أنزلوا بالاعداء الوبال و أحلوا بهم النكال

Dhāt al-Himma II.11.14 Kruk, "Warrior Women," part 2, translation of this passage is on 19.

21. *Dhāt al-Himma* II.11.15–17, Kruk, "Warrior Women," part 2, on 19–20.

22. الاميره المجاهدة الطاهرة

Dhāt al-Himma II.11. 24; Kruk, "Warrior Women," part 2, on 30.

23. *Dhāt al-Himma* I.4.2–9, I.5. 12–16, I.6. 19–20, II.13. 78–79, II.20. 17ff, III.24. 63–67, 73, III.33. 37–41, IV.37. 10–11; Lyons, *Arabian Epic*, vol. 3, paragraphs 9–10, 17, 47, 62, 75, 77, 93, 95–96, 110, 112, 113 on 311–13, 319–20, 346–47, 364–66, 380–82, 384–85, 403–04, 405–06, 423–24, 426, 427 respectively. Also see Kruk's discussion of this issue, "Warrior Women," part 1.

24. ʿImād al-Dīn al-Iṣfahānī, *Al-fatḥ al-qussī fī-'l-fatḥ al-Qudsī* (Cairo: al-Dar al-Qawmiyah lil-Tibaʿah wa-al-Nashr, 1965), 349; Gabrielli, *Arab Historians*, 206–07. Abū Shama, *Kitāb al-Rawdatayn* in *Recueil des Historiens des Croisades Orientaux* (Paris, 1872–1906), IV: 434; Hillenbrand, *Crusades*, 348–49.

25. Ibn Shaddad, *al-Nuwādir al-Sulṭāniyah wa al-maḥāsan al-Yūsufiyah* in *Recueil des Historiens des Croisades Orientaux*, III: 231–32. Hillenbrand, *Crusades*, 349.

26. Hillenbrand, *Crusades*, 348–49; Evans, " 'Unfit to Bear Arms' "; Keren Caspi-Reisfeld, "Women Warriors during the Crusades 1095–1254," in Edgington and Lambert, *Gendering the Crusades*, 94–107; H. J. Nicolson, "Women on the Third Crusade," *Journal of Medieval History* 23 (1997): 335–49; Megan McLaughlin, "The Woman Warrior: Gender, Warfare and Society in Medieval Europe," *Women's Studies* 17 (1990): 193–209.

27. Evans, " 'Unfit to Bear Arms.' " Of course Usamah wrote his account as an old man (ca. 1213 CE) once his own personal involvement with holy war had passed, however the lessons would have remained relevant. Usāmah ibn Munqidh, *Kitāb al-'Itibār*, 160–62; Usāmah ibn Munqidh, *Arab-Syrian Gentleman*, 13–14, 17, 190–92.

28. 'Imād al-Dīn al-Iṣfahānī, *al-fatḥ al-qussī*, 347–49; Gabrielli, *Arab Historians*, 204–206.
29. Hillenbrand, *Crusades*, 347–51; Evans, " 'Unfit to Bear Arms.' "
30. Evans, " 'Unfit to Bear Arms.' "
31. *Sīrat fāris al-Yaman al-malik Sayf ibn Dhī Yazan*, 4 vols. (Cairo: Maktabat al-Jumhuriyya al-'Arabiyya, 1970) 2:41–45; *Adventures of Sayf Ben Dhi Yazan*, 282–89; Kruk, "Clipped Wings."
32. Kruk, "Clipped Wings."
33. *Book of the Thousand Nights*, 1: 356, 363–64.
34. Ibid., 1:376–80.
35. *Qissat al-amīr Ḥamza al-Bahlawān al-ma'rūf bi-Ḥamzat al-'Arab*, 4 vols. (Cairo: Maktabat al-Jumhuriyya al-'Arabiyya, 1900) II.258; Lyons, *Arabian Epic*, vol. 3, paragraph 23, on 559; Kruk, "Back to the Boudoire."
36. On negative or controlling attitudes toward women warriors in *Sīrat Ḥamza*, see: Kruk, "Back to the Boudoire."
37. *Dhāt al-Himma* I.7.9–11; Lyons, *Arabian Epic*, vol. 3, paragraph 21 on. 323–24.
38. However, Zalīm, who helps her cousin Ḥārith in his desire to marry Fāṭima, does so because he wants to "curtail her activity and diminish her strength." *Dhāt al-Himma* I.6.33; Lyons, *Arabian Epic*, vol. 3, paragraph 17 on 320. Clearly one male character assumed (wrongly) that marriage and sex would negatively affect a female warrior.
39. ما قتلت الشمطا الاعلى شانكم لانكم اسود وشجعان وانتم تخدموا امراة عجوز
Dhāt al-Himma I.1.18; Lyons, *Arabic Epic*, vol. 3, paragraph 1 on 301.
40. وقالت يا ولدى ما أدعك تخرج الى هذه الملعونة لانها ان ظفرت بك فهو العار الاكبر و ان ظفرت بها لاتنال فخر ولاظفر و اننى ما امن عليك من شرها و مكرها فدعنى أخرج اليها و اهجم عليها
Dhāt al-Himma, II.11. 17. Translation by Remke Kruk in "Warrior Women," part. 2 on 21. Also see Lyon's summary: *Arabian Epic*, vol. 3, paragraph 38 on 338–39.
41. و لكن أنا أفديه من الرد او بروحى أقيه و ألقى عنه ربات الخرئد و أصحاب المقانع و القلائد
Dhāt al-Himma, II.11. 24. Translation is my own. For a different translation of the same passage, see: Kruk, "Warrior Women," part 2 on 30. Also see: Lyons, *Arabian Epic*, vol. 3, paragraph 38 on 338–39.
42. *Book of a Thousand Nights*, 1: 111–12, 354, 380, 447–60, 464–65, 470–71; *Dhāt al-Himma*, I.5. 12–13; Lyons, *Arabian Epic*, vol. 3, paragraph 12 on 315. For another example of the negative portrayal of old women as ugly (and over-sexed) from the late thirteenth century CE, see the first shadow play in Shams al-Dīn Muḥmmad b. Dāniyāl, *Ṭayf al-Khayāl: thalāt bābāt min khayāl al-ẓill*, ed. Paul Kahle, critical apparatus, Derek Hopwood (Cambridge: E. J. W. Gibb Memorial Leda House, 1992), 4–54.
43. *Dhāt al-Himma* I.6.36; Lyons, *Arabian Epic*, vol. 3, paragraphs 17, 19 on 320, 322 respectively.
44. لا حول و لاقوة الا بالله العلى العظيم سبحان الذى صوره فى ظلمات الا حشا و لا أخاف من الحق و لا أخشى و لا أقتل نفسى طاهرة من زواج صحيح و عقد رجيح عقده خليفة الله المنصور... و انا امرأة قد اشتغلت بالاخره عن الدنيا الساحره و ما لى حاجة فى زواج و لا فى غيره و انما اريد وجه الله العلى

Dhāt al-Himma, I.7.11 Compare with II.13.61 where she also states that she has never felt inclined toward men, desiring only the "King most High." For a discussion of this second passage in context see: Kruk, "The Bold and the Beautiful."

45. *Dhāt al-Himma*, II.13.47; Lyons, *Arabian Epic*, vol. 3, paragraph 46 on 345.

46. *Dhāt al-Himma*, III.24. 24; Lyons, *Arabian Epic*, vol. 3, paragraph 73 on 379.

47. *Dhāt al-Himma* III.26. 13–15, III.29.47–50; Lyons, *Arabian Epic*, vol. 3, paragraph 76 on 383, and paragraph 82 on 391.

48. *Dhāt al-Himma* I.3. 78 - I.4. 5; Lyons, *Arabian Epic*, vol. 3, paragraph 9 on 311; *'Alf laila wa laila* 1: 210–11, *A Thousand Nights*, 1: 352. For other examples of Christian women who belong to or are associated with a monastery before marrying a Muslim man see: *Dhāt al-Himma* I.5. 52–70; IV.33.24; Lyons, *Arabian Epic*, vol. 3, paragraphs 15, 92 on 317–18, 402–03. Another Christian princess, Marjāna, is traveling to a church with one hundred other women when she is accosted by the Muslims. *Dhāt al-Himma* summary in Lyons, *Arabian Epic*, vol. 3, paragraph 115 on 428.

49. *Dhāt al-Himma* summary in Lyons, *Arabian Epic*, vol. 3, paragraph 119 on 435.

50. و كانت هذا الملكه نورا تهوى النساء و تبغض الرجال

Dhāt al-Himma II.13.47; Lyons, *Arabian Epic*, vol. 3, paragraph 46 on 345.

51. و لكن و حق المسيح ما لى فى الرجال رغبة و لا يطلب قلبى الاربات الحجال

Dhāt al-Himma, III.24.67; Lyons, *Arabian Epic*, vol. 3 paragraph 75, pp. 382.

52. *Dhāt al-Himma* I.4.6.

53. فانها فرحت بأسر أبو محمد البطال و غلمانه و الملك شعشعونا و كان لها جارية يقال لها لنهار و ما كانت زنانير بشرب الا معها الليل استدعت بالجارية اليها و قعدوا يشر بون يتلذذون و يطربون

Dhāt al-Himma, III.24.80. In the text here the verb forms imply that the "they" includes at least one man. Kruk interprets this passage as a homoerotic one between Nahār and Zanānīr and cites a different, feminine form of the verb "watataladhdhadhā." Kruk, "Warrior Women," part 1, esp. 224.

54. *Dhāt al-Himma*, III.24.67.

55. Everett Rowson notes that Arab writers frequently associated *liwāṭ*, penetrative anal sex of one male with another man, with monks. See: Everett Rowson, "The Categorization of Gender and Sexual Irregularity in Medieval Arabic Vice Lists," in Julia Epstein and Kristina Staub, eds., *Body Guards: The Cultural Politics of Gender Ambiguity* (New York: Routledge, 1991), 50–79; Aḥmad ibn Muḥammad Jurjānī, *al-Muntakhab min kināyāt al-udabā' wa-ishārāt al-bulaghā'* (Hyderabad: Matba'at Majlis Dairat al-Ma'arif al-'Uthmaniyah, 1983), 28. The portrayal of female monastics in *Sīrat Dhāt al-Himma* suggest that the stereotype included same-sex love between nuns as well. My thanks to Sahar Amer of the University of North Carolina for pointing out these references to me.

56. As a rule, Islam did not celebrate celibacy as a spiritual ideal. However, some Sufis, such as the ninth-century Rabi'a did favor such behavior. See: Julian Baldick, *Mystical Islam: An Introduction to Sufism* (New York/London: New York University Press, 1989), 16, 29.

57. *Dhāt al-Himma*, I.4. 36; III.29.47; Lyons, *Arabian Epic*, vol. 3, paragraphs 9, 82, 115 on 312, 391, 429. For a discussion of a similar phenomenon in

medieval French epics see: Ramey, *Christian, Saracen and Genre in Medieval French Literature*, 40–42, 57.

58. *Dhāt al-Himma*, summary in Lyons, *Arabian Epic*, vol. 3, paragraph 32 on 333.
59. *Dhāt al-Himma*, III.25.13; Lyons, *Arabian Epic*, vol. 3, paragraph 75 on 380.
60. It is not clear what the original sexual preferences of the first Zanānīr are.
61. و كانت اكثر اقامتها عند ولدها حردوب ملك الروم لآجل الجوارى الآبكار, لانها كانت تحب السحاق و ان تأخر عنها تكون فى انمحاق, وكل جارية أعجبتها تعلمها الحكمة و تسحق عليها الزعفران فيغشى عليها من فرط اللذة مدة من الزمان, فمن طاوعتها أحسنت اليها و رعيت ولدها فيها و من لا تطاوعها تتحايل على هلاكها, و بسبب ذلك علمت مرجانة وريحانو واترجه جوارى ابريزة, وكانت الملكة ابريزة تكره العجوز و تكره ان ترقد معها لآن جسدها اخشن من الليفة, و كانت ترغب من يساحقها بالجوائر و التعليم, و كانت ابريزة تبرأ منها الى الحكيم العليم.

Alf laila wa laila, 1: 284; Mardrus and Mather's version (*A Thousand Nights*, 1: 447–48) is very different. On their interpolations especially with regard to sexual matters see: Irwin, *Arabian Nights*, 36–41. The word being used for sexual activity between women in this passage is *siḥāq*, and derivatives from it. The root verb *saḥaqa* means "to crush, pound, pulverize" but commonly designates sex between women. For more on this see: Fedwa Malti-Douglas, "Tribadism/Lesbianism and the Sexualized Body in Medieval Arabo-Islamic Narratives," in Francesca Canadé and Pamela Sheingorn, eds., *Same Sex Love and Desire among Women in the Middle Ages* (New York: Palgrave, 2001), 123–41; Saffron was also commonly associated with same-sex love between women. See: Aḥmad al-Tīfāshī, *Nuzhat al-Albāb fīmā lā Yūjad fī Kitāb*, ed. Jamāl Jum'a (London: Riyad al-Rayyis lil-Kutub wa-al-Nashr, 1992), 243; Aḥmad al-Tīfāshī, *Les Délices des Coeurs ou ce que l'on ne trouve en aucun livre*, trans. René R. Khawam (Paris: Phébus, 1981), 250–51; Sahar Amer, "Lesbian Sex and the Military: From the Medieval Arabic Tradition to French Literature," in Canadé and Sheingorn, *Same Sex Love*, 179–98; Irwin, *Arabian Nights*, 171.

62. *Dhāt al-Himma*, I.5. 12–13; Lyons, *Arabian Epic*, vol. 3, paragraph 12 on 315. On this personage see: Kruk, "Warrior Women" part 1; Canard, "Les Reines de Géorgie dans l'histoire et la légende Musulmanes."
63. *Dhāt al-Himma* summary in Lyons, *Arabian Epic*, vol. 3, paragraph 62 on 365.
64. و قام شعر بدنها كأنها شعر قنفذة . . . فصارت كأنها عفريت معطاء أو حية رقطاء

'Alf laila wa laila, 1:211, 212. For an alternate translation see: *A Thousand Nights*, 1: 354. The description here does seem a bit contradictory in making her both prickly and bald! The name Dhāt al-Duwāhā is translated as Mother-of-Calamity by Mathers however the root of "Duwāhā" also means cunning and wily.
65. Ibid.
66. Ibrīza converts to Islam: *Alf laila wa laila*, 1; *A Thousand Nights*, 1:367. For more examples of this phenomenon from *Sīrat Dhāt al-Himma* see further. Lynn Tarte Ramey and Jacqueline de Weever have noted similar patterns in *chansons de geste*. See Ramey's "Role Models? Saracen Women in Medieval French Epic," *Romance Notes*, 41.2 (2001): 131–41 and Ramey, *Christian, Saracen and Genre*, 45–50, and de Weever's *Sheba's Daughters*, 11, 54–75, 96–100.

67. و قد كنت لا أرضى الرجال حمية

    Dhāt al-Himma, IV.36.57; Lyons, *Arabian Epic*, vol. 3 paragraph 101 on 413.

68. و كان قد ألقا الله عز و جل محبة الاميره فى قلبها و عجبت من فعلها و حسن قتالها

    Dhāt al-Himma, IV.37.38; Lyons, *Arabian Epic*, vol. 3, paragraph 102 on 414.

69. The saga of Maimuna's pursuit of 'Abd al-Wahhāb begins in *Dhāt al-Himma*, IV.36. 50 and continues until IV.37.38, culminating in her conversion and marriage.

70. For example, Zananir indicates that she loves Lu'lu and favors him. She remains staunchly Christian and a military opponent of the Muslims for a long period during Lu'lu's pursuit of her. *Dhāt al-Himma*, III.24. 65 – III.29. 50; Lyons, *Arabian Epic*, vol. 3, paragraphs 75–82 on 380–91.

71. *Dhāt al-Himma* summary in Lyons, *Arabian Epic*, vol. 3, paragraphs 117, 118, 132 on 431–32, 455.

72. *Dhāt al-Himma* summary in Lyons, *Arabian Epic*, vol. 3, paragraph 136 on 460. Both women have dreams of their forthcoming battle with one another, but Maimuna's dream only shows her wounding Fāṭima (Maimuna assumes that this proves she will win) whereas Fāṭima also dreams she is wounded but is further shown that she will kill Maimuna with her own weapon.

73. *Dhāt al-Himma* IV.37. 9; Lyons, *Arabian Epic*, vol. 3, paragraph 101 on 413.

74. al-Tīfāshī, *Nuzhat*, 242; Malti-Douglas, "Tribadism/Lesbianism and the Sexualized Body."

75. Malti-Douglas, "Tribadism/Lesbianism and the Sexualized Body."

76. Jurjānī, *al-Muntakhab*, 34–35. Also see: Rowson, "Vice Lists."

77. al-Tīfāshī, *Nuzhat*, 238–41; al-Tīfāshī, *Délices des coeurs*, 262–65; Malti-Douglas, "Tribadism/Lesbianism and the Sexualized Body."

78. D. Cook, *Studies in Muslim Apocalyptic* (Princeton: Darwin Press, 2002), 13, 333–44.

79. و شارك النساء ازواجهن فى التجارة حرصا على الدنيا ... و ركب ذوات الفروج السروج, وتشبه النساء بالرجال, و الرجال بالنساء

    Muḥammad ibn 'Alī ibn Bābūwayh al-Qummī, *'Ikmāl al-dīn wa-'itmām al-ni'ma fī ithbāt at-raj'ah* (Najaf: al-Matba'ah al-Haydariyah, 1970), 490. The comment about saddles perhaps refers to women taking the top position in sexual intercourse.

80. Aḥmad ibn Ja'far ibn al-Munādī, *al-Malaḥim*, ed. 'Abd al-Karim al-'Uqayli (Qum: 1998), 301.

81. و رأيت الفسق قد ظهر و اكتفى الرجال بالرجال و النساء بالنساء .... و رأيت الغلام يعطى ما تعطى المرأة و رأيت النساء يتزوجن النساء .... و رأيت الرجال يتسمنون للرجال و النساء للنساء, و رأيت الرجل معيشته من دبره و معيشة المرأة من فرجها, و رأيت النساء يتخذن المجالس كما يتخذها الرجال ... . و رأيت الرجل يأكل من كسب امرأته من الفجور .... و رأيت المرأة تقهر زوجها

    Muḥammad ibn Ya'qub al-Kulaynī, *al-Uṣul min al-Kāfī*, eds. A. A. Ghaffari and M. Akhundi, 3rd ed. (Tehran: Maktabah al-Islami-yah, 1968–71), 8: 38–39. For a slightly different and more complete translation see: Cook, *Studies in Muslim Apocalyptic*, 333–38. "Fattening themselves" i.e., making themselves sexually attractive in a particularly feminine way. On this as well as attitudes toward anal sex and homosexuality see: Irwin, *Arabian Nights*, 167–77.

82. أطاع الرجل امرأة . . . . و استغنى الرجال بالرجال و النساء بالنساء . . . . فمها نكاح الرجل امرأة أو أمته

في دبرها , وذلك مما حرم الله رسوله , ويمقت الله عليه و رسوله؛ و منها مكاح الرجل الرجل و ذلك مما

حرم الله عليه و رسوله ؛ و منها نكاح المرأة المرأة و ذلك مما حرم الله و رسوله و يمقت الله عليه ورسوله

'Ali ibn 'Abd al-Malik al-Muttaqi al-Hindi, *Kanz al-'ummāl li sunan al-aqwāl wa-al-af'āl* (Aleppo: Maktabat al-Turath al-Islami, 1969), vol. 14, nos. 39239, 39240 on 574–71. Compare with Jalāl al-Dīn 'Abd al-Raḥim ibn 'Abi Bakr al-Suyūtī, *Durr al-manthūr fi al-tafsīr bi-al-ma'thūr . . . wa-bi-hāmishihi al-Qur'ān al-sharīf ma'a kitāb Tanwīr al-miqbās tafsīr . . . 'Abd Allāh ibn 'Abbās..* 6 vols. (Tehran: al-Maktabah al-Ja'fariyah, 1957), vol. 6 on. 52–55.

83. Irwin, *Arabian Nights*, 168–70; and more generally: H. Lutfi, "Manners and Customs of Fourteenth-Century Cairene Women: Female Anarchy versus Male Shari'i Order in Muslim Prescriptive Treatises," in Nikki R. Keddie and Beth Baron, eds., *Women in Middle Eastern History: Shifting Boundaries in Sex and Gender* (New Haven:Yale University Press, 1991), 99–121.

84. There are numerous passages in the Qur'an and subsequent elaborations of Muslim law that make this hierarchy between Islam and the other "religions of the book" clear. See: Qur'an 2:62–64, 112–23, 135–41, 3:20–26, 5: 12–19, 65–86; Mark Cohen, *Under Crescent and Cross: Jews in the Middle Ages* (Princeton: Princeton University Press, 1994).

85. Ramey argues that in medieval French epics, making the Saracen *princess* embody both beauty and military of the Muslim culture was a kind of feminization of those aspects of Muslim culture Westerners found desirable that served to make those co-opted aspects less threatening. (Ramey, *Christian, Saracen and Genre*, 64. Also see: de Weever, *Sheba's Daughters*, 30–34, 43–45, 115–17) The same might be said here of the Arabic epics' treatment of Christian princesses, however, given the frequency with which they continue to beat and outsmart men, both before and after their conversion, raises the question of how truly "non-threatening" these women seemed to be.

86. Sahar Amer, "Lesbian Sex and the Military: From the Medieval Arabic Tradition to French Literature," in Canadé and Sheingorn, *Same Sex Love and Desire*, 179–98. Compare with Robert Clark, "Jousting without a Lance: The Condemnation of Female Homoeroticism in the *Livre des Manières*," in the same collection, 143–77 and more generally in medieval Western literature: Kathryn Gravdal, *Ravishing Maidens: Writing Rape in Medieval French Literature and Law* (Philadelphia: University of Pennsylvania Press, 1991) 2–3, 66.

87. For examples from *Kitāb al-'Itibār* see earlier. Also see: Hillenbrand, *Crusades*, 285, 298.

88. وسيف قاطع ودم صبيب \ وكم من مسلم امسى سليا \ ومسلمة مها حرم سليب \ وكم من مسجد جعلوه ديرا

\ على محرابه نصب الصليب \ دم الخنزير فيه لهم خلوق \ و تحريق المصاحف فيه طيب

Abū Maḥāsin Yūsuf Ibn Taghrībirdī, *Al-Nujūm al-zāhira fī mulūk Miṣr, wa al-Qāhirah*, 16 vols. (Cairo: Matba'at Dar al-Kutub al-Misriyah, 1929–72), vol. 5

on 151–52, trans. in Hillenbrand, *Crusades*, 297–98 and see her analysis there. Compare with Ibn Khallikan, "Extraits de la vie du Sultan Salah ed-Din," in *Recueil des historiens des croisades orientaux*, vol. 3. (Paris: Imprimerie royale, 1884), 416 and Alexandra Cuffel, *Gendering Disgust in Medieval Religious Polemic* (Notre Dame, IN: University of Notre Dame Press, 2007), ch. 4.

89. Fidentius of Padua, *Liber de recuperatione terrae sanctae* in *Biblioteca biobibliographica della terra santa e dell'oriente francescano*, vol. 2 of 5. ed. Girolamo Golubovich (Quaracchi: Collegio di S. Bonaventura, 1906–27), 18–19, 21–23; Roger Bacon, *The Opus Majus of Roger Bacon*, 2 vols. trans. Robert Belle Burke (Bristol, UK: Thoemmes Presses, 2000), *Opus Majus, moralis philosophiae*, part 7 , vol. 2 on 814; Debra Higgs Strickland, *Saracens, Demons, and Jews: Making Monsters in Medieval Art* (Princeton: Princeton University Press, 2003), 174; Cuffel, *Gendering Disgust*, ch. 4.

90. *Dhāt al-Himma* I.3. 77– I.4.12; II.13.47; III.24. 64–67; IV.36. 50–57; Lyons, *Arabian Epic*, vol. 3, paragraphs 9–10, 46, 75, 101 on 311–13, 345, 380–82, 412; *Book of the Thousand Nights*, 1:376–80.

91. Qur'an 5:5. *Chapters on Marriage and Divorce: Responses of Ibn Ḥanbal and Ibn Rāhwayh*, trans with introduction and notes by Susan A. Spectorsky (Austin: University of Texas Press, 1993) 15, 61, 100, 103, 111–12, 153, 174, 183, 214, 234.

92. Spectorsky, *Chapters on Marriage and Divorce*, 15–16, 61, 153.

93. For example, Nura was to be sold before her conversion. *Dhāt al-Himma* II.19. 26–27, Lyons, *Arabian Epic*, vol. 3, paragraph 52 on 351–52.

94. *Dhāt al-Himma* III.23:35–43; Lyons, *Arabian Epic*, vol. 3, paragraph 72 on 376–77.

95. *Dhāt al-Himma* II.13. 53, 55, 80 and 20.16–18; Lyons, *Arabian Epic*, vol. 3, paragraph 47 on 346–47; Kruk, "The Bold and the Beautiful."

96. *Dhāt al-Himma* I.4. 2–12; Lyons, *Arabian Epic*, vol. 3, paragraph 9–10 on 311–13.

97. *Dhāt al-Himma* III.25.11, 14–15; Lyons, *Arabian Epic*, vol. 3, paragraph 75 on 380–82.

98. *Dhāt al-Himma*, II.11. 24.

99. *Dhāt al-Himma* III.26. 14–15; Lyons, *Arabian Epic*, vol. 3, paragraph 76 on 383.

100. *Dhāt al-Himma* II.19.49, II.20.36–38; Lyons, *Arabian Epic*, vol. 3, paragraph 60 on 363, paragraph 62 on 366.

101. رجعت تلك البغضة محبة

Dhāt al-Himma II.20. 38–39; Lyons, *Arabian Epic*, vol. 3, paragraph 62 on 366. This transformation does not occur immediately after forced intercourse as Lyon's summary implies; Al-Baṭṭāl talks to Nura afterwards and she is entranced by the beauty of his words.

102. *Dhāt al-Himma* II.19. 26–27; Lyons, *Arabian Epic*, vol. 3, paragraph 60 on 362.

103. *Dhāt al-Himma* I.7. 8–10; Lyons, *Arabian Epic*, vol. 3, paragraph 21 on 323–24.

104. In truth I have adopted the transliteration "Ṣalbān" because that is what Lyons chose in his summary, however, there is no reason in the Arabic text to suppose that her name is not to be vocalized as "Ṣulbān." In a minority of occasions, however, her name is spelled with a soft s, "Salbān" (or "Sulbān").

105. *Qur'an* 5:82.

Chapter 7

Hunters and Boundaries in Mande Cultures

Stephen Belcher

In Europe and the Americas, oral folktales are generally associated with subordinate social categories, and the ideology most often identified with such narratives is one of resistance and subversion: the clever farmer outwits the devil, the simpleton brother wins the princess, Brer Rabbit rides the fox, the slave fools the master. There, the folktale is defined as the property of the subordinate groups, set in some opposition to the normative structures and institutions of the society as a whole. The opposition of oral and written finds its equivalent in the power relations of social groups: those normative structures and institutions are defined and transmitted through writing, with a presumption of increasing reliance on reading and writing as one moves up the ladder, whereas what is oral is associated with the under-educated, the poor, and the powerless.

The equation changes somewhat when we shift our attention to Africa. The oral-written divide which marks social differences in the Occident loses much of its value as a social marker: the cultures of west Africa are marked far more by a pervasive orality at all levels of the "traditional" society (i.e., where there is continuation of precolonial structures and relations). For them, oral folktales serve a normative purpose, and they function as the vehicles for the expression of social expectations, rules, and behavior. Suggestions of subversion and resistance are not so universal. While west Africa offers its share of theriomorphic tricksters who define the limits of the human sensual appetites and find ways to evade the rules which govern the common run of mortals, these figures are not found everywhere.

Ananse the spider and Ajapa the tortoise are associated, respectively, with the Akan-Ashanti peoples of Ghana and the Yoruba of Nigeria. Leuck the hare is found among the Wolof of Senegal. But other regions, and particularly the world of the Mande peoples, are not so easily characterized by the rules-breakers; tricksters appear a minor element of their oral literature. Folktales may explore and question social norms, but almost invariably the outcome justifies and reinforces the current status quo.[1] This is not to say that the societies involved are without (consciously expressed) tensions, or that they see the status quo as an ideal condition. Mande societies are marked by strong social hierarchies and barriers, and their members are fully aware of the personal limitations which this system imposes upon individuals; the indigenous systems are also under considerable pressure from the forces of modernization and, increasingly, of imported forms of Islam. It does suggest that the boundaries of discourse are defined somewhat differently than within literate systems, and it may be useful to consider how these boundaries are defined and, at times, questioned. In what follows, we shall briefly consider how the epic traditions, narrated by specialized performers, and folktales, narrated by ordinary people, incorporate social norms, before looking at the ideology and narratives of hunters' associations as a possible site for challenges to the social boundaries laid down elsewhere.

Mande Society

It may be useful first to provide a brief description of the Mande cultural world.[2] "Mande" is an essentially linguistic term, describing a family of languages whose core population is associated with the medieval empire of Mali (thirteenth to sixteenth centuries). The principal languages involved would be Maninka, in Mali and Guinea, Mandinka in the Gambia, Bamana in central Mali, and Dyula in Côte d'Ivoire, which can all be considered regional variants of a single language; Soninke (Sarakholle) is also closely associated to this grouping linguistically and culturally. The geographic core of this empire lay on the Manding plateau and the headwaters of the Niger river, in a region now divided between the modern republics of Guinea and Mali. At its largest extent, the empire stretched east (down the Niger) as far as Timbuktu, west into Senegal and the Gambia, and south to the edge of the forest zones of Liberia, Côte d'Ivoire, and Ghana. Since the time of the empire, the peoples have spread somewhat further, either as satellite populations speaking distinct languages that can be related to the Mande family, or as part of a trading diaspora (the Dyula; the term means "trader") whose language (known as Dyula or Jula) is essentially a dialect of the central Maninka-Bamana core.

The central Maninka groups are marked by a strong social structure divided by class, lineage, age, and gender. The class oppositions, however, are not binary. While free (noble) and slave can be contrasted, these two groups also stand in opposition to the craft-status groups, sometimes called castes. The craft groups include blacksmiths, leather-workers, and most famously, the praise-singers and musicians (*jeli* or griots)who are carriers of the musical and oral historical traditions of the Mande peoples. The line between noble and slave (*horon* and *jon*) is relatively delicate and not immediately perceptible to the outsider: the different groups may share the same patronyms, and since slavery was outlawed under colonial rule, explicit recognition of slave status or ancestry has become a matter of insider knowledge. The distinction between these two groups and the craft-status groups, however, is much clearer: the craft groups are marked by distinct patronyms (e.g., Kouyate and Diabate are two of the best-known griot lineages; Kante is a smith's name) which allow easy identification. Some patronyms cross categories: the name Camara, for instance, applies both to blacksmith and to noble lineages. By and large, though, and especially at the local level, members of the societies are keenly aware of their social status and of the relative importance of their lineage.

Within the lineages, age is marker of authority and power. Mande society is considered gerontocratic, in that final authority within a lineage rests with the most senior male members. Succession is not by primogeniture, but rather passes from the deceased to the oldest living member of the lineage within a prescribed descent-group. The elders delegate authority to the males who are heads of households (usually polygamous), and these men in turn manage the labor and economic resources of their compounds. Generational lines and distinctions are strongly marked, and the younger members are always expected to defer to their elders, and to assume a subordinate role.

The oral literature of the Mande peoples has attracted a good deal of deserved attention, perhaps mostly because of the traditions of the *jelilu* or griots. These are genealogical and historical recitations or praise-songs which in narrative form are often termed epic; the best-known example is the "Epic of Sunjata," the story of the founder of the empire, of which we now have some thirty full-length versions from a variety of sources.[3] This epic, however, is not purely a literary document; its content is considered historical within the Mande world, and "sanctioned" performance is restricted to a select number of lineages who are considered authorized and informed. One will hear epic echoes in all forms of the Mande lyric tradition; these are largely the short praise-names which distinguish lineages and which are used by performers to honor (wealthy) patrons in the immediate audience. Other forms, such as the folktale, songs, and proverbs may seem to suffer by comparison, although they are represented in print.[4]

Historical Epics

The *jeli*, or griot, is a specialist of song, genealogy, and historical recitation.[5] The jeli does not perform folktales, and the jeli's art is not visualized in terms of poetic creativity. Fluency of speech, perception of nuances, and knowledge of the local Mande verbal heritage are rather the desired attributes. The jeli is thus also associated with the traditional power divisions of the society; a jeli's loyalty is to his or her noble patron family, although a jeli will also be opportunistic and praise any potential donor in the immediate vicinity. As a brief example of the jeli's support for traditional divisions of society, we might consider the commentary by Bamba Suso in his performance of the "Epic of Sunjata." The comment comes during the final opposition of Sunjata Keita, the destined king of the Manding, and his opponent, the usurper Sumanguru Kante, king of the Sossos, a blacksmith and a magician. Sumanguru is protected by powerful magic which Sunjata cannot defeat; Sunjata's sister goes to Sumanguru and seduces him into revealing his secret:

Night fell,
And he [Sumanguru] and the woman were in his house.
Now, a princess of the Manding
And a smith would not sleep together.
They were chatting,
Till the smith's mind turned in a certain direction.[6]

The sister then exploits the smith's interest to learn his secret. Almost no version of the story collected as an oral performance leads to an actual seduction or sexual act; only in a literary handling such as that of the Guinean novelist Camara Laye[7] will the seduction be consummated.

This respect for social divisions in the "Epic of Sunjata" is hardly surprising; the story serves as the chartering myth for much of Mande society. Lineages trace their descent and relations from the ancestors mentioned in the story; social institutions such as marriage, the sibling incest taboo, and the joking relationship (*senankuya*) which is such an essential force of social cohesion, linking disparate groups and dissipating frictions, all find their origin in the time and the actions of Sunjata. More telling examples may be found in an emerging tradition of epics dealing with more recent heroes. Jelis now sing of Samori Toure, a war-leader who established an empire over parts of Guinea, Mali, and Côte d'Ivoire during the nineteenth century and was a major figure of resistance to the French.[8] Curiously, though, Samori himself is not the dramatic focus of those texts I have seen, perhaps because memories of Samori can be grim: he is said to have buried his son alive, because the son (who had visited France) dared say they could not win against the French, and he depopulated entire regions by enslaving the inhabitants to sell for weapons. In the epics, the dramatic and emotive focus of the story is on Samori's younger brother Keme Brema, who, because he believed he had offended his older brother, went into battle without his magical protections and thus was killed. This is self-sacrifice in service of a recognized social value (the respect due from younger to older siblings), and the story thus avoids the historical, political, and ideological complications from a focus on the problematic Samori himself.

Another example involves an equally problematic historical figure, al-Hajj Umar Tal.[9] Al-Hajj Umar was originally a Tukolor (from the Futa Tooro, a region along the Senegal river) who rose to prominence as a Muslim religious leader; after he settled at Dingiraye, in upper Guinea, he came into conflict with the French and was driven east into what is now Mali, where his armies conquered the (Mande) Bamana states of Kaarta and Segu. He died in a revolt in 1853. A Maninka epic tells of his greatness; here again, though, much of the focus is displaced from the leader himself onto a figure who embodies traditional social values of submissiveness and fortitude: his mother. Her sufferings—humiliation because of childlessness, displacement by a co-wife, a period of servitude, and finally disbelief in the legitimacy of her son—take up half the narrative, but are the essential prequel to the son's greatness within the conceptions of Mande society. Mothers are fulfilled through their children: the pattern is repeated through many narratives.[10]

Such historical epic narratives are the product of specialized performers. They enjoy a certain prestige, reinforced by the interest of outsiders; whether or not they count as a truly popular entertainment may be a moot point. Certainly, recordings of epic performances are staple fare among the market cassettes. But the principal point to retain in this discussion is that the historical epics do not pose significant questions about social values; they may serve to model behavior, or in some cases to influence it through the evocation of ancestral glories, but they do not really cross boundaries. "A smith would not sleep with a noble," explains Bamba Suso, and in fact that principle is carried throughout the epic tradition: extant social boundaries are reinforced rather than questioned.

The epics do have a generic counterpart in hunters' narratives, which share many of the same performance features. But before turning to the hunters' narratives, it might be useful to further illustrate the normative function of oral tradition with a folktale; such tales are common property throughout the culture, although there are certain rules regarding their telling (not in certain seasons, preferably at certain times of day) which set up an opposition between productive labor (especially food-producing work) and the idleness associated with telling and listening to tales.[11]

Folktales

One of the most widespread narratives across west Africa, and amply represented in the collections of Mande folktales, is the story of the two step-sisters (or co-wives, and very occasionally step-brothers[12]). In this narrative, a first girl—usually an orphan, à la Cinderella—is sent on an errand or punished by being sent away; she comes to an older woman who sets her a variety of (domestic and occasionally disgusting) tasks which she accomplishes dutifully and without complaint. The older woman sends the child back to her family with packages which, when opened, turn into wonderful gifts and wealth. The step-mother then sends her own daughter to earn this rich reward, but the second child does everything wrong: she complains and criticizes, she doesn't finish the tasks. She also usually opens her packages on the path, rather than waiting to reach the home as she has been told, and they prove lethal: snakes and scorpions, or a lion that devours her.

The normative function of the story is perfectly clear. The story repeats its sequence of events: proper behavior is modeled in the first; the forms and consequences of misbehavior are given in the second. The first girl shows respect to the older woman, does not question her commands even when they appear absurd (e.g., cook a pot of rice with a single grain), and obeys her requests even when they are distasteful (e.g., to clean the old woman's boils, or to remove the lice from her hair). The second girl does not. In fact, her reactions may seem more normal (the wonder of producing a pot of rice from a single grain deserves comment), but in the context they are demonstrated to be inappropriate. The story also illustrates a point made by Veronika Görög, that many Mande folktales ground their entertainment value in the punishment received by the person who is violating the norms: that the appeal of the story is in fact to see that the norms are upheld.[13]

Of course, not every Mande folktale is quite so obviously prescriptive. There are humorous stories (the husband made of lard who had two wives, a cockroach and a chicken[14]) and adventurous stories of encounters with the beings of the spirit world. But by and large, and in some contrast to the recognized corpora of European folktales, the stories deal more with rule-breaking and consequent retribution than with such topics as initiation, maturation, and development. They also continue to be more grounded in every-day experience and expression than the largely literary texts of the European tradition, collected in the nineteenth century and earlier.

Hunters' Narratives

Against these two bodies of traditional material stands a third, which shares certain features of historical epics and folktales while still creating its own artistic space: the hunters' narratives. Hunters' narratives are, like the epics, performed by specialized performers to a musical accompaniment, and there is said to be an established repertoire of the narratives, although it has yet to be convincingly catalogued. While specialized, the performers are not selected through heredity; they choose the calling as part of their involvement with the hunters' association. The narratives, in turn, share much with folktales: they are creative and structured fictions.

Hunters' associations and narratives are found across the Mande world, from the Gambia in the west to northern Côte d'Ivoire in the south. The institution is much wider; one finds hunters' associations among the peoples of Ghana, Benin, and Nigeria. As such, they are evidence for a common cultural pattern, although there has been very little comparative work. Within the Mande world, hunters' associations have been gaining prominence as an ideological construct, just as their importance for organized economic activity has been diminishing. Led by the Malian scholar Youssouf Tata Cissé, researchers now see the hunters' associations as an expression of an authentic and ancient Mande culture, and as the repository of traditional values. This function is reinforced, despite the drastic decline in the value of hunting for food, by the new activity of healing which has been taken up, building on the reputed hunters' knowledge of the natural world.[15]

Two claims in particular, associated with membership in the associations, stand in contrast to the ordinary social principles grounded in family and status: first, that all hunters are equal in their membership, regardless of their original status, and second, that authority derives from one's seniority in the association, as well as one's accomplishments. The first claim dissolves the barriers of lineage, nobility, possible servile status, and ethnicity. The second strikes at the principle of gerontocracy which operates so strongly within the family structure. These claims present the associations as a form of virtual reality, so to speak, in which the normal social rules stand in abeyance, and in which socially divisive forces are suspended in favor of an idealized fraternity of the members.

These claims, however, deserve to be questioned. The work by Cissé, Camara, and others, is based to some extent upon a speculative reconstruction of the role of hunters' associations in the past. It is true that several major figures of the Mande past are portrayed as hunters: Sunjata Keita, founder of the empire of Mali, Daman Ngille, the Soninke founder associated with the kingdom of Nioro, and Mamari "Biton" Kulibali, founder of the later kingdom of Segou. But the continuities are questionable: each of them is actually portrayed as a solitary figure, travelling alone more often than not. The name "Biton" attached to Mamari Kulibali does mean "Leader of the association" (*bi-ton*), but the association in question, as recounted in the story of his rise to power, is not a hunters' association, but a drinking club which becomes an army of slave-raiders. There has been relatively little work done on modern hunters' associations to examine or support the claims.[16] It is also worth noting that the claims run somewhat counter to the current invocation of their value as an indigenous national tradition for the Mande peoples; it should instead be considered a pan-African, or at least regional, institution.

We might ask why the claims are being advanced, and the answer is: to fulfill a need. Mande culture is conservative, cohesive, and strong. But it is, of course, being challenged from the outside. The years of colonialism may have left less of a mark in Mali than in other parts of Africa (the situation in Guinea is complicated by forty years of corrupt dictatorships), but the challenges of modernity and globalization are still being felt. These challenges are compounded by the growth of Islam in the past century, and particularly by the more recent puritan movements that call into question the accommodations reached in past centuries by local clerics with local practices and beliefs.[17] Beset on two sides, the turn to an autochthonous tradition is only natural.[18]

We have some thirty hunters' narratives, or epics, in published form; many others circulate in the form of recorded cassettes.[19] The texts come from across the Mande world: from the the Gambia to Côte d'Ivoire, yet they recognizably belong to the same corpus. A narrative of the Bozo hunters of the middle Niger river echoes texts from the Mandinka hunters from the Gambia and from Baro in upper Guinea: it tells of a monstrous beast (a crocodile in form) who seizes newly-wed brides as they cross the river, until a hunter arises who learns the secret of its power and kills it.[20] A striking feature of these texts is the manner in which the natural world is less important than the human society: very few of the texts are centered in the conflict of hunter and prey. Instead, the relations of the human and natural worlds are translated into a social and often sexual relationship: a hunter is successful because of a bargain with a spirit, and is saved from paying with his life by the "despised co-wife" (a staple figure of Mande culture), or a hunter succeeds in slaying a beast that has terrorized a region, because his wife learns the secret of the beast's power (it is invariably a human who takes the shape of a beast). Animals may try to destroy an overly successful hunter by sending one of their number disguised as a seductive woman. And finally, several narratives tell of a tragic love between a hunter and a transformed antelope (a parallel to the Swan maidens of northern folklore) which ends in destruction for the couple but leaves children who in several narratives become the founders of the hunters' cult.

The narratives of the hunters' associations connect tenuously with the lineage-based historical epic of Sunjata through the figure of Manding Bori, the brother of the emperor. Manding Bori appears in one episode of the historical epic: he has a dispute with his sister over meat, and causes her skirt to fall down; his brother Sunjata rebukes him and tells him that his descendents will never be kings.[21] Within the hunters' narratives, however, Manding Bori is a more versatile figure and he appears in a number of what one might call the standard story types: the hunter who escapes the animal seductress, the hunter who rescues the stolen brides, and the hunter who marries the antelope. This last story, of which we have two versions,[22] may deserve to be given in slightly more detail, as it leads to useful material:

A hunter in the bush comes across a beautiful woman bathing, with her antelope skin nearby. He takes the antelope skin away, and the woman follows to retrieve it. They marry, on certain conditions: he will never reveal her origin, and he will never brandish fire at her. They have children. At length, however, they have a bitter argument (often because someone in the compound has learned her identity), and in the course of the quarrel, forgetting himself, the husband waves a firebrand at his wife. She retrieves her skin and vanishes into the bush. Some time later, the hunter kills an antelope. His children recognize the meat, and refuse the meal; the hunter, however, eats it with relish and then dies. The children (a boy and a girl) then grow up to become the founders, or deities, of the hunters' cult.

The story plays with identities and fundamental boundaries: most specifically between the human and animal, between the categories of food and non-food, and between human and natural space. When, in Ndugacè Samakè's version, the hunter waves a piece of burning wood at his wife, he is effectively changing her classification from human, female, and spouse to cookable food.[23] He has not only violated his promise, he has also completely redefined their relationship out of the human social sphere. The symbolic act is fulfilled in the end of the story, when the hunter does kill, cook, and eat his former wife, and it is probably significant that the part consumed, in both available versions, is the head, the most personalized part of the animal. In the version of Seydou Camara, the opposition of categories seems tied more to reproduction: Manding Bori and his antelope wife live in hiding in the bush, where she bears him four children, until Manding Bori's father performs a divination and enchantment because he is worried that his son has not yet married a (human) wife to produce human descendents. The diviners discover the couple's secret, and the wife runs away as a consequence.

Samakè also offers an interest twist, by which the hunter is a Fula named Maghan Jan who has turned his back upon his ethnic identity.[24]

While the story plays with oppositions and boundaries, one could argue that the ordinary order is affirmed: a marriage between human and animal is shown to be impossible. The story ends unhappily, even in the version of Seydou Camara where the offspring become the founders of the hunters' cult. Nor is this affirmation greeted with the satisfaction which accompanies the unhappy fate of the second sister in the tale of the two sisters; the tone is instead one of tragedy and sorrow.[25] The hunters' narratives establish a somewhat different narrative space than that either of the ordinary folktale or of the historical epic; it is one in which far more fundamental questions about the social order may be posed and other possibilities explored. Examination of a second narrative can help to illustrate the point.

"Nyakhalen la forgeronne" (Nyakhalen the blacksmith-woman) is a curious text performed by Seydou Camara, the great hunters' singer, who was also by birth in the blacksmith status group (a *numu*) and initiated into the Komo society.[26] It belongs to no easily defined category of narratives, neither hunters' epic nor historical narrative, not a folktale, not an initiatory text. But it seems to occupy much the same sort of narrative space as the hunters' epics: the story type fits into folkloric patterns, while the presentation and handling are those of the recited epic.

The story combines two separate narrative strands: in the first, the smith-woman Nyakhalen tries desperately to have a child, working with different diviners until she succeeds in becoming pregnant with the help of the spirits. Her son then grows up with the prohibition: he must never make love with a woman, or he will die. Naturally, he meets a woman, loves her, and dies. Nyakhalen runs wild into the bush, where she encounters the spirit who had helped her conceive; the spirit, in the form of a marabout (Muslim holy man) then offers to resuscitate the son if the mother will give her life for that of the dead youth. At the test, however, Nyakhalen withdraws: she cannot leave her husband alone. Then the son's lover accepts the sacrifice. She is untouched by the magic fire and the boy is brought back to life.[27]

This story plays with sex. We noted earlier the hesitancy of the historical epic to flesh out a seduction scene; there is no such hesitancy here, although neither is there any graphic detail. Nyakhalen first approaches two human diviners to ask their help in having a child; each of them sleeps with her:

> Bari made love with Nun Nyakhalen . . .
> "Nun Nyakhalen, come into my room,
> "Nun Nyakhalen, I am thinking of something,
> "Nun Nyakhalen, if you agree
> "Nun Nyakhalen, I would be very happy! . . .

He took Nyakhalen into his room, my friends!
"Noun Nyakhalen, see my bed there,
"Noun Nyakhalen, we can have some fun together."[28]

Each of the two humans who sleeps with her is then killed by Nyakhalen's husband, using special poisons known to blacksmiths. The spirit (or jinn) who assists her does not engage in surrogate activity; he consults a variety of oracles and then sends her to her husband, with whom she conceives. The son, in turn, is essentially seduced, although in a cursory manner.[29]

Ribaldry, however, is not the focus of the story, and in fact male sexuality is incidental. The story carefully juxtaposes distinct female relationships: one must be struck by the contrast between the frenzy with which Nyakhalen seeks to have a child and her hesitancy when it comes to sacrificing her life for that child, a hesitancy which in fact contradicts an earlier claim, made repeatedly to the jinn, that she would die for a child.[30] Her sexual conduct, performed in the name of procreation, is balanced by that of her son and his lover, performed in the name of passion, and to some extent the second act erases or nullifies the relationship formed through the first: once the son has engaged in intercourse with a woman, he apparently (by the logic of the story, at least) leaves the orbit of the mother for that of his sexual partner. In fact, Nun Sediman, the woman with whom he sleeps, does speak of trust and faith as she offers her life for his,[31] and she contrasts present loose mores with the trust shown in the past. So on one level, the story speaks for the childless mother seeking a child—a common theme in Mande oral literature—but also of the way in which that child will, to some extent, pass out of her control and form new social relationships if, indeed, the process of procreation which is so essential to the perpetuation of society is to continue.

Seydou Camara has thus defined a narrative space in which social issues can be presented and addressed. The message may still seem rather conservative—he expresses, rather than questions, the wife's yearning for offspring—but the novelty (certainly visible in terms of the extant corpus of texts collected at the time he himself was active) is that he, a male, does give a voice to a woman, and in fact produces a gynocentric text of sorts. His narratives lead to a perception of the ordering of society and a sense of its boundaries, in a way that other forms and genres seem not to do. What then makes this possible?

The significant trait, for this discussion, that unites both the story of "Manding Bori" and "Nyakhalen" is that they are set in a remote past, in a period of origins and the founding of institutions. The world portrayed is still very much the contemporary world (historical accuracy is not the point), but the characters involved are identified as the ancestral, type-setting figures whose actions have defined the world as we know it. In other words, the stories are set in a mythological time and space. It is a peculiarly Mande space, as opposed to the Muslim and European spaces which might be considered (although of course it is tinged with Islam, the dominant faith of the present in the area), and it is also a peculiarly nonhistorical space, distinct from the narratives associated with the lineage ancestors represented in the epic of Sunjata and other such narratives. As such, it can become the locale for a creative interrogation of social norms and boundaries. It is the place for an exploration of causes and possibilities: it is a space in which boundaries can be tested and crossed. The past holds the mirror up to the present, and the handling allows for a creative framing of the image.

In this process, modern Mande culture is drawing upon a far older cultural pattern, although perhaps somewhat unconsciously. The hunter is one of the central figures of creation mythology across the continent: he is the discoverer of new lands, the founder of communities, and the vehicle by which new skills travel from one group to another.[32] But despite this primordial function, in modern society hunters are not figures of authority. They are often considered rather despised and put-upon: they must suffer long hours in the bush, feeding mosquitoes and horseflies, for uncertain rewards. However, they appeal to the imagination. Seydou Camara sings:

> I've seen a hunter, I've seen my friend
> I've seen a hunter, I've seen my brother
> I've seen a hunter, I've seen my sharer of pleasures[33]

The construction is of the hunter as an everyman figure, a surrogate for the ordinary person caught in undesirable living conditions, who will nevertheless win through by merit and determination, or with the assistance of helpers (the folktale patterns at work). This is a figure that can appeal to the modern conscience, caught in a conflict of dynamics and daunted by the disparities between the outer world and the local space. This is the figure that can cross into new spaces and create new perspectives on the society.

Notes

1. Veronika Görög-Karady comments: "They [tales of the Bambara-Malinké group] carry rather simple explicit ideological messages which conform to prevailing social norms. They show in most cases a protagonist acting against the established laws of society and who will be punished accordingly." "Tales and

Ideology: The Revolt of the Sons in Bambara-Malinké Tales," in Graham Furniss and Liz Gunner, eds., *Power, Marginality, and African Oral Literature* (Johannesburg: Witswatersrand University Press, 1995), 83–91. Michael Jackson, dealing with Kuranko narratives from Sierra Leone (the Kuranko are a related Mande group), also focused upon the moral imperatives that are made quite explicit in the stories he assembles (*Allegories of the Wilderness* [Bloomington: Indiana University Press, 1982]).

2. The bibliography on the Mande world is now quite extensive; for a basic description of social structures, see Diango Cissé, *Structures malinké de Kita* (Bamako: Editions populaires, 1970), 57ff. On the Nyamakala, or craft groups, see David Conrad and Barbara Frank, eds., *Status and Identity in West Africa* (Bloomington: Indiana University Press, 1985). For references to later work, see Stephen Belcher, *Epic Traditions of Africa* (Bloomington: Indiana University Press, 1999), 64–141, with notes and bibliography.

3. For a general description of Mande epic traditions, see Belcher, *Epic Traditions* (see note 2), 64–141. Ralph Austen offers a series of studies focusing on the epic of Sunjata in his edited volume, *In Search of Sunjata: The Mande Oral Epic as History, Literature, and Performance* (Bloomington: Indiana University Press, 1999). The best-known English versions would be those of Djibril Tamsir Niane, *Sunjata: An Epic of Old Mali*, trans. G. D. Pickett (London: Longman, 1965) and John William Johnson, ed., *The Epic of Son-Jara According to Fa-Digi Sisoko: A West African Tradition* (Bloomington: Indiana University Press, 1986). There are now several new versions in print, most notably a recent text from Guinea edited by David Conrad: *Sunjata, a West African Epic of the Mande Peoples* (Indianapolis: Hackett Publishing, 2004).

4. Representative regional collections would include Gerard Meyer, *Contes du pays malinke* (Paris, Karthala, 1987); Katrin Pfeiffer, *Mandinka Spoken Art: Folk-Tales, Griot Accounts, and Songs* (Köln: Rüdiger Köppe Verlag, 1997), Michael Jackson, *Allegories*.

5. For discussions of historical epics in West Africa, see Lilyan Kesteloot and Bassirou Dieng, *Les Épopées d'Afrique Noire* (Paris: Karthala, 1997), 39–61, 67–92 and Belcher, *Epic Traditions*, 1–26.

6. Gordon Innes, ed. *Sunjata: Three Mandinka Versions* (London: School of Oriental and African Studies, 1974), 73, lines 723–28. It is worth observing that this performance was actually recorded at a school, and so Bamba Suso may have put on his pedagogical hat for the occasion. Also, the question of princesses and other social categories has a local resonance in the Gambia; the neighboring Sereer people, in Senegal, claim a Mande princess as founder of the royal lineage. But the princess had fled the Mande because she took a jeli as a lover. See Stephen Belcher, *African Myths of Origin* (London: Penguin, 2005), 428–29.

7. Camara Laye, *Le maître de la parole* (Paris: Plon, 1978). English translation by James Kirkup, *The Guardian of the Word* (New York: Aventura, 1980/1984). This novelization of the story is based on an oral account collected from Babu Condé of Fadama, in Guinea.

8. I am indebted to David C. Conrad for access to unpublished translations of versions of the epics of Samory. An excerpt is given in John W. Johnson, Thomas Hale,

and Stephen Belcher, eds., *Oral Epics from Africa* (Bloomington: Indiana University Press, 1997), 68–79. For some discussion of the epic of Samory, see Jan Jansen, "The Adventures of the 'Epic of Samori' in 20th-century Mande Oral Tradition" in Jan Jansen and Henk M. J. Maier, eds., *Epic Adventures: Heroic Narrative in Oral Performance Traditions of Four Continents* (Munster: Lit Verlag, 2004), 71–80. On Kèmè Brèma, see also Ansoumane Camara, "L'image de Kèmè Bouréma dans l'épopée samorienne," *Mande Studies* 3 (2001): 65–72.

9. The standard reference for the career of al-Hajj Umar is the work of David Robinson, *The Holy War of Umar Tal* (Oxford: Oxford University Press, 1985); French translation: *La guerre sainte d'Umar Tal* (Paris: Karthala, 1988).

10. See David Conrad, "Mooning Armies and Mothering Heroes" in Austen, *In Search of Sunjata*, 189–229.

11. See Meyer, *Contes*, 13.

12. See Jackson, *Allegories*, 242–46 and Meyer, *Contes*, 66–70;. The region offers interesting variants. From Senegal, Blaise Cendrars reproduces a story in which the hero (male) encounters people with enormous genitals on his way to and from the quest in his *Anthologie Nègre* (Paris: Buchet Chastel, 1947), 305–13. Ruth Finnegan recorded a story among the Limba of Sierra Leone in which the pair of women are co-wives, one of whom wants a child; the disgusting tests to which the old woman puts the aspirant are quite clearly drawn from every-day child care (Ruth Finnegan, ed. and trans., *Limba Stories and Storytelling* [Oxford: Oxford University Press, 1967], 249–54).

13. See Görög-Karady, "Tales and Ideology," 83–84.

14. Pfeiffer, *Mandinka Spoken Art*, 74–76.

15. The works of Youssouf Cissé are largely devoted to describing the rituals and explicating the narratives ("Notes sur les sociétés de chasseurs malinké," *Journal de la Société des africanistes* 34 (1964) 175–226; *La confrérie des chasseurs Malinké et Bambara: Mythes, rites, et récits initiatiques* [Paris: Arsan/ Editions Nouvelles du Sud, 1994]); work by other Malian scholars such as Brahima Camara (*Jägerliteratur in Manden: Gattungs-und Übersetzungsprobleme afrikanischer Oralliteratur am Beispiel von Baala Jinba Jakites Epos Bilakoro Mari (Teil 1)* [Bayreuth: Schultz and Stellmacher, 1998]) or N'Golo Konatè (*Jägererzählungen der Bamanan: Transcription, Übersetzung und literarischer Kommentar* [Bayreuth: Schultz and Stellmacher, 1998]) largely repeats Cissé's findings. The work of Foday Tounkara is independent (*La parole du serewa*, Stockholm, private printing, 1993), but largely a nostalgic panegyric. A paper by Sten Hagberg, presented in 2002, documents the ways in which a hunters' association near Bobo-Dioulasso, in Burkina Faso, is being used as an instrument of exclusion against incoming Peuls. Joseph Helweg is working on hunters' groups in northern Côte d'Ivoire, but I have not yet seen his work.

16. Virtually the only skepticism of Cissé's claims expressed by an African scholar is that of Karim Traoré, *Le jeu et le sérieux* (Koln: Rüdiger Köppe Verlag, 2000), 95ff.

17. The best-known local group is the Jakhanke (or Diakhanke); see Lamin O. Sanneh, *The Jakhanke* (London: International African Institute, 1979) or more generally Nehemia Levtzion's chapter on west African Islam in Levztion and Randall Pouwels, eds., *A History of Islam in Africa* (Athens: Ohio University Press,

2000). Their founder, Salim Souare, preached coexistence with nonbelievers and conversion by example.

18. The result is something of an escape from the normal limits of society. One popular example may illustrate the pattern. Salif Keita is a very popular singer in Mali, but had been subject to criticism because a member of the Keita lineage (nobles) normally should not be a public performer; that is the function of the *jeli* lineages. His response was to turn to hunters' music and take on the trappings of a hunters' singer, a *sere*, and the shift muted the criticism (see Cherif Keita, "A Praise Song for the Father: Family Identity in Salif Keita's Music," in Jan Jansen and Clemens Zobel, eds., *The Younger Brother in Mande Kinship and Politics in West Africa* [Leiden: Center for Non-Western Studies, 1996], 97–104).

19. See the discography in Karim Traore, *Le jeu*, 241–43.

20. For the Bozo version, see Shekh Tijaan Hayidara, ed. and trans., *La geste de Fanta Maa* (Niamey: CELHTO, 1987). For the Gambian version, see Gordon Innes and Bakari Sidibe, eds. and trans., *Hunters and Crocodiles: Narratives of a Hunters' Bard Performed by Bakari Kamara* (Sandgate: Paul Norbury/Unesco, 1990). For the version from Baro, see Ahmadou Kouyaté, Denise Aebersold, and Dramane Keita, eds. and trans., *Manden Mori Fasa: Récits de chasse* (Conakry: Bibliothèque Franco-Guinéenne, 1994), vol. 2.

21. This episode is not found in all versions of the epic. It is missing from some of the older texts we have, and it is not mentioned in versions from the Gambia. It does appear in versions recorded since independence in Mali, in the same areas where Manding Bori is associated with the origin of the hunters' cult.

22. There are two available bilingual editions of the story in print, one by Ndugacè Samakè, from the collection of Annik Thoyer, *Récits épiques des chasseurs Bamanan du Mali* (Paris: L'Harmattan, 1995; first published 1978),19–69, and the other by Seydou Camara, in Gerald Cashion's dissertation, "Hunters of the Mande: A Behavioral Code and Worldview Derived from the Study of their Folklore," 2 vols. (Indiana University, 1984), vol. 2 second appendix.

23. The food element is present in Seydou Camara's version, as witnessed by this revealing comment, "Her teeth had never touched cooked food," given in the course of his initial description of the beautiful woman/antelope (Cashion, "Hunters of the Mande," appendix II on 28); the theme is amplified by a discussion of what she eats (not meat, at any point) and how it is cooked.

24. There is in fact a group of Maninka/Bamana speakers known as the Fula of Manding, associated with the region of Wassulu, on either side of the border of Mali and Guinea. They have distinctive patronyms (Sidibe, Sangare, Diallo, Diakhite) and, if indeed originally Fula, have lost their distinctive culture to become completely assimilated with the dominant Maninka culture of the area. Several eminent hunters' singers are from the region, and it is now contributing a distinct and very popular mode of women's singing as well. In Seydou Camara's version of the story, the antelope, Dagwe (literally "white mouth," but this is also the name of the animal in Maninka), is described as a white, Arab woman, fat enough to have folds about her neck, and so here again there is an ethnic displacement. Fat is associated with wealth and beauty in west Africa.

25. Both available versions end with a lament for the death of the hunter, which moves the recitation into what may be the more usual discourse of hunters' singing. Cissé and others have noted that the usual occasion for a hunters' gathering and the singing that accompanies it is the funeral of a hunter, and references to the great hunters of bygone days (with regret for their passing) are a staple of the genre. This is not unique to the Mande; see also Bade Ajuwon, *Funeral Dirges of Yoruba Hunters* (New York: Nok Publishers, 1982).

26. Annik Thoyer, ed. and trans., *Nyakhalen la forgeronne . . . par Seyidou Kamara* (n.p.,1986).

27. The mother's quest for a pregnancy is almost standard in west Africa; Seydou Camara offers a parallel sequence in another recorded epic, *Kambili* (ed. and trans. by Charles Bird, Bourama Soumaoro, Gerald Cashion, Mamadou Kante [Bloomington: Indiana University Linguistics Club, 1974; Bamana text in 1976]). The prohibition of sex and rescue by the lover are not a standard tale-type. The pattern of serial refusals by family-members, culminating in rescue by the lover, corresponds to Child Ballad 95, the "Briery Bush." There are other regional examples, discussed by Görög-Karady, "Tales and Ideology," 87–88. One might also mention, while discussing prohibitions of sex, a story published in the N'ko writing system by Soulaymane Kante, in which a king forbids his three sons from having sex on pain of death; all three disobey, but only the youngest escapes punishment by demanding that the father admit his own guilt in the matter. The story is described and discussed in some detail by Valentin Vydrine, "Souleymane Kante, un philosophe-innovateur traditionnaliste Maninka, vu à travers ses écrits en N'Ko," *Mande Studies* 3 (2001) 99–131.

28. Thoyer, *Nyakhalen*, 25; my translation from the French.

29. The activity is initiated by the woman, who sees him and suffers a passion; she then enlists the services of an old woman to find the way to fulfill her desires. The function of the old woman here echoes the medieval European staple character of the *vieille*, the older intermediary in affairs of the heart, and the parallels probably deserve further study.

30. Thoyer, *Nyakhalen*, 37.

31. The Bamana word is "Lahadi," possibly from the Arabic *lahaja*, which denotes devotion leading into infatuation.

32. I know of no general regional or continental study on the figure; for representative narratives from a variety of groups, see my *African Myths of Origin*. There is also an excellent collection of narratives from the Fon (of modern Benin, formerly Dahomey) in the Herskovits' collection, *Dahomeyan Narrative* (Melville and Frances Herskovits, *Dahomeyan Narrative* [Evanston: Northwestern University Press, 1956]). Certain figures in Mande history, and most notably Sunjata, are credited with having been hunters before they were kings, and Seydou Camara remarks, in *Kambili*, that "Kings have always come from the hunters" (on 59, see note 27), but the quality of the hunter does not seem to translate well into royal power.

33. Seydou Camara, *Kambili*, 1, lines 16–18, repeated elsewhere in the text.

III

Early Modern Cultures

Chapter 8

Peripheral Inclusion: Communal Belonging in Suriname's Sephardic Community[*]

Aviva Ben-Ur

The Jews of Suriname in a Dutch Caribbean Context

The first Jews to permanently settle in the Caribbean arrived in the mid-seventeenth century and traced their origins to the Iberian peninsula, where many had lived for centuries as New Christians before reverting to Judaism in centers such as Amsterdam, Bayonne, and London. The place of Jews in colonial Caribbean societies is of particular interest since they were often among the first white settlers. Perhaps nowhere in the region has their impact been more pronounced than in Suriname and Curaçao, the longest-lived and historically largest Jewish communities in the early modern Caribbean.[1]

Both communities were established in the 1650s by Sephardim (the Hebrew-derived term for Jews of Portuguese and Spanish origin), peaked at just over 1,000 members in the eighteenth century, comprised one-third of the white population, and survive to this day, albeit in drastically reduced numbers.[2] Suriname, a former Dutch colony and today an independent republic roughly the size of the U.S. State of Georgia, and Curaçao, an island of 178 square miles that is part of the Netherlands Antilles (an autonomous region of the Kingdom of the Netherlands since 1954), are ideal for a diachronic exploration of relations between European-origin Jews and non-Jews of African descent in the Caribbean. The vast majority of Suriname's population (96 percent by the late eighteenth century) was both enslaved and of African origin.[3] Similarly, 79 percent of Curaçao's population by 1789 traced its roots to Africa.[4] These factors—demographics and communal longevity—form the context in which the black/Jewish nexus developed from the 1650s to the present day.

Only recently have the role and status of men and women of African descent in Caribbean Jewish communities received serious attention, particularly since Robert Cohen's groundbreaking *Jews in Another Environment* (1991).[5] This article seeks to fathom the transformation of communal membership and the place of Eurafrican progeny in the Jewish settlement of Suriname, with some attention to Curaçao.[6] In both cases, the linchpin of the early creolization of the colonies' Jews are the mostly nameless women of African descent, at once reviled and desired, who bore children fathered by their masters, setting into motion a Judeo-African syncretism that endures until today.

Defining Communal Membership

In his 1991 monograph, Robert Cohen explored the transformation of early modern Surinamese Jewish society as it sought to perpetuate traditional mores while responding to its new surroundings. The importance he placed on environment is especially pertinent in a comparison between Suriname and Curaçao.[7] Physical environment—particularly climate and its long-term consequences—played a central role in shaping the economies and societies of these two Jewish communities.

On the riverside shores of the jungle, Suriname's Jews established an agrarian settlement comprising dozens of plantations and centered around Jodensavanne, or Jews' Savannah, an autonomous village where members congregated for synagogue services, attended educational institutions, and were administered justice by a secular Jewish court. Dominating the stretch of the Suriname River, some thirty kilometers south of the capital city of Paramaribo, Jodensavanne and the dozens of surrounding Jewish plantations collectively formed, by the mid-eighteenth century, the largest Jewish agricultural community of its time and the only Jewish settlement in the Americas that was granted virtual self-rule. Under tolerant Dutch rule, Sephardim received rights, exemptions, and immunities both as an ethnic minority and as burghers, arguably the most liberal treatment Jews had ever received in the Christian world. The setting—a self-determining Jewish village—represents one of the few situations in Diaspora history where the highest form of social climbing meant becoming a Jew, rather than a Christian or a Muslim. Beginning in the last quarter of the eighteenth century, a combination of soil depletion, maroon attacks, and economic crisis led to the gradual demise of Jodensavanne, the abandonment of agricultural pursuits, and the definitive shift of Suriname's Sephardic community to the capital city.[8]

Curaçao's early Jewish settlers were drawn from the same streams as those who migrated to Suriname. While the first Jews to plant roots on the island were expected to engage in agriculture, the infertility of the soil and infrequency of rain quickly led them to abandon the earth for mercantile enterprises.[9] Because of their preference for trade over agriculture, Curaçao's Jews owned fewer slaves than their Surinamese brethren. This did not, however, affect their standing in the Dutch Caribbean social pyramid. Similar to Suriname, the island's Sephardim were among the white elite, occupying a social status just below that of Dutch Protestants.[10]

In both Suriname and Curaçao, colonial demographics cited earlier, dramatically skewed in favor of blacks, rendered miscegenation virtually inevitable. In the former colony, Jews were vastly outnumbered by the Africans they owned. As early as 1684, 4,200 African slaves resided in Suriname, and the colony's 232 Jewish householders, comprising 28.6 percent of Suriname's European population, owned slightly more (30.3 percent or 1,298) than their share of slaves.[11] On Curaçao, however, the "most complete list of Curaçaoan slave owners," dating to 1764–65, shows that only 16 percent (or 869) of the 5,534 slaves on the island were Jewish-owned.[12] Thus, the number of slaves owned by Jews roughly equaled the Jewish population of the time, though there were exceptional community members who owned dozens of slaves.[13]

Like many early colonial American settlements, the Jewish communities of both Suriname and Curaçao suffered a dearth of women in the early years of formation. 64.4 percent of Suriname's Jewish population in 1684 was adult male, comprising almost twice as many men as women. This approximates patterns in the gentile European population, where 74 percent of the community was male. Such gender imbalance helped open the doors to "Suriname marriage," described as "the informal, but still permanent relationship concluded with some form of ceremony and ending with the death or departure of the white male," a phenomenon typical of both the gentile and Jewish communities. This Caribbean form of concubinage was characterized by sexual double standards, leading to an Afro-European population that could claim white descent mainly through the paternal line.[14] While parallel statistics are not available for Curaçao, it is likely that a similar pattern was obtained.[15] Finally, the slave in colonial American society possessed no legal status. Official marriage between the enslaved and the free was impossible, again leaving concubinage as an obvious resort.[16] Extra-legal sexual relations between blacks and whites led to the rise of two separate Eurafrican classes that existed on the peripheries of white gentile and Jewish society. These marginal groups were key to the growth, survival, and redefinition of the white gentile and Sephardic populations.

Miscegenation between Jews and blacks in Suriname likely began during the earliest Jewish settlement in the colony. The first known evidence is a bylaw drafted by the Mahamad (Hebrew for "assembly"), the autonomous governing body of Suriname's Jews, alluding to unions between Euro-Sephardi Jews and their African-origin consorts. In 1662–63, Suriname's Jewish leaders explicitly defined the two subdivisions of the Sephardic community. The Hebrew term *jahid* referred to a full member of the Jewish community by virtue of his or her European descent. The second-class *congregante* (Portuguese for "congregant") denoted either a Eurafrican Jew or a first-class member, by virtue of his whiteness, who had been demoted to a lower social status as a penalty for marrying a Jewish female of African descent.[17]

More concrete evidence of sexual unions between Sephardim and women of African origin—both legal and extra-legal—are sprinkled throughout communal archives. The excavation and collation of these references has only just begun, and those relating to concubinage are particularly oblique. Among the earliest is the case of Joseph Pelegrino, who in 1720 appealed to local authorities to recognize the manumission of his children, all procreated outside of legal marriage.[18] Simha, Jacob, and Mariana, he declared, were all of the Jewish religion, adopted as members of Suriname's Sephardic community by its teacher (*leraar*) and properly manumitted according to the rules of the Jewish "nation." Inheritance issues prompted Pelegrino's request, for the laws of the Jewish community were at times contrary to those of the Dutch colonial government, and it was thus unclear whether the children's status and rights would be accepted outside Jewish circles. Pelegrino's request was nonetheless granted by the court and his three children were declared "free of all slavery" and legitimized as his true descendants.[19]

Here, it is important to note that a white Jewish woman would likely never have found herself in a position to produce Eurafrican children, convert them to Judaism, and appeal for their manumission. First of all, her children would have been automatically Jewish according to rabbinical laws, which stipulated that Jewishness is transmitted through the mother. Secondly, extramarital intercourse between European-origin women and (presumably enslaved) blacks or Indians was regarded a heinous crime by the larger ruling society. In a placard of 1711, colonial authorities named such aberrations "unnatural whoredom and adultery." Unmarried violators would be flogged and banished for life, while married women would also be branded, a punishment generally reserved for slaves.[20] The very existence of this law points to actual illicit unions between white women and their black or Indian consorts, but these were rare.[21] In 1721 two white Christian women were so accused, while ten years later, the daughter of a Jewish planter acknowledged having a sexual relationship with an Indian. The key is that the offending female was expelled from the colony, while the extramarital alliances of white Jewish men were not only on some level countenanced, but the resulting offspring at times legitimized through recognition of paternity, conversion to Judaism, and manumission.[22]

Thus, miscegenation in the Dutch and Jewish communities was outright prohibited only when the involved female was white. Her punishment entailed not a mere loss of social status (as in the case of *jehidim* demoted to *congregantes*), but rather her local eradication: complete elimination from community membership as well as physical removal from the colony. In Suriname, the Jewish tradition of women as determinants of an offspring's ethno-religious identity was therefore reversed. If Sephardic men had not sought to bring their enslaved children into the Jewish fold, the community would have had few, if any, Eurafrican Jews. The phenomenon of the so-called "mulatto" Jew—at least initially, before Eurafrican Jewesses complexified Jewish genealogical descent—was thus wholly an expression of a Caribbean patriarchy that suppressed one of the main matriarchal aspects of rabbinical Judaism.[23]

There are suggestions that in Suriname the conversion of slaves to Judaism entailed a formal ceremony carefully guided by rabbinical liturgical rites. The prayer book *Sefer Berith Yitshak* ("The Covenant of Isaac"), whose earliest known edition was published in 1729 in Amsterdam, includes instructions for circumcising and ritually immersing male and female slaves for conversion to Judaism. The ceremony, involving a ritual circumciser (*mohel*) for boys, Hebrew prayers, a glass of wine, and ritual immersion for both sexes, closely followed the biblical commandment, "He that is born in thy house, and he that is bought with thy money, must needs be circumcised: and my covenant shall be in your flesh for an everlasting covenant."[24]

Though published in Amsterdam, the prayer book was evidently meant not only for European, but also for Caribbean consumption. The appendix of ritual circumcisers at the end, arranged according to their city or colony of residence, names practitioners in the Sephardic communities of Amsterdam, The Hague, Naarden, London, Hamburg, and Bayonne, as well as Suriname and Curaçao, the only Caribbean centers included in this list. Significantly, another Amsterdam edition from 1764/1765, reprinted in 1803/1804, is housed in the synagogue archives of Congregation Mikvé

Israel-Emmanuel in Curaçao. While bereft of a list of ritual circumcisers, this volume does include the slave conversion ceremony.[25] The extent and geographical range of archival holdings (yet to be determined) is essential in providing an idea of the relevance of slave conversions for various early modern Jewish communities. The successive reprinting of this book—with the slave prayer unexpurgated—opens the question of the endurance of this practice through at least the early nineteenth century. The explicit evidence of slave conversion to Judaism unearthed for Suriname seems not to exist for Curaçao (or has not yet surfaced), leading most scholars to conclude that the phenomenon did not develop on that island.[26]

Peripheral Inclusion

The entrance of individuals of African descent into the Jewish community of Suriname granted them a second-class social status I have termed "peripheral inclusion." In this paradigm, Jewish elites extended official communal membership to individuals they considered fellow, albeit marginal, Jews. Typically, these individuals were the progeny of African mothers and Sephardic fathers who were legally recognized and converted to Judaism under the aegis of the Jewish patriarch, as well as their descendants (who, if born of Eurafrican Jewish mothers, did not need to convert). These individuals—the aforementioned *congregantes*—existed both metaphorically and literally at the limits of Sephardic society.

The synagogue, as a daily gathering spot offering social prestige and a sense of belonging, provided the most dramatic spectacles of *congregante* relegation. It is thus not surprising that some Eurafricans actively asserted their right to *jahid* status in this very space. The most coveted seats in the synagogue were between the pillars, and even *jehidim* who had a theoretical right to be seated there were obliged to petition the Mahamad for an official seat. In 1754, the Mahamad added an ordinance that seating for Eurafrican Jews was limited to the mourner's bench, just as in times past, and not anywhere else (that is, not between the pillars). This reaffirmation hints that by the mid-eighteenth century, Eurafricans had begun to petition for just those seats.[27] The article does not appear in the 1748 askamot, suggesting that the 1750s were a turning point for congregant activism. Peripheral inclusion had already existed in Amsterdam's Sephardic synagogue, where male converts to Judaism were never appointed to official posts in the Jewish community, rabbinical law stipulating that a convert not be given a post with coercive authority. Similarly, Amsterdam's Mahamad decreed in 1644 that "circumcised Negro Jews" were not to be called to the

Torah or given any honorary commandments to perform in the synagogue.[28] These examples indicate that peripheral inclusion was not exclusively a Caribbean phenomenon, but was perhaps an outcome of Atlantic slavery and its impact on Sephardi Diasporic communities.

Second-class status followed the manumitted and their nonwhite descendants to the grave, noticeable in Jodensavanne's cemetery, which preserves some 460 grave markers. The cemetery is spread over terrain that gently slopes downward from "top to bottom" (northwest to southeast) and from right to left (northeast to southwest). In the southeast extreme (the limit of the burial ground, near a no-longer extant fence) three tombstones, submerged several feet beneath the soil's surface, were unearthed by a cemetery expedition in 1999.[29] The individuals buried below, Jacob Peregrino (d. 1750), Joseph Pelengrino, and Joseph de Mattos (both d. 1751) share the family names of Jewish slaves manumitted by the first two decades of the 1720s and may be direct descendants. Joseph Pelengrino is perhaps the aforementioned petitioner who manumitted his three children.[30] Communal archives describing the relative position of deceased Eurafrican Jews in this cemetery reveal a concatenation of *congregantes* stretching from Luna, daughter of David Haim del Monte, to Joseph Pelengrino, all buried along the fence on the southerly slope of the hill.[31]

This liminal spot continued to be reserved for manumitted slaves through at least the late eighteenth century. In May of 1791 the free "mulata" Simha, who had been enslaved to Joseph Gabay Farro, was also buried in the "southern part" of the cemetery, near the fence. She was laid to rest with feet pointing to the east, in accordance with Jewish law, near the grave of the aforementioned Joseph, son of Gabriel de Mattos. The next month her sister, Jahel, also a free Eurafrican who had once served the same master, was buried at Simha's feet. Both graves were marked with a (presumably wooden) stake, rather than a carved stone slab, and have since disintegrated. Only the burial register and a passing reference to their manumission preserve their memory.[32]

A similar pattern of peripheral inclusion emerged in Paramaribo's oldest Sephardic burial ground. A plot book of that cemetery lists "rows of congregants," where the socially inferior were interred. The decedents bear well-known Eurafrican Jewish family names, such as Judio/Judia (Jew/Jewess) and Pelegrino, as well as names of founding Sephardic families, such as d'Avilar, Cohen Nassy, and Mendes Meza, revealing an increasingly intertwined African and European Jewish lineage.[33]

While in death Suriname's Eurafrican Jews were pushed into the margins of the Jewish cemetery, in life they had more options. In the mid-eighteenth century Eurafrican Jews formed separate institutions and developed their own ceremonies, closely modeled on those of their white Jewish counterparts.

This occurred as early as 1759, when Eurafrican Jews at Jodensavanne formed a brotherhood (*siva*) called the Path of the Righteous (*Darhe Jesarim*)[34] as well as a separate prayerhouse.[35] These separate institutions were not only sanctioned by whites Jews but also founded with the financial support of both Sephardim and Ashkenazim.[36] When Eurafrican Jews attempted to extend these parallel models to funereal ceremonies, they realized the limits of their Jewish independence.

On November 20th, 1787, evidently on his deathbed, Daniel Peregrino petitioned the governing leaders of the Liviat Hen brotherhood for permission to be carried in a funeral procession by his disciples. Evasively, the regents decided not to answer, instead placing the question in the hands of the brotherhood's leader.[37] Peregrino's last name suggests a Eurafrican Jewish identity, and indeed, his entry in the death register two days later identifies him as a congregant.[38] References to his "disciples" and the desire for a special procession suggest that Eurafrican Jews had their own leadership and ceremonies that paralleled those of the white Sephardic community.

A major fissure that split the Sephardic community in 1790 reveals that the Peregrino case was not an isolated incident. First studied by the late Robert Cohen, this was perhaps the first major rebellion against Jewish congregant status.[39] In April 1790, Joseph, son of David Nassy, a prominent member of the Jewish Eurafrican class, breathed his last breath. Given his stature, the Eurafrican mourners desired to inter him with the ceremonies reserved for a Sephardic community president (*Parnas Presidente*), carefully dictated in communal ordinances.[40] This entailed a procession with wax candles in which the mourners—rather than the cantor—would sing the memorial prayers. The problem was that Joseph was a Eurafrican Jew, and hence occupied the status of congregant. In demanding such protocol, Nassy's disciples expressed their desire to appropriate rituals reserved solely for leaders of the Mahamad, suggesting the development of an internal political structure that consciously mimicked that of the white Jewish community.

A regent present at the funeral observed this breach of social propriety and intervened to forbid the procession "as being contrary to the bylaws of the community."[41] Racial tensions resurfaced during the actual burial. The Eurafrican mourners were horrified to discover that Nassy's intended grave was located "in a swamp and only one foot deep." Their objections were silenced with the Mahamad's response: "You cannot give orders here, and if you folks do not shut up we will shut you up." The grave's condition confirms not only a designated location for deceased non-white Sephardim in the outer limits of the cemetery—similar to that of Jodensavanne—but also the Mahamad's discriminatory neglect of Eurafrican burial sites. The regents rejected the latter allegation, pointing to weather conditions in the months of April and May, which assured that "there will always be water on the outer grounds which are lying low and in which a hole has to be dug to serve as a grave."[42]

At the end of that year more unrest challenged the Mahamad's authority. On December 17, just before the Jewish Sabbath, the president (*Parnas Presidente*) of Jodensavanne's Congregation Beraha VeSalom dispatched the *samas*, Solomon Fereyra, to order a shroud and box for the recently deceased *congregante*, Simon de Meza. Fereyra presented the request before the congregation's brotherhood, Liviat Hen, which was in charge of funereal arrangements. However, the brotherhood official refused to comply, pointing to article 10 of the brotherhood's bylaws—approved by the Mahamad itself—that only members of the Portuguese Jewish nation, who were *jehidim* or *congregantes* from a "legitimate marriage," could receive these funereal necessities. Simon de Meza was not a *jahid*, nor a *congregante* of a legitimate marriage. Although his parentage is unknown, de Meza was likely conceived out of wedlock to Eurafrican Jewish parents or out of wedlock to a white Sephardi master and *congreganta*. The death register lists Simon de Meza only as a *congregante* who was buried in Paramaribo.[43]

So as not to be "considered disobedient," the brotherhood official paid a personal visit to the president of the Mahamad and reminded him of the articles that prevented the request from being fulfilled. In what was likely a heated argument, the president asked and then commanded that the order be carried out that one time, without consequences for the future. He promised to provide the explanation later. Recognizing the Mahamad was its superior, the brotherhood was forced to carry out the order, as there was no opportunity to convene a *junta* (ad-hoc meeting). Fissures were appearing in the community's foundation: the president had violated the Mahamad's own legislation.

The Tuesday following the Sabbath, the brotherhood convened a *junta* at which it was resolved to respectfully ask the Mahamad to allow the Liviat Hen to follow its own articles. One *junta* member, Abraham Bueno Bibaz, requested to be exempt from the meeting, suggesting either a fear of repercussions or his sympathy with the Eurafrican Jew's plight. The disruption over the funeral of Joseph Cohen Nassy earlier that year may have made the congregation's leaders more cautious about further offending the sensibilities of Eurafrican Jews. If this reading is correct, the Eurafrican community had a considerable degree of communal power, despite its second-class status. Moreover, the conflict suggests that there was no clear dividing line between white and Eurafrican Jews. Cross-group alliances show that the Mahamad itself was internally divided.

Meanwhile, fury over the treatment of Joseph Nassy's remains seemed to intensify with time. The protests of the Eurafrican mourners led the Mahamad to demand a written statement from Eurafrican leader Reuben

Mendez Meza, presenting his community's complaints. Meza's statement was interpreted by the regents as a demand for independence, and their response was intended to remind Eurafrican Jews of their place and prevent further social uprisings. The Mahamad responded that all "Mulattoes, Mestices and Castices who call themselves children of Portuguese [and] Spanish Jews will be *congreganten* of the Congregation *Beraha Ve Shalom*." Furthermore, the Mahamad reminded them that they were forbidden to maintain their brotherhood without permission and demanded the Eurafrican Jews present the brotherhood's constitution. They submitted these constitutional bylaws in May of 1791, over a year after the controversial funeral.

To the surprise of the Eurafrican Jews, the regent secretary, David Nassy (perhaps the white father of the deceased Eurafrican Jewish leader), returned a revised version of this constitution that severely limited the operations of *Darhe Jesarim*. Nassy curbed Eurafrican Jewish privileges in three areas: burial rites, financial aid, and *jahid* involvement in the running of *Darhe Jesarim*. Restrictions on funeral services conveyed a clear message that protests, such as those that interrupted Joseph Nassy's funeral, would not be tolerated. The white Nassy stipulated that no *congregante* would ever be buried in a procession carrying wax candles, and the funeral liturgy (*ascaba*) was to be recited by the cantor as opposed to the mourners. Furthermore, these prayers were to be uttered in the fraternity house, not in the cemetery. Lastly, the Mahamad would withdraw virtually all financial assistance to and involvement in the brotherhood. Such strictures helped ensure that *Darhe Jesarim* would remain purely a brotherhood and not a separate religious congregation.[44] They also dealt a huge blow to both the brotherhood and the status of Eurafricans in the Jewish community.

These setbacks did not inhibit Eurafricans from further rebellion. Not only did they refuse to sign this new constitution; they also threatened to withhold their taxes (*finta*) and to withdraw from the Jewish community by joining the Ashkenazim, leading the Mahamad to ban the brotherhood altogether. In 1793, the Eurafricans, perhaps naïvely, appealed to the non-Jewish authorities at Paramaribo to be admitted as full members (*jehidim*) of the Sephardic community. The detailed process of this appeal and reactions to it predictably ended in a triumph of the white Sephardic government. Eurafrican Jews were "to behave themselves in all respects with the subordination and the due respect" toward the leaders of the Mahamad, and the abolishment of *Darhe Jesarim* was confirmed. Furthermore, any further protests or uprisings would be punished as "disturbances of the peace."[45]

The threat posed by the Eurafrican Jews did not lay merely in their ritual challenge to time-honored traditions. The very existence of Jewish Eurafricans and their limbo racial status threatened the definition of white status. The communal bylaws bifurcated members into the categories of *jahid* and *congregante*, and seem ill suited to deal with the more complex social reality. Jewish Eurafricans referred to themselves as colored (*kleurlingen*), while the colonial and white Jewish leaders of the colony employed such terms as *negroes, karboegers, mulattos, mestices,* and *castices*.[46] Moreover, the issue of "legitimate marriage" further clouded the social status of second-class Jews. And, as we have seen, a white Jewish leader's personal sentiment or conviction could overturn the Mahamad's very regulations. In this panoply of ancestry, circumstances of birth, and personal bias, what precisely defined a Jew, a *jahid*, or a *congregante*?

Previous studies dealing with Suriname's "mulatto" Jews usually portray them as pitted against white Jews and fighting for autonomy or secession. In reality, the two groups more resembled concentric circles than separate spheres. The same communal records that detail racial conflict also reveal just how permeable boundaries could be. The case of the aforementioned Simon de Meza and his white Sephardi sympathizers is one example. Another is the recurring controversy surrounding seating arrangements in the synagogue. In 1794 the Mahamad of Beraha VeSalom complained of disorderly conduct among the *congregantes* who frequently claimed seats in the section reserved for *jahidim*. The resolution, imposing a fine of 100 guilders on any transgressor, also warned that the same punishment would be the lot of *jahidim*—male or female—who attempted to occupy the seats of *congregantes* or insisted on having second-class Jews sit beside them. The Mahamad believed that those in question were interested in "offending the orders of this College,"[47] but this was no mere rebellion. Like the aforementioned Joseph Pelegrino who manumitted his three children more than half a century earlier, many European-origin Jews may have wished to publicly claim *congregantes* as their own flesh and blood.

These "concentric circles" were part of a broader pattern emerging in Caribbean societies by the mid-eighteenth century. In 1752, Curaçao's Council argued that a number of free, prosperous, and powerful families of African origin who had intermarried with whites should be granted equal treatment with whites. In 1769 the West India Company's military commanders and the civil militia officers began a dispute about which organization should accept a group of some twenty or thirty soldiers of mixed African-European descent. The white militia officers maintained that these soldiers were not truly mulattoes and should thus not be incorporated into the free black and free mulatto militias, but rather into the white militia unit. By 1789, 214 mestizos were accordingly admitted into the white militia unit, comprised of 1,063 soldiers.[48] Similarly, in the Danish West Indies legislators in the second half of the eighteenth century grappled with the concept of "nearly white" and sometimes proposed that the status of these

Eurafricans be legally changed to white. Tellingly, the government never took a definitive position on this matter, an indication of its controversial nature and serious threat to white society.[49]

In Suriname, experiments with the social elevation of Eurafrican Jews had also proven controversial. Communal records hint that at one time, Eurafrican Jews were sometimes conferred *jahid* status. The regents' decision by at least 1748 to classify them solely as *congregantes* emanated from "the impropriety of admitting Mulattos as *jahidim*, and elevating them in this community, in which some have intervened in cases of government of the congregation."[50] Seven years later this locution was intensified to "the *harm* and impropriety of admitting mulattoes as *jahidim* [italics mine]."[51]

The circumstances leading to the bestowal of *jahid* status on Eurafrican Jews sometime before 1748 are not yet known. Perhaps the nepotism of white fathers who had sired "mulatto" children played a role. If this interpretation is correct, it may explain why the aforementioned Eurafrican Jewish leader, Joseph, son of David Cohen Nassy, who died in Paramaribo on April 17, 1790, was listed in the community's death records as a "mulatto and not a congregant."[52] If read as subversive, this entry, recorded by First Cantor David Hezkiahu Baruh Louzada, is another sure indication that displeasure with the status and treatment of *kleurlingen* was also shared among certain high-placed *jehidim*.[53]

Another factor encouraging alliances between white and Eurafrican Sephardim was the possibility of white demotion to the status of congregant (through marriage to a "mulatto" Jew), as stipulated by communal ordinances. Though not apparent in the community's bylaws (*ascamot*), a distinction between whites demoted to the status of *congregantes*, on the one hand, and ("mulatto") *congregantes*, on the other, did exist. It is likely that this legal nuance was formalized only in the second half of the eighteenth century. In the 1790s, community officials reaffirmed the distinction between "born congregants" (*congregantes de nacimento*) and *jehidim* relegated through marriage to a Jew of African origin. An announcement from 1797 stipulated that born congregants were obliged to sit on the bench behind the *tevah* and on the bench in front of the seat of the *samas*. *Jehidim* (perhaps indicating *jehidim* lowered to a congregant status) were strictly banned from these spaces.[54] If this reading is correct, the announcement demonstrates an attempt to publicly distinguish born congregants (presumably Eurafrican) from demoted congregants (presumably white), and to soften the social stigma of the latter, at least in regard to this racial game of musical chairs.

As it had been for Joseph Pelegrino in 1720, a key issue in defining the status of Eurafrican Jews continued to be inheritance. In 1797, the Mahamad issued an ordinance that required congregants to begin registering the births of their children. The issue that spurred it into being was the realization of "how damaging" it could be for both *congregantes* and the "nation in general" to be ignorant of birth dates in cases of inheritance. *Congregantes* were ordered at both Beraha VeSalom in Jodensavanne and Paramaribo's Congregation Sedek VeSalom to register the births of their children, proffering circumcision certificates as proof.[55] The law is a sure indication that the community had previously not recorded such births (at least systematically). Indeed, the earliest records of newborns specified as *congregantes* date to the 1770s.[56] Why would the community not have recorded these births previously? Perhaps this omission reflects a reluctance to record the undeniable evidence of "illegitimate" unions. Whatever the reason, at least some of these Eurafrican children had evidently long enjoyed an unofficial status as potential heirs within the organized Jewish community. The ordinance also suggests a sea change in the status of Eurafrican Jews. Second-class Jews were increasingly being named as inheritors, suggesting a rise in their social status and power. The demand for this came not only from within the Eurafrican Jewish population, but no doubt also from *jehidim* themselves. The nineteenth century was to usher in a new era of opportunity and inclusion for *kleurlingen* in the Caribbean, Jewish and Christian alike.[57]

The End of Peripheral Inclusion

As we have seen, challenges to the second-class status of *kleurlingen* intensified at the turn of the eighteenth century. In April of 1802 the Mahamad of Beraha VeSalom decided to abolish all differences in burial rites between *jehidim* and *congregantes*. They decided that "pious deeds must be carried out without prejudice," and that in the administration of last rites to the dead, "every distinction is improper and disagreeable." All charitable institutions, those already existing (gemilut Hasadim, Liviat Hen, and Hozer Holim) and those to be established in the future, were to identically serve *jehidim* and *congregantes* with respect to coffin, shroud, and procession and burial in the cemetery, without exception.[58]

By January of 1820 the practice of relegating deceased congregants to specific cemetery rows ceased. The Mahamad decreed that all baptized congregants be interred throughout the cemeteries, "without stipulation of the place of their graves."[59] The resolution fixed new attention on a "book of baptisms [conversions to Judaism]," listing the names of "congregants who are baptized and those who will be in the future." This book suggests the existence of a significant body of fringe members of the Jewish community, hovering in a spiritual no-man's land, neither Jew nor gentile. Alas, the record book does not make explicit the ethnic or circumstantial origins of these individuals.[60]

The end of peripheral inclusion among Suriname's Jews emerged alongside parallel developments elsewhere in the Caribbean, including the Danish West Indies. There, the phenomenon was uneven, reflecting conflicting interests. Frederik V's "Reglement for Slaverne" of 1755 stated in its last clause that the "freed are to enjoy all rights on par with the free-born subjects esteemed and respected in all regards equally with the free-born subjects of the Crown."[61] As in Suriname, the end of peripheral inclusion was partially a result of the exponential growth of the Eurafrican population. By 1775, in St. Croix, freed people comprised some 20 percent of the total free population, and by 1797 that number had increased to 35 percent (some 4 percent of the total population). Similar statistics are available for St. Thomas. By 1797, there was nearly one freedman for every two whites in the Danish West Indies (1,418 compared to a white population of 3,062).[62]

Identifying Eurafrican Jews

The birth and death records of Suriname's Sephardic community are among the richest sources for identifying Sephardic Jews of African-European origin. Before 1777, the starting date of the most comprehensive communal registers, it was superfluous (or perhaps indecorous) to racially identify decedents in birth and death registers. Matrilineal descent was also irrelevant: in terms of identifying the child, only the father was mentioned as parent. But in 1777, cantor Mendes Quiros died and passed on his administrative staff to cantor David Baruh Hezkiahu Louzada. The latter began to carefully note both racial and social status. This was about two decades after the Eurafrican Jewish *siva* was established (1759) and about a decade and a half before a group of Eurafrican Jews in Paramaribo were to assert themselves and rebel (early 1790s). In the registers kept from 1777, both father and mother were noted; in the case of most Eurafrican Jews, only the mother was mentioned. This demonstrates a transition back to matrilineal descent, offering another explanation for the apparent proliferation of Eurafrican Jews beginning in the late nineteenth century.

The record book maintained by cantor Baruh Louzada provides hard evidence of this proliferation. The 1,371 entries span from 1778 to 1835. Between 1779 and 1824 the deaths of 99 Jews of second-class status were recorded. The overwhelming majority was identified as *congregantes*, while three were named as "mulattoes" and one as a Jewish slave. Two of the congregants were converts and, for reasons suggested earlier, another individual

(Joseph, son of David Cohen Nassy) was a Eurafrican who was specifically designated as not a congregant.[63] Alas, Baruh Louzada did not differentiate in his records between born *congregantes* and *jehidim* demoted to congregant status.

The statistics of this community profile show that, at least officially, between 1778 and 1835, 7.2 percent of the members were lower status members. Most of these were likely of African origin. Phrased another way, more than one out of every fourteen Sephardic Jews in Suriname over the course of roughly half a century was certainly either of African origin or lowered to a congregant status through marriage to what was probably in most cases a Eurafrican Jew. This statistic, which cannot possibly reflect every fringe member of the community, nevertheless significantly exceeds official estimates, which place the Eurafrican members of Suriname's white gentile and Jewish communities between one and two and a half percent.

Particularly in light of Louzada's detailed records, official statistics tabulated by the colonial government do not seem useful for determining the size and composition of Surinames non-white Jewish population. A general population survey taken in 1817, claiming to be accurate for the Jewish communities, came up with a dubious 30 *kleurlingen* and no blacks living among a urban white Sephardic population of 592. What makes these figures all the more unreliable is the statement that community members owned no enslaved "coloreds" or blacks. In the rural district of Jodensavanne and its surroundings, the survey counted 99 free whites, but turned up nothing for freed and enslaved *kleurlingen* and *negers*. For Paramaribo's Ashkenazi community, there were supposedly 580 whites, 5 free colored, and no blacks, while in the outside districts there were only 26 whites and no *kleurlingen* or *negers*, whether enslaved or free.[64] These improbable statistics are rendered all the more dubious on the very next page, where the editor remarks that the ongoing dearth of white women has resulted in the reality that "Whites generally . . . live with women of color so that the closest relationships come about between white man and women of color."[65]

Another important consideration is the comparison between rural and urban areas. Two second-class Jews listed by cantor Baruh Louzada were buried on the Caxewinica Creek on the Cupij Plantation and just eight at Jodensavanne.[66] The vast majority (89 or about 90 percent) were buried in Paramaribo. It would be erroneous to thus conclude that the Eurafrican Jewish phenomenon was largely an urban phenomenon, for extant records focus on the late seventeenth century and beyond, precisely when Suriname's Jews were transitioning from the jungle interior to Paramaribo.

The identification of additional congregants and the details of the lives of those already recognized, has scarcely begun. To discover more information, the research methodology sometimes referred to as monks' work (*monnikenarbeid*) would be essential. This would involve tirelessly scanning hundreds of pages of Jewish marriage, birth, circumcision, and death records, for an African or unusual Jewish name (e.g., Jaba or Ismahel) or racial notation (e.g., *congregante, castiço,* or *escrava*). Poring through Dutch notarial archives with this goal in mind turned up our Joseph Pelegrino, while the thousands of pages of Jewish communal meeting minutes, dating from 1749 to the turn of the nineteenth century, are sprinkled with references to slaves and their conversion. Collectively, the individuals retrieved from these painstaking searches form a significant bunch, both in terms of relative size and impact, and are the key to understanding the phenomenon of Jewish Africanization in the Caribbean.

The second step is more subtle and complicated. Scrutinizing the silence demands a sensitive eye that detects *congregante* status when none is mentioned, and only sometimes implied. One of the main challenges is that the racial composition of Jews of African descent is often not mentioned, the aforementioned Joseph Peregrino, manumitter of his three children, being a possible example of this omission. Moreover, congregants existed at the margins of the community. Birth and death registers demonstrate that they are hardly mentioned at all until the late eighteenth century, though they were always crucial to the general community's development.

The consequences of these silences are also evident among Curaçao's Jews. Over the centuries, its members were so successful in cultivating "public secrets" (and censoring their official historian) that not one African-origin Jew appears in the two-volume history of the community, published in 1970.[67] Curaçao's elite Jews showed deep concern with maintaining decorum and family honor, and it is possibly in this light that we may interpret their social conventions. Nineteenth-century invitations to balls celebrating engagements and wedding anniversaries often concluded with the stern admonition: "servants are not permitted entrance ("No se admiten criados;" "No se admiten sirvientes").[68] A congratulatory anniversary card written in 1857 explicitly conveys this preoccupation. Lea J. M. Monsanto wished her friends A. J. and E. D. Jesurun happiness and sunny horizons, but most of all that they would forever conserve their family name as righteously and stainlessly as they had inherited it.[69] A systematic exploration of genealogy and reputation throughout the Jewish Caribbean will no doubt reveal much more information on "parallel lives" and "parallel wives," even if it means a substantial reliance on oral testimony and family traditions.

Casual conversations with community members whose families have lived on the island for seven generations reveal that most every Sephardic man led a "parallel life," with a public, white Jewish spouse and children, side-by-side with a covert black cohort and her Eurafrican children. In Curaçao the children of these "secret" unions are still known in Papiamentu as "yu di afo" (often pronounced, "yu ja-fo," from the Portuguese: hijo de afora"), "children of the outside." They and their mothers were permitted to visit the white patriarch once a year but could enter only via the back door.

The white spouse was entirely aware of the relationship and its offspring, but the matter was not a topic of open acknowledgment.[70]

Even if scholars are correct that the island's Jews did not permit conversion of African-origin people to Judaism, we must not discount alternative forms of communal membership. Fewer than six white families on the island could declare they had no Afro-Curaçaoan relatives, an island native observed in the 1950s, and it is difficult to imagine that Sephardim were exempt from this reality.[71] Gerardus Balthazar Bosch, pastor of the island's Protestant community from 1816 to 1825 and of the united Protestant community from 1825 to 1836 (when the church merged with the Lutheran community), confirmed this in 1829:

> Only the Jews in the West Indies can pride themselves—if it is any reason for pride—that they have not mixed their Asian origins with African or American races. Whereas one Christian family accuses the other of having some drops of black blood—as they usually call it—in their veins, and whereas there are a few who even consider it a badge of honor not to descend in the maternal line from the Negroes, but from the free-born Indians—it is certain that the Jews have preserved their species in a pure and unmixed form. The illegitimate children which they have conceived with black or colored women, and which one can see walk around in some parts of the West Indies in large numbers, to be recognized by their Asian noses, they have never attempted to bring into their church, and have even steadfastly refused this in the event that a petition was made. On Curaçao I know a colored man who for a number of years has been a diligent observer of the Jewish religion, who can shout out all Hebrew prayers as well as a born Jew, and closes his eye and mouth to bacon, turtle, and whatever else is non-kosher, indeed, does not want to eat from pots in which Christians have cooked. As a reward for all this he only requests to be incorporated among the number of Abraham's descendants; but that is out of the question. He is allowed constantly to observe the religion, but they refuse to introduce him into the community.[72]

The anecdote suggests that by at least the 1820s the community eschewed formal conversion of Afro-Curaçaoans to Judaism, but tolerated the existence of fringe people, existing on the extreme margins of the community, and neither clearly gentile nor legally Jewish.

Other evidence for this type of fringe existence also emerged in Suriname. It involves African-origin and Indian concubines, who perhaps understood that their prospect for upward mobility was through their hybrid children. Jodensavanne's communal ordinances, whose earliest extant version dates to 1748, include a prohibition against the synagogue attendance of "Negras, Mulatas ou Indias," with or without children, and indicate the responsibility of their masters to remove them. Perhaps these non-Jewish females were attempting to attain a higher social status, or even recognition as Jews, through participation in public communal prayer. The presence of these women in the company of children, coupled with the masters' responsibility to discipline them, moreover, suggests that the children may have been the issue of concubines and their masters.[73] If this reading is correct, this phenomenon parallels the aforementioned situation of unbaptized congregants in Suriname in the 1790s, some of whom seemed poised for official conversion and inclusion in the Sephardic community.

Conclusion

Suriname's autonomous community and unprecedented New World environment allowed for the development of conversion practices only indirectly informed by *halakha*, and more intensely conditioned by a society distant from centers of traditional Jewish authority. The Sephardi community of Suriname can be compared to other frontier or marginal societies that developed their own definitions of Jewishness. An example is eighteenth-century Ashkenazi male criminals in the Dutch Republic, who formed sexual liaisons with Gypsy women. Criminal proceedings suggest that their conversion to Judaism was informal, including the case of Fisone, who "had become a Jewess" during her relationship with the Jew, Levi Abrahams. One of her children produced during a previous relationship with a Christian man was given a new, Jewish name. Florike Egmond, who has studied this marginal subclass, classifies this phenomenon as the adoption of Jewish customs by a Christian/Jewish group.[74] Particularly in the case of frontier societies of the early modern Caribbean, which developed to some extent independently of the halakhic centers of the Jewish world in Europe and the Ottoman Empire, it is crucial to consider nontraditional ways of communal belonging that defy the strictures of normative Jewish law. This broader vision of community is critical for understanding the Jewish and Dutch gentile communities alike.

Notes

* All translations from the French, Hebrew, Portuguese, and Dutch are mine, except where noted. Abbreviations are as follows: NA = Nationaal Archief, The Hague; GAA = Gemeentearchief Amsterdam.

1. Perhaps the most dramatic imprint has been economic and linguistic. See Linda Marguerite Rupert, *Roots of our Future: A Commercial History of Curaçao* (Curaçao, Netherlands Antilles: Curaçao Chamber of Commerce & Industry,

1999) and "Trading Globally, Speaking Locally," *Jewish Culture and History* 7:1/2 (2004): 109–22; Jacques Arends, "The History of Surinamese Creoles I: A Sociohistorical Survey," 115–30, 118–19 and Norval Smith, "The History of Surinamese Creoles II: Origin and Differentiation," 131–51, 140 and 146–47, both in Eithne B. Carlin and Jacques Arends, eds., *Atlas of the Languages of Suriname* (Leiden: KITLV Press, 2002). Ashkenazim, present in Suriname since the late seventeenth century and in significant numbers on Curaçao only since the 1930s, fall outside the parameters of this article. Eva Abraham-van der Mark, "The Ashkenazi Jews of Curaçao, a Trading Minority," *New West Indian Guide/Nieuwe West-Indische Gids* 74. 3 & 4 (2000): 257–80.

2. Each community has about 200 members.

3. This data is derived by the author from Cornelis Christiaan Goslinga, *The Dutch in the Caribbean and in the Guianas, 1680–1791* (Assen/Maastricht, The Netherlands and Dover, New Hampshire: Van Gorcum, 1985), 279, 291, 309, 341, and 519.

4. This data is derived by the author from Wim Klooster, "Economische malaise, politieke onrust en misdaad op Curaçao in de Patriottentij," in *Breekbare Banden: Feiten en visies over Aruba, Bonaire en Curaçao na de Vrede van Munster, 1648–1998* (Bloemendaal, The Netherlands: Stichting Libri Antilliani, 1998), 108, table 1. The population of 20,988 included 3,714 free blacks; 12,864 slaves; and 4,410 whites (including 1,095 Jews and assuming servants were white).

5. Robert Cohen, *Jews in Another Environment: Surinam in the Second Half of the Eighteenth Century* (Leiden: E. J. Brill: 1991). More recent studies include Jonathan Schorsch, *Jews and Blacks in the Early Modern World* (Cambridge, UK: Cambridge University Press, 2004), Alan F. Benjamin, *Jews of the Dutch Caribbean: Exploring Ethnic Identity on Curaçao* (London and New York, Routledge, 2002), which alludes to Eurafrican Jewish identity in passing, and a dissertation in progress by Wieke Vink, tentatively entitled "Suriname Jews: Creolisation Strategies of Group-Identities in a Global Environment, 1800–2000," as cited in her, "Over migranten, suikerplanters, Joodse kleurlingen en religieuze tolerantie," *Oso: Tijdschrift voor Surinaamse Taalkunde, Letterkunde, Cultuur en Geschiedenis* 21.1 (May 2002): 35–57.

6. The term Eurafrican refers to an individual of mixed European and African descent and is borrowed from George E. Brooks, *Eurafricans in Western Africa: Commerce, Social Status, Gender, and Religious Observance from the Sixteenth to the Eighteenth Century* (Athens, OH: Ohio University Press; Oxford: James Currey, 2003).

7. Cohen, *Jews in Another Environment*, 1 and 4.

8. Aviva Ben-Ur and Rachel Frankel, *Remnant Stones: The Jewish Cemeteries and Synagogue of Suriname* (Cincinnati: Hebrew Union College Press, forthcoming).

9. Charles T. Gehring and J. A. Schiltkamp, eds., *Curacao Papers, 1640–1665*, vol.17 (Interlaken/New York: Heart of the Lakes Publishing, 1987), 58, 61, 62, 92.

10. By the nineteenth century, however, Dutch Protestants and Sephardic Jews each saw themselves as the elite of the island. Frances P. Karner, *The Sephardics of Curaçao* (Assen, The Netherlands: Van Gorcum, 1969), 32–33.

11. The figure of 232 Jews (including 105 men, 58 women and 69 children, presumably mostly settled along the Suriname River) is from a census conducted by the Society of Suriname in 1684 and cited in Claudia Schnurmann, *Atlantische Welten: Engländer und Niederländer im amerikanisch-atlantischen Raum, 1648–1713* (Köln: Böhlau, 1998), 382. Victor Enthoven states that 1,158 individuals resided in Jodensavanne in 1684, with Africans outnumbering Jews 6 to 1. Statistics for slaves do not reflect natural increase, but rather the constant replenishment by "saltwater slaves." Victor Enthoven, "Suriname and Zeeland: Fifteen Years of Dutch Misery on the Wild Coast, 1667–1682", in J. Everaert and J. M. Parmentier, eds., *International Conference on Shipping, Factories and Colonization* (Brussels: Koninklijke Academie voor Overzeese Wetenschappen, 1996), 249–60, 255. Comparable figures for Suriname's European and enslaved populations are provided in Johannes Postma, *The Dutch in the Atlantic Slave Trade, 1600–1815* (Cambridge; New York: Cambridge University Press, 1990), 185.

12. Appendix 22 in Isaac Emmanuel and Suzanne Emmanuel, *A History of the Jews in the Netherlands Antilles*, 2 vols. (Cincinnati: American Jewish Archives, 1970), 1036–45. (Emmanuel's list on 1045 indicates 867 Jewish-owned slaves, including 23 separately listed. However, if these 23 are added to the alphabetical list he provides the number jumps to 869.)

13. Curaçao's Jewish community never numbered over 1,100. See the 1789 Curaçao census, showing a tally of 1,095 Jews on the island, in Maritza Coomans-Eustatia, "Het oog van de Engelsen gericht op Curaçao, Aruba en Bonaire," in *Breekbare Banden: Feiten en visies over Aruba, Bonaire en Curaçao na de Vrede van Munster, 1648–1998* (Bloemendaal, The Netherlands: Stichting Libri Antilliani, 1998), 142. Avraham and Isaac de Marchena owned eighty slaves, and Francisco Lopes Henriquez, Isaac Mendes, and Jeosuah Henriquez, are each listed as owning forty. Appendix 22 in Emmanuel and Emmanuel, *A History of the Jews in the Netherlands Antilles*, 1036–45.

14. Enriqueta Vila Vilar with Wim Klooster, "Forced African Settlement: The Basis of Forced Settlement: Africa and its Trading Conditions," in P. C. Emmer, ed., *General History of the Caribbean*, 6 vols. (London and Basingstoke: UNESCO, 1999), 2: 159–71, 170; Cornelis Christiaan Goslinga, *The Dutch in the Caribbean and in the Guianas*, 358 ("Surinam Marriage"); R. A. J. van Lier, *Frontier Society: A Social Analysis of the History of Surinam* (The Hague, The Netherlands: Martinus Nijhoff, 1971), 78 ("marriage Surinam-style"). For statistics see Wim Hoogbergen, *'De Bosnegers zijn gekomen!': Slavernij en rebellie in Suriname* (Amsterdam: Prometheus, 1992) and Schnurmann, *Atlantische Welten*, 382. On the endurance of concubinage (male infidelity and double sexual standards) in the modern Caribbean, see Christine Barrow, "Male Images of Women in Barbados," *Social and Economic Studies* 35.3 (1986): 51–64, 53 and 58.

15. As in Suriname, the gender ratio had likely equalized by the second half of the eighteenth century. In Willemstad proper the number of Jewish families in Curaçao in 1789 was 259. Taking into account that the average family counted four members, and assuming that the vast majority probably had a matriarch

and at least one girl, there would have been perhaps 500 females. This data is derived by the author from Klooster, "Economische malaise, politieke onrust en misdaad," 108, table 1.

16. Van Lier, *Frontier Society*, 74.

17. "em Este kaal ay huma escama feita no ano 5423 que Prohibe a cual quer Jahid so pena de herem a circonsidar os filhos do que sedespidue de Jahid. Esta escama que foy feita com Prudencia pelos Primeiros fundadadores deste kaal (adterorem)." GAA, no. 334, folio 1029, Stukken betreffende gemeenten te Amsterdam, Curaçao, Suriname en Constantinopel, 1650–1798, on 428–29. The earliest known definitions of *jahid* and *congregante* in Suriname's Sephardic community are provided in NA, Portugees Israelitische Gemeente in Suriname, no.99, Minuut-Askamoth voor de gemeente B.V.S. 1748 [Minutes-Askamoth for Congregation Beraha VeSalom 1748], tractate 26. The racial terms used are "mulattos" and "Jehidim." The androcentric locution of the bylaws became more gender inclusive by the mid-eighteenth century. At least by the 1750s, intramarriage between Sephardi men and Ashkenazi women, which lowered the couple to congregant status, was sufficiently frequent as to merit mention in the communal ordinances (Tractate 26, article 4). By at least the 1780s, the gender-sensitive locution of the ordinance reveals that Sephardi women had also begun to intramarry in significant numbers. Fragment van een concept-vertaling in het Nederlands van de Askamoth, no.111, chapter 1, article 2, 1789. "Tanto homen como mulheres" appears in superscript over the words, "Todo Jahid."

18. Given the wording of the petition, Pelegrino obviously produced these children outside of Dutch marital law, but perhaps according to Jewish law. Surinamese Jews had obtained a special privilege in the 1650s to arrange their own marriages under the jurisdiction of their religious leaders. After 1703, however, Dutch law required Jewish marriage contracts be approved by Dutch officials and registered with the state archives. On the repeal of exclusive autonomy in Jewish marital laws see Ralph G. Bennett, "The Blacks and Jews of Surinam," *African Notes: Bulletin of the Institute of African Studies, University of Ibadan* 17.1–2 (1993): 62–82, 69; P. A. Hilfman, "Some Further Notes on the Jews in Surinam," *Proceedings of the American Jewish Historical Society* 16 (1907): 10–13; and Jacob Rader Marcus, *The Colonial American Jew, 1492–1776*, 3 vols. (Detroit: Wayne State University Press, 1970), I: 150–54. The family name appears variably throughout the archives as Pelegrino, Pelengrino, and Peregrino.

19. NA, Oud Archief Suriname, Request of Joseph Pelegrino to Governor General Johan Coetier [Jean Coutier], Paramaribo, July 17, 1720, 83–87.

20. Goslinga, *The Dutch in the Caribbean and in the Guianas*, 359; J. A. Schiltkamp, J. Th. de Smidt, T. van der Lee, eds., *West Indisch Plakaatboek, Suriname*, Deel I (Amsterdam: S. Emmering, 1973), 277 (plakaat 240). On Curaçao this taboo is preserved through oral tradition. See A. F. Paula, *From Objective to Subjective Social Barriers: A Historico-Philosophical Analysis of Certain Negative Attitudes among the Negroid Population of Curaçao* (Curaçao: Curaçaosche Courant, 1972), 33.

21. The phenomenon was also rare in North American British colonies. See, for example, Johann Martin Bolzius, "Reliable Answer to some Submitted

Questions concerning the Land Carolina," *William and Mary Quarterly*, Third Series, 14: 2 (April 1957): 223–61, 235. Compare Martha Hodes, *White Women, Black Men: Illicit Sex in the Nineteenth-Century South* (New Haven: Yale University Press, 1997).

22. In North America's frontier societies Jewish men sometimes raised their halakhically gentile children as Jews. The children of Samson Levy (Philadelphia) and Michael Judah (Connecticut), both of whom intermarried, were ritually circumcised in the eighteenth century. Marcus, *Colonial American Jew*, III: 1228–29. In the French Caribbean, too, children of Sephardic men and gentile African women were sometimes raised as Jews, though this was counter to traditional Jewish law requiring Jewish descent to be traced via the mother. In St. Louis, Saint-Domingue, one M. de Paz spawned several male and female children with a black woman "to whom he is very loving." She was emancipated years before, but he did not marry her. He was "very tender" to the children and sent them to his parents in Bordeaux to be educated. Abraham Cahen, "Les juifs dans les colonies françaises au XVIIIe siècle," *Revue des Études Juives* 4 (1882): 127–45, 141.

23. Eurafrican women born to Jewish mothers could, according to Jewish law, automatically transmit Jewish status.

24. The translation is from Harold Fisch, ed., *The Holy Scriptures* (Jerusalem: Koren Publishers, 1989), 16. Abraham and Solomon Levy Maduro, eds., *Sefer Berit Yitshak* (Amsterdam: Gerard Johan Jansen in the shop of Israel Mondove, 5528 [1767/1768]), 16. Copies consulted for this article are located at the John Carter Brown Library in Providence, Rhode Island, and the Ets Hayim library in Amsterdam, and represent the edition published nearly forty years later. It is apparently a reprint of the 1729 edition, cited in Moritz Steinschneider, *Catalogus Librorum Hebraerum in bibliotheca Bodleiana jussu curatorum digessit et notis instruxit M. Steinschneider* (Berlin: Welt-Verlag, 1931), entry 3222. For an alternative interpretation of this ritual see Schorsch, *Jews and Blacks*, 225–26.

25. *Sefer Berit Itshak* (Amsterdam: Belinfante and de Vita, 1803/1804 [Amsterdam: Solomon Levy Maduro, 1764/1765]).

26. J. Hartog, *Curaçao: From Colonial Dependence to Autonomy* (Aruba: De Wit, 1968), 148; Emmanuel, *Jews of the Netherlands Antilles*, 1:146; Jacob Rader Marcus, *The Colonial American Jew: 1492–1776*, 3 vols. (Detroit, MI: Wayne State University Press, 1970), 1: 200; all cited in Schorsch, *Jews and Blacks*, 222 and 237–38. Schorsch, basing himself partly on Isaac S. Emmanuel's silence about black or mulatto converts in the island's Jewish cemetery (in Emmanuel, *Precious Stones*), concludes that Jews "did not convert their slaves." However, scholarly censorship must be considered; Emmanuel himself reveals that "the parnassim made it a condition *sine qua non* to control the manuscript before delivery to the printer" (Emmanuel and Emmanuel, *History of the Jews of the Netherlands Antilles*, 1: 8). One wonders what a thorough perusal of Curaçao's early modern documents might further reveal on black/Jewish relations. As is the case for Suriname, this work has scarcely begun. Moreover, one important eighteenth century source for Curaçao (NA, Oud Archief Curaçao) is in poor

condition and often illegible (author's personal communication with Wim Klooster).

27. NA, Nederlandse Portugees Israëlitische Gemeente in Suriname, no.102, 1754, tractate 19, articles 3 and 4 on 43–44.

28. Kaplan, "Political Concepts," 57–58.

29. Ben-Ur and Frankel, *Remnant Stones*.

30. If so, the spelling of his last name would be interchangeable with Pelegrino.

31. The others are Miriam Nassy; Abigail, daughter of Simha de Meza; Ishmael Judeo; Matatia de Robles; Moses Rodrigues del Prado, Joseph de G[abriel?]. de Mattos (d.751?); and Jacob Peregrino (d. 1750). Three others, the brothers Jacob and Isaac Garcia, and a "morito, son of Isaac Naar Meza," were likely buried in the vicinity. Ben-Ur and Frankel, *Remnant Stones*.

32. NA, Nederlandse Portugees Israëlitische Gemente in Suriname, no. 423, Register van begravenen op de kerkhoven van de Savanne, 1777–1833 [Register of graves in the cemetery of the Savanna, 1777–1833], p.19; N.A., microfilm reel 67a, n. 785, undated will of Joseph Gabay Farro. Simha died May 1, 1791 (27 Nissan 5551); Jahel June 19, 1791 (17 Sivan 5551). *Congregantes* were permitted burial in the Cassipora Cemetery by at least 1819, but no register of burials there has survived. NA, Nederlandse Portugees Israëlitische Gemeente in Suriname, Minuut-notulen van vergaderingen van de Senhores de Mahamad (Parnassijns) en van de Junta (Parnassijns en ouderlingen), [Minutes of the meetings of the Gentlemen of the Mahamad (Parnassim) and of the Junta (Parnassim and elderly)], September 7, 1819, on 7.

33. NA, Nederlandse Portugees Israëlitische Gemeente in Suriname, Grafboek van het kerkhof te Paramaribo (1849) [Grave register of the cemetery at Paramaribo], no. 137. While burials are generally undated, many seem to date from the late eighteenth century onward. A few Ashkenazi names, such as Samson and Goedschalk, also appear among *congregantes*, suggesting Sephardi/Ashkenazi unions.

34. Cohen, *Jews in Another Environment*, 164.

35. Van Lier, *Frontier Society*, 81; J. Wolbers, *Geschiedenis van Surinam* (Amsterdam, H. de Hoogh, 1861), 256; Willem F. L. Buschkens, *The Family System of the Paramaribo Creoles* ('s-Gravenhage : M. Nijhoff, 1974), 70; Goslinga, *The Dutch in the Caribbean*, 366.

36. Cohen, *Jews in Another Environment*, 166.

37. NA, Nederlandse Portugees Israëlitische Gemeente in Suriname, no. 435, Minutes of meetings, Liviat Hen Society, 1778–1790, November 20, 1787, on 65 [b].

38. NA, Nederlandse Portugees Israëlitische Gemeente in Suriname, no. 420, on 18. He is listed as "Danl. Pelengrino (congregante)."

39. NA, Oud Arch. Sur. Gouvernements secretaries, no. 528; Cohen, *Jews in Another Environment*, 163–74.

40. NA, Nederlandse Portugees Israëlitische Gemeente in Suriname, no. 102, tractate 55 (1755). The only "Joseph Cohen Nassy" listed in the Old Sephardi Cemetery burial register and identified as a *congregante* appears in an undated entry for the *carreira dos congregantes* in row 6, grave number 68. NA,

Nederlandse Portugees Israëlitische Gemeente in Suriname, Grafboek van het kerkhof te Paramaribo (1849), no. 137.

41. Cohen, *Jews in Another Environment*, 163.

42. Ibid., 170. Ironically, the plot on which the cemetery lay was sold in 1959 and the gravestones transferred to a newer Sephardi burial ground, where they were haphazardly piled in the back of that graveyard in a "tumbled heap," disrupting the social distinctions that had been so carefully arranged in rows since the eighteenth century. Adriana van Alen-Koenraadt and Philip Dikland, "Brief History of the old Sephardic cemetery," unpublished article, 2002.

43. NA, no. 420, December 18, 1790 (11 Tebet 5551), 93.

44. Cohen, *Jews in Another Environment*, 165.

45. Ibid., 172.

46. Ibid., 170.

47. NA, Nederlandse Portugees Israëlitische Gemeente in Suriname, no. 36, Bijlagen tot de notulen van Mahamad en Junta (ingekomen stukken en minuten van uitgegane stukken) [Bylaws of the minutes of Mahamad and Junta (incoming pieces and minutes of outgoing pieces)], 337.

48. Wim Klooster, "Subordinate but Proud: Curaçaos Free Blacks and Mulattoes in the Eighteenth Century," *New West Indian Guide* 68. 3/4 (1994): 283–300.

49. Neville A. T. Hall, *Slave Society in the Danish West Indies: St. Thomas, St. John, and St. Croix*, ed. B. W. Higman (Baltimore and London: The Johns Hopkins University Press, 1992), 152–53 and 160–61.

50. NA, Nederlandse Portugees Israëlitische Gemeente in Suriname, no. 99, Ascamot, 1748, Tractate 26, article 1, "On not admitting Mulattoes as Jehidim to the synagogue nor whites married to mulattoes." The locution is, "Avendo alianiado pr. experiencia o Improprio q'he Admeter mulatos p. Jehidim & sublimalos nesse gremio (. . .)." NA, Portugees Israelitische Gemeente in Suriname, No. 99, Minuut-Askamoth voor de gemeente B.V.S. 1748, tractate 26, article 1.

51. The locution is "Havendo mostrado aexperiencia o danozo, e improprio que he admittir Mulatos por Jahidim, e colocalos em esse gremio, em oqual alguns se entremetera'o em Cazos do governo do Kaal (. . .)."

52. NA, Nederlandse Portugees Israëlitische Gemeente in Suriname, no. 418, Registro Mortuorio [Death Register], 49.

53. Alternatively, this may indicate that Joseph was conceived outside of "legitimate marriage" and thus qualified as neither *Jahid* nor *congregante*.

54. NA, Nederlandse Portugees Israëlitische Gemeente in Suriname, no. 36, 187. The ordinance does not mention the *Jehidim* as relegated, but the term *congregantes de nacimento* implies that there were *congregantes* who were formerly *jahidim*.

55. NA, Nederlandse Portugees Israëlitische Gemeente in Suriname, no. 36, Mosseh Davilar, sworn clerk, October 2, 1797, 251. This bylaw seems to imply that only sons were concerned. If so, one wonders how the community dealt with young *congregantas* claiming an inheritance.

56. The earliest birth register contains no specific references to congregantes. NA, Nederlandse Portugees Israëlitische Gemeente in Suriname, no. 416, Alfabetische staten van geborenen over 1662–1723 en 1723–1777 (commenced

by Mendes Quiros, who died June 21, 1777); no. 417 (commenced June 16, 1777); no. 419 (commenced June 16, 1777).

57. The question of entitlement of Eurafricans to equality with whites had emerged in the Danish West Indies as early as the 1750s, when in a slave conspiracy, a freedman of St. Croix apparently conspired to make himself governor general in a new society bereft of whites. This is evidence that before the end of the eighteenth century "a certain sense of individual, if not communal, self-esteem" had emerged. This self-consciousness intensified during the nineteenth century. Hall, *Slave Society*, 156–57.

58. NA, Nederlandse Portugees Israëlitische Gemeente in Suriname, no. 437, Extracto do Registro de Notulas & Rezolucoems do Collegio dos Sres ao MM & Deputados da Nacao do KKBVS [Extract form the Register of Minutes and Resolutions of the College of the Gentlemen to the Mahamad and Deputies of the Nation of Holy Congregation Beraha VeSalom], April 13, 1802.

59. NA, Nederlandse Portugees Israëlitische Gemeente in Suriname, no. 11 on 13. The bylaw reads in part: "que todos os Congregantes que forem banhados, poderao ser enterrados por todo o lugar no Beth-ahaim sem particularizar lugar de seus Sepulcros."

60. NA, Nederlandse Portugees Israëlitische Gemeente in Suriname, no. 11, October 30, 1820, 13; November 20, 1820, 15. The book was kept by the secretary of the community. In response to this announcement, former First Cantor David Baruh Louzada offered his testimony that two congregantes, Gabriel Davilar and Moses de Pina, had been baptized under his aegis, demonstrating that these conversions were not always strictly recorded (NA, Nederlandse Portugees Israëlitische Gemeente in Suriname, no. 11, November 20, 1820, 15). Alternatively, the First Cantor may have fabricated his testimony due to some sort of personal bias. Davilar appears as a "molato" in the communal death register (April 14, 1824/16 Nissan 5584); de Pina does not.

61. See Hall, *Slave Society*, 146.

62. Ibid., 145.

63. NA, Nederlandse Portugees Israëlitische Gemeente in Suriname, no. 418, Registro Mortuorio [Death Register], 49. He is listed as "Molato & nao congregante."

64. N.a., *Surinaamsche Almanak voor het jaar 1821* (Paramaribo and Amsterdam: E. Beijer & C. G. Sulpke, 1821), 30. "Alleen van de Joodsche Gemeenten, en vooral van de Portugesche, heeft men eene juiste opgaaf kunnen bekomen" [We have obtained an accurate listing only of the Jewish communities and especially of the Portuguese].

65. Ibid., 31. "De Blanken wonen vrij algemeen, (daar de vrouwen van hunne kleur in zulk een gering getal voorhanden zijn) bij de vrouwen-Kleurlingen, zoodat er de naauwste betrekking tuschen de Blanke mannen en de Kleurlingen-vrouwen onstaat."

66. Interestingly, none lay buried at the Cassipora Cemetery, perhaps exclusively reserved for elite descendants of the leading families. As noted earlier, *congregantes* were theoretically permitted burial in the Cassipora Cemetery by at least 1819. NA, Nederlandse Portugees Israëlitisch Gemeente in Suriname,

Minuut-notulen van vergaderingen van de Senhores de Mahamad (Parnassijns) en van de Junta (Parnassijns en ouderlingen), [Minutes of the meetings of the Gentlemen of the Mahamad (Parnassim) and of the Junta (Parnassim and elderly), September 7, 1819, 7].

67. Isaac Samuel Emmanuel and Suzanne Amzalak Emmanuel, *A History of the Jews in the Netherlands Antilles*, 2 vols. (Cincinnati: American Jewish Archives, 1970), 1: 8–9; Benjamin, *Jews of the Dutch Caribbean*, 27–28.

68. Mongui-Maduro Library, Uitnoodiging map [invitation album], Book 1, 1854–1932, Curaçao. I thank Ena Dankmijer-Maduro for permission to view her collection.

69. Lea J. M. Monsanto to A. J. and E. D. Jesurun, March 6, 1857, Mongui-Maduro Library, Uitnoodiging map [invitation album], Book 1, Curaçao. The letter reads in part: "surtout que vous conserverez toujours vos noms aussi just et sans tache, que les ont laisses ceux dont vous l'avez hérités."

70. The term, its meaning, and the ubiquity of such arrangements among the island's Jews until just a few generations ago were shared in a casual conversation during a recent trip to Curaçao. The informant, whose family had dwelled on the island for seven generations, requested I conceal her identity. I have heard similar stories from former members of Suriname's Jewish community, again, in casual conversation. See also Eva Abraham-Van der Mark, "Marriage and Concubinage among the Sephardic Merchant Elite of Curaçao," in Janet Henshall Momsen, ed., *Women and Change in the Caribbean: a Pan-Caribbean Perspective* (London: James Currey Ltd., 1993), 38–49.

71. Abraham-Van der Mark, "Marriage and concubinage," 43, who cites H. Hoetink, *Het patroon van de oude Curaçaose samenleving: een sociologische studie* (Assen: Van Gorcum, 1958), with no page number.

72. Gerardus Balthazar Bosch, *Reizen in West-Indië*, 2 vols. (S. Emmering, 1985 [Utrecht: N. van der Monde,1829]), 1: 230–31.

73. NA, Nederlandse Portugees Israëlitische Gemeente in Suriname, no. 101, Ascamot, 1748, tractate 2, article 6.

74. Florike Egmond, "Contours of Identity: Poor Ashkenazim in the Dutch Republic," in *Dutch Jewish History: Proceedings of the Fifth Symposium on the History of the Jews in the Netherlands*, vol. III (Jerusalem: The Institute for Research on Dutch Jewry/Assen and Maastricht, The Netherlands: Van Gorcum, 1993), 205–25; 217–18.

Chapter 9

The Vain, Exotic, and Erotic Feather: Dress, Gender, and Power in Sixteenth- and Seventeenth-Century England

Catherine Howey

Around the year 1532, Hans Holbein sketched Mary Howard, Duchess of Somerset and Richmond. At first glance, there is nothing particularly striking about this simple, but elegant chalk outline of the widow of Henry VIII's illegitimate son, now part of the Royal Collection housed in London. Yet, there is something very unusual about this image: it is the first one of an English woman wearing a feather. Although few scholars from any of the disciplines of dress history, early modern English history, literature, or gender studies have made any weighty remarks about this fashion accessory, it caused grave concern among some sixteenth- and seventeenth-century contemporaries. The anonymous author of *Hic Mulier* angrily accused women, "from the other, you haue taken the monstrousnesse of your deformities in apparell, exchanging the modest attire of the comely Hood, Cawle, Coyfe, handsome Dresse or Kerchiefe, to the cloudy Ruffianly broad-brim'd Hatte, and wanson feather."[1] The outrage of this unknown individual seems incomprehensible to modern eyes, because the twenty-first century perception of the role of clothing has changed since the sixteenth century, and more importantly, because today the feather is a completely feminine fashion accessory.

The concept of a feminine feather, however, is a modern one. Originally, only men wore feathers, and women committed the horrid crime of cross-dressing in sixteenth- and seventeenth-century England when they decided to wear them. This transformation of the feather's connection from the masculine to the feminine has so far only warranted a short and now dusty footnote in a book on English costume written by C. Willet Cunningham: "It is curious, however, that the use of feathers as ornamental additions to costume, introduced near the end of the thirteenth century, remained until the eighteenth exclusively a masculine habit. Since then it has, of course, become a material exclusively used by women."[2] Even though it has been over fifty years since that footnote was written, little attention has been paid to the gradual feminization of the feather and the controversy initially produced by the feminine theft of the feather from the male wardrobe.

This essay explores both the process by which the feather switched from a masculine fashion accessory to a feminine one as well as the social consequences produced by this transformation. The female theft of the feather was an alarming one for some individuals in sixteenth- and seventeenth-century England because of clothing's intimate connection to power and its role in structuring early modern English society. This study will be divided into three main sections: the first section will outline the way in which women wore feathers in the sixteenth and seventeenth centuries. Secondly, I focus on the changing significance of the feather with regard to the English love of emblems and their exploration of the New World. The last section of the paper addresses the rather contradictory consequences of the female adoption of the feather: by 1620 although it was still considered too masculine for women to wear, it was now also considered too feminine an accessory for men.

The Fashionable Feather and Fashions of the Feather

A rather important premise of this paper rests upon the assertion that up until 1532 in England the feather was an exclusively masculine dress accessory. This seems to have been accepted simply as a self-evident truth in dress history, which no one has bothered to firmly root as fact. Indeed, from a cursory glance at English portraiture and medieval manuscript illuminations, women throughout the centuries had covered their heads with veils, jeweled cawls and nets, high conical head-dresses and, by the sixteenth century, the hood.[3] Hats, and the feathers that adorned them, were left to men. As illustrated with the anonymous author's statement concerning women's cross-dressing, the feather was defined as masculine and could (as we will see later in the essay) masculinize a woman. Despite the fact that *Hic Mulier* was printed in 1620, English women had been wearing feathers for close to ninety years—demonstrating that opinions about and meanings of the feather were slow to change.

Opinions and associations were not the only things to alter about the feather, but the ways in which the feather was being used, and who was using it, changed over time. Women first adopted the feather from the male wardrobe in the form of hat trimmings. As stated in this essay's introduction, one of the earliest, if not the first, image of an English woman wearing a feather is Hans Holbein's drawing, *Mary Howard, Duchess of Somerset and Richmond* dated circa 1532, presently part of the Royal Collection at Windsor Castle. Images of women wearing feathers are literally few and far between; the next surviving image of a woman wearing a feather is that of *Catherine Parr* painted by an unknown artist circa 1545 now at the National Portrait Gallery in London. Both the Duchess of Richmond and Queen Consort Catherine Parr wear a cap designed exactly like the fashionable male cap of the period; the only notable difference about how men and women wore these caps is that women donned them straight across their brow over a female white undercap, whereas men wore their caps directly on their hair and tilted to one side.[4]

Images of women wearing feathers are more the exception rather than the rule. Most women wore a variant of the English gable hood, or after the 1530s, the rounded French hood. A possible explanation for the majority of portraiture displaying women in more traditional feminine headdress could reflect that wearing men's hats and feathers was too informal to be deemed acceptable to be preserved in a portrait. Wearing hats adorned with feathers was probably first adopted by women because they would be easier to wear when participating in outdoor activities such as horseback riding.[5] In later portraits, such as George Gower's 1573 portrait of *Elizabeth Cornwallis, Lady Kytson,* now located in the collection of the Tate Gallery in London, women tend to wear masculine hats with feathers in conjunction with other articles of clothing that denote outdoor activity. For example, in addition to wearing a man's hat with a tall crown adorned with a feather, Lady Kyston also wears a pair of leather gloves.[6]

The two constants that can be found in women's portraits depicting their use of feathers, therefore, are the connotation that outdoor activities are about to ensue and that women always wore an undercap or cawl underneath the plumed hat—perhaps a means to mute the heavy masculine overtone of the hat- and- feather combination. Queen Elizabeth I was recorded as wearing headgear similar to that of Lady Kyston's in 1564 when she traveled to Cambridge where she wore, "a call upon her head, set with pearles and pretious stones; a hat that was spangled with gold, and a bush of feathers."[7] At this point in the account, she had been outdoors, traveling to Cambridge.

Although it is not clear if the hat was as tall-crowned as that of Lady Kyston's, by the 1570s it was fashionable for both men and women to wear hats trimmed with one or multiple plumes. Women also started to wear the male doublet along with their growing acceptance of the male feather; Queen Elizabeth, England's female fashion leader, started wearing doublets around 1575.[8] Women's adoption of hats, feathers, and doublets, all male articles of dress, denotes a more general trend of women's fashions borrowing from the male wardrobe. Another factor, too, that might have made wearing feathers more fashionable in the 1570s was the introduction of brighter colors into English attire.[9] Feathers, which were often dyed, fit nicely with the trend for more colorful embellishment.

By the mid-1570s women's hair was being brushed out into a rounded smooth heart-shape. This rounded shape was pushed out quite wide by the mid-1580s, demanding pads or a wire support underneath the hair in order to maintain the shape. Whatever head-dress women did wear, including hats, was pushed to the back of the head. Again, a feather was still almost exclusively worn with a hat, and the trend for women from the mid-1570s until the mid-1580s was to wear a hat, usually bejeweled, with a feather on the right side. From 1588 onwards, the feather moves from the right side to the middle of the headdress with a large jewel pinned directly in front of the plume, all still attached to a hat or cap. However, by the turn of the century, a woman was not circumscribed to only wearing plumes with a masculine hat or cap. Hair grew much taller during the 1590s as it was combed straight up and slightly rounded on the very top, and feathers could also be worn directly in the hair.

Women's hair had lowered itself by 1610, but it was still very full and styled in a way so that it looked like a smooth, round ball or halo. A portrait of Queen Anne of Denmark, the consort of Elizabeth's successor to the English crown, James I, painted by Marcus Gheeraedts the Younger ca. 1611–14, now in a private collection, shows the round hair on top of which lay a jeweled head-dress holding a feather in the middle. By 1619, however, hair was losing its height in the middle, but keeping a roundness and fullness at the side. Feathers appear to have come into their own at this point, and by July 1618 the Venetian ambassador described the various ways women wore feathers: "the plume on the head, sometimes upright, sometimes at the back of the head and sometimes even transverse."[10] Lady Margaret Aston, in her portrait painted by an unknown artist around 1619 and currently located at the Tate Gallery in London, wears a jeweled band trimmed with feathers, perhaps illustrating one of the fashions mentioned by the Venetian ambassador. No new feather fashions were introduced by 1625, the close of this study; women could wear feathers, either on masculine hats or directly in their own hair.[11]

Hats and hair were now trimmed with both feathers and jewels, and sometimes the two were combined into a feather-shaped jewel. Women treated these feather-shaped jewels just like actual plumes and pinned them directly into their hair. Men wore feather-shaped jewels to embellish their hats. Perhaps the most famous example of a feather jewel was an English crown jewel, simply called the Feather, which was made explicitly for James I as a hat jewel.[12] An entry found in the "Schedule of Royal Jewels, &c 1606" described The Feather as "Item, one fayre jewell, like a feather of goulde, contayning a fayre table-diamond in the middest, and fyve-and twenty diamondes of divers forms made of soundrous other jewells."[13] Aigretts were another feather-form of jewelry also used to decorate hats that could be found in male fashion. As with actual feathers, women could wear feather-shaped jewelry directly in their hair or on a hat, but men could only use them as hat trimmings.

One other feather fashion in the sixteenth and seventeenth century was the plumed fan. Queen Elizabeth popularized them as a fashion accessory among English women. The earliest portraits of Elizabeth I holding a fan are in the 1570s, the same time when she started receiving feather fans as New Year's Gifts. Among the items she received as gifts for the 1574 New Year there is "a fanne of white fethers, sett in a handell of golde; the one side thearof garnished with dyamondes and rubyes; and the backe syde a white beare and twoe perles hanging, a lyon ramping with a white moseled beare at his foote. Geven by therle of Lecetor."[14] Fans consisted of multiple, long, white or different colored ostrich feathers, or shorter feathers arranged in layers and "of sundry collers."[15] The shapes of feather fans ranged from circular, triangular to even rectangular, varying in size as well. Although, the majority of the fans listed as gifts did not mention the types of feathers used, from portraiture it can be deduced that ostrich plumes were the most popular choice. Queen Elizabeth, however, did receive "a ffane of Swanne Downe, wth a maze of greene velvett, ymbrodered w^t seed pearles."[16] By the mid-1580s onwards the feather fan was a familiar feature in female portraiture, and it survived well into the seventeenth century with the sizes ranging from large rectangles to fans consisting of only one or two plumes.

Unlike feathers that trimmed hats, the plumed fan was an exclusively female accessory. One Elizabethan satirist had few kind comments for men "when a plum'd Fanne may shade thy chalked face."[17] Bishop Hall, the author, believed that a man who used feathered fans was effeminate, for the act of wearing cosmetics was also considered a purely feminine activity— and a questionable one at that. Thus, men wearing cosmetics and holding fans, were guilty of being both a poor excuse of a man as well as a foolish and vane woman. Indeed, women too were criticized for possessing fans. Steven Gossen, a Puritan polemicist, complained that "fannes, and flappes of feathers fond . . . they are wives such tooles as bables are in playes for fooles."[18] Although Gossen identifies the fan as a female accessory, it is not the accessory of a good woman but one who is foolish and shallow. This theme of women's vanity and weakness for luxury goods presents itself repeatedly in the sixteenth- and seventeenth-century debate about feathers, and fashion in general, and so will be discussed in greater length further on in the essay.

A more ambiguous feather fashion was embroidery. Both male and female clothes were lavishly embellished in a number of ways, including embroidery, during the Elizabethan and Jacobean periods. In 1563, Queen Elizabeth owed a bill "for Enbraud of a fflaunders gowne of Black velvet wrought allov^r wth a ffaire worke of Estriche ffethers."[19] Another example of embroidered feathers decorating a woman's dress can be found in the previously mentioned Marcus Gheeraedts' portrait of Queen Anne of Denmark in which she wears a dress adorned with embroidered peacock feathers, a reference to the Classical goddess Juno, consort of the chief god, and goddess of the home and hearth. As will be discussed later, symbols were an important source of meaning and re-enforcement of people's perception of themselves and their social position. The embroidered feathers on Queen Anne of Denmark's dress colorfully state her role as wife to the King of England, James I.[20] Men, too, wore elaborately embellished clothes, often with three-dimensional forms of decoration such as embroidery, jewels, pinking, and slashing. I have not as yet discovered any references to men wearing or ordering articles of dress embroidered with a feathered motif, but because it was a unisex fashion to wear heavily decorated clothing, there is not enough evidence either way to claim that an embroidered feather was an exclusively feminine motif.

Regardless of the purchaser's gender, if an individual wanted to buy one or a number of feathers for a hat, he or she had a choice to go either to a haberdasher, a milliner, or a feather-maker. While both haberdashers and milliners sold readymade goods, haberdashers tended to sell hats and trimmings, whereas milliners sold the more luxurious accessories such as jewels, fans, and perfumes. Ostrich plumes could be bought dyed in any color and combined with other types of feathers, often with an osprey or a heron feather, or they could also be encrusted in gold or silver spangles.[21] Many of these haberdashers and feather sellers were housed in the Royal Exchange, the main point for commercial activity once it opened in 1571.[22] Buying feathers was quite an investment, which is perhaps why Philip Stubbes, another Puritan writer displeased with most aspects of late Elizabethan society, simply remarked that "[m]any get good liuying by diying and sellyng of them."[23] If one compares what the haberdasher, Peter Bonyvale, needed to be paid by the Office of the Revels in 1558, to what the tailors employed by the court were being paid, it is quite clear that feathers were expensive. Bonyvale must have supplied different types of feathers (perhaps from different types of birds, or some were dyed, or maybe one group was spangled) because the accounts list two groups of feathers at different prices, but without any description of what made the two groups different, "di. dozen of fethers at ij *s.* the pece—xij *s.*; vj other fethers at xij *d.* the pece."[24] The cheapest feather was an equivalent to an entire day's wage of the tailors who worked for "ij*s.* by daye."[25] Feathers were expensive imported goods, often coming from places such as Morocco, making one ostrich feather directly off the boat worth five days work on a laborer's wage.[26]

Since feathers were so expensive, they made worthy gifts for a queen. Queen Elizabeth I received feathers not only as gifts in the forms of fans, but also in the form of hat trimmings. The New Year's Gift roll for 1600 lists two hats bedecked with feathers.[27] Especially in the case of fans, it was not only the costly plumes that were valued, but the usually elaborate bejeweled fan handles. The feathers themselves, however, were expensive enough to be carefully maintained. Special fan cases were often used, like the ones ordered for Queen Elizabeth in 1575: "one case for a Plume of Fethers coverid with lether lyned with tapheta; one Case for Fanne coverid with leyther lyned with red paper."[28] Therefore, whether the feather was being bought for a queen or a gentleman, its purchase was an expensive endeavor.

Although we can understand the outrage of some of the critics of female feather-wearers since women were spending a great deal of money for foolish fans and lascivious feathers, price alone does not explain the anger felt by writers who were so deeply disturbed at women's adoption of the feather. Indeed, what did it mean for a woman to wear a feather? Therefore, the next step to better understanding the feminization of the feather, with its implications and consequences for both men and women, is to examine the associations and meanings held by the feather. As discussed in the next section, women were not simply wearing a new object, but one laden with meanings and anxieties, thereby giving the act of appropriating the feather meanings of its own.

The Vain, Exotic, and Erotic Feather

It was only fitting to commence this study by examining the visual journey the feather made from the male wardrobe into the female one through an inspection of portraiture. Tudor and Jacobean England was a very visual culture. In addition to feathers, most portraiture, especially during the reign of Elizabeth I and that of her Stuart successor, James I, displays male and female figures encased in rich clothes encrusted with jewels, embroidery, and spangles from their heads to their toes. This love of three-dimensional decoration reflected more than an aesthetic; it reenforced that a person had to illustrate their political power and social dominance—or their lack of it. Rulers demonstrated their power publicly to their subjects and their foreign rivals through grand civic pageants, lavish banquets, splendid palaces, and expensive clothing.[29] Clothing, in particular, was a very important element of displaying one's social position. In early modern England, if a person elevated his/her status, the event often would be commemorated with a portrait and a new set of clothes.[30]

However, power was distributed in a very particular way. Tudor and Stuart society and government were organized along a strict hierarchy, with the most powerful, the ruler, at the top. Moreover, hierarchy was not perceived to be fabricated by man, but a God-given truth, as revealed in this Elizabethan homily:

> Every degree of people in their vocation, calling, and office, hath appointed to them in duty and order: some are high in degree, some in low; some Kings and Princes, some Inferiors and Subjects . . . Masters and Servants . . . Husbands and Wives . . . so that in all things is to be praised the goodly order of God; without which no house, no city, no commonwealth, can continue and endure, or last. For where there is no right order, there reigneth all abuse, carnal liberty, enormity, sin and Babylonical confusion.[31]

In short, society was based on degrees of power, and if those gradations were forgotten, breached, or abandoned, chaos and destruction would ensue. Consequently a society that demanded visibility of power also insisted upon the visibility of lack of power. A servant had to dress more simply than his/her master/mistress. The hierarchy had to be illustrated and enforced by clothing. The power of dress was considered important enough to be a matter for legislation in the form of sumptuary laws. Sumptuary laws divided society into groups and then dictated what items made of what material could be worn by which group. Hierarchy, and each individual's place in it, had to be sartorially demarcated.

The Elizabethan period was typical in that sumptuary laws broke down as a rule, rather than as an exception. Although Elizabeth I ordered no new sumptuary legislation, she constantly reissued decrees titled "Enforcing Statutes of Apparel" that had been originally drawn up under her father, Henry VIII, or her elder half-sister, Mary I. In the first half of her reign, 1558–80, these "Enforcing Statutes of Apparel" were issued seven times, revealing the importance rulers still attached to sumptuary legislation. The Statute of 1566 declared that this particular decree was passed because of the "excess in apparel, both contrary to the laws of the realm and to the disorder and confusion of the degrees of all estates . . . and finally to the subversion of all good order by reason."[32] Clothing functioned within this hierarchical framework by visually expressing social status.[33] Fashion may have changed the styles of dress, but clothes still had to express the correct amount of power or lack of power that a person held. Literally, people had to be what they wore.

In a society that was trying to fix individuals in their places, in part by their clothing, it is interesting that the feather, a fashionable accessory, was actually in the process of becoming unfixed and shifting in its meaning and use, as it switched from being a solely masculine accessory, to a unisex, to finally a feminine one. How do we know what these meanings were? In order to answer this question, the Elizabethan and Jacobean love of emblems and symbols must be addressed. More than just the literal truth of one's social status was demanded of English subjects' clothing. Although dress, at least in theory, was supposed to sartorially demarcate social ranks and occupations, dress also incorporated signifiers that held additional layers imbued with deeper meanings. Therefore, in order to understand the significance in the shift of the feather's role in fashion, the associations held by the feather must first be explored.

In order to determine what the feather symbolized, one must turn to the Elizabethan and Jacobean love of allegory.[34] The feather had four main associations: vanity, exoticism, eroticism, and masculinity. Allegorical figures were often present in public celebrations such as royal progresses and civic pageants. One of the most popular manifestations of this love of allegory was the emblem. An emblem consisted of a picture with a few verses, all of which was encapsulated by a motto.[35] The first emblem books to circulate throughout England were foreign ones published in Italy and France. Two of the most popular were Claude Paradin's *Devises Herioques* (1557) and Cesare Ripa's *Iconologia* (1593).[36] Eventually, England produced its own emblem book with Geffrey Whitney's 1586 *A Choice of Emblems*, which borrowed many of its images from other sources, Paradin in particular.[37] Concepts such as virtue were illustrated by a few key characteristics, with a moral message taught to the reader through the motto. As will be presented further along in the paper, sometimes a solitary object could stand in for a larger concept, such as wisdom or even a continent.

Emblems not only decorated the pages of books, but easily lent themselves to other areas in the decorative arts of the period. These simple images, which projected a concise message, fulfilled for Elizabethans and Jacobeans both the general love of allegory and the specific fondness for three-dimensional embellishment of dress. Emblems inhabited a place in the English wardrobe in two main areas: in jewelry and in embroidery that decorated dress. Queen Elizabeth received many jewels that were emblems; in 1578 she received one New Year's Gift described as "Item, a Juell of golde, being a woman ennamuled, called virture standing upon a Raynebowe, the boddy garneshed wth spcks of Diamonds and Rubyes."[38] The tag of "virture" (what must be an early modern spelling for virtue) was probably unnecessary because her mind, trained in allegorical thinking, and her eye, familiar with the emblem of the figure of Virtue, would have recognized the jeweled figure.[39] In the case of embroidery, there were two types: professional embroidery and domestic craft. Surviving examples of domestically produced embroidery suggest that emblems were very popular sources for designs.[40] Queen Elizabeth I and her successor's wife, Queen Anne of Denmark, wore dresses and other garments decorated with emblems professionally embroidered. One such example can be found in the previously discussed portrait of Anne of Denmark, which presents her as wearing a dress embroidered with peacock feathers, the emblem of the goddess Juno, consort to the Jupiter, the king of all the Roman gods, thereby reenforcing her position as the royal consort.

Queen Anne's dress illustrates how birds and feathers played two key roles in emblemtry; either they stood as emblems in and of themselves, or they were one key element in an emblem formed from multiple components. Not all birds, however, had positive connotations, and as in the case of the peacock feathers, they held both positive and negative associations. The peacock's plumes not only signified Juno, but like feathers in general, were associated with vanity and folly. In Ripa's *Iconologia*, the figure of "Arroganza," the emblem of arrogance takes the form of a woman holding a peacock. Ripa explains that "[t]he peacock signifies arrogance being an example of pride."[41] In sixteenth-century England, just as in the twenty-first century, people who are too concerned with their appearance and very involved in following fashion are compared to peacocks. When contemporary writer Stephen Gossen wanted to upbraid the women of his time for being too preoccupied with fashion, he scolded: "to peacocks I compare them right, that glorieth in their feathers bright."[42]

Feathers in general, however, were also aligned with pride and sin. In Paradin's *Devises Heroiques* is the emblem, "*Renouata iuuentus*," which is illustrated by a bird flying to the sun, visibly shedding its feathers. In its explanatory verse, feathers are equated with sins, and according to Paradin, the bird "purges itself of its bad feathers just as we must do with our vices."[43] As illustrated in the figure of "Arroganza," feathers represented the vice of pride. Negative sentiments about feathers were expressed outside the emblem books, such as in Philip Stubbes' 1583 *Anatomie of Abuses*. In his work, he shares his disgust over the fashions of the day with his readers, and even the plumed hat could not escape his condemnation:

> And another sort . . . are content with no kind of Hat, without a greate bunche of feathers of diuers of sondrie colours, peakyng on top of heades, . . . as sternes of Pride and ensignes of vanitie, and these fluttering sailes and feathered flagges of defiaunce of vertue.[44]

Stubbes' choice of vocabulary is noteworthy; these feathers, deemed to be "ensignes of vanity," were the very embodiment of pride. For him there was no mistake that feathers were the emblem of vanity. Moreover, feathers were a public renouncement of humility and virtue and a visual declaration of the wearer's acceptance of sin. Feathers, "sternes of Pride," would lead their wearers astray from an upright lifestyle. Indeed, clothes, as will be discussed in the next section, not only reflected a person's social status or spiritual state, but also played a part in creating a person's social, mental, and religious position.

As if being an emblem for pride and vanity were not enough, the feather also had associations with the exotic and the erotic. The feather was a key visual component in the emblem of the newly discovered continent, America. Many emblem and costume books contained images of the allegorical figure of America. Two of the most popular costume books in late sixteenth- and early seventeenth-century Europe were Jean Jacques Boissard's *Habitus Variarum Orbis Gentium* published in 1581 and Abrham de Bruyn's 1581 *Omnium Pene Europe, Asiae, Aphricae Atque Americae Gentium Habitus*, and both frontispieces have the four allegorical figures of the four known continents. The two frontispieces feature America as a woman, almost completely nude, with the exception of either a strategic piece of drapery in Boissard's version or a feather mantle and odd bits of jewelry on de Bruyn's figure, but both Americas wear a feather head-dress while holding a bow and arrow.[45] The connection between feathers and the Americas was as old as the European discovery of the Americas themselves.

Most of Europe became fascinated with the exotic natural inhabitants of the New World, namely Native Americans and parrots. On his return from his first voyage, Columbus brought back a small group of both the indigenous human and bird population to Spain.[46] Brazil became known as the "land of parrots" and the featherwork of the Amerindians was very much admired; many European rulers such as the Emperor Ferdinand I, his two sons, and Cosimo I collected Mexican art with featherwork making up a significant part of those collections.[47] Familiarity with feathers and Native Americans was not reserved for European royalty, but the common people also were exposed to the discoveries found in the New World. By 1512, people dressed as Amerindians joined the ranks of allegorical and exotic figures presented to the masses in civic pageants across Europe. In the Triumph of the Emperor Maximilian I in 1512, the figures of Native American were represented by men wearing colorful plumed head-dresses and feather bases (strips of material sewn together at the end of a tunic), creating a feather skirt, and feathers connected to a band which was tied around the leg, right below the knees.[48]

This image of America, an Indian bedecked with feathers, was not only found on the Continent, but across the Channel in England as well. In 1620, a civic pageant was given in London to celebrate the inauguration of the new mayor. One of the triumph wagons held people dressed as "the Four Parts of the World, Asia, Africa, America and Europa" with America presented as "a tawney moore, upon her head a crowne of feathers, and bases of the same, at her back a quiver of shafts, and in her hand a Parthian bow."[49] Whether on the Continent or in England, Europe had a common allegorical construction of America: a female Indian with a bow, an arrow, and feathers.

The New World and its inhabitants were not only depicted as exotic, but soon shades of eroticism were added to the canvas. Amerigo Vespucci wrote about his supposed discoveries on his trips to the New World, which was aptly titled *Mundus Novus*, first printed in 1505 in Latin. Over the next ten years, it had been translated into five languages and reissued in thirty editions all throughout Europe, including England.[50] Perhaps one of the reasons why Vespucci's work was so popular was due to its description of the Amerindians' purported sexual appetites. The explorer recounted that the Indians wore no clothes, but were not ashamed of their nudity. The women, according to Vespucci, were "immoderately libidinous, and the women much more so than the men, so that for decency I omit to tell you the artifice they practice to gratify their inordinate lust."[51] Europeans considered all Indians to be hyper-sexed, and accused Indian men of practicing sodomy, pederasty, and polygamy.[52]

It is important to note here that Vespucci only had contact with the peoples of South America, whereas England had more dealings with the Native Americans of North America, especially after 1603 when the first successful English colony was established in Virginia. To the early modern English, the North American Indians appeared to refrain from the more shocking sexual practices of their South American counterparts. Yet this could be accounted for by the fact that many of the people writing about Virginia were trying to encourage settlers and did not want to scare away prospective emigrant families.[53] Despite any perceived differences that were made between the indigenous people of South America from those of North America, the emblem for America, the allegorical female figure, stood for both continents, thereby collapsing any distinctions, including any gender differences, made between their peoples.

The emblematic image of America was so tightly linked to the feather that it was used as an emblem in and of itself to represent America. An example can be found in Robert Peake's portrait of Lady Elizabeth Pope painted around 1615, now part of the Tate Gallery's collection in London. The portrait presents Lady Pope as the allegorical figure America. The visual keys that decode the meaning behind this portrait are the ostrich feathers made of pearls, encrusting her purple mantle, and her head-dress constructed from the same material as her mantle, which is then trimmed with a real ostrich feather that had been dyed purple. Ellen Chirelstein's analysis of this portrait and the evidence produced by her investigation into the sitter's background further supports the idea that Lady Pope personifies America. Her father had invested heavily in the Virginia Company, which ran the colony that shared the company's name.[54] In addition to her natal family's links to the Virginia colony, Lady Pope was also connected to America through her husband, who commissioned the portrait. Chirelstein argues that "Lady Elizabeth's image as America opens the possibility of considering a husband's possession of his wife . . . as an object of desire" just as America was sexualized in much the same way—as a husband's sexual possession of a virgin bride.[55]

It was not only in terms of Europeans' discussion of Amerindians' sexual habits that eroticized the indigenous peoples of the Americas—the very land was sexualized. John Smith, who lived and explored the Virginia colony in the first decade of the seventeenth century, described Virginia in terms of sex: "the soil is fat and lusty."[56] Smith used similar terms when describing the female Indians: "We saw but three of their women, and they were . . . fat and well favoured."[57] Both the people and the land were discussed in language that accentuated their sexuality and their fertility. Whether it was a literary passage or an illustration, America was sexualized and feminized. The frontispiece of Boissard's costume book (figure 9.1) also articulates America in erotic terms. The frontispiece imagery contains four figures representing the four known continents. The figure representing America is almost completely naked. America is dressed (or undressed) in striking contrast to Europe. The female figure that represents Europe has the most flesh covered. Europe wears clothes that correspond with the general lines of the fashions worn by Western European women of this period. Her unbuttoned doublet has long sleeves which cover her arms, and a collar to hide most of her neck. Underneath the doublet is a laced bodice and long skirt which falls to the floor, only exposing a few toes of one foot. Below Europe is Asia, who wears a loose dress, one based more on imagination than fashionable dress, which exposes her arms and her neck. Across from both Europe and Asia is Africa and America. Africa appears to be half out of her dress. Her breasts are fully exposed as are her shoulders, arms, and neck.

Figure 9.1   The engraved frontispiece of Jean Jacques Boissard's 1581 *Habitus Variarum Orbis Gentium*. Originally the engraving was just black and white; this particular example was colored in at a later date. The figures starting with the top left and moving clockwise: Europe, Africa, America, and Asia. Reproduced with the permission of the Anne S. K. Brown Military Collection, Brown University Library, Rhode Island.

A small piece of fabric is twisted around her upper left arm. Although she wears a voluminous skirt, it has a high slit, exposing her left leg from the mid-thigh to her toes. Whereas Africa is half-naked, America is almost completely nude, except for her enormous feather head-dress and a piece of drapery situated over the very top of her left thigh. The only other articles of dress that cover her body are an armlet and a necklace. Surely it was no coincidence that the lands with which Europeans were the least familiar with and over which they hoped to gain economic control were depicted in exotic and erotic terms. Civilization, sexuality, and empire are discussed in the language of the body, articulated through clothes and flesh. Since America was sexualized, so too was the feather, which could act as an emblem for America all by itself.

The portrait of Lady Pope borrowed symbols from English culture to represent herself as the figure of America. However, Lady Pope's unusual choice to not wear fashionable, real garments must be explained. Chirelstein claims that the sitter is depicted in a "fictive masque."[58] The masque was yet one more area that Elizabethans and Jacobeans could indulge in their love of allegories and emblems. Masques were a type of court entertainment, which first appeared in England in its earliest form under Henry VIII. By the reign of James I, the masque was a much more formal event that included a show of verse, singing, and dancing, which was performed by a mixture of courtiers, professional actors, and musicians, all masked and dressed in exotic costumes. At the very end of the masque, the remaining courtier spectators were expected to join the performers in the final, formal dance.[59] Lady Pope's portrait is one example of a small, but definitive, trend of individuals who chose to represent themselves in fictive or real masque outfits.[60] Stephen Orgel and Roy Strong in their exhaustive work on the early Stuart masque explain that the sources for these masques are "allegory, symbol and myth."[61] Ben Jonson wrote the majority of the masques performed for the Jacobean court, and Inigo Jones designed the stage, costume, and other props. Together they assembled a moving emblem book with Jones providing the text and Jones building the picture through his stage sets and costumes. Jonson mined Ripa's *Iconologia* as a source in conjunction with Jones' use of costume books such as Boissard and de Bruyn to design his costumes.[62] Jones used the costume books in order to gain ideas about the dress of peoples from different times and places in order to create exotic characters. According to Francis Bacon, a late sixteenth-century contemporary noted that the costumes should be "not after examples of known attire, [but] Turks, soldiers, mariners, and the like."[63] Since the masque contained elements of allegory and exoticism, America and Indians made suitably exotic characters.

The masque, like America and the feather, had connotations of both exoticism and eroticism. The erotic elements of the masque lay primarily in female masque dress. The integral part of a female masquer's costume was the *camicia*, which was a loose lawn chemise that stopped before the ankle, thereby creating a much shorter hemline than found on normal skirts.[64] In Inigo Jones' costume designs, the *camicia* is transparent, revealing the breasts and large portions of leg. Dressing a woman in these short, see-through garments was the very epitome of an early modern man's sexual fantasy, for "what man would not gladly see a beautifull woman naked, or at least with nothing but a lawne, or some loose thing ouer her?"[65] Indeed, some courtiers such as Dudley Carleton felt that masque clothes were quite inappropriate for Queen Anne and her aristocratic ladies, who were often the performers, to wear "theyr apparel rich, but too light and curtizan like."[66] Another part of the masque dress was the consistent use of feathers. Surviving inventories of the props produced for the masques give ample evidence that feathers were frequently used in constructing masque costumes. Jones' various and numerous costume designs are full of feathered head-dresses. Thus, the masque, with its overtones of strangeness and sex, compounded the exotic and erotic charge of the feather.

The feather's links to America and Native Americans were illustrated in masques. Performed in 1613, "The Memorable Masque" by George Chapman featured "Virginian priests" and "Virginian princes," (Virginia stands for America, so the priests and the princes are Amerindians) with both groups covered in a multitude of feathers:

Their robes were tucked up before, strange hoods of feathers and scallops about their necks, and on their heads turbans, stuck with several coloured feathers . . . Then rode the chief masquers in Indian habits all of a resemblance: the ground-cloth of silver richly embroidered with golden suns . . . their bases of the same stuff and work, but betwixt every pane of embroidery went a row of white ostrich feathers . . . and about their necks ruffs of feathers spangled with pearl and silver. On their heads high sprigged feathers, compassed in coronets, like the Virginian princes they presented.[67]

The "Virginian priests and princes" were defined by their use of feathers. Jones probably turned to any of the costume books of his time in order to find a suitable design for the Virginian costumes. A surviving sketch by Jones of a "Torchbearer: An Indian" currently part of the Devonshire Collection at Chatsworth, wears feathers. The feather was eroticized through its use in depicting the concept of America and its use in the masque. The masque in turn often reenforced the feather-America/American Indian association.

The masque, "News from the New World Discovered in the Moon," by Jonson, performed in 1620, was set on the moon, veiling the actual setting, the New World of the Americas. The tie between the moon and the Americas was drawn even tighter as the masque's explorers describe some of the things they witnessed in this "New World." One of their discoveries is related in the same erotic overtones as Vespucci's *Mundus Novus*:

1st Herald

Only one island is called the Isle of the Epicoenes, because there under one article both kinds are signified; for they are fashioned alike, male and female the same, notheads and broad hats, short doublets and long points; neither do they ever untruss for distinction, but laugh and lie down in the moonshine, and stab with their poniards; you do not know the delight of the Epicoenes in moonshine.

2nd Herald

And when they ha' tasted the springs of pleasure enough, and billed and kissed, and are ready to come away, the shes only lay certain eggs (for they are never with child there) and of those eggs are disclosed a race of creatures like men, but are indeed a sort of fowl, in part covered in feathers (they call 'em Volatees).[68]

There are three points in this passage that suggest that this masque is referring to America as opposed to a purely invented fictional moon-land: the feathers, the similarity of dress between the sexes, and the stress on sexual pleasure as opposed to sexual reproduction. The feathers had such a powerful connection to the Americas that they could stand alone as an emblem to represent the New World. This America-feather connection is also reenforced with the Volatees characters. These creatures not only have plumes, but the head of a bird, once again making the connection between America and exotic birds, such as the New World parrots.[69]

Secondly, the similarity of dress between the sexes also alludes to the Americas as the true scene of this masque. Early modern costume books, such as de Bruyn's *Omnivum Pene Europe, Asiae, Aphricae Atque Americae Gentium Habitus*, presents the dress of Indian men and women as interchangeable. In de Bruyn's page on the dress of American Indians, the top male and female figures are both dressed and undressed in an almost identical fashion. The top left figure is labeled a woman, but the only signifier of her gender is the child fastened to her back, for like her male companion, she is topless, wears a skirt, a feathered head-dress, and feather garters. While she holds a child and a jug, he holds what might at first be categorized as more masculine accessories, a bow and arrow, until one remembers the emblem of America—where it is a female figure who holds the bow and arrow. The male Indian's masculinity is further compromised by the two Indian figures on the bottom of the page. Again, both figures, despite their gender, wear skirts, feathered mantles, feathered head-dresses, feather garters, and ankle bracelets. The major difference is that the female figure, instead of her male counterpart, wears the feather skirt. According to this illustration, feathers, skirts, and mantles are all unisex Amerindian clothing. John Smith also commented upon the lack of sartorial gender distinction: "We saw but three women . . . attired in skins like men."[70]

This sartorial blurring of the demarcation of gender difference brings us to the third point, that the Americas were considered a European fantasy land of sexual pleasure. Cross-dressing was also another source of eroticism that became associated with the feather. In the selected passage from "News of the New World Discovered on the Moon," the speakers state that the men and women dress the same, but the clothes that are listed, especially the broad hats and short doublets, were male articles of clothing. This returns us to a passage cited at the beginning of this essay, that early modern writers, such as the anonymous author of *Hic Mulier*, complained that women, in general, were dressing like men, by appropriating traditionally male articles of dress, such as the "broad-brim'd Hatte, and wanson feather." The feather was just one manifestation of the overall problem of cross-dressing that the author labeled "wanton and lascivious" which in turn made any cross-dressed woman "guilty of lust."[71]

Although the feather was a symbol of the Americas, the American Indians, and the masque, it had first been an emblem of masculinity. However, when a member of the wrong gender wore the feather, the symbol became sexually perverted. When a woman wore a feminine headdress, such as a cawl or a hood, an article of clothing that hid her hair, her choice of dress was deemed "modest." Once she chose a feather, her head-dress was no longer considered modest, but "wanson" for wearing an item that would bring attention to her, compelling men to look at her and lust after her. Philip Stubbes explains that when women cross-dress, the clothing becomes, "wanton, leud kind of attire, proper onely to manne" because she is subverting the true purpose of clothing which was given us as a signe distinctiue, to discerne betwixt sexe and sexe, and therefore one to weare the apparell of an other sexe, is to particiate with the same, and to adulterate the veritie of his owne kind."[72] Thus, a woman wearing men's clothing cancels her female gender. In an age that demanded an individual visually declare his or her social rank, occupation and gender through clothing, cross-dressing undermined the sartorial supports of this hierarchical society.

Furthermore, cross-dressing was linked to illicit sexuality. This connection is made most clearly by art historian Anne Hollander who asserts "that when clothing no longer demarcates men from women, "it is sexual *pleasure*, set up in visible defiance of the clear male and female signals designed to further procreation, that is emphasized by any hint of homoerotic fantasy in clothes; and it frightens many."[73] In the "News from the New World Discovered on the Moon," sexual pleasure is also emphasized by the "New World" men and women wearing similar dress and the ease of childbirth. In the masque, the women simply lay eggs instead of giving birth. The ease of birth, moreover, was another association attached to Native American women.[74] This emphasis on the ease of reproducing children, along with the absence of clothing signifiers to demarcate male and female, shifts the focus of sex from procreation to that of sexual pleasure.

Blurring sexual reproduction and sexual pleasure along with blending genders frightened many like Philip Stubbes and the unknown author of *Hic Mulier*. In a society where a person was supposed to be what they wore, the female adoption of the feather as a fashion accessory could only be problematic. The female theft of the feather from the male wardrobe produced two alarming consequences: the vain, exotic, erotic, and masculine feather not only fashioned masculine women, but created feminized men.

Contradictory Consequences

The significance of women wearing feathers is two-fold: it created an unacceptable form of femininity, which then, in turn, produced an equally socially unacceptable type of masculinity. Although the feather was deemed as too masculine for women to wear, the female theft of the feather started a process that made it too feminine for men to continue wearing. Just as preachers and Puritan polemicists alike denounced clothing that collapsed social distinctions, a parallel problem arose that "there is left no difference in apparel between an honest matron and a common strumpet."[75] Whereas the feather was associated with being vain, exotic, erotic, and masculine, women were supposed to be chaste, silent, and obedient as described in J. L. Vives' 1528 conduct manual, *A Very Frutefull and Pleasant Boke Called the Instruction of a Christian Woman*. All women, but especially married women, were admonished to be chaste. However, a woman's chastity was not her own: instead, her "chastitee and honestie whiche thou hoste is not thyne but committed and betaken unto thy kepyng by thy husbande," and before marriage, a woman's chastity was her father's property.[76] Chastity was of the utmost importance in a society where a man's wealth passed on to his heirs, because the only way for a man to ensure the children were his was by controlling his wife's sexuality.[77] Keeping silent went along with being obedient; according to Vives, "Saint Paule wrytynge vnto Tymothe speaketh of womanes duetie in thys wyse: Let the woman lerne with all obedience, kepyng silence."[78] It was considered a law of nature as well as a Divine commandment that women owed men their obedience, "all lawes, both spyrituall and temporall, and Nature hir selfe cryeth and commaundeth that the woman shallbe subiecte and obedient to the man."[79] The ideal woman, however, was not an easy being to make.

The tension of the "good" woman wearing the "bad" feather lay in the now familiar theme of the sixteenth- and early seventeenth-century desire for clothing to visibly demarcate one's station, occupation, gender, and even inward character. Women, even without wearing the feather, were contradictory enough. Despite the feminine ideal of chastity, silence, and obedience, early modern people believed that women by their very nature were weak and easily succumbed to lasciviousness, unruliness, emotions, and deceitfulness, and therefore subject to the logical male.[80] One way to ensure women behaved appropriately was to dress them appropriately. Clothing did not simply reflect whether a woman was "an honest matron" or "a common strumpet," but dress had the power to fashion an ideal woman and enforce the tenets of correct femininity. According to Phillip Stubbes, the best way to teach women how to behave properly was for parents to dress them properly while still young children, because "so long as a sprigge . . . or branche is young, it is flexible and bowable to any thyng a man can desire, but if we tarie till it bee a greate tree, it is in flexible."[81] If parents neglected to dress their daughters modestly, Stubbes claims this lack of sartorial discipline was "what maketh them so soone Whores, Strumpets and Bawdes."[82] Once women were married, they were advised that "also raymente lykewyse as all other thynges oughte to be reffered vnto thyne husbandes wyll."[83] Women needed proper clothing in order for them to overcome their inconstant nature and become chaste, silent, and obedient.

Dress contained the power to fashion people's actions; therefore, if gender roles were to be properly enacted, the players had to dress in the proper costume. The feather, however, provided no help in this regard; instead it undermined any attempts to fashion a good woman. One problem with women wearing the feather was that it was a symbol of vanity. Women, due to their weaker nature, were very susceptible to vanity, even if they did not wear plumes. Vanity was the outward manifestation of pride, one of the seven deadly sins. Pride was viewed as a dangerous disease: "Pride is infectious, and breeds prodigality: Prodigalite after it has runnne a little closes vp and festers, and then turns to Beggerie."[84] Women were perceived to be particularly prone to extreme cases of vanity, inspiring Vives to write that women, "robbe bothe theyr husbandes and their children, to clothe them selfe wyth, and leaue hunger and pouertee at home, that they maye go forth them selfe laden with sylke and golde."[85] Whether male or female, people who wore sumptuous clothing reflected their "wanton appetites of . . . lasciuios mindes."[86]

Vanity also led women astray from chastity. In "An Homily Against Apparel" all women who wore costly clothes were compared to prostitutes:

> No less, truly is the vanity that is used amongst us in these days. For the proud and haughty stomachs of the daughters of England are so maintained with divers disguised sorts of costly apparel, that . . . there is left no difference in apparel between an honest matron and a common strumpet.[87]

Therefore, in order to maintain a woman's chastity, she needed to dress modestly so that she drew no attention to herself. Modest dress, which covered a woman's body, was another way of silencing women, whereas immodest dress called attention to the exposed flesh of a woman. The anonymous author of *Hic Mulier* provides an example: "the vpper parts of a concealing straight gowne, [as opposed to] the loose, lascivious ciuill embracement of a French doublet, being all vnbutton'd to entice."[88] Feathers, by contrast, were "ensignes of vanitie . . . and feathered flagges of defiaunce to vertue" and unfitting attire for a chaste, modest woman. Vanity, however, was the least of the feather's offenses.

Exoticism was another fault of the feather, because "all acquisite, externall, exotique, and artificiall varnishes, cultures, dressings and attires, which anywayes, sophisticate, or alter the naturall feature, forme comelinesse . . . is so farre from adding comeliness . . . that it doeth more deturpate and der-forme vs."[89] In a society that presumes to "see" everything such as a person's social status by his/her clothes or a woman's chastity by her appearance, anything that acts as a disguise cannot be tolerated. The feather was further tainted by exoticism with its links to the Americas and the masque. If the feather was being worn in everyday fashion, then other elements of the masque, such as disguising, might become commonplace. Thomas Nashe, another early modern contemporary, lamented "England . . . the continuall Masquer in outlandish habilements, great plenty-scanting calamities art thou to await for wanton disguising thy selfe."[90] Disguise was dangerous, because it made the known into the unrecognizable. Furthermore, if the masque spilled onto the streets, then so too did the otherwise contained eroticism of the masque. As noted in the previous section, the female masque costume was considered risqué. The feather, a visual signifier of the exotic and the erotic connotations of the masque, challenged the more suit-able modest attire of a chaste woman.

Feathers assaulted chastity from all sides, especially since contemporaries believed that "apparraile, more then any thing, bewrayeth his wearers minde."[91] Thus, when a woman wore a "wanson feather," she advertised her sexual desire.[92] Yet, as already established, a woman's sexuality was not hers to control. To compound matters, since women, by their innate nature, were considered to have an insatiable sexual appetite, she needed to wear modest attire that would prevent her from giving into her desire. The feather would not only publicly proclaim her lust, but there would be no sartorial restraints to keep her from satisfying her sexual urges. Again, the early modern belief that clothes did not merely reflect things about the wearer, but actually influenced behavior is brought to light. The fear that women, by not wearing modest, feminine attire, could not be distinguished as whores or chaste maidens did not just stem from the fact they would be dressing in the same way, but that they would be behaving in the same way.

This argument, that clothing determined action, becomes even more evident when discussing the implications of women wearing feathers in order to cross-dress. In *Hic Mulier*, the fact that women were dressing like men was only half the problem. Cross-dressed women were "Masculine in Moode, from bold speech, to impudent action . . . they were, are and will be most Masculine."[93] When women behaved like men, they were no longer obediently or silently accepting their inferiority to men. Women wearing the feather, or any article of male dress, were committing the same offense as a knight dressing like an earl; cross-dressed women were transgressing boundaries of power and privilege. In a hierarchical society, power could not be shared; there would be discord. The analogy used to teach women their place in the household presented the married couple as one person in body and in mind, but "in wedlocke the man resembleth the reason, and the woman the body. Nowe reason ought to rule, and the body to obey."[94] Consequently, if a woman considered herself equal to her husband, the household would fall apart, "for if it haue many heddes or many bodies it is lyke a monster."[95] The destruction or disunity of a household held larger implications for the whole of society, because the household was the microcosm of both the political and the social order of early modern England. A king was considered a father to his subjects, and fathers were deemed kings of their families. If people forgot their place in the family, they would forget their place as political subjects.[96] Gender was one of the many categories that defined the amount of power an individual could receive and exercise in the social hierarchy of sixteenth- and seventeenth-century England—categories that had to be sartorially enforced.

The anonymous author of *Hic Mulier* also wrote *Haec-Vir: Or The Womanish-Man: Being an Answer to a late Booke intitled Hic Mulier*, which argued that the only reason women were wearing masculine attire, such as the feather, was due to the fact that all the men had become effeminate. Whereas the effeminate man accuses the masculine woman of stealing the male doublet and the "most prophane Feather" in addition to other items, the masculine woman counters, "why doe you rob vs of our Ruffes, of our Earetings . . . of our Fannes and Feathers?"[97] The feather, by 1620, when *Hic Mulier* and *Haec-Vir* are published, was in a liminal state of being too masculine for women, but too effeminate for men. Plumes, however, were just one example of men paying too close attention to fashion, which was seen as the result of the sixteenth- and seventeenth-century's courtier's lifestyle. Throughout the Tudor and early Stuart era, the aristocracy was expected to live extravagantly, especially in their dress, since it was an outward display of their wealth, power, and privileges.[98] If an individual desired such power and privileges, he/she needed to go to the royal court. Once there, courtiers required lavish dress, in order to create a visually magnificent setting that would allow the monarch to impress foreign powers.[99] Subsequently, once a person achieved power and rank that individual had to maintain that image, such as dressing as sumptuously as one's rank allowed.

A complication for male courtiers arose because wearing these luxurious clothes was considered to effeminate men. Stubbes provides the contemporary logic behind this process: "For be sure this pamperyng of their bodies, makes them weker, tenderer . . . then otherwise thei would be if thei were used to hardnesse."[100] Luxurious clothing was part of living the soft life of the court, and resulted in an "effeminacie of condition, as we maie seeme rather nice dames, and wanton girles, then . . . manly men."[101] In 1609, Thomas Dekker wrote *The Guls Horne Book*, a satire about the dress and behavior of these effeminate, overly fashion conscious men. A "Gul" was a young man who followed fashion's every whim, including growing his hair long, wearing perfume, and spending prodigious amounts of money. Another questionable fashion they practiced was to "weare fethers then chiefly in their hates, being one of the fairest engines of their brauery."[102] His long hair was equated with feathers, which "in sommer, [act] a coolong fanne of fethers."[103] Dekker facetiously remarks "O no, long hair is the only nette that thy women spread to entrappe men in: why should not men be as far aboue women in that commodity?"[104] Long hair was considered one of the main features women used to attract men; therefore, men who grew their hair long and wore feathers were proclaiming their effeminacy. The feather, once a declaration of manhood, was now deemed effeminate.

Even by 1620, the transition of the feather from the male wardrobe to the female one was far from complete. Men did wear feathers well into the eighteenth century. This was due, in part, because everything, especially dress and its accessories, held meanings and shaped (as well as reflected) particular beliefs. Just because feathers were being used in new ways did not mean that the old associations were quickly discarded for new ones. Instead, new and contradictory associations of the feather existed simultaneously. Nor were feathers the only male article of clothing that was appropriated by women. During the same period, when women started wearing masculine headgear, they also appropriated the male doublets. The feather with its changing role in fashion was problematic, but it was not an anomaly; it was a symptom of broader fashion and social changes. Perhaps the feather best symbolizes the breakdown of visual labeling through dress. Women who wore the feather were dressing above their station by crossing the power barriers of gender. Society, in general, seemed to be dressing above its station, otherwise the sumptuary laws would not have needed to be reissued so frequently, nor would Philip Stubbes have been left with such an acute case of writer's cramp.

It is no coincidence that sumptuary laws were repealed in 1604, the middle section of the period this paper covers.[105] The case study of the feather is more than just a story of the breakdown of sartorial labeling. Studying the transition of the feather from a masculine dress accessory to a female article of dress reveals the process of mutual constructions of gender and how items become gendered—that gender is a concept that is created, maintained, and perpetuated by props. According to some sixteenth-century writers, clothing was more than just a mirror that reflected a person's body, mind, and soul, but in fact fashioned those very entities. Clothes literally made the man or the woman. Therefore, when feathers crossed the gender boundaries, not only did the feathers themselves change gender, from being considered masculine to being considered feminine, but they contained the dangerous potential of changing gender norms. Instead of women being chaste and modest, the feather would create wanton women. Instead of men being hard, by wearing the feather, they would become soft and effeminate. Instead of clothing revealing a person's place in society, clothes, like the feather, would disguise a person's social standing.

Lastly, it is important to note that the process of the feminization of the feather was a slow one which produced confused understandings of this article of dress, and by 1620 the feather was fit neither for women nor for men. The feather came to inhabit a dangerous gray area, a no-man's land and a no-woman's land. This gradual feminization of the feather illustrates that the concept of gender in the early modern period could easily move from a strict binary, male or female, to encompassing a spectrum of potential genders. However, these broader and more protean possibilities did not fit into a hierarchical society that demanded strict and visible distinctions. Ideas about gender were not only challenged when clothes crossed the gendered boundaries of the wardrobe, but when the feather crossed geographical boundaries. Discoveries made in the New World challenged the status quo of the Old World. Europe placed its anxieties about gender, power, and sexuality onto the indigenous people and the indigenous commodities of the Americas. The New World feather added new layers of meaning and anxieties onto an item that had already existed for centuries in the Old World. The feather, in sixteenth- and seventeenth-century England, was one such site of negotiation where boundaries of gender, race, class, and religion were both established and transgressed.

Notes

1. *Hic Mulier: Or, The Man Woman: Being a Medicine to Cure the Coltish Disease of the Stagers in the Masculine-Feminines of our Times* (London, 1620), not paginated.
2. This footnote can be found in C. Willet Cunningham, *The Art of English Costume* (London: Collins Clear Type Press, 1948), 164.
3. Female hoods, worn from the end of the fifteenth century until the end of the sixteenth century, came in two forms. These hoods were not like the hood of a cloak or cape, but a structured headdress. From 1490–1530, most English aristocratic women wore an English, or gable, hood, so named because there was a band, shaped like a gable, that framed the face, and had lappets that covered the sides and back of the head. Hoods started to move further to the back of the head, exposing more of the hair and face. The French hood which was rounder and worn around the middle of the head, replaced the English hood completely,

albeit often in modified form, by the 1540s in England. For a general outline of English women's fashions see Valerie Cumming and Aileen Ribeiro, eds., *A Visual History of Costume* (London: B. T. Batsford Ltd., 1997); for a more specific examination of women's fashion in the sixteenth century, see Jane Ashelford, *A Visual History of Costume: The Sixteenth Century* (London: B. T. Batsford Ltd., 1983; reprinted 1993); for the seventeenth century, see Valerie Cumming, *A Visual History of Costume: The Seventeenth Century* (London: B. T. Batsford Ltd., 1984; reprinted 1987).

4. The white undercap worn by these women were worn by all sixteenth-century women, regardless of the type of headdress worn.

5. Amanda Straw, "An Investigation into the Work of Hans Holbein the Younger as a Source for Understanding Englishwomen's Headwear, c. 1526–1543," (MA thesis, Courtauld Institute of Art, 1995), 30. When discussing the possible reasons why the Duchess of Richmond might have chosen to wear as hat with a single ostrich feather Straw posits this idea that male attire was more suitable for outdoor activity. This theory would make sense; most of the female thefts of male dress stemmed from the need to have comfortable clothes that allow more movement. Another example that comes from the late seventeenth century is the female riding suit that was based upon the male three piece suit.

6. Ashelford, *A Visual History of Costume*, 82.

7. John Nichols, *The Progresses and Public Processions of Queen Elizabeth*, 3 vols. (London: John Nichols and Son, 1823), 1:160.

8. Janet Arnold, *Queen Elizabeth's Wardrobe Unlock'd* (Leeds: W. S. Maney & Sons Ltd., 1988), 142.

9. Jane Ashelford, *The Art of Dress: Clothes and Society 1500–1914* (London: National Trust Enterprises Limited, 1996), 28.

10. Allen B. Hinds, ed., *Calendar State Papers Venetian* (London: Anthony Brothers, Limited, 1909), vol. 25, 270.

11. The time period 1530–1625 was chosen because one of the earliest images of a woman wearing a feather is dated at ca.1532 and with the dawn of the Caroline Age in 1625 there is a new fashion aesthetic that would drastically alter this study. Indeed, the reign of Charles I witnessed many changes not only in fashion, but in society at large, bringing too many complications to the limited scope of this paper.

12. Roy Strong, *The Tudor and Stuart Monarchy: Pageantry, Painting, Iconography* 3 vols. (London: Boydell Press, 1995), 3:72.

13. John Nichols, *The Progresses, Processions, and Magnificent Festivities of King James the First, His Royal Consort, Family and Court*, 4 vols. (London: John B. Nichols, 1828), 2: 47.

14. Nichols, *The Progresses and Public Processions of Queen Elizabeth*, 1:380.

15. Ibid., 2:75.

16. Lansdowne Roll 17, New Years Gift Roll for 1588, British Library, London.

17. Bishop Joseph Hall, *Virgidemiarvm* (London: Thomas Creede, 1597), 31.

18. Steven Gossen, *Pleasant Quippes For Upstart New Fangled Gentlewomen* (London: Richard Johnes, 1596), 7.

19. LC5/33 f.54, Wardrobe of the Robe Accounts, National Archives, London.

20. Karen Hearn, ed., *Dynasties: Painting in Tudor and Jacobean England 1530–1630* (London: Tate Publishing, 1995), 192.
21. Jane Ashelford, *Dress in the Age of Elizabeth I* (London: B. T. Batsford Ltd., 1988), 51.
22. Ibid., 50–51 and Ashelford, *The Art of Dress*, 48.
23. Philip Stubbes, *The Anatomy of Abuses* (London: Richard Jones, 1583), 22v.
24. Albert Feuillerat, "Documents Relating to the Office of the Revels in the Time of Queen Elizabeth," in *Materialien Zur Kunde Des Alteren Englischen Dramas* (London: David Nutt, 1908), 84.
25. Ibid., 84.
26. Ashelford, *Dress in the Age of Elizabeth I*, 51 compares the price of feathers to a laborer's pay and T. S. Wilian, *Studies in Elizabethan Foreign Trade* (Manchester: University of Manchester Press, 1959), 111, 113, 266, lists a few locations from where feathers were imported.
27. R. P. 294/I, New Years Gift Roll for 1600, British, Library, London.
28. The original passage from Egerton 2806, f.19v, British Library, London as quoted in Arnold, *Queen Elizabeth's Wardrobe Unlock'd*, 230.
29. Sydney Anglo, *Spectacle, Pageantry and Early Tudor Policy* (Oxford: Clarendon Press, 1969), 104; Jasper Ridley, *The Tudor Age* (London: Constable & Company, Ltd., 1988), 183–84.
30. Ashelford, *The Art of Dress*, 31.
31. "An exhortation Concerning Good Order and Obedience to Rulers and Magistrates," in *Sermons or Homilies, Appointed to be Read in Churches in the Time of Queen Elizabeth of Famous Memory* (1817), 95–96.
32. "Enforcing Statues of Apparel," in Paul L. Hughes and James F. Larkin, eds., *Tudor Royal Proclamations*, 3 vols. (London: Yale University Press, 1969), 2: 278–279.
33. Both Ashelford, *Dress in the Age of Elizabeth I*, 108 and Ridley, *The Tudor Age*, 165 stress how clothes demarcated social and occupational status.
34. G. W. Digby, *Elizabethan Embroidery* (London: Faber and Faber, 1963), 45; and Ashelford, *Dress in the Age of Elizabeth I*, 90 are just two of the many sources that emphasize the pervasive love of allegory in all aspects of Tudor and Jacobean life from embroidery to civic pageants.
35. Ashelford, *Dress in the Age of Elizabeth I*, 90.
36. Claude Paradin's *Devises Heroiqves* was first published in France in 1557 although not translated into English until 1591, and Cesare Ripa's *Iconologia* which was first published in Rome in 1593.
37. Rosemary Freeman, *English Emblem Books* (London: Chatto & Windus, 1948), 47 and Alison Saunders, "Introduction" in Claude Paradin's *Devises Heroiqves* (Aldershot, Hants: Scholar's Press, 1989), 10. Ripa's *Iconologia* had a later impact after Ben Jonson used it as a source when writing court masques, see Freeman, *English Emblem Books*, 95. However, the connection of emblems and masques will be discussed in another section.
38. MS 537, New Years Gift Roll for 1578, Society of Antiquaries, London; Digby, *Elizabethan Embroidery*, 46 goes on to explain that the rainbow signified peace.

39. John Nichols also describes these jewels and transcribes "virture" for virtue, see Nichols, *The Progresses and Public Processions of Queen Elizabeth*, 2:79. Nichol's description is a little different, and I am uncertain what document exactly he was examining. He states that another copy of this New Years Gift Roll said Virgo instead of virtue. Currently, I am aware of only one extant New Years Gift Roll for 1578 at the Society of Antiquaries in London, which is the one I examined and the one from which I quoted. It should be noted I could not clearly discern if the word is spelled virture or virtuce in MS 537, Society of Antiquaries, London.

40. Digby, *Elizabethan Embroidery*, 22, 46.

41. This is my translation of Ripa 36: "Il pauone significa l'arroganza essere una spetie di superbia."

42. Gossen, *Pleasant Quippes For Upstart New Fangled Gentlewomen*, 6.

43. Paradin, *Devises Heroiqves*, 172; the original French was "se purge de ses meschantes plumes: Ainsi deuons nous faire des vices."

44. Stubbes, *The Anatomy of Abuses*, 22r–22v.

45. Ripa's emblem of America also had the mandatory feather head gear, see Ripa, *Iconologia*, 353–354.

46. Hugh Honour, *The Golden Land: European Images of America from the Discoveries to the Present Time* (London: Allen Lane, 1975), 34.

47. Ibid., 30, 34.

48. Ibid., 13–14.

49. Nichols, *The Progresses and Public Processions of Queen Elizabeth*, 4: 619, 620.

50. Honour, *The Golden Land*, 8.

51. Amerigo Vespucci, *The First Four Voyages of Amerigo Vespucci. Reprinted in Facsimile and Translated from the Rare Original Edition (Florence 1505–6)*, (London, 1893), 10.

52. Honour, *The Golden Land*, 21, 58. For example, according to *The Pleasant Historie of the Conquest of the Weast India now called new Spayne, Atchieued by the worthy Prince Hernando Cortes, Marques of the Valley of Huaxacac, most delectable to Reade: Translated out of the Spanishe tongue by T.N.* (London, 1578), 402 lamented that it was only "through greate punishmente that haue left off the horrible sinne of sodomy, although it was a great griefe to put away their number of wiues."

53. Honour, *The Golden Land*, 67, 72.

54. Ellen Chirelstein, "Lady Elizabeth Pope: The Heraldic Body," in Lucy Gent and Nigel Llewellyn, eds., *Renaissance Bodies: The Human Figure in English Culture c. 1540–1660* (London: Reaktion Books, Ltd, 1990), 41 where she makes the links between feathers and America; 43, where she discusses Elizabeth Pope's personal connection to the Virginia colony.

55. Chirelstein, "Lady Elizabeth Pope," 43–44.

56. John Smith, "The General History of Virginia, New England and the Summer Isles," in E. A. Benians, ed., *The True Travels, Adventures and Observations of Captain John Smith in Europe, Asia, and Africa and America, and the General History of Virginia, New England and the Summer Isles*, 3 vols. (Cambridge: Cambridge University Press, 1908),1:86.

57. Smith, "The General History of Virginia, New England and the Summer Isles," 1:87.
58. Chirelstein, "Lady Elizabeth Pope," 40.
59. Jane Ashelford, "Female Masque Dress in Late Sixteenth-Century England," *Costume* (1978): 41.
60. For other examples of portraits depicting their sitters in masque dress see Ashelford, *Dress in the Age of Elizabeth I*, 122–35; Hearn, *Dynasties* 176, 190.
61. Stephen Orgel and Roy Strong, *Inigo Jones: The Theatre of the Stuart Court*, 2 vols. (Sotheby Parke Bernet: University of California Press, 1973), 1:11.
62. For Jonson using Ripa, see Freeman, *English Emblem Books*, 95; Jones and costume books see E. E. Veevers, "Sources of Inigo Jones's Masquing Designs," *Journal of the Warburg and Courtauld Institutes* 22 (1959): 373–74.
63. Francis Bacon, "Of Masques and Triumphs," in John Pitchner, ed., *The Essays* (Suffolk: Penguin Books, 1985), 176.
64. Ashelford, "Female Masque Dress in Late Sixteenth-Century England," 41–42.
65. Thomas Dekker, "The Guls Horne Book," in Alexander B. Grosart, ed., *The Non-Dramatic Works of Thomas Dekker*, 5 vols. (London: Hazell, Watson & Viney, Ltd., 1885), 2:221; originally it was published in 1609.
66. *State Papers, Domestic* 14/12/6 used on microfilm at Rutgers, The State University of New Jersey's Alexander Library, New Brunswick, New Jersey.
67. George Chapman, "Memorable Masque" in Stephen Orgel and Roy Strong's *Inigo Jones: The Theatre of the Stuart Court*, 2 vols. (Sotheby Parke Bernet: University of California Press, 1973), 1:256.
68. Ben Jonson, "News from the New World Discovered on the Moon" in Stephen Orgel and Roy Strong's *Inigo Jones: The Theatre of the Stuart Court*, 2 vols. (Sotheby Parke Bernet: University of California Press, 1973), 1:31.
69. Orgel and Strong, *Inigo Jones*, 1:312.
70. Smith, "The General History of Virginia, New England and the Summer Isles," 1:87. In other accounts, such as the one written by a relation of the explorer John Verarzanus in 1524, when dress is described, there is little or no sexual division noted, as in this passage describing one group of Native American women in Richard Hakluyt, *Divers Voyages Touching the Discouerie of America, and the Ilands Adiacent Vnto the Same* (London: 1582) not paginated: "they are all naked saue their priuie partes whiche they couer with a Deares skinne braunched or embodered as the men use: . . . and when they are married they weare divers toyes, according to the vsage of the people of the Cast as well men as women."
71. *Hic Mulier*, not paginated. One scholar in particular, Susan Vincent in her book, *Dressing the Elite: Clothes in Early Modern England* (New York: Berg, 2003) takes on the past scholarship on early modern English cross-dressing. Vincent argues that "Scholars have been mis-led, then, in imagining a subculture of cross-dressed men, and particularly women, who appropriated the apparel of the other gender in order to make some kind of social or political point. It was fashionable rather than cross-gendered, apparel that was being vilified" (172). While I agree with Vincent that scholars should not inflate the

extent and nature of cross-dressing in this period, I do not believe that the anonymous author of *Hic Mulier* and Phillip Stubbes were only railing against innovation and novelty in dress. As will be discussed later in this essay, the writings that decried cross-dressing were very concerned with the fact that when men and women exchanged garments, they also inverted the behavior that was socially acceptable for each sex. This emphasis on dress and behavior, I believe, complicates Vincent's stance on cross-dressing in this period.

72. Stubbes, *The Anatomy of Abuses*, 37v, 38 r.
73. Anne Hollander, *Sex and Suits: The Evolution of Modern Dress* (New York: Kodansha International, 1995), 40, the italics is Hollander's.
74. Honour, *The Golden Land*, 58.
75. "A Homily Against Apparel," in *Sermons or Homilies, Appointed to be Read in Churches in the Time of Queen Elizabeth of Famous Memory* (1817), 287.
76. J. L. Vives, *A Very Frutefull and Pleasant Boke Called the Instruction of a Christian Woman*, (1528) trans. Richard Hyrd in *Distaves and Dames: Renaissance Treatises for and About Women*, ed. Diane Bornstein (Delmar, New York: Scholars' Facsimiles and Reprints, 1978), not paginated.
77. Laura Gowing, *Common Bodies: Women, Touch and Power in Seventeenth-Century England* (New Haven: Yale University Press, 2003), 177–78; Margaret R. Sommerville, *Sex and Subjection: Attitudes to Women in Early-Modern Society* (London: Arnold, 1995), 147.
78. Vives *A Very Frutefull and Pleasant Boke Called the Instruction of a Christian Woman*,, not paginated.
79. Joseph Swetnam, *The Arraignment of Lewd, Idle, Froward, and Vnconstant Women: Or The Vanitie of Them, Choose You Whether* (London: George Purstowe and Thomas Archer, 1615), 55.
80. Ian Maclean, *The Renaissance Notion of Woman: A Study in the Fortunes of Scholasticism and Medical Science in European Intellectual Life* (Cambridge: Cambridge University Press, 1980), 42; Sommerville, *Sex and Subjection*, 17; Thomas Laqueur, *Making Sex: Body and Gender from the Greeks to Freud* (Cambridge, MA: Harvard University Press, 1990), 4, 108.
81. Stubbes, *The Anatomy of Abuses*, 39v.
82. Ibid.
83. Vives, *A Very Frutefull and Pleasant Boke Called the Instruction of a Christian Woman*, not paginated.
84. Thomas Dekker, "The Seuen Deadly Sinnes of London," in Alexander B. Grosart, ed., *The Non-Dramatic Works of Thomas Dekker*, 5 vols. (London: Hazell, Watson, & Viney, Ltd., 1885), 2:59. Originally this work was published in 1606.
85. Vives, *A Very Frutefull and Pleasant Boke Called the Instruction of a Christian Woman*, not paginated.
86. Stubbes, *The Anatomy of Abuses*, 13v.
87. "A Homily Against Apparel," 287.
88. *Hic Mulier*, not paginated. The words in the brackets are mine.
89. William Prynne, *The Unlouelinesse of Love-lockes* (London: 1628), 53.

90. Thomas Nashe, "Christ's Teares Over Jerusalem," in Ronald B. McKerrow, ed., *The Works of Thomas Nashe*, 5 vols. (Oxford: Basil Blackwell, 1966; originally published in 1593), 2:143.

91. Ibid., 2:143.

92. *Hic Mulier*, not paginated.

93. Ibid.

94. Vives, *A Very Frutefull and Pleasant Boke Called the Instruction of a Christian Woman*.

95. Ibid.

96. D. M. Palliser, *The Age of Elizabeth: England under the Later Tudors 1547–1603*, (London: Longan Group UK Limited, 1992), 75; Gowing complicates the family as microcosm scenario by arguing that there were other forces that divided the household, not only was their a wife-husband dichotomy, but women mistresses often claimed power over their female servants, or village women assumed power over poor beggar women's bodies, see Gowing, *Common Bodies*, 7–10.

97. *Haec-Vir*, not paginated.

98. Lawrence Stone, *The Crisis of the English Aristocracy, 1558–1641* (New York: Oxford University Press, 1967), 27.

99. Ashelford, Dress in the Age of Elizabeth I, 109–10; Lisa Hopkins, *Queen Elizabeth I and Her Court* (London: Vision Press, 1990), 45.

100. Stubbes, *The Anatomy of Abuses*, 24v.

101. Ibid.

102. Dekker "The Guls Horne Book," 2:227.

103. Ibid., 2:229.

104. Ibid., 2:227.

105. Gowing, *Common Bodies*, 32.

Chapter 10

S(m)oothing the Savage('s) B(r)east: Covering and Colonialism in the Age of Euro-American Expansion

Adam Knobler

In 1498, on his third voyage across the Atlantic, Christopher Columbus was moved to describe the new land mass he had just come upon as "una teta de muger": the nipple of a woman.[1] Having earlier likened the entire globe to a woman's breast, his reference to South America as its nipple, something of its crowning glory, might not be so terribly surprising.[2] Coming from a society in late fifteenth-century Latin Europe where the breast was highly eroticized, and often described as the "crown jewel of femininity," Columbus' words were apt.

The relationship between Western male fascination with the female breast, and the imperial enterprise was not merely limited to metaphor. For just as European expansion was a venue for the exchange, interaction, encounter and transfer of peoples, pathogens, and politics, so too was it a point of encounter between different constructions of beauty, the body and the erotic. What one society came to view as sexualized and seductive, another might well have viewed as unerogenous and commonplace. This connection has not been lost on scholars, and works such as Anne McClintock's *Imperial Leather: Race, Gender, and Sexuality in the Colonial Contest* have explicitly attempted to address the larger questions of the colony *qua* body and body *qua* colony.[3]

There can be little doubt, however, that the portrayals of non-European women found in the chronicles, paintings, prints and diaries of Europeans found an absolute fascination with female nudity: its abundance, its sensuality and its eroticism, and much of this occidental fantasy came to center around the portrayal of the female breast as somehow emblematic of the nature of the women they encountered.

The European fascination with women's bodies, and the breast in particular, colored Western portrayal of non-Western societies. The mission to Europeanize or "civilize" the savage's breasts thus became an important component in the broader imperial enterprise. The feminine and the exotic merged.[4] Indeed, I would argue that the discourse regarding the covering and uncovering of the female torso has been central to the Western gaze of the "tropical" other from the early sixteenth century. We can identify three distinct phases of interest: an initial phase which relates the bodies of non-Western women to their "natural" or "unadorned" state, often in positive contrast to the adorned women of the West; a second phase where the castigations of clergy and moralists condemn all female nudity as sinful and quite non-conducive to proper, Christian behavior; and finally, the use of the nude or partially nude form as an inducement to attract Western men to come to the non-Western world for sensual pleasure, as a means of economic empowerment for the emerging nation or state. In examining these three phases of development, I shall draw my examples from Brazil and Polynesia, from the early modern period to the present day. These points of contact, while in different parts of the world, display quite similar patters of body-geography discourse in the context of Western expansion and imperialism.

How have Europeans conceived of the eroticized body? The Western fascination with nudity cannot be properly examined without reference to clothing. As Anne Hollander has noted, in our clothed society, what we see on a daily basis—what conditions us—is the "body-and-clothes unit": the body as clothed, draped, wrapped, and adorned.[5] While some societies, where clothing is neither obligatory or, indeed, even a commonplace, might not associate the naked body with what it lacks in terms of covering, Westerners do. The naked body—its portrayal—is eroticized through what is known to be missing: clothing. As a consequence, Western notions of what is beautiful or erotic about the naked body—shape, size, proportion—is often conditioned by how that body is shaped when clothed, rather than when it is nude.

This notion was clearly true in Columbus' time. By the mid-fifteenth century, in France and Spain, the breast had become publicly eroticized and featured as erotic in fashion through its draping or concealment. Women's breasts had come to be supported by corsets which molded, confined, flattened, or emphasized their form. The natural shape of the breast, which varies of course from woman to woman, was not in and of itself a matter of much concern. Rather, its constructed shape, created by clothing, came to be the standard by which feminine beauty was judged. The beautiful woman was, by Columbus' time, one whose natural small, white, round, hard firm breasts, wide apart, looked as if they had been corsetted.[6] The attempts to conform to this ideal were, not surprisingly, legion, and just as today's Wonderbra grants instant and deep cleavage—a phenomenon generally not possible without some form of binding—so too did corsets, plunging necklines, infusions and pomades promise to give women of the elite classes of the early sixteenth century the fashionable breasts they (or their male admirers) so desired and which were described in the so-called "blasons anatomiques" (male gaze poetry collections devoted to the female body) in extraordinary detail.[7] Clement Marot's classic *Le blason du beau tetin* (1535) emblematically proceeds:

Tetin refaict, plus blanc qu'un oeuf,
Tetin de satin blanc tout neuf,
Tetin qui fait honte à la rose,
Tetin plus beau que nulle chose;
Tetin dur, non pas Tetin, voyre,
Mais petite boule d'Ivoire,
Au milieu duquel est assise
Une fraize ou une cerise,
Que nul ne voit, ne touche aussi,
Mais je gaige qu'il est ainsi.
Tetin donc au petit bout rouge
Tetin quijamais ne se bouge,
Soit pour venir, soit pour aller,
Soit pour courir, soit pour baller.
Tetin gauche, tetin mignon,
Tousjours loing de son compaignon,
Tetin qui porte temoignaige
Du demourant du personnage.
Quand on te voit il vient à mainctz
Une envie dedans les mains
De te taster, de te tenir;
Mais il se faut bien contenir
D'en approcher, bon gré ma vie,
Car il viendroit une aultre envie.
O tetin ni grand ni petit,
Tetin meur, tetin d'appetit,
Tetin qui nuict et jour criez
Mariez moy tost, mariez !
Tetin qui t'enfles, et repoulses
Ton gorgerin[8] de deux bons poulses,
A bon droict heureux on dira

Celluy qui de laict t'emplira,
Faisant d'un tetin de pucelle
Tetin de femme entiere et belle.[9]

[Breast remade, whiter than an egg
Breast of white satin, all new
Breast that shames the rose
Breast more beautiful than anything else
Firm breast that is not a breast, verily,
But a little bowl of ivory
In the midst of which sits
A strawberry or a cherry,
That no one either sees or touches
But I would bargain that it is indeed so
Breast, thus, with a little red tip
Breast that never moves
Neither to go or to come
Or to run or to dance
Left breast, little breast
Always far from its companion
Breast that reveals
The rest of the person
Upon seeing you many feelings
A desire in their hands
To touch you; to hold you
But it is necessary to restrain oneself
From approaching them, good grief
Because there would come another desire
Oh, breast, neither big nor little
Mature breast, breast of appetite
Breast that cries night and day
Marry me soon, marry!
Breast that swells and pushes through
Your *gorgerin* two inches away
For good reason, happy, one will say
Is he who fills you with milk
Making from the breast of a girl
The beautiful, complete breast of a woman.]

The poem makes evident the specific appeal of the ideal breast in sixteenth century France: the word "petite" is repeated emphasizing small size, whereas the phrase "Tousjours loing de son compaignon" implies that the ideal breasts are far apart and flat. Likewise, breast-feeding, encouraged by doctor's and clerics alike, fell out of fashion among elites, where small, upper-class breasts meant for male delight were prized over the full, lactating, working-class breasts whose size emphasized utility.[10] The pendulous breast came to be associated with age, poverty and, ultimately, evil, as the portrayal of witches clearly demonstrated.[11]

This breast cult of the sixteenth century had, of course, its critics, though they blamed the movement of breasts upward and neckline downward on the natural lasciviousness of women. The clergyman Olivier Maillard assured revealing women that they would be strung up, as he put it, by their udders in Hell.[12] Others stated that those who made meager attempts to cover their flesh were like lepers who went about with small noisemakers to alert passers-by of their dangerous presence.[13]

The initial European and Euro-American reactions to the bodies of Tupinamba and Guarani women of early sixteenth-century Brazil and the women of the Hawai'ian Islands of the eighteenth-century were clearly conditioned upon such preconceived notions of the meaning of the naked breast in the Western context. Here lay something of a paradox: the women of Brazil, because of their nudity, were described most frequently in the most sexualized of terms. Amerigo Vespucci, for example, wrote of them as living lives of sexual liberty and sexual willingness. Yet, in contrast to the European standard where only prostitutes and women of the lower orders— women whose beauty did not conform to court standards—exhibited such lack of sexual inhibition, Vespucci notes that "although libidinous" the women of Brazil are "pretty and well shaped." "We were amazed," he wrote, "that among those we saw we noticed none with fallen breasts. Those who had given birth . . . were no different from virgins and resembled them in other parts of their bodies."[14] In essence, these were women whose beauty clearly conformed to the Western male standard of the time. Likewise, William Ellis, who served as a surgeon and naturalist on Captain Cook's voyages to Hawai'i (1776–80), noted that he "saw some . . . females who might really be called fine women . . . [but, he added] there are no people in the world who indulge themselves more in their sensual appetites than these: in fact they carry it to a most scandalous and shameful degree, and in a manner not proper to be mentioned."[15] These women thus combined both the desirability of any woman of the European elite with the sexual abandon of the European prostitute. In both the Polynesian and Brazilian cases we are presented with what Bernard Smith has termed as a "soft primitivism."[16] This unthreatening "softness" initially allowed both Brazilian and Hawai'ian native peoples to be judged as physically and, in some cases, morally and intellectually superior to most other non-European peoples.

The nude women of first encounter are thus, in their natural state, no less beautiful than the corsetted figures of European women, yet they are not, in and of themselves, especially seductive. Their sexuality is somehow savage and not especially appealing. According to the French traveler Jean de

Léry, it was the addition of frills, ruffs, paint, wigs and trifles which transform the European woman into an object of true eroticization.[17] As Torgovnick has said, primitivism is constructed in accordance with the needs of the society which describes, not to the needs of the society under description.[18] To carry this argument one stage further, if the bare-breasted woman becomes emblematic of places such as Brazil and Hawai'i, the very point of conquest is the physical body of the women as well as the physical geography of the locale.

With the entrance into Brazil and Hawai'i of missionaries, the commentaries and gaze of Western observers move away from the admiration of the nude female form to warnings regarding the dangers inherent in nudity. As beautiful as these women were perceived to be in their unclad state, they had to be clothed: to be circumscribed, bound, and controlled in body as in spirit, as the mark of civilization and conversion. Most Tupi and Hawai'ian women resisted initial attempts to adopt European clothing styles, which they viewed as suitable for ornament but not for regular use, and attempts to forcibly clothe them were met with hostility.[19] There were abundant reports of women, corsetted in their finest Western fashions, who would march into church, only to disrobe upon the end of the service when out of sight of missionaries' eyes.[20] However, those Brazilian and Hawai'ian women brought into association with European society through their contact, marriage, or sexual encounter with European men, often adopted European styles which were intended both to hide and simulate the shape, size and proportions of the breasts earlier explorers claimed they possessed naturally. In Hawai'i, the reach of the missionaries became quite significant, particularly in the banning of the *hula*. The most important story-dance of Hawai'ian culture, the *hula*, performed by both male and female dancers, in its precolonial form, was often undertaken without any torso coverings. By the mid-1820s, the dance had nearly disappeared entirely from public performance due to the work of missionaries such as Hiram Bingham.[21]

But the desire to cover indigenous women, so promoted by moralists and missionaries, contrasted sharply with the continuing images of male fantasy of the disrobed exotic female propagated by such immigrants to the region as the French painter Paul Gaugin (who moved to French Polynesia toward the end of his life and often used indigenous women in various states of nudity as subjects for his work) and, increasingly, as there was to be money made from a tourist trade.[22]

Between postcards, photographs, and stereopticon, the early twentieth century brought an image of a clearly eroticized and beckoning Hawai'i.[23] The image of the "*hula* girl," often portrayed as bare-breasted (although bare-breasted dancing had been banned by missionary-influenced governments), induced potential male tourists to see the Hawai'i of the early twentieth century as a place of free love.[24] Brazil's first beach resort at

Copacabana in Rio de Janeiro, began to draw celebrity tourists from North America and Europe with the construction of the Copacabana Palace Hotel in 1923.[25]

Today, both Hawai'i and Brazil lure tourists with fantasy images of scantily clad women: again, paradise is portrayed as supple and passive female. *Sports Illustrated* magazine's swimsuit issue, published annually since 1964, has featured its models posing at beach locations including Hawai'i (in 1970 and 1977) and in Brazil (1978).[26] Current tourism brochures and books emphasize beach culture, and some specifically focus on the sexual potential of tourism.[27] Brazilian authorities attempted to ban topless bathing in January 2000, but retracted when hundreds of topless women appeared in protest. The news, which was disseminated globally, only added to the preexisting global belief in Brazil as the home of thong and "dental floss" beach attire.[28] Nude bathing is banned in Hawai'i, but today Hawaii lures tourists with watered-down versions of the traditional hula performed by young women whose proportions correspond to contemporary Western male ideas of svelte beauty, rather than the larger women who correspond to traditional Polynesian beauty image. The women wear contemporary Western, two-piece swimwear fashion.[29] For example, a 2006 calendar entitled "Hula Honeys" invites the purchaser to "Welcome the topical mystique, exotic allure, and enduring myth of the Polynesian hula girl into your home or office with this vibrant wall calendar."[30]

The colonial and postcolonial discourses about the breasts of indigenous women in Brazil and Hawai'i has never focused on the breasts' lactating function, but rather, as an emblematic sign of feminity in its purest state. For Europeans, for whom the "public beast" is always covered, the uncovered breasts of Hawai'ian and Brazilian women have always marked a distinct contrast: something alien, other, and exotic. Much of the eroticism attached to the breast came with the covering and uncovering of the torso. The revelation of what European women possessed but dared not show. Within the Western context, a body which never knew drapery, clothing, or covering was totally outside the realm of European comprehension. Even those women who lived on the eroticized margins of society, such as prostitutes, did so through the act of disrobing—consciously rejecting the clothing conventions.

But in Brazil and Hawai'i there were women for whom Western clothing conventions initially held no meaning, To European observers, this was incomprehensible, and could only be understood as a moral weakness or as some sign of libidinousness. To make the conquest complete, the non-European body had to be brought into the context of clothing; the Hawai'ian body, the Tupi breast, had to be covered, or at least, thought of as if it were covered. Thus covered, it could be controlled, even to the point of future undressing for Western male touristic and voyeuristic gaze. The "soft primitivism" of the sixteenth, seventeenth, or eighteenth centuries was thus revitalized as part of the continuing appeal of the women of Brazil and Hawai'i, as something both beckoning and "other." At such a point, therefore, could the breast be understood and seen as truly civilized and thus become acceptably erotic and a suitable subject for uncovering: soothing the savage beast by smoothing the savage's breasts.

Notes

1. Christopher Columbus, *Textos y documentos completos: relaciones de viajes, cartas y memorials*, ed. Consuelo Varela (Madrid:Alianza, 1982).

2. Ibid.

3. Anne McClintock, *Imperial Leather: Race, Gender, and Sexuality in the Colonial Contest* (New York: Routledge, 1995); See too, Catherine Keller, "The Breast, the Apocalypse, and the Colonial Journey," *Journal of Feminist Studies in Religion* 10.1 (1994); Ann Laura Stoler, *Carnal Knowledge and Imperial Power: Race and the Intimate in Colonial Rule* (Berkeley: University of California Press, 2002); Lenore Manderson and Margaret Jolly, eds., *Sites of Desires, Economies of Pleasure: Sexualities in Asia and the Pacific* (Chicago: University of Chicago Press, 1997).

4. See Marianna Torgovnick, *Gone Primitive: Savage Intellects, Modern Lives* (Chicago: University of Chicago Press, 1990), 156.

5. Anne Hollander, *Seeing Through Clothes* (New York: Viking Press, 1978), 83ff.

6. Ironically, one of the most classic portrayals of this beauty were the paintings by Sando Botticelli and Piero di Cosimo of Simonetta Vespucci, the cousin of Columbus' contemporary, the explorer Amerigo Vespucci. See Nicoletta Pons, *Botticelli: Catalogo Completo* (Milan: Rizzoli, 1989); Anna Forlani Tempesti and Elena Capretti, *Piero di Cosimo: Catalogo Completo* (Florence: Octavo, 1996).

7. Pascal Laîné and Pascal Quignard, *Blasons anatomiques du corps féminin* (Paris: Gallimard, 1982).

8. "Gorgerin" or "Gorgerette" was part of a woman's collar, covering her throat and the area just above the breasts. See Paul Robert, *Dictionnaire alphabétique et analogique de la langue française*, 4 vols. (Paris: Presses Universitaires de France, 1951–64), 4/1: 325.

9. http://fr.wikisource.org/wiki/Blason_du_Beau_T%C3%A9tin, accessed December 18, 2005. I wish to thank Alexandra Cuffel and Diane Brown, both of Macalester College, and Sahar Amer of University of North Carolina for help with the translation.

10. See the contrast between mistress and servant in the portrait of Gabrielle d'Estrées, mistress of Henri IV, held at the Musée Condée, Chateau de Chantilly, France. See Michel de Decker, *Gabrielle d'Estrées* (Paris: Pygmalion, 2003).

11. On this, see Bernadette Bucher, *Icon and Conquest: A Structural Analysis of Illustrations of de Bry's Great Voyages* (Chicago: University of Chicago Press, 1981), which was first published in France under the title *La sauvage aux seins pendants* (Paris: Hermann, 1977).

12. Olivier Maillard, *Oeuvres françaises: sermons et poesies*, ed. Arthur de La Borderie (Nantes, 1877; reprinted Geneva: Slatkine Reprints, 1968); Dominique Gros, *Le sein dévoilé* (Paris: L. Pernoud, 1987), 27.

13. Michel Menot, *Sermons choisis de Michel Menot (1508–1518)*, ed. Joseph Nève (Paris: E. Champion, 1924).

14. Amerigo Vespucci to Lorenzo de Medici (1503) in *La terra del Brasile*, ed. Gabriella Airaldi (Verona: Cassa di risparmio di Verona, Vicenza, Belluno e Ancona, 1991), 107. "le donne, como te ho dicto, benchè nude vagano et libidinose sianno, . . . una cosa miraculosa a nui è parso, che infra de quelle niuna se vedeva che havesse le tette cadute; et quelle che haveano parturito per la forma del ventre et contracture niente erano differentiate da le vergene."

15. William Ellis, *Polynesian researches: Hawaii* (London: Peter Jackson, Late Fisher, Son & Co, 1842; new ed. Rutland, VT: C.E. Tuttle Co., 1969).

16. Bernard Smith, *European vision and the South Pacific*, 2nd ed. (New Haven: Yale University Press, 1985).

17. Jean de Léry, *History of a Voyage to the Land of Brazil, otherwise Called America*, trans. Janet Whatley (Berkeley: University of California Press, 1990), 67; *Histoire d'un voyage fait en la terre du Brésil*, ed. Jean Claude Morisot (Geneva: A. Chuppin 1580; reprinted Geneva: Droz, 1975).

18. Torgovnick, *Gone Primitive*, ch. 1, 4, 5.

19. Patricia Grimshaw, "New England Missionary Wives, Hawaiian Women and 'The Cult of True Womanhood,' " *Hawaiian Journal of History* 19 (1985): 81.

20. Jean de Léry, *History*, 66.

21. Otto von Kotzebue, *Puteshestvie vokrug svieta* [A New Voyage Round the World in the Years 1823–1826] (London: H. Colburn & R. Bentley, 1830; reprinted Amsterdam: N. Israel, 1967), 2: 254–57.

22. See the classic work of Bengt Danielsson, *Gauguins Söndershavsår* [Gaugin in the South Seas] (Garden City: Doubleday, 1966); also George Shackleford and Claire Frèches-Thory, eds., *Gauguin Tahiti: The Studio of the South Seas* (London: Thames & Hudson, 2004).

23. See Lynn Davis, *Na Pa'i Ki'i: The Photographers in the Hawaiian Islands, 1845–1900* (Honolulu: Bishop Museum Press, 1980).

24. Elizabeth Bentzel Buck, *Paradise Remade: The Politics of Culture and History in Hawai'i* (Philadelphia: Temple University Press, 1993), 2.

25. David Cleary, Dilwyn Jenkins, Oliver Maxwell, and Jim Hine, *Brazil: The Rough Guide* (London: Rough Guides, 1994), 81.

26. http://sportsillustrated.cnn.com/swimsuit/collection/covers accessed March 23, 2006.

27. See Cristiano Nogueira, *Rio for Partiers* (Rio de Janeiro: Solcat Editura, 2003); *Salvador for Partiers* (Rio de Janeiro: Solcat, 2003); and the first half of Jane Desmond's *Staging Tourism: Bodies on Display from Waikiki to Sea World* (Chicago: University of Chicago Press, 1999).

28. Rodolfo Espinoza, "The Summer of the Topless," *Brazil Magazine* (January 1, 2002), viewed at http://www.brazzil.com/content/view/6860/73 on March 23, 2006.
29. See Desmond, *Bodies* and Buck, *Paradise Remade*.
30. Jim Heiman, *Hula Honeys 2006 Wall Calendar* (San Francisco: Chronicle Books, 2005); Heiman has also published a series of coasters and of postcards on the same theme.

Chapter 11

European Family Law and the People of the Frontier

James Muldoon

Scholars who study the expansion of Europe can list a large number of effects that contact with Europeans has had on non-European societies over the past 500 years. When examining these effects, writers can point to economic, political, military, and, in recent years, biological effects that resulted from the impact. In the nineteenth century, Europeans and North Americans routinely described the long-term effects of European overseas expansion in positive terms, even if there were significant negative effects in the short run. The celebration of the quincentennial of Columbus's first voyage, on the other hand, generated a number of books and articles excoriating Europeans for going overseas in the fifteenth and sixteenth centuries because of the dire consequences that contact with Europeans had upon many of the newly encountered societies—consequences said to continue into the present day.[1]

The emphasis on the economic, political, military, and biological causes for the changes that occurred in the lands that Europeans encountered after 1492 has, however, overshadowed the implications of late-medieval family law on non-European societies. That is to say, while economic pressures, wars, and changes of government, not to mention diseases, had an enormous impact on the lives of those who came under European control or were affected by contact with Europeans, the impact of European family law on these newly encountered societies has been less noted. In reality, changes in family law have been one of the most important agents of long-term change in non-European societies as European civilization has expanded over the past thousand years.

At first glance, the notion that family law has played a significant role in reshaping non-European societies, a role comparable to that played by armies or disease, may be hard to accept. After all, the term "family law" seems benign or even bland and suggests all kinds of good things to the modern listener. The image of family law is therefore one of a liberal, progressive force to improve the lives of the oppressed in society. This is especially true if we limit our conception of family law to laws protecting children from abuse and providing financial support for women and children in families broken by divorce.

This benign and bland image that the concept of family law presents is misleading, as recent American experience demonstrates. In the United States the realm of family law, taken in its broadest sense, has become the arena within which a number of significant social and cultural battles have been waged. The very definition of family is at present undergoing transformation as the partners in same-sex relationships seek the legal status and economic benefits of spouses in traditional marriages. The question of whether homosexual marriages should be recognized as legitimate marriages with all of the implications that such recognition would entail has arisen with some force. Should the children of a divorce be placed in the custody of a gay parent? Should gay or lesbian couples be allowed to adopt children? Who should be the legal guardian of a dying person in the absence of a spouse, the individual's parents or the individual's lesbian lover? These and myriad other problems with significant consequences for society as a whole make family law a highly contested topic at the moment.

The changes, affected and demanded, in family law are not, however, limited to situations that arise from changing definitions of the family. The law as it affects traditional families is also undergoing challenges that will no doubt lead to significant changes. The relationship between parents and children is being challenged as children have sought to divorce themselves from their parents. In one particularly difficult case, a young girl who was switched at birth with another girl who subsequently died sought to remain with the father who raised her rather than be required to spend time with her biological parents. The divorce rate has also led to the legal question of the rights of grandparents in cases where the divorced parent who has custody of the child refused to allow the parents of the divorced spouse to visit the child. Do grandparents have a right to see their grandchildren after the parents have divorced?[2]

These and other questions, such as the abortion debate, that currently roil American society demonstrate that family law, far from being settled and benign, has enormous potential for causing societal turmoil. Changes in the laws affecting family life and structure reflect changes in the life of an entire society. Once incorporated into the legal system, these changes generate new situations that in turn generate new demands for reform. For example, the economic consequences of laws granting spousal economic benefits to same-sex partners or to unmarried partners of the opposite sex may generate opposition from employers who fear the impact of increased health-care and insurance costs in a time of economic belt-tightening. Furthermore, the actual costs may appear only after the laws have been changed and produce consequences that the legislators had not intended.

These legal issues are at the core of the current American debate about family values, making the courts the arena within which the cultural debate, the family values debate, is played out. The passions that these issues generate have a number of real and alleged consequences: attacks on abortion clinics, the murder of a doctor who performed abortions, gay-bashing on the one hand and dramatic public demonstrations by extremist supporters of the gay-rights movement designed to intimidate their opponents on the other. The vehemence with which changes in family values and laws are both supported and attacked is a painful reminder that changes in family law will appear subversive of the entire social order, even revolutionary, to some groups, while judged as justice-long-denied by others.

If family law can play such a disruptive role within a society whose members presumably share many of the same values, consider the impact of new rules of family law on members of a society that is forced to accept European rules as the result of military conquest, peaceful religious conversion, or social and economic forces beyond its control. The obvious case, of course, is the situation in the Americas where all of the European conquerors criticized the sexual practices of the indigenous population and required changes to be made.

If we accept the premise that family law has the potential for causing significant changes in those societies that came under European domination after 1492, then the next question to consider is the nature of the family law that Europeans sought to impose on these peoples. That is, European family law was itself the product of long historical experience and had been imposed on other peoples well before Europeans went overseas at the end of the fifteenth century. Like the motives that impelled them (the goals that they sought, the technology that they possessed) Columbus and his successors dealt with the peoples they encountered based on the 500 years of experience that Europeans had acquired in the first stage of European expansion.

When I employ the phrase "the expansion of Europe" I do not mean simply the expansion that followed Columbus's first voyage. In fact, medievalists, if no one else, are aware that the expansion of Europe falls into two phases, pre- and post-1492. The post-1492 period of European expansion overseas built upon the pre-1492 experience of expansion—what one scholar described as the internal colonization of Europe, in almost every way.[3]

Just as the motivations, the goals, the technology, and the other aspects of Columbus' career were rooted in medieval expansion, so too the perceptions that Europeans had about non-Europeans were rooted in medieval perceptions of Others.[4] The same principles of family law that European Christians had imposed upon the peoples whom they converted to Christianity (either peacefully as in the case of Britain and Ireland, for example, or as the result of conquest, as Charlemagne did with regard to the Saxons) were similar to the principles that they imposed on the peoples of the Americas and Asia in the sixteenth and seventeenth centuries.

Because family law is obviously a large topic, I will restrict this discussion to some particular aspects of the law of marriage, the matter of divorce, and the question of legitimacy of offspring. When one considers these issues, it becomes clear that while the heroic and dramatic elements of the expansion of Europe generally draw the most attention, the imposition of European, Christian family law upon non-European societies was clearly one of the most important forces in transforming those societies. After all, when monogamy replaces polygamy as the basis of marital relations, there are a number of consequences, not all of which are positive. In a society that becomes Christian and whose members agree to live by Christian principles, what happens to the women whose status as wife is now reduced to that of concubine? What is the effect on the children who are now deemed illegitimate because their mothers were not the lawful spouses of their fathers? What are the implications for a society that has traditionally accepted divorce once it becomes Christian and officially accepts the Church's ban on the practice? (This is especially relevant in a society where one's identity is linked to the survival of the family over time. If a couple has not produced a child, especially a son, and if the wife is seen as responsible for the failure to provide a heir, then following a religion that does not allow divorce could lead to the end of the family line, a form of social extinction.)

Christian family law then would thus appear to be a powerful agent of change, but it must also have appeared quite frightening to those for whom its imposition would lead to significant, barely understood, social changes. Furthermore, the social changes that conversion to Christianity would have required must have been a very difficult hurdle for missionaries to surmount. One might even raise the question of the degree to which any of the participants in the process of change had any clear understanding of the problems and issues involved. In the modern world, anthropologists and sociologists would be available to discuss these issues, but neither existed in the Middle Ages.

The reason for the importance of Christian family law in the process of European expansion is that unlike most other expanding and conquering societies, Christians not only sought conquest and economic or political domination, they also sought the spiritual and moral transformation of those whom they encountered as well. That transformation meant not simply worshipping the Christian God in some formal ritual; it also meant that the individuals who composed the society would undergo an inner transformation and live according to the rules of the Christian Church. The public law of the society would be brought into agreement with Christian law in order to encourage the process of transformation and to ensure that the converts remained constant in their faith and in the practice of the Christian life.

In this chapter, I will deal with three specific examples of the way in which Christian family law affected peoples on the frontiers of medieval Christian Europe and then suggest some implications of these experiences for subsequent European overseas expansion. The first is a papal decretal dealing with polygamy in Muslim society. The second is a series of criticisms of the marital practices of the presumably Christian Irish. The third concerns papal attempts to convert the Mongols.

Can a Muslim Convert Remain Polygamous?

Probably the most common criticism that European Christians made of non-Christians concerned their marriage practices, with two traditions in particular attracting attention. The first was polygamy; the second was marriage between individuals who were related within the canonically forbidden degrees. One might see these issues simply as reflecting prurient interest in the sexual practices of non-Christians, but that would underestimate the significance of the law of marriage and its implications in medieval Christian society. Marriage law was an important part of the canon law, and both of these issues generated a good deal of legal analysis and a number of judicial decisions. The tradition of commentary on the law encouraged popes to explain the reasoning that underlay their decisions with the result that commentators could then criticize the reasoning and identify its problem areas.

The issue of polygamy was important in Christian discussions of marriage law because of the number of Muslims who were either under direct Christian rule or who were the object of Christian missionary efforts, although these were not very extensive, as Professor Benjamin Kedar has pointed out.[5] Around 1200, in response to a letter from the Bishop of Tiberias in the Holy Land, Pope Innocent III (1198–1216) issued two decretals, *Quanto te* (X.4.19.7) and *Gaudemus* (X.4.19.8 and 4.17.15), that dealt with polygamy and became the basis for the legal discussion of the subject.[6] In the first of these decisions, *Quanto te* (1199), Innocent III observed in passing and without any explanation of his position that a marriage between two infidels "exsistat, non tamen est ratum," (was a valid marriage but not a sacramental marriage) while a marriage between two baptized Christians was both "verum quidem et ratum" (that is both valid and sacramental). That being the case, the pope could dissolve a marriage between infidels while he could not do so in the case of a marriage between Christians. At the same time, he insisted upon the validity of marriages between infidels.

What Innocent III did not explain in *Quanto te* was why the marriages of infidels were not *ratum* and why the pope had any right to judge the validity of such marriages anyway. Furthermore, Innocent appears to have taken for granted that marriage was always monogamous. To some extent he responded to these issues in another decretal, *Gaudemus*, responding to the Bishop's letter. At the same time, the pope raised some new problems as well. The bishop was concerned that the Church's rules on consanguinity and affinity were causing a great deal of difficulty in the efforts to convert Muslims. Muslims commonly married individuals related to them in the second or third degree of consanguinity, a situation forbidden to Christians without a dispensation. Were Muslim converts required to separate from spouses related to them within the forbidden degrees? Apparently some potential converts were hesitating for just this reason. Innocent responded that "the sacrament of marriage existed among Christians and non-believers" equally, an opinion he attributed to St. Paul. The only reason for dissolving a valid marriage involving converts was the case in which one partner became a Christian while the other did not and interfered with the other's practice of the Christian faith. This exception to the general rule about the indissolubility of valid marriages was the so-called Pauline Privilege rooted again in an opinion of St. Paul.[7] This privilege was allowed lest the convert's new faith be endangered by the opposition of the non-believing spouse. Nevertheless, the pope pointed out, this privilege should be employed only sparingly because the purpose of becoming a Christian was to become spiritually better—not to provide a justification for dissolving a marriage.

Innocent's decretal considered a series of other points about the marriages of infidels and the implications of these for potential converts. In the first place, he pointed out that the ban on marriages between those related in the second and third degrees existed only in canon law and thus could not have been known to or applicable to infidels before their baptism. Furthermore, Innocent added that the children of such marriages were to be recognized as legitimate for "reasons of public utility," a curious argument if the parents' marriage was actually valid in the first place.[8]

Returning once again to the letter from the Bishop of Tiberias, Innocent went on to raise two other points about the marriages of non-Christians, clearly Muslims in this case. They were polygamous and they allowed divorce. He then offered the interesting example of the Muslim convert who wished to retain all of his wives who were willing to remain with him. Could an exception be made here, on the grounds of public utility, so to speak? There was, after all, the biblical precedent of the Hebrew patriarchs who had more than one wife. That example might have provided a basis for tolerating polygamy for the first generation of converts, seeing it as part of an early stage of religious and social development, a part of the Old Law that the New Law of Christ had supplanted. But Innocent III, understandably enough, was not a student of comparative anthropology and argued that as Christ had described marriage as "two in one flesh," not "three or four," it was clear that polygamy could no longer be tolerated unless God Himself decreed it.[9]

Innocent III then made a similar argument about divorce. That is, he admitted that the Bible did allow a man to dismiss his wife for fornication, but he added that this did not authorize the man to take a new wife during the lifetime of the dismissed wife. In fact, should a Muslim become a Christian, he was obliged to return to the former wife unless she was unwilling to have him back. In the event that the unconverted spouse was not interested in returning he could request dissolution of the marriage on the grounds of the Pauline Privilege.

These Innocentian decretals generated several commentaries by various canonists anxious to clarify what the pope had said. The general theme of these commentaries was that Innocent III was claiming too much power for the pope in these matters. Particularly, the commentators were not always comfortable with his assertion that the pope could determine whether or not the marriages of non-Christians were valid. At the same time, because the situations that Innocent III described existed within Christian-controlled lands, it was possible to argue that Christian rulers had the right to impose some rules of social behavior on all of their subjects even if that meant that such people were forced to act according to canonical principles. One commentator used the example of restrictions on the practice usury by Jewish money-lenders living in Christian societies. Jewish law did not forbid usury but Christian law did, so Christians would be in the position of enforcing that law on their Jewish subjects.[10] By analogy, canonical rules on marriage could also to some extent be imposed on non-Christian subjects. Polygamy and divorce could, for example, be forbidden to Muslim subjects of Christian rulers. Before considering some of the implications of this discussion of polygamy and marriage within the forbidden degrees, I wish to consider the problems associated with Christian marriage law within Christian societies. In the bull *Laudabiliter* (1155), Pope Adrian IV authorized Henry II of England to invade Ireland "to root out the growths of vice from the field of the Lord."[11] While the particular vices to be eliminated were not identified in this bull, other sources give us some indication of the problems that Henry II's advisors suggested needed addressing in Ireland.

Almost a century earlier, Lanfranc, Archbishop of Canterbury, had written to Turlough O'Brien, whom he called "magnificent king of Ireland," pointing out areas in which the Irish did not live up to the practice of the faith that they embraced long ago. The first criticism that the archbishop pointed out in this letter concerned the marriage practices of the Irish.

> It is reported that in your kingdom a man will abandon his lawfully wedded wife at his own will, without any canonical process taking place and with a temerity deserving of punishment, takes to himself some other wife who may be of his own kin or of the kindred of the wife whom he has abandoned, or whom another has abandoned with similar wickedness, according to a law of marriage which is rather a law of fornication.[12]

In 1172, the year in which Henry II entered Ireland, a synod held at Cashal spelled out the reforms that had to be made in the Irish Church. At the head of the list came the following: "That all the faithful throughout Ireland shall eschew concubinage with their cousins and kinfolk, and shall contract and adhere to lawful marriages." The same synod also declared that a man must draw up a will granting one-third of his movables to his wife and another third to his children.[13] And again, in 1172, Pope Alexander III condemned the marriage practices of the Irish in even more belligerent terms than did Lanfranc. Among other things, the Irish were now said to marry their stepmothers and have been known to live with and then dismiss a woman in order to do the same with her daughter.[14]

When looked at from Rome, the marriage practices of the Muslims and especially the Irish would appear to be the product of ignorance or sinful desires. Polygamy, marrying women within the forbidden degrees, and divorcing wives when the husbands tired of them all deserve condemnation, which the popes issued. Was it possible, however, to see these practices in other terms? Was it possible that these forms of behavior were reasonable responses to particular social circumstances, and that the ending of these marriage practices could only come when the entire structure of the society was transformed? Was it possible for medieval observers to view the marriage practices of other societies in something like a comparative manner? In other words, could the twelfth and thirteenth centuries have seen the birth of comparative anthropology?[15]

Monogamy, Polygamy, and Social Reality

There are some hints that medieval observers of non-Christian or insufficiently Christian societies had some awareness of the role of social circumstances in the marriage practices of other societies. Usually it was those on the scene—missionaries or, as in Ireland, colonial officials—who articulated these views, but they were not the only ones. Even Innocent III, as he condemned polygamy, recognized that God allowed the Hebrew patriarchs to engage in this practice, and he was clearly uncomfortable about it. Was it possible, then, to tolerate polygamy on the grounds that it was likely to exist at a particular stage of social development and that as a society evolves to a more civilized level of existence (by European Christian standards) the practice will disappear?[16]

In the middle of the thirteenth century, the experience of Christian missionaries with yet another polygamous people, the Mongols of Central Asia, suggested that at least some Christians recognized that polygamy was not simply a sign of immorality but was, in fact, a rational response to certain social conditions. The missionaries who went out to the Mongol world in the middle of the thirteenth century, the Mongol Mission that Pope Innocent IV (1243–54) initiated, encountered yet another polygamous society. Both John of Plano Carpini (d. 1252) and William of Rubruck (thirteenth century) who wrote descriptions of the Mongols mentioned their marriage practices. Plano Carpini noted the existence of polygamy and of marriages within the forbidden degrees. He pointed out that a man could marry any woman, excepting only his natural mother, daughters, and sisters. As the Mongols did not recognize the nature of spiritual affinity, they could also marry their sisters-in-law. While these practices were forbidden to Christians, the missionary appears to have been somewhat less judgmental. In the first place, at least some of these marriages resulted from the death of a man. The women of his household then passed to the care of a male relative. For example, "a younger brother may marry his brother's wife after his death; or another younger relation is expected to take her."[17] The existence of polygamy among the Mongols also meant that there could be a Christian woman within the khan's household and as such was a possible channel for missionaries to reach the highest levels of Mongol society.[18]

Observing the Mongol marriage practices, William of Rubruck seems to have had some understanding of why the Mongols married as they did but was, at the same time, more judgmental about the situation than Plano Carpini. Not only were they polygamous, but a son also had the positive obligation to marry his father's widows. Rubruck realized that Mongol society was a network of families, clans, and tribes, and each of these was headed by a man. What would happen to the women of a man's household if he was killed in battle or succumbed to disease? Who would care for them? Under those circumstances, the polygamous extended family would seem to be a reasonable solution to the problem of caring for and protecting these women, especially because women in this situation were forbidden to marry otherwise. Eventually, after death, they would then be reunited with their original husband.[19] To convert these people to Christianity under these circumstances would be extraordinarily difficult without radically transforming the entire economy and social structure of the Mongol world, a daunting task. To some extent, the failure of the Mongol mission and the failure to convert the Muslims ought to take into account the inability of the Christian Church to accommodate itself to the marriage practices of these societies.

When we look at the situation in medieval Ireland, we find that there were some English figures who recognized that marriage practices had significant social and political consequences. In 1366, the English government issued the Statutes of Kilkenny designed to force the Irish to become anglicized by refusing the protection of the Common Law to those who did not live in English fashion. The Statutes were particularly aimed at those Englishmen who had, as it were, gone native, becoming as one observer reported "more Irish than the Irish."

> But now many English of the said land, forsaking the English language, fashion, mode of riding, laws, and usages, live and govern themselves according to the manners, fashion, and language of the Irish enemies, and also have made divers marriages and alliances between themselves and the Irish enemies aforesaid; whereby the said land and the liege people thereof, the English language, the allegiance due to our lord the King and the English laws there are put in subjection and decayed and the Irish enemies exalted and raised up contrary to right.[20]

Further along in the document, the importance of marriage becomes clearer. "Also it is ordained and established that no alliance by marriage, gossipred, fostering of children, concubinage or amour or in any other manner be henceforth made between the English and Irish on the one side or the other."[21] Such marriage alliances and the practice of great families raising or fostering the children of other families were the basis of political and military networks in Ireland—and in England for that matter.

What the English faced in governing Ireland was the emergence of the great families that had gone native, in effect becoming the chiefs of Irish families and opposing English efforts at imposing English order on the entire country. One of the most important techniques for this was the marriage alliance between a member of one of the Anglo-Norman families resident in Ireland and a daughter of one of the important Irish families. Another was the practice of fostering. The families thus created, the Fitzgeralds being the most prominent, were a constant threat to English control of Ireland.

It would appear that to some extent at least, medieval observers of the marriage practices of societies that differed from their own had at least some understanding of the social and political consequences of marriage. It must have been apparent to at least some of the friars who went to Asia that without some concessions on the law of marriage, the conversion of the Mongols and others would be quite difficult, if not impossible. Likewise, the English in Ireland recognized that marriage practices, even when both parties were Christians, differed significantly and had consequences in the political realm.

But these glimmerings of awareness about the social implications of marriage and family law did not lead to the emergence of comparative anthropology or to a consideration of the relationship between law and society. In fact, it would seem that when Europeans began to appreciate cultural differences in marriage practices and other cultural forms, something that only appeared extensively after 1492, the law had already codified the medieval experience. As a result, at least on issues of marriage law, the Catholic Church was unwilling to make any serious concessions to existing practices. As for the English, it can be argued that their experience in Ireland made them cautious about intermarriage with indigenous peoples. In Massachusetts Bay colony at least, the Puritans were strongly opposed to interracial marriages and may well have feared the emergence of a mixed race, like the Fitzgeralds, who could block any further expansion.

Conclusion

In the final analysis, family law has played an important role in the expansion of Europe for the past millennium. While a great deal of attention has been paid to the effects of conquest and disease on the indigenous population of the Americas after 1492, less has been paid to the implications of the imposition of European laws of marriage, divorce and so on in these societies. About a dozen years ago, Constance Bouchard published an article on the issue of marriage within the forbidden degrees that pointed out the implications of the imposition of the rule forbidding marriages between individuals related within seven degrees of consanguinity.[22] She concluded that these rules had enormous consequences for the noble class, as royal families and the great noble houses found it increasingly difficult to find wives of their own social level to whom they were not related. In the eleventh century, a French king had to reach out to the princely house of Kiev to find a legally acceptable wife. The consequences of this, she argued, was to encourage marriages between the higher and lower nobility, reaching down vertically rather than out horizontally for marriage partners.

If the canon law of marriage had the importance for the European nobility that Bouchard finds, it should be no surprise at all that when European Christian societies imposed their law of marriage on those whom they wished to convert to Christianity, peoples who not only married within the forbidden degrees but were polygamous and so on, the Europeans were, in effect, subverting the existing social order in ways that they did not appreciate. In other words, the law of marriage is not necessarily gently uplifting; it often is subversive, even revolutionary in its consequences.

Notes

An earlier version of this paper was originally presented at the Twenty-Second University of British Columbia Medieval Workshop, November 12–15, 1992. I wish to thank Professor De Lloyd J. Guth for inviting me, and the members of the audience for their comments.

1. The most critical evaluation is Kirkpatrick Sale, *The Conquest of Paradise* (New York: Knopf, 1990). There are several surveys of the literature that the quincentennial celebration has generated. One of the most recent is Marvin Lunenfeld, "Columbus Bashing: Culture Wars over the Construction of an Anti-Hero," in *Columbus: Meeting of Cultures, Forum Italicum: Columbus Supplement* (Stony Brook, NY: Forum Italicum, 1993), 1–12.

2. A regular reader of the *New York Times* or of any other metropolitan newspaper could add to this list without much difficulty. The *New York Times* for Sunday, August 9, 1993, contained three articles dealing with issues of family law: "Testing Newborns for AIDS Virus Raises Issue of Mothers' Privacy" (1, 44) dealt with the conflict posed by recent laws protecting those with AIDS having their condition made public with the desire of public health and medical officials to provide care for children with AIDS. "The Strain on the Bonds of Adoption," (Section 4: 1, 5) dealt with the following issues: the conflict between the birth parents of a young girl and the couple that wished to adopt her; the desire of a girl switched at birth to divorce her birth parents; the widespread inability of adoptive parents to obtain medical insurance for an adopted child until the adoption is finalized. The third article, "Custody Trial Explores Backgrounds of Rivals" (20), centered on the right of a girl to divorce her birth parents but also raised the issue of the right of grandparents to visit a grandchild. It should be pointed out that these issues of family law are not restricted to the state and federal courts. Canon lawyers practicing in the marriage courts maintained by each

diocese of the Catholic Church also face challenges to existing law. See, for example, Paul K. Thomas, "Marriage Annulments for Gay Men and Lesbian Women: New Canonical and Psychological Insights," *The Jurist* 43 (1983): 318–42.

3. See the seminal article by Archibald Lewis, "The Medieval Frontier," *Speculum* 33 (1958): 473–83, esp. 476.

4. The quincentennial of Columbus's first voyage generated a good deal of interest in the relationship between medieval and early modern expansion. See J. R. S. Phillips, *The Medieval Expansion of Europe*, 2nd. ed. (Oxford: Oxford University Press, 1998); Felipe Fernndez-Armesto, *Before Columbus: Exploration and Colonization from the Mediterranean to the Atlantic, 1229–1492* (Philadelphia: University of Pennsylvania Press, 1987); Robert Bartlett, *The Making of Europe: Conquest, Colonization, & Cultural Change, 950–1350* (Princeton: Princeton University Press, 1993); Robert Bartlett and Angus MacKay, *Medieval Frontier Societies* (Oxford: Oxford University Press, 1989); Valerie Flint, *The Imaginative Landscape of Christopher Columbus* (Princeton: Princeton University Press, 1992). See also, James Muldoon, *The Expansion of Europe: The First Phase* (Philadelphia: University of Pennsylvania Press, 1977).

5. Benjamin Z. Kedar, *Crusade and Mission: European Approaches toward the Muslims* (Princeton: Princeton University Press, 1984), 7.

6. James Muldoon, "Missionaries and the Marriages of Infidels: The Case of the Mongol Mission," *The Jurist* 35 (1975): 125–141; James Brundage, *Law, Sex, and Christian Society in Medieval Europe* (Chicago: University of Chicago Press, 1987), 339–40.

7. Muldoon, "Missionaries," 125–26; Donald J. Gregory, *The Pauline Privilege*, Canon Law Studies, no. 68 (Washington, DC: The Catholic University of America,1931); John T. Noonan Jr., *Power to Dissolve* (Cambridge, MA: Harvard University Press, 1972), 345–47; for the application of the Pauline Privilege in the Americas, see Noonan, *Power to Dissolve*, 347–59.

8. Muldoon, "Missionaries," 128–29.

9. Ibid., 129. The question of tolerating polygamous marriages has been raised again in recent years: see Robert E. Rodes Jr., "Natural Law and the Marriage of Christians," *The Jurist* 35 (1975): 409–30 at 427–29.

10. Ibid., 131.

11. Edmund Curtis and R. B. McDowell, eds., "Laudabiliter," in *Irish Historical Documents 1172–1922* (London: Methuen & Co., 1943; reprint ed., New York: Barnes and Noble, 1968), 17–18 at 17.

12. John A. Watt, *The Church in Medieval Ireland, The Gill History of Ireland*, vol. 5 (Dublin: Gill and Macmillan, 1972), 6.

13. Curtis and McDowell, "The Constitutions of the Synod of Cashal, 1172," in *Irish Historical Documents*, 18–19.

14. Curtis and McDowell, "Three Letters of Alexander III . . ." in *Irish Histroical Documents*, 19–22 at 21.

15. There has been a debate among anthropologists concerning whether or not anthropology and ethnology existed, at least in rudimentary fashion, before the modern world. Margaret T. Hodgen, *Early Anthropology in the Sixteenth and Seventeenth Centuries* (Philadelphia: University of Pennsylvania Press, 1964;

reprint ed., 1971) argued that Herodotus began a tradition of anthropological writing that survived, if only in "fractional and mutilated" fashion during the Middle Ages (29). John H. Rowe, on the other hand, argued that "the anthropological tradition of interest in differences among men had its beginnings in the Italian Renaissance . . . specifically in Renaissance archaeology." John H. Rowe, "The Renaissance Foundations of Anthropology," *American Anthropologist* 67 (1965): 1–20. Also, see his "Ethnography and Ethnology in the Sixteenth Century," *The Kroeber Anthropological Society Papers* 30 (Spring, 1964): 1–19. For a critique of Rowe's position, see John W. Bennett, "Comments on 'The Renaissance Foundations of Anthropology,'" *American Anthropologist* 68 (1966): 215–20. John H. Rowe, "Further Notes on the Renaissance and Anthropology; A Reply to Bennett," *American Anthropologist* 68 (1966): 220–22.

16. Muldoon, "Missionaries," 129.
17. John of Plano Carpini, "History of the Mongols," in Christopher Dawson, ed., *Mission to Asia* (New York: Harper & Row, 1966), 3–76 at 7.
18. The presence of Christians, most often Nestorians, at the various Mongol courts, is well-documented. Both John of Plano Carpini and William of Rubruck mention them. Rubruck mentions that one of the wives of Mangu Chan "had been a Christian." "The Journey of William of Rubruck," in Dawson, *Mission to Asia*, 89–220 at 163.
19. Rubruck judges the practice of a son marrying the widows of his father "a shameful custom." Dawson, *Mission to Asia*, 104.
20. "The Statutes of Kilkenny, 1366," *Irish Historical Documents*, 52–53 at 52.
21. Ibid., 53. 53.
22. Constance B. Bouchard, "Consanguinity and Noble Marriages in the Tenth and Eleventh Centuries," *Speculum* 56 (1981): 268–87.

Contributors

Sahar Amer is Associate Professor of Asian and International Studies at the University of North Carolina, Chapel Hill. She is a specialist in medieval French literature and in the relations between Arabs and French, Muslims and Christians from the Middle Ages to the present day. She has published *Esope au féminin: Marie de France et la politique de l'interculturalité* (Rodopi, 1999), and *Border Crossings: Love between Women in Medieval French and Arabic Literatures* (forthcoming).

Carlin Barton is Professor of Ancient History at the University of Massachusetts, Amherst. Her work focuses on concepts of emotion and their cultural roles in republican and early imperial Rome. She is the author of two books: *The Sorrows of the Ancient Romans: The Gladiator and the Monster* (Princeton University Press, 1993) and *Roman Honor: Fire in the Bones* (University of California Press, 2001). Her recent articles include: "Being in the Eyes; Shame and Sight in Ancient Rome" in David Frederick, ed. *Roman Gaze: Vision, Power and the Body* (Johns Hopkins University Press, 2002); and "Honor and Sacredness in the Roman and Christian Worlds," in Margaret Cormack, ed., *Sacrificing Self: Perspectives on Martyrdom and Religion* (Oxford, 2002).

Stephen Belcher has taught at the University of Nouakchott, the Pennsylvania State University, and the University of Kankan in Guinea. He is the author of *Epic Traditions of Africa* (Indiana University Press, 1999) and *African Myths of Origin* (Penguin Classics, 2005), and coeditor of *Oral Epics from Africa* (Indiana University Press, 1997). He currently works with the Humphrey Fellowship Program at the Pennsylvania State University, and is coeditor of *Mande Studies*, the journal of the Mande Studies Association.

Aviva Ben-Ur is Associate Professor in the Department of Judaic and Near Eastern Studies at the University of Massachusetts, Amherst. She is the author, with Rachel Frankel, of *Remnant Stones: The Jewish Cemeteries and Synagogue of Suriname* (Hebrew Union College Press, forthcoming). Her book, *Sephardic Jews in America: Where Diasporas Met*, is forthcoming with New York University Press.

Brian Britt is Professor and Director of Religious Studies in the Department of Interdisciplinary Studies at Virginia Tech. His research on literary and theoretical approaches to the Bible combines the analysis of biblical texts with questions of contemporary culture. In addition to articles in biblical and religious studies journals, his work includes two books: *Walter Benjamin and the Bible* (Continuum, 1996; Edwin Mellen Press 2003), and *Rewriting Moses: The Narrative Eclipse of the Text* (T and T Clark, 2004). He is currently working on biblical curses and their modern legacy.

Alexandra Cuffel is Assistant Professor in the History Department of Macalester College. Her research focuses on the intersections of Jewish, Christian, and Muslim relations, gender, and medical theories in the Middle Ages. She has one book forthcoming in 2007 with the University of Notre Dame Press entitled: *Gendering Disgust in Medieval Religious Polemic* in addition to having published articles in Jewish, Islamic, and/or Mediterranean studies journals. She is currently working on two books, one dealing with shared saints and festivals among medieval Jews, Christians, and Muslims, and another, *Imagining the Ten Lost Tribes*, coauthored with Adam Knobler. She received her PhD from New York University.

Catherine Howey received her MA in Art History at the Courtauld Institute of Art working under Aileen Ribeiro in Dress History, and this essay stems from her Courtauld Masters thesis. Currently she is working on her PhD dissertation at Rutgers, The State University of New Jersey with Alastair Bellany in the fields of Early Modern Europe and Women's and Gender History. In her dissertation she plans to examine the role Elizabethan court women played in the construction of Queen Elizabeth I's monarchical image as well as how Elizabethan female courtiers understood their own position at the court of the last Tudor monarch.

Kenneth F. Kitchell, Jr. is Professor of Classics at the University of Massachusetts. Prior to this he was an Alumni Distinguished Professor of Classics at Louisiana State University in Baton Rouge, LA., where he taught for 22 years. He received his BA from College of the Holy Cross (Worcester, MA) in 1969 and his MA and PhD in Classics in 1976 from Loyola University of Chicago. He is the author of over 45 articles. He coauthored a translation and annotation of the Latin text of Linnaeus' most important work on reptiles, and *De Animalibus: A Medieval Summa Zoologica*, the first translation and annotation of the *De Animalibus* of Albertus Magnus, with Irven M. Resnick. He is the editor of *Entering the Stadium: Approaches to Ancient Athletics* (*The Classical Bulletin* 74, 1998) and the coauthor, with

Sean Smith, of *Catullus: A Legamus Reader* (Bolchazy-Carducci, 2006). He is founder and coeditor of the *Legamus* series and is at work on a textbook of medieval Latin and a new introductory textbook of Latin for the college level. He is the immediate past-president of The American Classical League and has spearheaded a program to recruit Latin teachers nationally.

Ann-Marie Knoblauch is Associate Professor in the Department of Art and Art History at Virginia Tech, where she specializes in the art of the ancient Mediterranean world. Her areas of research include ancient Cyprus, and she has been involved with the archaeological excavations at the site of Idalion on Cyprus since 1998. She is currently preparing for publication the limestone sculpture found at the site in 1992. She received her PhD in Classical Archaeology from Bryn Mawr College in 1997, and her dissertation on Greek satyrs led to an interest in their female counterparts, the nymphs. Recent publications include: "Defining the Satyr in the Archaic and Classical Periods: The Numismatic Evidence" Proceedings of the 12th International Numismatic Congress Berlin, September 1997 (Berlin 2000); "Votives and Votaries on Ancient Cyprus" in the Catalogue of the Diniacopoulos Collection at the Montréal Museum of Fine Arts (Montreal: forthcoming) and "Rethinking the Satyr on Greek Coins" *Minerva* 14 (September–October 2003).

Adam Knobler is Associate Professor of History at the College of New Jersey (formerly Trenton State College), where he has taught since 1992. A graduate of Wesleyan University (BA, 1985) and the University of Cambridge (PhD, 1990), he has published widely on the subject of cross-cultural contact in the age of expansion. He has recently completed a book manuscript, *The Power of Distance: Mythology and Diplomacy in the Age of Exploration, c1250-c1550.*

James Muldoon is Professor Emeritus at Rutgers and a research fellow at the John Carter Brown Library on the campus of Brown University. A specialist in medieval legal and ecclesiastical history, Professor Muldoon has a particular interest in the relations between Christian and non-Christian societies in the medieval and early modern world. His publications on this subject include: *The Expansion of Europe: The First Phase* (1977); *Popes, Lawyers, and Infidels: The Church and the Non-Christian World 1250–1550* (1979); *The Americas in the Spanish World Order: The Justification for Conquest in the Seventeenth Century* (1994) all through the University of Pennsylvania Press; *Varieties of Religious Conversion in the Middle Ages* (University Press of Florida, 1997); *Empire and Order: The Concept of Empire, 800–1800* (Macmillan, 1999) and *Identity on the Medieval Irish Frontier* (University Press of Florida, 2003).

Irven M. Resnick is Professor of Philosophy and Religion and holds an endowed chair in Judaic Studies at the University of Tennessee at Chattanooga. His research interests include medieval Jewish-Christian relations, and his publications include *Albertus Magnus on Animals: A Medieval Summa Zoologica*, with Professor Kenneth Kitchell (John Hopkins University Press, 1999), 2 vols.; *Two Theological Treatises of Odo of Tournai: On Original Sin, and a Debate with the Jew, Leo, Concerning the Advent of Christ, the Son of God* (University of Pennsylvania Press, 1994); and *Power, Penance, and Possibility in St. Peter Damian's De divina omnipotentia* (E. J. Brill Publishers, 1992).

Index